Introduction to Psychometric Theory

Introduction to Psychometric Theory

Tenko Raykov
Michigan State University

George A. Marcoulides
University of California at Riverside

Routledge
Taylor & Francis Group
New York   London

Routledge
Taylor & Francis Group
270 Madison Avenue
New York, NY 10016

Routledge
Taylor & Francis Group
27 Church Road
Hove, East Sussex BN3 2FA

Printed in the United States of America on acid-free paper
10 9 8 7 6 5 4 3 2 1

International Standard Book Number: 978-0-415-87822-7 (Hardback)

Library of Congress Cataloging-in-Publication Data

Raykov, Tenko.
    Introduction to psychometric theory / Tenko Raykov, George Marcoulides.
        p. cm.
    Includes bibliographical references and index.
    ISBN 978-0-415-87822-7 (hardcover : alk. paper)
    1. Psychometrics. I. Marcoulides, George A. II. Title.

BF39.R34 2011
150.1'5195--dc22   2010032526

Visit the Taylor & Francis Web site at
http://www.taylorandfrancis.com

and the Psychology Press Web site at
http://www.psypress.com

Contents

Preface

This book arose from our experiences accumulated over a number of years in teaching measurement, testing, and psychometric theory courses. Throughout this time, we have not been able to identify a single textbook that would consistently serve all our instructional purposes. To meet these objectives, we developed a series of lecture notes whose synthesis this text represents. In the meantime, measurement and test theory evolved further into a very extensive field, which is challenging to cover in a single course. With this in mind, our book is meant to introduce behavioral, social, educational, marketing, business and biomedical students and researchers to this methodological area. To this end, we have identified a set of topics in the field, which are in our view of fundamental importance for its understanding and permit readers to proceed subsequently to other more advanced subjects.

Our pragmatic goal with this text is to provide a coherent introduction to psychometric theory, which would adequately cover the basics of the subject that we consider essential in many empirical settings in the behavioral, social, and educational sciences. We aim at a relatively non-technical introduction to the subject, and use mathematical formulas mainly in their definitional meaning. The audience for which this book is most suitable consists primarily of advanced undergraduate students, graduate students, and researchers in the behavioral, social, educational, marketing, business and biomedical disciplines, who have limited or no familiarity with the mathematical and statistical procedures that are involved in measurement and testing. As prerequisites for the book, an introductory statistics course with exposure to regression analysis and analysis of variance (ANOVA) is recommended, as is initial familiarity with some of the most widely circulated statistical analysis software in these sciences (e.g., IBM SPSS, SAS, STATA, or R; a brief introduction to R is provided in Section 2.8 of Chapter 2; see also Appendix to Chapter 11).

We believe that it is not possible to introduce a reader to psychometric theory, as available to us currently, without repeated use of statistical software. After the first couple of chapters, we utilize nearly routinely the latent variable modeling program M*plus* that is becoming increasingly popular and widely used across the social and behavioral sciences, in addition to our use of R, IBM SPSS, and SAS on a number of occasions in several of the chapters. On the webpage for this book (www.psypress.com/psychometric-theory), we provide essentially all data used in the text formatted in such a way that it can be used with IBM SPSS, SAS, M*plus*, or R. To enhance comprehension, the software codes and associated outputs are also included and discussed at appropriate places in the book. In addition, instructors will find helpful PowerPoint lecture slides and questions and problems for each chapter in the book, which are also available at the above webpage.

Our hope is that readers will find this text to present a useful introduction to and a basic treatment of psychometric theory, as well as prepare them for studying more advanced topics within this rich and exciting scientific field. There are two features that seem to set apart our book from others in this field: (i) the extensive and consistent use of the comprehensive framework of latent variable modeling (LVM); and (ii) the concern with interval estimation throughout, in addition to point estimation of parameters of main interest and model fit evaluation. We believe that in the coming years the applied statistical methodology of LVM will gain even further in popularity and utilization across the social and behavioral sciences. For this reason, we anticipate that LVM will be particularly helpful to students and researchers who embark on their journey into the theoretically and empirically important subject of measurement and test theory in these sciences.

This book has been substantially influenced by the prior work of a number of scholars. We are especially grateful to J. Algina and R. P. McDonald for valuable discussions in various forms on measurement and related topics. Their contributions to psychometrics and books (Crocker & Algina, 1986; McDonald, 1999) have markedly impacted our understanding of the field and this text that can in many respects be seen as positioned closely to theirs. We are also thankful to P. M. Bentler, K. A. Bollen, M. W. Browne, K. G. Jöreksog, C. Lewis, S. Penev, M. D. Reckase, and R. Steyer for many valuable discussions on measurement related topics, as well as to T. Asparouhov, D. M. Dimitrov, G. Mels, S. Penev, P. E. Shrout, and R. E. Zinbarg for their important contributions to our joint research on reliability and related issues in behavioral and social measurement. We are similarly indebted to the M*plus* support team (L. K. Muthén, B. O. Muthén, T. Asparouhov, and T. Nguyen) for instrumental assistance with its applications. Tenko Raykov is also thankful to L. K. Muthén and B. O. Muthén for valuable instructions and discussions on LVM. George A. Marcoulides is particularly grateful to R. J. Shavelson and N. M. Webb for their years of guidance and discussions on a variety of measurement related topics. A number of our students provided very useful and at times critical feedback on the lecture notes we first developed for our courses in psychometric theory, from which this book emerged. We are also grateful to several reviewers for their critical comments on an earlier draft of the manuscript, which contributed substantially to its improvement: M. Meghan Davidson (University of Nebraska–Lincoln); Robert Henson (The University of North Carolina at Greensboro); Joseph J. Palladino (University of Southern Indiana); Scott L. Thomas (Claremont Graduate University); Andre A. Rupp (University of Maryland); and Jennifer Rose (Wesleyan University). Thanks are also due to Debra Riegert and Erin Flaherty from Taylor & Francis for their essential assistance during advanced stages of our work on this project, and to Suzanne Lassandro for valuable typesetting assistance. Last but not least, we are more than indebted to our families for their continued support in lots of ways. The first author thanks Albena and Anna; the second author thanks Laura and Katerina.

Tenko Raykov,
East Lansing, Michigan

George A. Marcoulides,
Riverside, California

1

Measurement, Measuring Instruments, and Psychometric Theory

1.1 Constructs and Their Importance in the Behavioral and Social Sciences

Measurement pervades almost every aspect of modern society, and measures of various kinds often accompany us throughout much of our lives. Measurement can be considered an activity consisting of the process of assigning numbers to individuals in a systematic way as a means of representing their studied properties. For example, a great variety of individual characteristics, such as achievement, aptitude, or intelligence, are measured frequently by various persons—e.g., teachers, instructors, clinicians, and administrators. Because the results of these measurements can have a profound influence on an individual's life, it is important to understand how the resulting scores are derived and what the accuracy of the information about examined properties is, which these numbers contain. For the social, behavioral, and educational sciences that this book is mainly directed to, measurement is of paramount relevance. It is indeed very hard for us to imagine how progress in them could evolve without measurement and the appropriate use of measures. Despite its essential importance, however, measurement in these disciplines is plagued by a major problem. This problem lies in the fact that unlike many physical attributes, such as, say, length or mass, behavioral and related attributes cannot be measured directly.

Widely acknowledged is also the fact that most measurement devices are not perfect. Physical scientists have long recognized this and have been concerned with replication of their measurements many times to obtain results in which they can be confident. Replicated measures can provide the average of a set of recurring results, which may be expected to represent a more veridical estimate of what is being appraised than just a single measure. Unfortunately, in the social, behavioral, and educational disciplines, commonly obtained measurements cannot often be replicated as straightforwardly and confidently as in the physical sciences, and there is no instrument like a ruler or weight scale that could be used to directly measure, say, intelligence, ability, depression, attitude, social cohesion, or alcohol dependence, to name only a few of the entities of special interest in these and related disciplines. Instead, these are only indirectly observable entities, oftentimes called constructs, which can merely be inferred from overt behavior (see discussion below for a stricter definition of 'construct'). This overt behavior represents (presumably) the construct manifestation. More specifically, observed behaviors—such as performance on certain tests or items of an inventory or self-report, or responses to particular questions in a questionnaire or ability test—may be assumed to be indicative manifestations of these constructs. That is, each construct is a theoretical entity represented by a number of similar manifested behaviors. It is this feature that allows us to consider a construct an abstraction from, and synthesis of, the common features of these manifest behaviors.

We can define a construct as an abstract, possibly hypothetical entity that is inferred from a set of similar demonstrated or directly observed behaviors. That is, a construct is abstracted from a cluster of behaviors that are related among themselves. In other words, a construct represents what is common across these manifested behaviors. In this role, a construct is conceptualized as the hidden 'source' of common variability, or covariability, of a set of similar observable behaviors. We note that a construct may as well be a theoretical concept or even a hypothetical entity and may also not be very well defined initially on its own in a substantive area.

There is a set of general references to the notion of construct that have become popular in the social and behavioral sciences. At times constructs are called latent, unobserved, or hidden variables; similarly, a construct may be referred to as an underlying dimension, latent dimension, or latent construct. We will use these terms synonymously throughout the text. Each of them, and in particular the last two mentioned, emphasize a major characteristic feature of constructs used in these disciplines. This is the fact that in contrast with many physical attributes, constructs cannot be directly observed or measured.

In this book, we will treat a construct as a latent continuum, i.e., a latent or unobserved continuous dimension, along which subjects are positioned and in general differ from one another. The process of measurement aims at differentiating between their unknown positions along this dimension and possibly attempting to locate them on it. Because the constructs, i.e., these latent dimensions, are not directly observable or measurable, unlike, say, height or weight, it is easily realized that the above-mentioned major problem of measurement resides in the fact that the individuals' exact locations on this continuum are not known. In addition, as we will have ample opportunities to emphasize in later chapters, the locations of the studied subjects on a latent continuum are not directly and precisely measurable or observable. For this reason, examined individuals cannot be exactly identified on the latent dimension corresponding to a construct under consideration. That is, we can think of each studied subject, whether in a sample or population of interest, as possessing a location—or a score, in quantitative terms—on this dimension, but that location is unknown and in fact may not be possible to determine or evaluate with a high level of accuracy.

Most entities of theoretical and empirical interest in the behavioral and social sciences can be considered latent constructs. Some widely known examples are motivation, ability, aptitude, opinion, anxiety, and general mental ability, as well as extraversion, neuroticism, agreeableness, openness to new experience, and conscientiousness (the so-called Big Five factors of human personality, according to a popular social psychology theory; e.g., McCrae & Costa, 1996). The constructs typically reflect important sides of behavioral and social phenomena that these disciplines are interested in studying. Despite our inability (at least currently) to measure or observe constructs directly in them, these constructs are of special theoretical and empirical relevance. Specifically, the study of their relationships is of particular interest in these sciences. Entire theories in them are based on constructs and the ways in which they relate, or deal with how some constructs could be used to understand better if not predict—within the limits of those theories—other constructs under consideration. Progress in the social, behavioral, and educational disciplines is oftentimes marked by obtaining deeper knowledge about the complexity of relationships among constructs of concern, as well as the conditions under which these relationships occur or take particular forms.

Although there are no instruments available that would allow us to measure or observe constructs directly, we can measure them indirectly. This can be accomplished using proxies of the constructs. These proxies are the above-indicated behavior manifestations, specifically of the behaviors that are related to the constructs. For example, the items in the Beck Depression Inventory (e.g., Beck, Rush, Shaw, & Emery, 1979) can be considered proxies for depression. The subtests comprising an intelligence test battery, such as the Wechsler Adult Intelligence Scale (WAIS; e.g., Chapter 3), can also be viewed as proxies of intelligence. The questions in a scale of college aspiration can be treated as proxies for the unobserved construct of college aspiration. The responses to the problems in a mathematics ability test can similarly be considered proxies for (manifestations of) this ability that is of interest to evaluate.

A widely used reference to these proxies, and in particular in this text, is as indicators of the corresponding latent constructs. We stress that the indicators are not identical to the constructs of actual concern. Instead, the indicators are only manifestations of the constructs. Unlike the constructs, these manifestations are observable and typically reflect only very specific aspects of the constructs. For example, a particular item in an anxiety scale provides information not about the entire construct of anxiety but only about a special aspect of it, such as anxiety about a certain event. An item in an algebra knowledge test does not evaluate the entire body of knowledge a student is expected to acquire throughout a certain period of time (e.g., a school semester). Rather, that item evaluates his or her ability to execute particular operations needed to obtain the correct answer or to use knowledge of a certain fact(s) or relationships that were covered during the pertinent algebra instruction period in order to arrive at that answer.

No less important, an indicator can in general be considered not a perfect measure of the associated construct but only a fallible manifestation (demonstration) or proxy of it. There are many external factors when administering or measuring the indicator that are unrelated to the construct under consideration this indicator is a proxy of, which may also play a role. For instance, when specific items from a geometry test are administered, the examined students' answers are affected not only by the corresponding skills and knowledge possessed by the students but also by a number of unrelated factors, such as time of the day, level of prior fatigue, quality of the printed items or other presentation of the items, and a host of momentary external (environment-related) and internal factors for the students. Later chapters will be concerned in more detail with various sources of the ensuing error of measurement and will provide a much more detailed discussion of this critical issue for behavioral and social measurement (see in particular Chapters 5 and 9 on classical test theory and generalizability theory, respectively).

This discussion demonstrates that the indicators of the studied constructs, as manifestations of the latter, are the actually observed and error-prone variables on which we obtain data informing about these constructs. Yet collecting data on how individuals perform on these indicators is not the end of our endeavors but only a means for accomplishing the goal, which is evaluation of the constructs of concern. Indeed, we are really interested in the underlying constructs and how they relate to one another and/or other studied variables. However, with respect to the constructs, all we obtain data on are their manifestations, i.e., the individual performance on the construct indicators or proxies. On the basis of these data, we wish to make certain inferences about the underlying constructs and their relationships and possibly those of the constructs to other observed measures. This is because, as mentioned, it is the constructs themselves that are of actual interest. They help us better understand studied phenomena and may allow us to control, change, or even optimize these and related phenomena. This lack of identity between the indicators, on the one hand, and the constructs with which they are associated, on the other hand, is the essence of the earlier-mentioned major problem of measurement in the behavioral and social sciences.

Whereas it is widely appreciated that constructs play particularly important roles in these sciences, the independent existence of the constructs cannot be proved beyond any doubt. Even though there may be dozens of (what one may think are) indicators of a given construct, they do not represent by themselves and in their totality sufficient evidence in favor of concluding firmly that their corresponding latent construct exists on its own. Furthermore, the fact that we can come up with a 'meaningful' interpretation or a name for a construct under consideration does not mean that it exists itself in reality. Nonetheless, consideration of constructs in theories reflecting studied phenomena has proved over the past century to be highly beneficial and has greatly contributed to substantial progress in the behavioral, social, and educational sciences.

1.2 How to Measure a Construct

Inventing a construct is obviously not the same as measuring it and, in addition, is far easier than evaluating it. In order to define a construct, one needs to establish a rule of correspondence between a theoretical or hypothetical concept of interest on the one hand and observable behaviors that are legitimate manifestations of that concept on the other hand. Once this correspondence is established, that concept may be viewed as a construct. This process of defining, or developing, a construct is called operational definition of a construct.

As an example, consider the concept of preschool aggression (cf. Crocker & Algina, 1986). In order to operationally define it, one must first specify what types of behavior in a preschool play setting would be considered aggressive. Once these are specified, in the next stage a plan needs to be devised for obtaining samples of such aggressive behavior in a standard situation. As a following step, one must decide how to record observations, i.e., devise a scheme of data recording for each child in a standard form. When all steps of this process are followed, one can view the result as an instrument, or a 'test' ('scale'), for measuring preschool aggression. That is, operationally defining a construct is a major step toward developing an instrument for measuring it, i.e., a test or scale for that construct.

This short discussion leads us to a definition of a test as a standard procedure for obtaining a sample from a specified set of overt behaviors that pertain to a construct under consideration (cf. Murphy & Davidshofer, 2004). In other words, a test is an instrument or device for sampling behavior pertaining to a construct under study. This measurement is carried out under standardized conditions. Once the test is conducted, established objective rules are used for scoring the results of the test. The purpose of these rules is to help quantify in an objective manner an examined attribute for a sample (group) of studied individuals. Alternative references to 'test' that are widely used in the social and behavioral sciences are scale, multiple-component measuring instrument, composite, behavioral measuring instrument, or measuring instrument (instrument). We will use these references as synonyms for 'test' throughout the remainder of this book.

As is well-known, tests produce scores that correspond to each examined individual. That is, every subject participating in the pertinent study obtains such scores when the test is administered to him or her. These scores, when resulting from instruments with high measurement quality, contain information that when appropriately extracted could be used for making decisions about people. These may be decisions regarding admission into a certain school or college, a particular diagnosis, therapy, or a remedial action if needed, etc. Because some of these decisions can be very important for the person involved and possibly his or her future, it is of special relevance that the test scores reflect indeed the attributes that are believed (on theoretical and empirical grounds) to be essential for a correct decision. How to develop such tests, or measuring instruments, is an involved activity, and various aspects of it represent the central topics of this book.

The following two examples demonstrate two main types of uses of test scores, which are interrelated. Consider first the number of what could be viewed as aggressive acts displayed by a preschool child at a playground during a 20-minute observation period. Here, the researcher would be interested in evaluating the trait of child aggression. The associated measurement procedure is therefore often referred to as trait evaluation. Its goal is to obtain information regarding the level of aggression in a given child, i.e., about the position of the child along the presumed latent continuum representing child aggression. As a second example, consider the number of correctly solved items (problems, tasks, questions) by a student in a test of algebra knowledge. In order for such a test to serve the purpose for which it has been developed, viz., assess the level of mastery of an academic subject, the test needs to represent well a body of knowledge and skills that students are expected to acquire in the pertinent algebra subject over a certain period (e.g., a school semester or year). Unlike the first example, the second demonstrates a setting where one would be interested in what is often referred to as domain sampling. The latter activity is typically the basis on which achievement tests are constructed. Thereby, a domain is defined as the set of all possible items that would be informative about a studied ability, e.g., abstract thinking ability. Once this definition is complete, a test represents a sample from that domain. We notice here that the relationship of domain to test is similar to that of population to sample in the field of statistics and its applications. We will return to this analogy in later chapters when we will be concerned in more detail with domain sampling and related issues.

We thus see that a test is a carefully developed measuring instrument that allows obtaining meaningful samples of behavior under standardized conditions (Murphy & Davidshofer, 2004). In addition, a test is associated with objective, informative, and optimal assignment of such numerical scores that reflect as well as possible studied characteristics of tested individuals. Thereby, the relationships between the subject attributes, i.e., the degree to which the measured individuals possess the constructs of interest, are expected to be reflected in the relationships between the scores assigned to them after test administration and scoring.

We emphasize that a test is not expected to provide exhaustive measurement of all possible behaviors defining an examined attribute or construct. That is, a test does not encapsulate all behaviors that belong to a pertinent subject-matter area or domain. Rather, a test attempts to 'approximate' that domain by sampling behaviors belonging to it. Quality of the test is determined by the degree to which this sample is representative of those behaviors.

With this in mind, we are led to the following definition of a fundamental concept for the present chapter as well as the rest of this book, that of behavioral measurement. Accordingly, behavioral measurement is the process of assigning in a systematic way quantitative values to the behavior sample collected by using a test (instrument, scale), which is administered to each member of a studied group (sample) of individuals from a population under consideration.

1.3 Why Measure Constructs?

The preceding discussion did not address specific reasons as to why one would be interested in measuring or be willing to measure constructs in the social and behavioral sciences. In particular, a question that may be posed at this point is the following: Because latent constructs are not directly observable and measurable, why would it be necessary that one still attempt to measure them?

To respond to this question, we first note that behavioral phenomena are exceedingly complex, multifaceted, and multifactorially determined. In order to make it possible to study them, we need special means that allow us to deal with their complexity. As such, the latent constructs can be particularly helpful. Their pragmatic value is that they help classify and describe individual atomistic behaviors. This leads to substantial reduction of complexity and at the same time helps us to understand the common features that interrelated behaviors possess. To appreciate the value of latent constructs, it would also be helpful to try to imagine what the alternative would imply, viz., not to use any latent constructs in the behavioral, social, and educational disciplines. If this alternative would be adopted as a research principle, however, we would not have means that would allow us to introduce order into an unmanageable variety of observed behavioral phenomena. The consequence of this would be a situation in which scientists would need to deal with a chaotic set of observed phenomena. This chaos and ensuing confusion would not allow them to deduce any principles that may underlie or govern these behavioral phenomena.

These problems could be resolved to a substantial degree if one adopts the use of constructs that are carefully conceptualized, developed, and measured through their manifestations in observed behavior. This is due to the fact that constructs help researchers to group or cluster instances of similar behaviors and communicate in compact terms what has in fact been observed. Moreover, constructs are also the building blocks of most theories about human behavior. They also account for the common features across similar types of behavior in different situations and circumstances. For these reasons, constructs can be seen as an indispensable tool in contemporary behavioral, social, and educational research.

This view, which is adopted throughout the present book, also allows us to consider a behavioral theory as a set of statements about (a) relationships between behavior-related constructs and (b) relationships between constructs on the one hand and observable phenomena of practical (empirical) consequence on the other hand. The value of such theories is that when correct, or at least plausible, they can be used to explain or predict and possibly control or even optimize certain patterns of behavior. The behavioral and social sciences reach such theory levels through empirical investigation and substantiation, which is a lengthy and involved process that includes testing, revision, modification, and improvement of initial theories about studied phenomena. Thereby, an essential element in accomplishing this goal is the quantification of observations of behaviors that are representative of constructs posited by theory. This quantification is the cornerstone of what measurement and in particular test theory in these sciences is about.

1.4 Main Challenges When Measuring Constructs

Given that the constructs we are interested in are such abstractions from observed inter-related behaviors, which can be measured only indirectly, the development of instruments assessing them represents a series of serious challenges for the social, behavioral, or educational researcher. In this section, we discuss several of these challenges, which developers of multiple-component measuring instruments—e.g., tests, scales, self-reports, subscales, inventories, testlets, questionnaires, or test batteries—have to deal with when attempting to measure constructs under consideration.

First, there is no single approach to construct measurement, which would be always applicable and yield a satisfactory measuring instrument. This is because construct measurement is based on behaviors deemed to be relevant for the latent dimension under study. Hence, it is possible that two theorists having in mind the same construct may select different types of behavior to operationally define that construct. As an example, consider the situation when one wishes to measure elementary school students' ability to carry out long division (e.g., Crocker & Algina, 1986). To this end, one could decide to use tests that are focused on (a) detecting errors made during this process, (b) describing steps involved in the process, or, alternatively, (c) solving a series of division problems. Either of these approaches could be viewed as aiming at evaluating the same construct under consideration, the ability to conduct long division.

A second challenge emerges from the fact that construct measurement is typically based only on limited samples of behavior. The reason is that in empirical research, it is impossible to confront individual subjects using a given instrument with all situations in which a certain construct is presumed to be indicated, demonstrated, or manifested. How many such situations must be included in a test, and of what kinds would they need to be, in order to provide an adequate sample of the pertinent behavioral domain? This is a major problem in developing a sound measurement procedure, specifically one in which domain sampling is involved. For example, an educational researcher cannot ask examined students to solve all possible division problems when he or she is interested in measuring, say, ability to carry out number division. Instead of that, the researcher will need to sample from the domain consisting of all these problems.

As a third challenge, behavioral and social measurements are typically subject to error, i.e., they are error prone rather than error free. Error of measurement results in part from inconsistencies in obtained individual scores, some of which are due to sampling of tasks and/or the actual process of measurement. Main contributors to this error are effects of factors that are unrelated to the studied construct but affect individual performance on a given measure (indicator) of it. Measurement error encompasses such factor effects and will be the subject of further and more detailed discussion in a later chapter of this book dealing with classical test theory (see Chapter 5), which represents a main approach to behavioral measurement. As we will see in that chapter, a persistent problem in measurement is how to evaluate the extent of error present in a given set of observations pertaining to a construct in question. The concepts of reliability and validity, which we will discuss in detail subsequently, are in particular concerned with this problem.

A fourth challenge results from the lack of (substantively) well-defined units as well as origins, or zero points, on used measurement scales in most behavioral and social measurements. For instance, is an individual score of 20 obtained on an aggression test indicative of twice as much aggression than that in a person with a score of 10? Furthermore, does an individual score of 0 on an ability test demonstrate no ability at all? None of these and many other similar questions can necessarily be answered affirmatively because of this lack of well-defined units and origins of measurement in most of present-day behavioral and social research.

Last but not least, constructs cannot be defined only in terms of operational definitions but must also demonstrate relationships (or lack thereof) with other constructs and observable phenomena. Typically, a construct is considered for use in a subject-matter domain where there has been prior theoretical work as well as other constructs studied previously. Hence, this new construct should demonstrate relationships (or, if appropriate, lack thereof) to those already available constructs in that substantive area. With this in mind, there are two levels at which a construct should be defined (e.g., Lord & Novick, 1968). One is operational, which deals with how measurement of a considered construct is to be obtained, i.e., how that construct relates to observable behavior. Another equally important level of construct definition is nomothetic. Accordingly, the construct should fit well into an already existing theoretical 'net' of other, previously established constructs and their relationships in the substantive area of concern. That is, a new construct should demonstrate predictable relationships (whether strong or weak, none, positive or negative) with other constructs available in the subject-matter domain of concern. When this is indeed the case, these relationships provide a basis for interpreting measurements obtained on the proposed construct. If there are no such relationships between the new and earlier established constructs, however, i.e., if there is no empirical evidence for them, there is little value if any in a newly proposed construct.

As an example, consider a test of abstract thinking ability for high school students. That is, suppose this ability is the construct of interest. The nomothetic level of construct definition requires here that scores obtained with this test should exhibit (a) notable relationships with scores on existing tests of algebra, geometry, inductive reasoning, and figural relations and (b) not nearly as strong relationships with scores on tests of knowledge of a foreign language, or history knowledge, as well as other weakly or essentially unrelated on theoretical grounds constructs. In other words, scores on the test of abstract thinking ability should be related markedly with scores on the tests of algebra, geometry, inductive reasoning, and figural relations and at the same time should be only up to marginally related with scores on tests of foreign language or history knowledge.

We will return to this last challenge for behavioral measurement in a later chapter of this book (Chapter 8). We will see then that this challenge has fundamental relevance for most of what measurement is about, i.e., validity of measurement, which can be viewed as the bottom line of behavioral and social measurement. In particular, we will observe that this challenge is of special importance for the most encompassing form of validity, called construct validity.

1.5 Psychometric Theory as a Scientific Discipline

The preceding discussion in this chapter allows us to define now the subject of test theory and more generally that of behavioral measurement, which is often referred to as psychometric theory. (In this text, we will use frequently 'test theory' and 'psychometric theory' as synonyms.) Specifically, psychometric theory is a scientific discipline that is concerned with the study of the above and related pervasive problems and challenges of human behavior measurement (see Section 1.4), using a particular set of methods developed to systematically manage or resolve them (cf. Crocker & Algina, 1986). That is, psychometric theory deals with (a) evaluating the degree to which these problems affect behavioral measurement in a given situation and (b) developing methods to overcome or minimize the adverse impact of these and related problems and challenges.

As a scientific discipline, psychometric theory is based on formal logic as well as mathematical and statistical methods and models (cf. McDonald, 1999). These also underlie standard practices in the process of construction, development, and revision of measuring instruments, as well as in their applications. Becoming aware of these models and underlying methods as well as their assumptions and limitations, in order to ensure improved practice in test construction and use of test information in decision making, is the primary goal of most measurement and test theory treatments, including the present book.

For the purposes of this text, we also need to draw a distinction between (a) psychometric theory and (b) behavioral assessment. Psychometric theory (test theory) is a theoretically oriented field of study, which is of general relevance regardless of the particular test, scale, or measuring instrument used in a given situation where evaluation of behavioral attributes is required. This book is concerned with psychometric theory. In contrast to it, behavioral assessment is primarily an applied, rather than theoretical, subject that is usually focused on administration and interpretation of particular tests used as measuring instruments under certain circumstances. Hence, the subject of behavioral assessment has relevance with regard to specific measuring instruments. This text will not be concerned with behavioral assessment, and we will not discuss it any further. Instead, we emphasize that psychometric theory provides a general framework for behavioral measuring instrument development, including instrument construction, revision, and modification. In order to be in a position to accomplish this goal, psychometric theory is based on general mathematical and statistical approaches, methods, and models that are valid irrespective of any behavioral theory that a researcher may be adopting. Being this general, psychometric theory is useful for measurement of any behavioral construct, such as an attribute, ability, trait, attitude, or aptitude. Although being based on generally valid mathematical and statistical principles, psychometric theory at the same time has been uniquely developed as a scientific discipline to meet the specific needs of behavioral, social, and educational measurement.

With these goals, psychometric theory provides essential input into research in the behavioral and social sciences, especially as far as development and selection of instruments and procedures for quantification of observations on studied variables are concerned. Psychometric theory has some of its major applications in the process of 'pretesting' and improvement of measuring instruments so as to minimize possible error and ensure highest validity with regard to variables involved in examined research hypotheses and questions. In this way, psychometric theory contributes to the provision of a set of high-quality, pretried measuring instruments with known characteristics, from which a scientist can select for use in a given research situation. Psychometric theory is a scientific discipline dealing with the study of how general epistemological problems related to measurement impact the process of quantification of aspects of behavioral phenomena under investigation, as well as with methods aimed at providing information of highest quality about associated constructs from their indirect observations (cf., e.g., Crocker & Algina, 1986).

1.6 Initial Steps in Instrument Construction

As has been indicated on a few occasions in this chapter, our concerns in this book will be with what is oftentimes referred to as subject-centered (person-centered) measurement. In this activity, the goal is to 'reveal' the location of individuals on a (presumed) quantitative continuum with respect to a particular behavioral construct, such as aggression, ability, intelligence, motivation, depression, aspiration, etc. Similarly, instruments of interest to us can also aim to provide information with regard to the level of mastery or proficiency that individuals or examinees possess in a particular subject-matter area.

The remainder of this text deals with a systematic approach to measuring instrument construction with wide applicability to various types of instruments that can be used across the behavioral, social, and educational disciplines. We will treat test construction as a principled approach to the development of behavioral measuring instruments. This process includes a number of stages that we will briefly review in this section. For a more detailed discussion, we refer readers to Allen and Yen (1979), Crocker and Algina (1986), Guilford and Fruchter (1978), McDonald (1999), and Suen (1990); these sources have also significantly influenced the following discussion in this section.

One of the earliest steps in this process is to decide for what purpose the resulting test (instrument) scores will be utilized. A main question a developer should ask initially is whether the instrument is supposed to differentiate among individuals with regard to a given construct or whether the test is to provide scores that describe in some sense absolute (as opposed to relative) levels of proficiency in a given content area. The former is the question raised when an instrument is supposed to evaluate an underlying trait—an activity that is often referred to as trait evaluation—whereas the latter is the query of relevance when one is interested in obtaining information about the level of achievement accomplished by studied subjects and is at times referred to as achievement testing. Within the achievement evaluation approach, the specific goal of the instrument needs to be clarified next. For instance, if an educational diagnostic test is to be designed, areas of specific weaknesses for low-ability students should be identified, and within them items that are relatively easy to solve for the general population should be developed. Alternatively, if a test is required to discriminate well among subjects over a broad range of ability, then items of medium difficulty level are needed, whereas a test measuring high levels of achievement should be composed of more difficult items.

At the next stage of instrument development, the researcher needs to identify behaviors representing the underlying (presumed) construct or define the subject-matter domain of relevance if involved in achievement evaluation (cf. Crocker & Algina, 1986). Either activity requires a thorough content analysis, which should include a critical review of available research. At times, types of behaviors most frequently studied by other scientists can be used when defining a construct of interest, or alternatively delineating extremely low or high performance levels can be of particular help when outlining the domain of knowledge and/or skills to be evaluated by the test under development. Input from substantive experts then will be especially helpful in narrowing down types of behavior pertaining to the construct of interest. Similarly, when developing tests of achievement, researchers should also take instructional objectives into account.

Whenever interest lies in measuring proficiency—as in achievement and aptitude tests—one becomes involved in what is referred to as criterion-referenced measurement, unlike the norm-referenced measurement that is usually conducted when one is concerned with trait evaluation. The underlying basis for the former type of measurement is the activity of domain sampling, which we briefly discussed earlier. The meaning of resulting test scores is then obtained by reference to the criterion (acceptable level of mastery), not to the scores of other individuals. Conversely, the meaning of test scores resulting from norm-referenced measurement is derived from their comparison with other individuals' scores on the same test.

In order to engage in domain sampling, an item domain needs to be available. This is a well-defined population of presumably homogeneous items (measuring the same ability) from which one or more test forms may be constructed by selection of a sample(s) of items. The creation of the item domain is facilitated by producing a set of item-domain specifications so structured that items written according to them could be considered to be interchangeable. In some cases, an item domain could be defined by certain algorithms for item creation, as in mathematics ability testing. More generally, the generation of an item domain is a sophisticated process that requires professional expertise and special training. The specific activity of item writing that is involved thereby will not be a concern of this text. For extensive discussion on the topic we refer the reader to Thissen and Wainer (2001) and Haladyna (2004; see also McDonald, 1999).

In a next step of the process of test construction, an early form of the instrument is tried out (piloted) on a small sample of subjects from the intended population (cf. Suen, 1990). Thereby, one invites comments from participants on how they perceived each item in the test. Following that, the descriptive statistics for the response distributions on each item are examined. This preliminary tryout can help make decisions about revision of some items, upon which usually a 'field test' on a larger sample from the studied population is conducted. Statistical properties of the items are examined then, possibly using procedures known as item analysis—frequently referred to as classical item analysis—which we will be in part concerned with in Chapters 2 and 4. At this stage, it may be decided that some items should be removed from the test. A study of reliability and validity of the instrument is then to be carried out, based on results of this field test. Corresponding revisions are usually undertaken then, with the aim of producing an improved version of the instrument. Establishing guides for test score interpretation is the next step, which is an involved process requiring professional attention. This process is part of the subject behavioral assessment, which as mentioned before will not be of concern in this book.

This section aimed only to provide a brief discussion of some of the steps involved in the process of instrument (test, scale) construction. Subsequent chapters will be concerned with how one can study important properties of the resulting instrument and how to improve these. Before we turn to them, however, we take another look at measuring instruments used in the behavioral and social sciences, with the particular aim of making a few observations with regard to their building blocks.

1.7 Measuring Instrument Scores as Composites

The earlier discussion in this chapter indicated that because of a number of difficult problems and challenges in behavioral and social measurement, one typically aims at obtaining multiple sources of information about a studied construct. They are usually furnished by distinct measures of construct manifestations, and their interrelationships may permit evaluation of that latent dimension.

Such an evaluation is also often aimed at in empirical research by a composite score (overall score) obtained from the multiple measures, or construct indicators, frequently referred to as components of the composite. They are typically individual testlets, items, subscales, subtests, or questions. Hence, a 'composite' can be viewed as synonymous to a 'test' consisting of multiple components or, more generally, to a 'test battery'. An alternative reference to a composite is scale, multiple-component measuring instrument, or just measuring instrument. Each of its components yields a separate score, and usually their sum furnishes an overall score, often referred to as the sum score. For example, the score on a depression test is usually the sum of the scores a person obtains on each of its items. The score on an algebra knowledge test is often the number of correct answers on the set of problems to be solved by the examined students, which is the sum of formal indicators for a true versus false response on these tasks. Once obtained, the composite score may be considered an indirect measure of the underlying latent construct.

More generally, a composite is a sum of scores on subtests (items, components, testlets, subscales, questions), whereby this sum may be directly resulting from their simple addition or such after their multiplication with some component-specific weights. In the former case, the composite is also referred to as unit weighted or unweighted, whereas in the latter case it is typically called a weighted composite (or weighted scale). This book deals predominantly with unweighted composites and will use the term 'test', 'scale', or 'multiple-component measuring instrument' ('instrument') as synonymous to 'composite' or 'sum score'. The majority of the procedures discussed in this book are also applicable to weighted scales with known weights, and extensions for some of them are available in case of unknown weights (e.g., Li, 1997; Li, Rosenthal, & Rubin, 1996; Raykov, 2004, 2005; Raykov & Hancock, 2005; Raykov & Penev, 2006, 2009, and references therein).

When administered and scored in empirical research, behavior measuring instruments give rise to a table called 'person–item score matrix' that contains the raw data, i.e., the data collected from the examined individuals. In this table, the rows correspond to persons and the columns correspond to the items, with a possibly subsequently added last row and last column as totals for items and for persons, respectively. Oftentimes, the entries of this table are 0s and 1s, corresponding to correct or false response, respectively (or to present–absent, endorsed–not endorsed, yes–no, agree–disagree answers). To analyze the so-obtained raw data set, one needs to make use of certain statistical concepts, methods, and models. A brief review of some important notions in this respect is provided in the next chapter.

2

Basic Statistical Concepts and Relationships

As a scientific discipline of inquiry, psychometric theory makes extensive use of statistical and mathematical methods and models. There are two primary purposes that statistics is utilized for in psychometric theory and its applications—description and inference. This chapter reviews a number of important statistical concepts, which will be of relevance in the rest of this book.

2.1 Behavioral Characteristics as Random Variables

In social and behavioral research, we are typically interested in person variables and their relationships. In applications of psychometric theory, such variables are often referred to as 'measures'. We will reserve this reference for variables whose individual realizations are observed, i.e., when their values collected from examined individuals are available. An alternative reference will be as observed variables (observed measures) or manifest variables.

More generally, a variable is a behavioral characteristic that takes individual-specific values in a given sample (population) and as such is generally not expected to be equal across studied persons. That is, variable is a concept that is the opposite to that of constant. We are not interested really in studying constants in social and behavioral research, because they do not vary across persons and thus typically do not contain information of relevance when behavioral phenomena are of concern. We mention, though, that some special mathematical constants will be important for us, such as the numbers $e = 2.718...$ and $\pi = 3.1415....$ As one may recall, the former constant is used as the natural logarithm base, whereas the latter constant represents the ratio of the circumference of a circle to its diameter. These two constants appear also in the definition of the normal distribution density function (Section 2.3).

Whenever variables are discussed throughout this book, we will imply they are random variables (e.g., Agresti & Finlay, 2009). These are variables whose values in a given group of subjects (sample or population) are unknown before a study is carried out that involves collection of data from the subjects on their corresponding characteristics. In other words, a random variable is such a variable whose individual scores (i.e., individual realizations) do not exist prior to the actual conducting of the study for which it is of relevance but become available only after that study has been carried out.

As it could be anticipated from Chapter 1, random variables can be either observed or latent. Observed variables will frequently represent manifestations, or indicators, of constructs (latent variables) in this book. For instance, observed measures can be obtained with an intelligence test battery, e.g., the 11 measures of the Wechsler Adult Intelligence Scale (WAIS; Chapter 3). Alternatively, latent variables have individual scores (realizations) that are not available to us, i.e., cannot be directly observed and thus are in a sense hidden from us; although these variables are not directly observed, their (presumed) manifestations are demonstrated in overt behavior and can thus be used as indicators or proxies of the latent variables. We will use the concept of latent variable mostly to denote a construct in this text (see Chapter 1). We stress that even though they are not observed, it is meaningful to talk about latent constructs as variables. This is because their scores also vary from subject to subject in general, despite the fact that we cannot measure them directly. We also emphasize that both observed and latent variables in this text are random variables. Their only distinction is that although both types of variables obtain individual realizations for all persons participating in a given study (sample or population), the realizations of the latent variables are not available, even after the study has been completed; i.e., they are inherently unobservable, unlike the realizations of the observed variables that are available in the collected (recorded) data set.

We note that the stated definition of latent variable includes, but is not limited to, latent constructs (as used in this text). As a simple example, an error term commonly encountered in a statistical model, for instance, a regression model, is a latent variable. However, we will not consider in this book such latent variables to be constructs, as they typically are without specific substantive meaning. Further examples of latent variables will be provided in Chapter 4, where we will be discussing the comprehensive applied statistical methodology of latent variable modeling.

In this book, we will also oftentimes refer to dependent and independent variables. As is well-known from research method texts (e.g., Graziano & Raulin, 2009), dependent variables are those of major interest when addressing a particular research question. Independent variables are the ones that are used to explain variability in the dependent variables. We will frequently use alternative references, such as response or outcome, for dependent variables or measures, and predictors, explanatory variables, or covariates for the independent variables (measures).

Another important distinction between random variables in psychometric theory and its applications derives from their nature. Specifically, we will differentiate between continuous and discrete variables, especially when these are dependent (response, outcome) variables. Generally, a variable that can take on any value between two given scores in its range is called continuous. Alternatively, a variable that can take on only a finite (or strictly speaking up to a countable) number of scores is called discrete. In psychometric theory, it will often be appropriate to consider as approximately continuous a variable that takes at least a certain number of distinct values in a study (preferably, say, 15 or more). Examples of such variables are scores from an intelligence test, age, or overall scores obtained from a depression inventory or mathematics ability test, to mention only a few. Conversely, we will typically consider as discrete a variable that can take a very limited number of scores in a given study. For instance, a binary measure that takes on the values of 'yes' or 'no', or alternatively 'endorsed' or 'not endorsed', 'true' or 'false', 'correct' or 'incorrect', 'present' or 'absent', is clearly a discrete variable. The responses to a question in a survey, which has as only possible answers the categories *strongly disagree, disagree, agree,* and *strongly agree,* will also be considered discrete. We will have more to say on this distinction later in this book, but for now we emphasize only its relevance with respect to the response (outcome, dependent) variables. The reason is that (approximately) continuous response variables require the use of particular types of statistical methods, which are distinct from the ones needed for analyzing data from discrete outcome variables. From a pragmatic viewpoint, the easiest way to find out which variable is of which kind, if not known beforehand, is to examine its associated observed score frequencies (frequency table or stem-and-leaf plot). They are easily obtained using widely circulated statistical software, such as SPSS (PASW), SAS, STATA, or R, to name a few. These particular activities will not be of concern in this book, and we refer readers to the manuals of these or other statistical analysis programs or numerous sources discussing their applications on data (e.g., McCall, 2005; Raykov & Marcoulides, 2008; Shavelson, 1996).

2.2 Variable Distributions and Parameters

Each random variable of concern in this book will be associated with a distribution. A variable distribution reflects the way in which its scores relate to one another. In behavioral and social measurement, these scores usually are the recorded (measured) observations on multiple individual realizations of the random variable, which are obtained from studied individuals (or aggregates of such if used as units of analysis)—e.g., subjects participating in an empirical investigation or potentially the members of a population under consideration. Important information about a variable's distribution can be readily rendered, once data are available on the variable, using for example popular statistical software like those mentioned in the preceding section. Statistical tests could also be used to ascertain some types of distributions. The discussion of these tests will not be of concern in our text, and we refer to other sources for them (e.g., Krishnamoorthy, 2006).

Often in this book, a variable distribution will be characterized by measures of central tendency or location, such as the mean, and of variability or dispersion, such as the variance. (Further measures of central tendency, variability, and related variable characteristics, which will not be used explicitly in this text, are discussed in alternative treatments, and we refer to them here; e.g., King and Minium [2003].) These measures typically take unknown values in a studied population and are commonly referred to as parameters. More precisely, a parameter is a number or a set of numbers that characterize a specific aspect(s) of a population distribution of a given variable(s), e.g., mean(s), variance(s), correlation or covariance coefficient(s), regression slope, intercept, etc.

2.2.1 Mean and Item Difficulty

For a particular random variable, denoted X, its mean in a population of N subjects (N being typically large and finite, as usually the case in current behavioral and social research and assumed in this book) is defined as

$$\mu_X = \frac{1}{N}(X_1 + X_2 + \cdots + X_N) = \frac{1}{N}\sum_{i=1}^{N} X_i,$$

where X_1 through X_N denote the values of X for the members of the population (the sign Σ in the right-hand side is used to denote summation across the subindex range indicated at its bottom and top). The mean can be estimated by the arithmetic average of the scores on X obtained in a given sample, i.e., by

$$\hat{\mu}_X = \bar{X} = \frac{1}{n}(X_1 + X_2 + \cdots + X_n) = \frac{1}{n}\sum_{i=1}^{n} X_i, \tag{2.1}$$

where X_1 through X_n symbolize these scores, n is sample size, and a caret is used to denote estimate (estimator), a practice followed throughout the rest of this text.

The mean is of particular relevance in behavioral and social measurement when a studied random variable is binary. Such a variable can take on as mentioned one of only two possible values—e.g., correct–incorrect response on an item from a test, yes–no response on a question from a survey, present–absent for a symptom in a clinical study, or a 0–1 response as a more general notation (with 1 used to denote a correct response). In this case, as is well-known from introductory statistics discussions, the mean of the variable is the probability of response symbolized as 1 (e.g., Agresti & Finlay, 2009). In psychometric theory, this probability can be of special importance when constructing and revising multiple-component measuring instruments and in particular achievement tests. The reason is that this probability is in fact that of correctly solving an item under consideration. As such, that probability reflects the difficulty (actually, the 'easiness') of the item, and this is why it is frequently and traditionally referred to as difficulty of the item. In an empirical study, this probability is estimated by the average response on the item, i.e., by Equation (2.1) where a 0 or 1 is inserted in its right-hand side for the incorrect or correct individual answers, respectively. Routine evaluation of item difficulty in an instrument consisting of binary (as well as more general) components is an important component of what has been traditionally referred to as item analysis (also at times called classical item analysis; e.g., Crocker & Algina, 1986). In fact, item difficulty estimation is often performed as a first step in this analytic activity and can be readily carried out with widely circulated statistical software like the ones mentioned in the Section 2.1. We return to this issue later in this book (Chapter 4).

2.2.2 Variance and Standard Deviation

In a more general setting, to what extent is the mean on a random variable informative of the possible scores that it can take in a group of studied individuals? For distributions with a wide spread around the mean, obviously the latter is far less informative than in distributions for which the majority of the scores are tightly clustered around the mean. The degree to which the mean is representative of most scores in a population on a variable under consideration, i.e., the extent to which its values are dispersed around its mean there, is captured at the individual level by the deviation scores $x_i = X_i - \mu_X$ ($i = 1, 2, \ldots, N$) and at the population level by the variance or standard deviation of X:

$$\sigma_X^2 = \frac{1}{N} \sum_{i=1}^{N} x_i^2,$$

or

$$\sigma_X = \sqrt{\frac{1}{N} \sum_{i=1}^{N} x_i^2},$$

respectively (with positive square root taken in the last equation). The standard deviation becomes of special interest when interested in evaluating precision of measurement in behavioral and social research. In particular, within the framework of the so-called classical test theory (Chapter 5), the standard deviation of an observed score is directly related to the standard error of measurement that may be viewed as the error involved in predicting an individual score on a construct of interest using the available observed score.

The last two definitional equations allow one to determine the variance and standard deviation of a random variable if an entire (finite) population of concern were available. This will rarely be the case in empirical social and behavioral research that typically works, because of a number of reasons, with samples from populations of interest (e.g., Agresti & Finlay, 2009). Then the variance and standard deviation are estimated in an available sample correspondingly by

$$\hat{\sigma}_X^2 = s_X^2 = \frac{1}{n-1} \sum_{i=1}^{n} (X_i - \bar{X})^2, \tag{2.2}$$

and

$$\hat{\sigma}_X = s_X = \sqrt{\frac{1}{n-1} \sum_{i=1}^{n} (X_i - \bar{X})^2}$$

(with a positive square root taken in the last equation).

In conclusion of this section, we note that in applications of psychometric theory, and for the purposes of this book, it can be assumed without (significant) loss of generality that means and variances always exist for studied variables (cf. Lord & Novick, 1968).

2.2.3 z-Scores

Different variables in behavioral and social research are typically measured using different scales whose units are not readily comparable, if at all, with one another. These units of measurement are in addition often arbitrary and perhaps meaningless, if not irrelevant. This makes comparison of subject performance across variables (e.g., subtests, components, subscales) very difficult if not impossible. To allow some comparability of individual scores across variables (measures), the z-scores are useful. In a studied population and for a given variable X, these scores are defined as

$$z_{X,i} = \frac{X_i - \mu_X}{\sigma_X},$$

for each subject ($i = 1, 2, \ldots, N$). In an available sample, the z-scores are estimated as

$$\hat{z}_{X,i} = \frac{X_i - \hat{\mu}_X}{\hat{\sigma}_X} = \frac{X_i - \bar{X}}{s_X} \tag{2.3}$$

($i = 1, 2, \ldots, n$; frequently in behavioral research the caret above z in the last equation is left out when estimated z-scores are used, in case no confusion can arise). We note that the mean of the z-scores on any variable is 0 whereas their variance is 1. The utility of the z-scores derives from the fact that they equal the distance of an observed score, for a given variable and subject, to the variable's mean, whereby this distance is measured in standard deviation units of that variable. We stress that z-scores are unitless or 'pure' numbers. Comparison of individual performance across studied variables is somewhat more facilitated when using z-scores, although it can be meaningless if only raw scores are used for this purpose.

2.3 The Normal Distribution

Many scores on multiple-component measuring instruments (tests, scales) follow approximately a normal distribution in a given sample and could be reasonably assumed to follow (approximately) a normal distribution in a studied population. This can be seen as a consequence from the so-called central limit theorem. Accordingly, the sum of a large number of random variables, whereby none dominates the others (in terms of its variance), approximately follows a normal distribution (e.g., King & Minium, 2003).

The normal distribution, for a given random variable X, is a continuous distribution that, as is well-known, is characterized by a bell-shaped curve of its density function. The latter is defined as follows (the argument u used next is unrestricted, i.e., covers all real numbers):

$$f_X(u) = \frac{1}{\sigma_X \sqrt{2\pi}} e^{-.5(u-\mu_X)^2/\sigma_X^2}. \tag{2.4}$$

This density expression can be used to work out the probability of a randomly drawn person to obtain a score falling within a given interval or above or below a particular value. The probability referred to is the area below the pertinent density curve and within the corresponding interval or across the respective range above or below that threshold. This probability is obtained by integrating, using numerical methods, the normal distribution density (2.4) across the corresponding range of u and is readily carried out in practice using statistical software. From Equation (2.4) it is also seen that there are infinitely many normal distributions, each characterized by its own mean and standard deviation. One of them, the standard normal distribution, plays a special role. This distribution has a mean of 0 and variance of 1, and its density is obtained from (2.4) by substituting these values for the mean and variance, respectively, appearing there. This special distribution is tabulated in most introductory statistics textbooks (e.g., Agresti & Finlay, 2009; McCall, 2005).

We conclude this short section by mentioning that the entire area below the normal density curve is conventionally assumed to equal 1. Also, some 68% of the area below the normal density curve is within 1 standard deviation from the mean; some 95% of it within 2 standard deviations; and some 99% of that area lies within 3 standard deviations from the mean. That is, it is very rare that a score from a normal distribution could be further away than 3 standard deviations from the mean, but such cases should not be unexpected in large samples from a normal distribution.

2.4 Variable Relationship Indexes

There are many instances in theoretical and empirical research when one is interested in examining how scores on two or more measures relate to one another. In psychometric theory, as in many other fields of quantitative science, variable relationships are of fundamental relevance. They become of particular interest when, for instance, questions like the following are asked: How does the SAT Verbal score relate to an intelligence test score? Or how is social support related to depression, or how does a mathematics ability test score relate to that on a reading ability measure? One possible way to understand this relationship is to use scatterplots that provide a graphical display of bivariate relationships. Scatterplots are widely used in practice, although their interpretation is eventually subjective, and the procedures to obtain them have received ample discussion in alternative textbooks (e.g., Cohen, Cohen, West, & Aiken, 2002; Kerlinger, 2001; King & Minium, 2003).

In addition to graphical representation, oftentimes it is desirable to have a numerical index of variable relationship, in particular of possible linear relationship. Such indexes are the covariance coefficient and the correlation coefficient. In a studied (finite) population, for a pair of variables X and Y, the covariance coefficient can be defined as

$$Cov(X, Y) = \frac{1}{N} \sum_{i=1}^{N} (X_i - \bar{X})(Y_i - \bar{Y}).$$

This coefficient is estimated in a given sample by

$$c_{X,Y} = \frac{1}{n-1} \sum_{i=1}^{n} (X_i - \bar{X})(Y_i - \bar{Y}). \tag{2.5}$$

We note in passing that the variance estimate results from the last equation by setting $X = Y$ (because the variance of any random variable is its covariance with itself; e.g., Agresti & Finlay, 2009). Unlike the covariance coefficient that is a nonnormed measure of linear relationship—and thus can take on any value, whether positive, negative, or zero—the correlation coefficient lies within the closed interval [–1, +1]. In the population, the correlation coefficient is defined as

$$\rho_{X,Y} = \frac{Cov(X, Y)}{\sqrt{Var(X)Var(Y)}}, \tag{2.6}$$

where $Var(.)$ denotes variance (as in the rest of this book) and can be estimated in a sample by

$$\hat{\rho}_{X,Y} = \frac{1}{n-1} \sum_{i=1}^{n} \hat{z}_{X,i} \hat{z}_{Y,i}, \tag{2.7}$$

which estimate is frequently denoted alternatively by $r_{X,Y}$. We note that the correlation coefficient is not defined if any of the variables have zero variance (see Equation (2.6)). That is, if at least one of the variables is a constant (which is equivalent to its variance being 0), then its correlation does not exist, and its covariance is 0.

According to its definition, the correlation coefficient is a unitless quantity, i.e., a 'pure' number that is also a symmetric measure or linear relationship. We interpret it in empirical research by paying attention to the following questions. One, what is its sign? If it is positive, then larger (or smaller) values on X tend to 'go together' with larger (smaller) values on Y; if it is negative, then larger values on X go together with smaller values on Y, and conversely. Two, what is its value? To make better sense of it, we square the correlation coefficient (estimate) to obtain in this way the percentage of variance in one of the variables that is explained in terms of its linear relationship with the other variable (e.g., Agresti & Finlay, 2009). As a third possible point worth noting here, if one were interested in testing the null hypothesis of the corresponding population correlation coefficient being 0, the question asked when looking at its sample estimate would be if the latter is 'significant'. The answer to this question responds to the query whether the difference from 0 of the observed correlation coefficient could be explained by chance effects only. Detailed discussions concerning how to conduct this test, as well as how to obtain, alternatively, confidence intervals for correlation coefficients, are provided elsewhere (e.g., King & Minium, 2003; McCall, 2005; see also Chapter 4 regarding interval estimation of some correlation coefficients).

We note that a relatively small value of a correlation coefficient may be the result of restriction of range, not necessarily of lack of discernible linear association in the population between the two variables involved (e.g., King & Minium, 2003). One could check for restriction of range by examining how the sample standard deviations of studied variables relate to what may be known about them in the population. In addition, one should revisit the data collection procedure, because a ceiling or floor effect may have been operating during the observation process (e.g., Graziano & Raulin, 2009). Similarly, one should examine whether any restriction could have been in place when selecting sample subjects. In particular, one may have chosen samples from prespecified groups without being aware of it (e.g., only students going to college, rather than all high school seniors, may have been administered the tests or measures under consideration). Last but not least, one should look also at the scatterplot that may indirectly point to a threshold operating in the sample.

In conclusion of this section, we emphasize that, as is well-known from introductory statistics discussions (e.g., McCall, 2005), correlation does not imply causation. Similarly, correlation is a measure only of linear relationship, with no information about possible nonlinear relationship between studied variables. In order to rule out the latter possibility, one can regularly check the data scatterplots in an attempt to spot patterns of nonlinear relationships if present.

2.5 Variances and Covariances of Linear Combinations of Random Variables

As indicated in Chapter 1, measuring instruments used in applications of psychometric theory very often represent composites, i.e., in general linear combinations of random variables reflecting performance on test (scale) components or items. Several straightforward rules can be used to obtain indices of variability and covariability for the resulting overall test scores (e.g., Raykov & Marcoulides, 2006a). To describe these rules, denote by $X_1, X_2, ..., X_p$ a given set of random variables ($p \geq 1$). For example, these could be considered components of a test (test battery) under construction. Then the variance of their linear combination is

$$Var(a_1X_1 + a_2X_2 + \cdots + a_pX_p) = a_1^2Var(X_1) + \cdots + a_p^2Var(X_p) + 2\sum_{i<j} Cov(X_i, X_j), \qquad (2.8)$$

where the *a*s are prespecified constants (weights for this linear combination). Similarly, the covariance of two linear combinations of $X_1, X_2, ..., X_p$ and of another set of random variables $Y_1, Y_2, ..., Y_p$, is

$$Cov(a_1X_1 + a_2X_2 + \cdots + a_pX_p, b_1Y_1 + b_2Y_2 + \cdots + b_pY_p)$$

$$= \sum_{1 \leq i,j \leq p} a_i b_j Cov(X_i, Y_j) \qquad (2.9)$$

where also the *b*s are a set of constants. (The expression in the right-hand side of Equation (2.9) is readily modified for the case of different numbers of variables in these variable sets, say *p* and *q*, with $p \neq q$, $p \geq 1$, $q \geq 1$.) We note in passing that setting all *a*s and all *b*s equal to 1 in Equations (2.8) and (2.9) leads directly to the following variance and covariance expressions for test scores resulting as overall sums from scores on a set of components ($p \geq 1$, $q \geq 1$):

$$Var(X_1 + X_2 + \cdots + X_p) = Var(X_1) + Var(X_2) + \cdots + Var(X_p) + 2[Cov(X_1, X_2) + Cov(X_1, X_3)$$
$$+ Cov(X_1, X_4) + \cdots + Cov(X_{p-2}, X_p) + Cov(X_{p-1}, X_p)], \tag{2.10}$$

and

$$Cov(X_1 + X_2 + \cdots + X_p, Y_1 + Y_2 + \cdots + Y_q) = Cov(X_1, Y_1) + \cdots + Cov(X_1, Y_q) + \cdots + Cov(X_p, Y_1)$$
$$+ \cdots + Cov(X_p, Y_q).$$

We will use the relationships in Equations (2.8) through (2.10) on a number of occasions later in this book.

2.6 A Short Introduction to Matrix Algebra

In psychometric theory and its applications, we are often interested in relationships between several sets of scores either resulting from instrument components or representing their overall scores. To be in a position to deal with such multiple sets of random variables, which quite often will also be interrelated among themselves, we will need more powerful techniques that allow one to simultaneously handle them. These techniques are provided by matrix algebra (MA). We will briefly discuss in this section some important facts from MA; for further detail we refer the reader to more comprehensive discussions available in the literature (e.g., see Raykov & Marcoulides, 2008, for a nontechnical discussion of main concepts and relations in MA).

The reason why MA is so important for this book, like many others dealing with behavioral and social measurement and its applications, is that MA furnishes a compact language that unifies important aspects of univariate and multivariate statistics. In this way, MA allows one to understand multivariable techniques using their univariate analogues and counterparts. Also, and no less important, MA permits one to quickly obtain insights about and in particular communicate ideas that are based on multiple random variables and their interrelationships.

2.6.1 Types of Matrices

Matrix algebra operates with various types of matrices. A matrix is defined as a rectangular set (table, array) of numbers, which as a special case can be in the form of a square—when the matrix is referred to as a square matrix. In this book, matrices will mostly represent indexes of interrelationship between studied variables or reflect relationships between sets of random variables (vectors). Special cases of matrices, viz., vectors, will represent sets of observed or latent variables.

As a general notation for matrix, denoted A, we will use the following:

$$
A = \begin{bmatrix}
a_{11} & a_{12} & \cdots & a_{1p} \\
a_{21} & a_{22} & \cdots & a_{2p} \\
\cdot & \cdot & \cdot & \cdot \\
a_{n1} & a_{n2} & \cdots & a_{np}
\end{bmatrix},
\tag{2.11}
$$

for short also symbolized $A = [a_{ij}]$ ($i = 1, 2, ..., n$; $j = 1, 2, ..., p$; $n \geq 1$, $p \geq 1$). We will refer to such a matrix as being of size $n \times p$, i.e., having n rows and p columns. (That is, 'size' refers to the number of rows and number of columns of the matrix.)

Often in this text, the rows of a matrix will correspond to persons and its columns to variables. Then a_{ij} will denote the score that the ith person has received on the jth variable. At other times, a square matrix (i.e., a matrix with $n = p$ rows and columns) will consist of all covariance coefficients, or all correlation coefficients, among a set of p studied variables. We note that these variables need not all be observed, and in fact some if not all of them may be latent. Alternatively, a matrix may consist of all possible regression coefficients when regressing a set of dependent variables upon several independent variables. Thereby, one or more latent variables may be used in either role, not only observed ones. Later chapters of this book will frequently utilize matrices of various kinds that involve observed and latent variables.

A special type of matrix, which will frequently be used in this book, is the vector. There are two types of vectors—row vectors and column vectors. (If we use only the reference 'vector', we will mean a column vector, a widely adopted convention in the literature.) A row vector is a matrix of size $1 \times p$, whereas a column vector is a matrix of size $q \times 1$ ($p, q \geq 1$). We will designate vectors using underscoring (underlining) of their symbol. The following are examples of a row vector and of a column vector, x and y, respectively:

$$\underline{x} = [1, 3, 5]$$

and

$$
\underline{y} = \begin{bmatrix}
6 \\
1 \\
4 \\
5
\end{bmatrix}.
$$

A further special case is that of a matrix of size 1×1, which is referred to as scalar. For instance, the matrix $H = [h]$, where h is a real number, is a scalar. Obviously, such a matrix consists of a single entry (element) and can also be considered a special case of a row vector or of a column vector, viz., when correspondingly $p = 1$ or $q = 1$ (in the respective of the above definitions of these types of vectors).

2.6.2 Matrix Operations

Before we discuss specific matrix relationships, we need to define when we will consider two matrices equal or unequal to one another (cf. Raykov & Marcoulides, 2008). Two or more matrices are equal if (a) they are of the same size (i.e., have the same number of rows and the same number of columns) and (b) each element of one of them is identical to the element in the other, which is in the same position. The following is an example of two equal matrices, denoted A and B:

$$A = \begin{bmatrix} 2 & 3 \\ 3 & 2 \\ 4 & 2 \end{bmatrix}$$

and

$$B = \begin{bmatrix} 2 & 3 \\ 3 & 2 \\ 4 & 2 \end{bmatrix}.$$

More generally, if $A = [a_{ij}]$ and $B = [b_{ij}]$ are of the same size and in addition $a_{ij} = b_{ij}$ for all i and j (i.e., for all elements of A and B), then A and B are equal, and we symbolize this relationship by $A = B$. When two matrices C and D are of different size, or if for at least one pair of i and j it holds that $a_{ij} \neq b_{ij}$, then C and D are referred to as unequal, symbolized as $C \neq D$. For example, the following two matrices are not equal:

$$C = \begin{bmatrix} 2 & 3 \\ 3 & 2 \\ 4 & 2 \end{bmatrix} \neq \begin{bmatrix} 2 & 2 \\ 3 & 3 \\ 4 & 2 \end{bmatrix} = D.$$

We note that even though C and D consist of the same numbers (elements), because these numbers are positioned at different places, these two matrices are not equal.

Having defined matrix equality, we are ready for a brief discussion of some matrix operations that will be used later in this book. Two of the simplest are matrix addition and subtraction. In order for these operations to be possible to execute on two or more matrices, they all must be conform, i.e., of the same size. In other words, the matrices need to have the same number of rows and the same number of columns. When this is the case, addition and subtraction are defined as addition and subtraction, respectively, carried out on their corresponding elements. For instance, the following two matrices are added by adding each of their elements that are located at the same position (row and column):

$$\begin{bmatrix} 3 & 7 & 4 \\ 2 & 4 & 5 \\ 1 & 4 & 3 \end{bmatrix} + \begin{bmatrix} 11 & 13 & 14 \\ 2 & 4 & 5 \\ 2 & 3 & 4 \end{bmatrix} = \begin{bmatrix} 14 & 20 & 18 \\ 4 & 8 & 10 \\ 3 & 7 & 7 \end{bmatrix},$$

and similarly for their difference holds:

$$\begin{bmatrix} 3 & 7 & 4 \\ 2 & 4 & 5 \\ 1 & 4 & 3 \end{bmatrix} - \begin{bmatrix} 11 & 13 & 14 \\ 2 & 4 & 5 \\ 2 & 3 & 4 \end{bmatrix} = \begin{bmatrix} -8 & -6 & -10 \\ 0 & 0 & 0 \\ -1 & 1 & -1 \end{bmatrix}.$$

This definition is readily extended to any number of matrices to be added or subtracted. We note in passing that the matrices involved do not need to be square, as they happen to be in these two examples, but need only to be conform.

To multiply a matrix with a number, we just multiply each element of the matrix by that number, as exemplified next (with '×' symbolizing multiplication):

$$
3 \times \begin{bmatrix} 2 & 4 \\ 3 & 2 \\ 1 & 5 \end{bmatrix} = \begin{bmatrix} 6 & 12 \\ 9 & 6 \\ 3 & 15 \end{bmatrix}.
$$

We stress that there is no requirement on matrix size for any matrix involved in order for addition, subtraction, and multiplication with a number to be carried out; however, for addition and subtraction, the matrices must be of the same size (i.e., they must have the same number of rows and the same number of columns).

We will frequently carry out in this book another relatively simple operation on a given matrix, which is called transposition. This operation consists of exchanging rows with columns (or vice versa) and is exemplified as follows, with the prime symbolizing transposition:

$$
\begin{bmatrix} 4 & 3 & 5 \\ 2 & 6 & 7 \\ 3 & 5 & 6 \end{bmatrix}' = \begin{bmatrix} 4 & 2 & 3 \\ 3 & 6 & 5 \\ 5 & 7 & 6 \end{bmatrix}.
$$

That is, the kth row (column) of the transposed matrix is the kth column (row) of the original matrix, where $k = 1, 2, 3$ in the last example and $k = 1, \ldots, p$ in the general case of a matrix of size $p \times p$ (see below). We note that the transposed matrix of one that is the result of an initial transposition is the starting matrix, i.e., $(A')' = A$. Also, we stress that the definition of transposition does not require that a matrix be quadratic (like the one in the last example happens to be; see below).

A special kind of matrix is the one that remains unchanged when transposed. Such a matrix is called symmetric. As is well-known from introductory statistics courses, any covariance or correlation matrix is symmetric. (For symmetric matrices, we will usually present only their elements on the main diagonal and beneath it.) We note that only square matrices can be symmetric, because the transposed of a nonsymmetric matrix has obviously a different size than that of the initial matrix.

Row vectors and column vectors are readily transposed (as are rectangular matrices, more generally) by simply using the above definition of this operation. Thereby, the transpose of a row vector is a column vector with the same elements, and vice versa. As an example, if $\underline{x} = [3, 5, 7]$ is a given row vector, then its transpose is

$$
\underline{x}' = \begin{bmatrix} 3 \\ 5 \\ 7 \end{bmatrix},
$$

i.e., a column vector. Similarly, if

$$
\underline{y} = \begin{bmatrix} 6 \\ 1 \\ 4 \\ 5 \end{bmatrix}
$$

is a (column) vector of interest, then its transpose is $y' = [6, 1, 4, 5]$, i.e., a row vector. (At times, it may be preferable to present a column vector, like y, by attaching the transpose sign to its symbol, i.e., $y' = [6, 1, 4, 5]$ in the last example.) We also note that for any scalar h, it is true that it represents a symmetric matrix, i.e., $h' = h$.

The matrix operation that will be quite often used in this book is matrix multiplication. In order to carry it out, the matrices involved must be multiplication conform (m.c.). Two matrices of size $n \times p$ and $s \times q$ are m.c. when $p = s$, i.e., when the number of columns of the first listed matrix equals the number of rows of the second listed matrix. (There is no limitation on n and q, as long as they are integer numbers, i.e., whole positive numbers; in particular, the matrices need not be of the same size, and none of them need be square.) That is, unless $p = s$, matrix multiplication is not defined, i.e., one cannot multiply the two matrices in question.

If A and B are two m.c. matrices, then the ijth element of their product $C = AB$ is the sum of products of corresponding elements in the ith row of A with those of the jth column of B. As an example, consider the following matrices A and B:

$$A = \begin{bmatrix} 3 & 5 \\ 4 & 7 \end{bmatrix}, \quad B = \begin{bmatrix} 7 & 4 \\ 5 & 3 \end{bmatrix}.$$

Then the element in the first row and first column of their product $C = AB$, i.e., c_{11}, is $3 \times 7 + 5 \times 5 = 46$ (with '$\times$' denoting multiplication of the two numbers involved). Similarly, the entry in the first row and second column of C is $c_{12} = 3 \times 4 + 5 \times 3 = 27$. Furthermore, the element in the second row and first column of C is $c_{21} = 4 \times 7 + 7 \times 5 = 63$. Finally, the last entry of C is $c_{44} = 4 \times 4 + 7 \times 3 = 37$. Hence,

$$C = AB = \begin{bmatrix} 46 & 27 \\ 63 & 37 \end{bmatrix}.$$

An important fact to keep in mind is that matrix multiplication is not commutative, unlike, say, multiplication of real numbers (e.g., $6 \times 7 = 7 \times 6 = 42$). Specifically, the product AB may but need not equal the product BA. In fact, if the product AB is defined (i.e., exists), then the product BA need not even be defined or exist, because B and A may not be m.c. (in this order of multiplication). Notice also that in the last example

$$BA = \begin{bmatrix} 37 & 63 \\ 27 & 46 \end{bmatrix} \neq AB = C.$$

That is, order of multiplication of two (or more) matrices does matter, unlike the case of real numbers when it does not. As another example, consider the case when AB exists but BA does not:

$$A = \begin{bmatrix} 4 & 33 \\ 21 & 23 \\ 32 & 3 \end{bmatrix}, \quad B = \begin{bmatrix} 12 & 3 & 4 & 5 \\ 3 & 66 & 5 & 79 \end{bmatrix}.$$

Here, because the number of columns of A equals that of rows of B, the product AB does exist. However, because the number of columns of B (which is 4) is unequal to the number of rows of A (which is 3), the product BA does not even exist.

Therefore, when speaking of matrix multiplication, one should be clear whether one means that A is to be postmultiplied with B, i.e., if one is referring to C = AB (if this product exists), or one alternatively means to postmultiply B with A, i.e., one is referring to the product D = BA (if BA exists). In general, as mentioned above, this matrix D need not equal C (if both matrices exist). This fact is a result of the observation we made above that matrix multiplication is not commutative.

In this book, (post-)multiplication of a matrix with a vector will be very important and often used. That is, if, say, a matrix A and a (column) vector $\underline{f}$ are given, such that the number of columns of A equals the number of elements (rows) of $\underline{f}$, we will often be interested in the product $A\underline{f}$, regardless whether A and $\underline{f}$ are in numeric or symbolic form. To exemplify, let

$$A = \begin{bmatrix} 3 & 7 \\ 5 & 11 \\ 44 & 6 \end{bmatrix}$$

and

$$\underline{f} = \begin{bmatrix} 9 \\ 4 \end{bmatrix}.$$

Then obviously

$$A\underline{f} = \begin{bmatrix} 55 \\ 89 \\ 420 \end{bmatrix}.$$

Most of the time when we consider vectors in this book, they will consist of random variables. Some vectors will comprise only observed random variables, and others will comprise only latent random variables. When considering a vector of observed variables, say $\underline{x}$, we will denote the associated covariance matrix by $Cov(\underline{x})$ (e.g., Raykov & Marcoulides, 2008). Oftentimes, we will be interested in random variables resulting as linear combinations of other random variables. For instance, for a given vector of random variables, $\underline{f}$, consider the set of linear combinations of its elements, which are obtained using corresponding rows of a matrix A consisting of constants, $A = [a_{ij}]$, i.e., consider the vector $\underline{x} = A\underline{f}$. Then using the earlier-discussed rules for variance and covariance of linear combinations of random variables, one can obtain the following compact relationship between the covariance matrices of $\underline{f}$ and $\underline{x}$:

$$Cov(\underline{x}) = Cov(A\underline{f}) = A\, Cov(\underline{f})\, A'. \tag{2.12}$$

Equation (2.12) can be viewed as the multivariate extension of the earlier Equation (2.9). Furthermore, if the vectors of random variables $\underline{x}$ and $\underline{y}$ are uncorrelated, i.e., any two pairs of variables from these vectors (with one variable taken from each of them) are uncorrelated, then similarly to the univariate case it can be shown that

$$Cov(\underline{x} + \underline{y}) = Cov(\underline{x}) + Cov(\underline{y}). \tag{2.13}$$

In particular, if $\underline{x} = A\underline{f} + \underline{v}$, where $\underline{v}$ is uncorrelated with $\underline{f}$, then through an application of Equations (2.12) and (2.13), one obtains the covariance matrix of the vector $\underline{x}$ as follows:

$$Cov(\underline{x}) = A\ Cov(\underline{f})\ A' + Cov(\underline{v}). \tag{2.14}$$

We will often use the variance and covariance expressions given in this section, and in particular their compact matrix forms in Equations (2.12) through (2.14), in later chapters related to factor analysis and latent variable modeling that represent the methodological foundations of this book.

2.7 Prediction of Individual Performance

Psychometric theory, as mentioned previously, is especially interested in variable relation-ships. Once it has been ascertained that there is a marked linear relationship between two measures (random variables), it may be desirable to predict individual values on one of them using the other. For example, a person may have a value on only the X variable, but one may also wish to have a good 'guess' of his or her value on another measure, denoted, say, Y. As a simple example, consider the familiar college admission situation. Admission officers may be interested then in predicting university freshmen grades (say, Y scores) for applicants for admission, based only on knowledge of their SAT score, denoted X.

Prediction of individual scores, for some goals in this book, could be carried out using regression analysis. Specifically, in case of a single explanatory variable, the predicted score, as shown in most introductory statistics texts (e.g., King & Minium, 2003), is

$$Y_i' = \mu_Y + b_{Y.X}(X_i - \mu_X), \tag{2.15}$$

where the subindex i serves to remind that these are individual values (to which it is attached, as opposed to the other quantities without such a subindex that are population specific). In the last equation, the regression coefficient, also frequently referred to as slope, is

$$b_{Y.X} = \rho_{X,Y}\frac{\sigma_Y}{\sigma_X}.$$

In an empirical setting, to obtain a predicted score on a response variable, one needs to substitute the sample estimates of the parameters appearing in Equation (2.15) in order to render the sought predicted (estimated outcome) score as

$$\hat{Y}_i' = \bar{Y} + r_{X,Y}\frac{s_Y}{s_X}(X_i - \bar{X}). \tag{2.16}$$

In behavioral and social research, two variables will rarely if ever be characterized by a perfect linear relationship. Hence, the question that naturally arises is, What is the amount of error incurred by using Equation (2.16) for prediction purposes? This query is answered using the concept of prediction error, formally referred to as standard error of estimate and commonly denoted $\sigma_{Y.X}$ (King & Minium, 2003):

$$\sigma_{Y.X} = \sigma_Y\sqrt{1 - \rho_{X,Y}^2}. \tag{2.17}$$

We note from Equation (2.17) that the higher the correlation between the two measures involved, other things being the same, the lower the prediction error, and vice versa. Also, the less varied studied individuals are on the Y measure, the lower this error, and vice versa (other things being the same). We also observe that the standard error of estimate, and in particular its sample estimate $s_{Y.X}$ (obtained by plugging into the right-hand side of (2.17) sample estimates of the correlation coefficient and standard deviation of Y), tells us what the uncertainty is when we make predictions using Equation (2.16). This error estimate is based on the assumption that the dispersion (variance), around the regression line, of all Y scores for persons that have a given X value is the same regardless of the position of X (e.g., King & Minium, 2003). When this assumption is not tenable, resulting predictions and error estimates may be misleading, and the degree to which they can be so depends on the extent of this assumption violations.

After this short review of important statistical concepts and relationships for the remainder of this book, we are ready to move on to discussion of major modeling frameworks for psychometric theory and measurement in the social, behavioral, and educational sciences. Before we do that, however, it is fitting to introduce an increasingly popular statistical software that we will utilize on a number of occasions in the remainder of this book.

2.8 A Brief Introduction to the Statistical Analysis Software R

R is a comprehensive statistical analysis package that can be used to conduct various estimation, modeling, and computational activities ranging from simple to very complicated procedures. This software is readily obtained with a search engine—e.g., by Googling with the letter 'R' (or the term 'R-project'); following the prompts then will complete the downloading process (see also Venables, Smith, and The R Development Core Team, 2004). In this last section of the present review chapter, it will be helpful for the purposes of this book to describe how one can use R to evaluate in an empirical setting a number of quantities and parameters discussed in the preceding sections. At the same time, such a demonstration will prepare us for more involved estimation and modeling activities, some of which will be of particular relevance in following chapters. (An introduction to some of the graphical capabilities of R, which are used on several occasions in the rest of this book, is provided in the appendix to Chapter 11.)

Some of the simplest procedures that R can be used for involve the estimation of the mean (average), variance, standard deviation, and z-scores for a given set of observed scores. Suppose one were interested in finding out these statistics for the following IQ test scores, which are presented next as elements of the vector $\underline{x}$ (as usual, formally assumed to be a column vector):

$$\underline{x} = (110, 112, 95, 96, 79, 92, 102, 81, 84, 92)'.$$

To achieve these aims, after starting R, at its prompt—which is the sign '>' that is displayed in red on the computer screen—we enter

```
> x = c(110, 112, 95, 96, 79, 92, 102, 81, 84, 92)
```

(In the rest of this book, for completeness we will include the R prompt, '>', at the beginning of each command line that needs to be submitted to the software; the prompt does not obviously need to be typed when the command is actually presented to R. Furthermore, we will use a different font to present commands to be input into R and its associated output or output sections. Also, we emphasize that R is case-sensitive software, so one needs to ensure that proper case is used with each symbol utilized.)

In the last command line, we prefix by 'c' the set of scores that represent the elements of x—placed within parentheses and delineated by commas—to signal that we wish to 'concatenate' them into a single entity. This entity, or object, is the vector x of concern to us here. Once we have defined this vector with IQ scores, x, we are ready to estimate the above-mentioned statistics of interest. To estimate its mean, we use the command 'mean(.)' as follows:

```
> mean(x)
```

This yields the following result (we use in this book a different font from that of the main text, for presenting also software output):

```
[1] 94.3
```

This output line commences with the symbol '[1]' because it contains only 1 row consisting in this case of a single number, the average of the components of x that is 94.3 in the present example.

To obtain the variance of these IQ scores, we use the command 'var(.)':

```
> var(x)
```

that furnishes the output

```
[1] 127.7889
```

Similarly, to render the standard deviation of these scores, we use the command 'sd(.)':

```
> sd(x)
```

that returns

```
[1] 11.30437
```

(This estimate, 11.30, can also be alternatively furnished by square rooting the above-presented variance estimate, 127.79, after rounding off to the second decimal place.)

To get the individual z-scores, we use the definitional Equation (2.3) of z-scores, employing '/' as a symbol of division (after placing the mean deviation, x - mean(x), in parentheses):

```
> z = (x - mean(x))/sd(x)
```

If we wish to print these z-scores on the computer screen, all we need to do is request the vector z of z-scores just obtained:

```
> z
```

This displays the individual z-scores corresponding to the above IQ scores:

```
[1] 1.38884284  1.56576550  0.06192293   0.15038426  -1.35345831 -0.20346105
[7] 0.68115222 -1.17653566 -0.91115167  -0.20346105
```

We note that the second line of this output commences with the symbol [7], which signals that the immediately following score (.68115222) is the seventh in the sequence of individual z-scores of concern (that are in total 10 here).

Suppose that we had access to the same subjects' algebra test scores, say, placed in the vector $\underline{y}$:

$$\underline{y} = (10, 12, 9, 9, 8, 10, 11, 9, 8, 10)'.$$

To obtain the covariance of the two available measures—the algebra knowledge and intelligence test scores—we first define the vector y in analogy to the vector x above:

```
> y = c(10, 12, 9, 9, 8, 10, 11, 9, 8, 10)
```

We can then look at their covariance that we obtain with R as follows:

```
> cov(x, y)
```

which yields

```
[1]  11.68889
```

As mentioned before, because the covariance is a nonnormed measure of linear relationship, its magnitude (absolute value) is hard to interpret. To aid interpretation of the degree to which there may be a linear relationship between these intelligence and algebra knowledge measures, we can examine their correlation:

```
> cor(x, y)
```

that is then rendered as

```
[1]  0.8174603
```

This estimate indicates moderately strong linear tendency of high (or low) IQ scores to be associated with high (low) scores on the algebra test. To further enhance interpretability, we square this correlation, denoting the result for now as 'r_square':

```
> r_square = 0.8174603^2
```

(Note the use of the symbols '^2' to raise the immediately preceding number to second power.) To inspect the result, we simply type

```
> r_square
```

which renders

```
[1]  0.6682413
```

That is, about two thirds of the variance in either of the two measures involved can be explained in terms of variance in the other (through their discernible linear relationship; e.g., Agresti & Finlay, 2009).

If we wanted to examine the regression of algebra test score upon IQ score, we could use a linear modeling procedure that is available via the command 'lm' as follows:

```
> lm(y~x)
```

We note that in this procedure we first state within parentheses the dependent variable, followed by the '~' symbol, and then the independent variable. This command produces the following output:

```
Call:
lm(formula = y ~ x)

Coefficients:
(Intercept)              x
    0.97435        0.09147
```

The regression output first presents the formula for the analysis conducted, which here is linear modeling of the relationship between the variables whose data are stored in y and x, and then provides the intercept and slope parameters (last line of this output section). Based on this result, the estimated regression equation is (after rounding off to the second decimal)

$$Y = .97 + .09\, X.$$

Hence, if one wished to make a prediction about the algebra test score of someone with an IQ score of say 110, employing this model, the following command could be used (note the use of asterisk for multiplication):

```
> y_prime = .97435 + 110*.09147
```

To view the result, we request the predicted score:

```
> y_prime
```

which yields

```
[1] 11.03605
```

That is, one could take 11 as the sought predicted score on the algebra test.

One of the most fascinating features of R is the ease with which matrix operations can be carried out using it. To demonstrate some of these capabilities, let's revisit the earlier examples in Section 2.6 (see Subsection 2.6.2). To define the matrix A utilized initially there, one could first define each of its columns and then concatenate them. The first of these activities is accomplished as follows, as we can already figure out based on the preceding discussion in this section:

```
> a1 = c(2, 3, 4)
> a2 = c(3, 2, 2)
```

Once this is done, we 'create' the matrix A by placing these two columns next to each other (and requesting thereby three rows for the resulting matrix):

```
> A = matrix(data = c(a1, a2), nrow = 3)
```

Similarly for the matrix B,

```
> b1 = c(2,3,4)
> b2 = c(3,2,2)
> B = matrix(data = c(b1, b2), nrow=3)
```

We can ascertain that these are indeed the matrices A and B from Subsection 2.6.2 by simply stating

```
> A
```

and then

```
> B
```

A simple way to ascertain if A = B (in addition to 'eyeballing' their entries) is to take their difference, C = A − B, and print it to the screen:

```
> C = A - B
> C
```

This returns the following matrix (the symbols placed formally in the first row and first column are just the numbers of pertinent columns and rows):

```
      [,1]   [,2]
[1,]    0      0
[2,]    0      0
[3,]    0      0
```

This output confirms that the difference matrix C = A − B is the zero matrix, i.e., that A = B. The sum of A and B is readily printed, too:

```
> A + B
```

which furnishes

```
      [,1]   [,2]
[1,]    4      6
[2,]    6      4
[3,]    8      4
```

A straightforward way of obtaining the transpose of a matrix is as follows:

```
> t(A)
```

which yields

```
      [,1]  [,2]  [,3]
[1,]    2     3     4
[2,]    3     2     2
```

Although these are fairly simple operations, R is equally at ease with far more complicated ones. It is beyond the scope of this section and chapter to discuss them in more detail, but it would suffice for our purposes here to use R for matrix multiplication. For example, although A cannot be multiplied with B, because A and B are not multiplication conform (in this order), the product of A with the transpose of B, viz., AB', exists and is readily obtained with R (note the matrix multiplication sign '%*%' used next):

```
> A%*%t(B)
```

This multiplication furnishes the matrix

```
      [,1]  [,2]  [,3]
[1,]    13    12    14
[2,]    12    13    16
[3,]    14    16    20
```

A special case of matrix multiplication is the multiplication of two vectors and that of a matrix with vector. To describe how this can be easily done with R, consider the following two vectors of scores, denoted $\underline{u}$ and $\underline{v}$, which consist of the same number of elements:

$$\underline{u} = (5, 7, 9, 22)'$$

$$\underline{v} = (15, 12, 19, 13)'.$$

As discussed at length in some multivariate statistics texts (e.g., Raykov & Marcoulides, 2008), the product $\underline{u}'\underline{v}$ is a single number that results by adding the products of the numbers at the same position within the two vectors involved ('×' denotes number multiplication next):

$$\underline{u}'\underline{v} = 5 \times 15 + 7 \times 12 + 9 \times 19 + 22 \times 13. \tag{2.18}$$

The result of this vector multiplication is readily obtained with R. We first need to define in R the vectors $\underline{u}$ and $\underline{v}$ (unless of course they are already available in R as results of preceding computational activities carried out with it). Then we use the matrix multiplication command for them:

```
> u = (5, 7, 9, 22)
> v = (15, 12, 19, 13)
> w = t(u)%*%v
```

To view the result of this activity, as mentioned before, we request the resulting scalar w to be printed to the screen:

```
> w
```

which yields

```
      [,1]
[1,]   616
```

That is, $\underline{u}'\underline{v} = 616$, as can also be verified by adding the four number products in the right-hand side of the above Equation (2.18). We stress that 616 is the product $\underline{u}'\underline{v}$. If we were interested, however, in the product of $\underline{u}$ with $\underline{v}'$, i.e., in $\underline{u}\underline{v}'$, then the result is a matrix rather than a scalar:

```
> u%*%t(v)
```

which renders

```
       [,1] [,2] [,3] [,4]
[1,]     75   60   95   65
[2,]    105   84  133   91
[3,]    135  108  171  117
[4,]    330  264  418  286
```

When multiplying a matrix with a vector, we first need to define each of them in R (unless they are already available internally, as a result of previous computational activities with the software or definitions) and then multiply them. To illustrate, consider the earlier example in Section 2.6:

$$A = \begin{bmatrix} 3 & 7 \\ 5 & 11 \\ 44 & 6 \end{bmatrix}$$

and

$$\underline{f} = \begin{bmatrix} 9 \\ 4 \end{bmatrix}.$$

To obtain their product $A\underline{f}$ using R, we can define this matrix and vector as follows:

```
> a1 = c(3, 5, 44)
> a2 = c(7, 11, 6)
> f = c(9, 4)
> A = matrix(data = c(a1, a2), nrow = 3)
```

Then postmultiplication of A with $\underline{f}$ is furnished with the command

```
> A%*%f
```

yielding

```
     [,1]
[1,]   55
[2,]   89
[3,]  420
```

which is their product (in this order). If we wish to obtain their product in reverse order, we first note that $\underline{f}$ and A are not multiplication conform. The product of $\underline{f}'$ and A' exists, however, and if of interest one can obtain it as follows:

```
> t(f)%*%t(A)
```

which furnishes

```
      [,1]  [,2]  [,3]
[1,]    55    89   420
```

that is the transposed product (A$\underline{f}$), as could be expected (e.g., Raykov & Marcoulides, 2008).

In conclusion of this chapter, we reviewed in it a number of important statistical concepts and relationships, as well as provided a brief introduction to the increasingly popular and widely circulated comprehensive statistical analysis software R. (An introduction to some of its graphical capabilities is provided in the appendix to Chapter 11, which may be viewed as a continuation of this Section 2.8 as far as this software is concerned.) The following chapters will be concerned with major modeling frameworks for measurement and testing in the behavioral and social sciences, using at appropriate places applications of popular statistical software.

3

An Introduction to Factor Analysis

3.1 What Is Factor Analysis?

The discussion in Chapter 1 clarified that psychometric (test) theory is concerned with latent constructs and their evaluation. A statistical methodology with a rich history, which deals with indirectly observable variables like latent constructs, is factor analysis (FA). This methodology can be considered in some sense the backbone of the present book. In this chapter, we introduce the basics of factor analysis. Our treatment is purposely at an introductory level, because we use FA more as a means throughout this book rather than as an end in itself. For more extensive and detailed discussions of FA, we refer readers to McDonald (1985), Johnson and Wichern (2002), and Cudeck and MacCallum (2007). Later chapters in the text deal with various additional applications of FA that address specific psychometric-theory-related concerns.

Whenever measurement is conducted in the behavioral and social sciences, typically several types of behavior manifestation are observed. (As before, we will often refer to the resulting observed variables as 'measures'.) For example, when a test is administered, these measures represent its components or items. When such measures are collected from a sample of subjects, a question that naturally arises is whether they assess the same underlying construct or perhaps more than one latent dimension. In the latter case, one would also be interested in knowing which of the measures indicate which latent variable.

This question is essentially the same as asking whether there is one or more clusters of observed variables on which subjects display notably related performance, whereby within cluster individuals would give rise to markedly correlated scores, unlike across clusters—if the latter are more than one—when their relationships would be considerably weaker. For instance, if a battery of intelligence tests is given to a group of subjects, it would typically be desirable to know whether the pattern of interrelationship indexes among these measures supports the hypothesis that there are, say, two different clusters of measures, one pertaining to fluid intelligence and the other pertaining to crystallized intelligence (e.g., Horn, 1982), or alternatively to performance and verbal intelligence (e.g., Wechsler, 1958). In order to respond to this question, one would seek subsets of measures with the property that variables from the same subset exhibit marked interrelationships whereas variables from different subsets show considerably weaker relationships.

This type of query can be addressed via use of FA. FA has a relatively long history. Its beginnings can be traced back at least to the turn of the 20th century when the English psychologist Charles Spearman proposed it as a method for investigating his bifactor theory of human intelligence (Hayashi & Marcoulides, 2006; Spearman, 1904). Spearman (1904) stipulated that there was a general intelligence factor (construct), called g, which was involved in performance on any intelligence test. In addition, each intelligence measure was characterized by a 'unique' factor that was specific only to that measure. An alternative reference to this theory of intelligence, under which it has been also widely known, is 'g-theory'. (We note that this reference should not be confused with the one often used for generalizability theory, or G theory [Cronbach, Gleser, Nanda, & Rajaratnam, 1972; Shavelson & Webb, 1991]; see Chapter 9.)

Over the past century, FA has become a highly popular statistical method in the behavioral and social sciences. In fact, it is especially relevant for test construction and development, as we will see throughout the rest of this book. In particular, we will be interested in using FA for examining the underlying dimensionality of sets of measures under consideration, as well as in the process of constructing and developing (revising) multiple-component measuring instruments.

3.2 A Simplified Start-up Example

To highlight the main ideas underlying FA, we will use a contrived setup and data set. Suppose that scores are available for a studied population of university freshmen on 11 subtests of the Wechsler Adult Intelligence Scale (WAIS; Wechsler, 1958; cf. Crocker & Algina, 1986). This intelligence test battery consists of 6 verbal and 5 performance measures, which can be considered approximately continuous random variables. On the basis of this rough categorization into verbal versus performance subtests, one might hypothesize that the correlations among them would suggest two clusters of subtests, with higher correlations between subtests within clusters and weaker correlations across clusters. FA is well suited to explore this hypothesis of two latent constructs being measured by the set of 11 subtests in question.

First let us inspect the matrix of intercorrelations between these 11 observed variables that is presented in Table 3.1 (where for our purposes as mentioned we use artificial data).

Table 3.1. Correlations among WAIS subtests(first six are verbal,remaining are performance measures; see note for their names).

Measure:	1.	2.	3.	4.	5.	6.	7.	8.	9.	10.	11.
1.	1										
2.	.65	1									
3.	.66	.67	1								
4.	.65	.64	.65	1							
5.	.67	.63	.67	.65	1						
6.	.66	.68	.66	.68	.69	1					
7.	.16	.15	.13	.15	.13	.14	1				
8.	.17	.14	.15	.13	.16	.16	.53	1			
9.	.13	.16	.16	.16	.17	.17	.52	.50	1		
10.	.16	.18	.15	.17	.16	.16	.51	.52	.53	1	
11.	.15	.17	.17	.15	.15	.15	.55	.51	.52	.51	1

Note: 1. = Information; 2. = Comprehension; 3. = Arithmetic; 4. = Similarities; 5.= Digit Span; 6. = Vocabulary; 7. - Digit Symbol; 8. = Picture Completion; 9. = Block Design; 10. = Picture Arrangement; 11. = Object Assembly.

Looking at the entries of Table 3.1, we see that the pattern of variable correlations is consistent with our above hypothesis. Indeed, each pair of verbal measures (see first six variables) correlates markedly, as does each couple of performance measures (see last five variables). Furthermore, any verbal measure correlates notably weaker with any performance measure. With this observation, one may suggest that there may be two underlying constructs—typically referred to as factors in the context of examining observed variable correlations, as in FA—which are evaluated by the 11 subtests under consideration. One of these factors seems to explain the marked interrelationships among subtests 1 through 6 and thus may be labeled Vocabulary factor. The second factor seems to explain the interrelationships among the remaining measures (subtests 7 through 11) and may be labeled Performance factor. By way of contrast, if all correlations in Table 3.1 were in the vicinity of .6 or .7, say, then it might be suggested that they indicate only a single construct (factor) underlying the 11 observed measures. (There are also other values for their correlations, with which the hypothesis of a single latent construct may be consistent.)

This example was deliberately chosen to be a fairly straightforward one, so as to emphasize the ideas and particularly the motivation behind usual applications of FA in the behavioral and social disciplines. However, one should not expect in empirical research to be dealing frequently with such 'neatly ordered' correlation matrices consisting partly of marked and partly of small correlations, where simple 'eyeballing' reveals clusters of adjacent measures that correlate at least considerably. Most of the time, even if one is dealing with a well-defined underlying structure, higher correlations (if any) will be scattered throughout the entire matrix. (Simplistically speaking, and of less relevance at this point, one could view at times FA also as a means of 'reshuffling' the order of observed variables so as to get higher correlations repositioned into separate clusters of adjacent variables.)

After this introductory discussion of the ideas underlying FA, we are now ready to move on to a presentation of the fundamentals and model of FA, which are of particular relevance for much of what follows in this book.

3.3 The Traditional Factor Analysis Model

In many applications of psychometric theory, observed variables are used to provide multiple, distinct pieces of information about underlying latent constructs. The traditional FA model accomplishes this by a particular assumption about the relationships between manifest measures, assumed to be continuous random variables, and presumed factors (underlying constructs) that are similarly assumed to be continuous latent variables. Accordingly, the model consists of as many equations as there are measures. For p observed variables, $X_1, X_2, ..., X_p$, and m factors, $f_1, f_2, ..., f_m$, this FA model is as follows ($p > 1, m \geq 1, p > m$):

$$X_1 = a_{11}f_1 + a_{12}f_2 + \cdots + a_{1m}f_m + u_1 \tag{3.1}$$

$$X_2 = a_{21}f_1 + a_{22}f_2 + \cdots + a_{2m}f_m + u_2$$

$$\cdots$$

$$X_p = a_{p1}f_1 + a_{p2}f_2 + \cdots + a_{pm}f_m + u_p.$$

In Equations (3.1), all variables are assumed to possess zero mean, with the observed variables and factors also assumed to have unit variance. Thereby, the as are unknown constants that reflect the relationship between corresponding observed variable and factor and for this reason are called factor loadings. Furthermore, the residual variables u_1, $u_2, ..., u_p$ are called unique factors (residual terms), which are assumed uncorrelated among themselves and with the factors $f_1, f_2, ..., f_m$. Each residual term comprises (a) random error of measurement as well as (b) all sources of variance in its corresponding observed variable, which are not captured by the last-mentioned m factors.

According to the model in Equations (3.1), the factors $f_1, f_2, ..., f_m$ are assumed to explain part of the variance in each observed variable. This is the reason why f_1 through f_m are also frequently referred to as common factors (latent factors). As such, they can be considered the sources of all shared (common) variability among the p observed variables. (We note that strictly speaking the unique factors are also latent, i.e., unobserved variables, but we reserve the name 'latent factors' only for the common factors, which at times for simplicity we also call just 'factors'.) Typically, it is desirable that the number of common factors, m, is considerably smaller than that of observed measures, p. In most measurement-related contexts in social and behavioral research, m is fairly small, oftentimes 1 or only marginally larger. We emphasize that the FA model (3.1) assumes that none of the unique factors (residual terms) is related to any other unique factor or to a common factor. Sometimes, in addition to these assumptions, one also makes that of normality of the observed variables and all factors. The normality assumption for observed variables will be in particular relevant when we are interested in conducting statistical inference and applying a specific method of FA, that of maximum likelihood, as we will discuss later.

It is worthwhile emphasizing that Equations (3.1) do show some resemblance to those of the well-known regression analysis model, specifically multivariate multiple regression (MMRA, or general linear model; e.g., Timm, 2002). Indeed, multiple dependent variables appear on their left-hand sides, and in their right-hand sides we see the common factors playing the role of predictors (explanatory variables), whereas the unique factors play that of regression model error terms. This resemblance of FA to MMRA, whereas quite useful conceptually, is not full, however. The reason is that the explanatory variables in Equations (3.1) are not observed, because no data are available on the common factors, as they cannot be directly measured, being latent variables. This is a main distinction between FA and regression analysis, and one that has a number of important consequences to be dealt with later in this book. Yet we stress that it is quite helpful to keep in mind this conceptual relationship between FA and regression analysis.

We also emphasize that like conventional (multivariate) multiple regression, FA is based on a linear model, as is evident from Equations (3.1). Indeed, we observe from their right-hand sides that the common factors are multiplied by constants, the as, and then added up (and to the residual terms), rather than transformed nonlinearly to produce the observed variables or related quantities in the left-hand side of those equations. Later in this book we will be dealing with latent trait models (also often referred to as item-response models), which are conceptually quite similar to FA but exhibit the important distinction that they are nonlinear models.

3.3.1 Model Parameters

The analogy to regression analysis just mentioned is also useful in finding out the parameters of the FA model under consideration (see Equations (3.1)). Using this resemblance of FA to regression analysis, we realize that these parameters are

1. the factor loadings, as counterparts of the (partial) regression coefficients;
2. the variances of the unique factors, as counterparts of the model error variance(s) (standard error of estimate, in case of univariate regression);

and, in addition, the following unique to FA parameters:

3. factor correlations (covariances), if any.

These parameters will be of particular relevance in the next chapter where we will be using specialized software to conduct FA, as well as when we employ FA for purposes of measuring instrument construction and development.

It is instructive to note at this point that the FA model in Equations (3.1) can be more compactly represented using matrices and vectors (see Section 2.7. in the preceding chapter for a brief introduction to matrix algebra):

$$\underline{X} = A\,\underline{f} + \underline{u}, \tag{3.2}$$

where $A = [a_{jk}]$ is the matrix of factor loadings whereas $\underline{X} = (X_1, X_2, ..., X_p)'$, $\underline{f} = (f_1, f_2, ...,f_m)'$, and $\underline{u} = (u_1, u_2, ...,u_p)'$ are the vectors of observed variables, common factors, and unique factors (residual terms), respectively, with all above-mentioned distributional assumptions of the FA model (3.1).

From Equation (3.2), using the rules for working out variances and covariances of linear combinations of random variables (see Chapter 2), one obtains in compact matrix terms

$$\Sigma_{xx} = A\,\Phi\,A' + \Theta, \tag{3.3}$$

where Σ_{xx} is the covariance matrix of the observed variables, Φ is that of the common factors, and Θ is the covariance matrix of the unique factors (which is diagonal, as assumed earlier). With the previously mentioned assumption of unitary variances for all observed variables and common factors, the same decomposition (3.3) holds also formally for the correlation matrix of the observed variables if Σ_{xx} were to denote that matrix and Φ were to denote the correlation matrix of the common factors—we readily observe that under this variance assumption, correlation equals covariance for each pair of variables involved (see Chapter 2; this equality between correlation and covariance coefficient when the involved variable variances are set at 1 will be often used later in the book). Equation (3.3) per se does not impose any particular restrictions on the factor covariance (correlation) matrix Φ—other than, of course, it being positive definite (as any covariance or correlation matrix of real-valued random variables; e.g., Raykov & Marcoulides, 2008). When Φ is the identity matrix of size $m \times m$, consisting of 1s along its main diagonal and 0s off it, Equation (3.2) defines the so-called orthogonal FA model, with all remaining distributional assumptions mentioned earlier in this section.

Equation (3.2) represents compactly the traditional FA model and will be frequently referred to in the rest of this book. From its following Equation (3.3), we also see easily that the unknown parameters of this model are

1. the elements of the factor loading matrix A (factor loadings),
2. the elements of the covariance (correlation) matrix Φ of the factor vector $\underline{f}$, and
3. the diagonal elements of the covariance matrix Θ of the unique factor vector $\underline{u}$.

Equation (3.3) in addition lets us realize at a glance what FA technically is about—viz., finding out values for the associated model parameters, with which the right-hand side of (3.3) becomes as close as possible to the correlation (covariance) matrix of the observed variables that is in its left-hand side. In empirical research, we do not know the population correlation (covariance) matrix, denoted Σ_{xx}, but know only its sample counterpart, designated generically as S. Then the task of FA becomes one of finding out such values of the parameters of the FA model in question, which have the property that with them the right-hand side of (3.3) 'emulates' as closely as possible the pertinent sample matrix of interrelationship indexes, S (cf. Raykov & Marcoulides, 2006a, Chap. 1). We will return to this issue later in this book.

3.3.2 Factor Analysis and Principal Component Analysis

FA bears notable resemblance to a statistical method often used in the behavioral and social sciences mainly for purposes of data reduction, which is called principal component analysis (PCA; e.g., Raykov & Marcoulides, 2008). In PCA, the major goal is explaining observed measure variance in terms of a few (as few as possible) linear combinations of the original variables. In FA, as we saw above, the aim is typically to explain the correlations among a given set of measures. Because a chief purpose of PCA is data reduction, interpretation of principal components is not essential, although still desirable. In the latter feature, however, FA and PCA are clearly distinct because an essential aim in FA is common factor interpretation, in addition to reduction of complexity.

In this context of differences and similarities between PCA and FA, one of the most important distinctions between the two is that FA is based on an a priori postulated model whereas PCA is not. In fact, PCA may be considered a mathematical (deterministic) technique, as opposed to FA that can be viewed as a statistical method. A look at the FA model in Equations (3.1) reveals further differences between the two techniques. Noteworthy among them is the fact that the unique factors are essential elements of the FA model, whereas no such elements are involved (explicitly) in routine applications of PCA.

3.3.3 Factor Analysis and Conditional Independence

If we revisit Equations (3.1) with regard to just two observed measures, say X_1 and X_2, we will also realize a very important feature of FA that relates it to a number of contemporary statistical methods. Indeed, for these variables, the equations

$$X_1 = a_{11}f_1 + a_{12}f_2 + \cdots + a_{1m}f_m + u_1$$

and

$$X_2 = a_{21}f_1 + a_{22}f_2 + \cdots + a_{2m}f_m + u_2$$

hold, which we restate here for completeness of the following argument. Suppose now that we fix the values of the m factors involved, i.e., assume we consider only individuals who have all the same values on these latent constructs, say $c_1, ..., c_m$, respectively (the cs need not be equal among themselves). Then these two equations for X_1 and X_2 take the form

$$X_1 = a_{11}c_1 + a_{12}c_2 + \cdots + a_{1m}c_m + u_1$$

and

$$X_2 = a_{21} c_1 + a_{22} c_2 + \cdots + a_{2m} c_m + u_2.$$

If we work out next the covariance (correlation) of these two measures (see Chapter 2), we will obtain

$$Cov(X_1, X_2) = a_{11} a_{21} Cov(c_1, c_1) + \cdots + a_{1m} a_{2m} Cov(c_m, c_m) + Cov(u_1, u_2) \qquad (3.4)$$

$$= Cov(u_1, u_2)$$

$$= 0,$$

because any of the covariances involved in the right-hand side of the first line of this equation chain are such of constants and thus 0, or assumed to be 0 (viz., the residual or error term covariance; see earlier in this chapter).

Equation (3.4) demonstrates that the observed measures X_1 and X_2 are uncorrelated for subjects who do not differ on the common factors. In other words, X_1 and X_2 are conditionally uncorrelated (and, with normality, conditionally independent), given the factors. A conditional property like this is one of the most fundamental characteristics of many latent variable modeling approaches, such as latent class analysis, latent profile analysis, and item response theory, along with factor analysis. This property allows us to look here at FA in a slightly more advanced manner. In particular, the typical question that underlies FA is how one could find as few as possible latent dimensions (factors) that explain the relationships between a given set of observed variables in the above sense. In other words, this FA question is, What is the minimal number m, with the property that given the m factors (i.e., fixing their values) the observed p variables are uncorrelated? Further details pertaining to this fundamental property and its relation to latent variable models are provided in Bartholomew and Knott (1999).

3.4 Factor Loadings and Observed Measure Interrelationships

From Equations (3.1) representing the traditional FA model, it can be readily seen that the factor loadings reflect important relationships between factors and observed measures. These relationships can be further explicated by making the following observations for the orthogonal FA model (i.e., the model where the factors are assumed to be uncorrelated). Specifically, taking covariance of two observed measures from Equations (3.1), say X_j and X_k ($1 \leq j < k \leq p$), keeping in mind that their variance like that of the common factors is assumed 1, and denoting the correlation of X_j and X_k by ρ_{jk}, we obtain via use of the pertinent formulas from Chapter 2 the following relationship (cf. Equation (3.4)):

$$\rho_{jk} = a_{j1} a_{k1} + a_{j2} a_{k2} + \cdots + a_{jm} a_{km}. \qquad (3.5)$$

Equation (3.5) represents this manifest variable correlation as a linear combination of the factor loadings of one of the measures, where the weights in that combination are the corresponding loadings of the other observed measure. With this equation in mind, when we consider a single of Equations (3.1), say for X_j, and using the rules for covariance algebra from Chapter 2, we readily obtain the observed-latent correlation $Corr(X_j, f_k) = a_{jk}$. Thus, with uncorrelated factors, a factor loading equals the correlation of pertinent observed measure and latent factor.

Oftentimes in applications of test theory, the case of $m = 1$ factor is of particular interest. This is typically referred to as the unidimensionality (homogeneity) case, because there is a single latent construct or factor underlying several measures under consideration. Then we readily notice that Equation (3.5) reduces to

$$\rho_{jk} = a_{j1}a_{k1} = a_j a_k.$$

(We observe that in this case—unlike in (3.5)—we do not really need the second subindex for the factor loadings, viz., 1, and so we can drop it.)

Similarly, another special case of Equation (3.5) is frequently of interest in empirical research, including test construction and development settings. Specifically, when dealing with $m = 2$ factors—which correspond to the case of bidimensionality (multidimensionality), as in the above WAIS example—from (3.5) it follows that

$$\rho_{jk} = a_{j1}a_{k1} + a_{j2}a_{k2}$$

holds for the orthogonal factor model. More generally, if the assumption of orthogonal factors is not made, similar expressions hold to those in Equation (3.5) and its discussed special cases for $m = 1$ and $m = 2$, but in order to obtain them explicitly, one needs to add the products of involved factor loadings and pertinent factor correlations (i.e., the correlations of the factors that these loadings relate observed variables to). This observation, along with Equation (3.5), demonstrates the particular relevance of the factor loadings in the FA model.

3.5 Factor Rotation

Equation (3.3) (see also Equation (3.5)) reveals an important limitation of the FA model. Although at the outset of a factor analysis all that one is presented with is a set of observed measure interrelationship indexes, such as correlation coefficients, the model parameters appearing on its right-hand side can be chosen in more than one way. In fact, in general there are infinitely many choices for the parameters for which the FA model (3.1) is equally consistent with a given correlation matrix (of corresponding size). For any such choice, the involved set of factor loadings will be called a solution in this and later chapters. Thus, in general, FA is associated with infinitely many solutions. (There is a formal, mathematical proof of this statement using the concept of orthogonal matrices, which we will not be concerned with in this text; for more details, see, e.g., Johnson and Wichern [2002].)

This problem of multiple (in fact, infinitely many) solutions has been for years a widely criticized feature of FA, especially in its early decades. The problem results from the fact that the factor loading coefficients relate observed to latent variables (viz., manifest measures to common factors), yet the latter are not observed themselves. Hence, the multiplicity of possible solutions of the factor loadings cannot be unexpected. Moreover, from any one of these solutions a researcher can obtain another solution through a linear transformation. So, which one of the infinitely many possible, equally 'good' solutions should one choose?

3.5.1 The Idea of Rotation

The last question can be addressed by using the so-called technique of factor rotation (at times referred to only as 'rotation'). With rotation, one chooses that set of factor loadings satisfying Equations (3.1), which leads to the most meaningful substantive interpretation of the underlying factors. Carrying out factor rotation is best left to the computer, for the purposes of this discussion, and we note that its technical details received ample attention throughout the history of FA (e.g., Browne, 2001; Hayashi & Marcoulides, 2006; Jennrich, 2007). Rotation starts with an initial solution (similarly obtained with specialized software) and then changes direction of the initial factors so as to optimize a particular function that reflects distance to what is referred to as 'simple structure', which would permit a meaningful substantive interpretation. The notion of simple structure was introduced by Thurstone in the middle of the 20th century and could be considered, for our goals here, synonymous with 'ease of interpretation'. We will discuss further the concept of 'simple structure' later in this section.

Rotation has an instructive geometric meaning. Specifically, a rotation can be viewed as equivalent to a change of the positioning of the axes of the space spanned by the latent factors, called latent space, in which also the observed measures can be thought of—for our purposes here—as being (approximately) positioned. Rotation tries to find such a positioning of the axes of that space, which is as close as could be to possible clusters of observed variables in that space. Figure 3.1, used only for illustrative purposes in this section, demonstrates the general idea underlying the notion of factor rotation (e.g., Raykov & Marcoulides, 2008).

Figure 3.1 aims to illustrate in a simplified manner the process of rotation, for the case of two common factors with altogether 10 indicators. The axes are meant to represent the coordinates of the initial solution's latent space, and the crosses observed variables. (Such a clear configuration would not always be the case in behavioral and social research, however, and the extent to which it would be in a given study is indicative of the degree to which FA may be a meaningful and appropriate method to apply on its data. The crosses in Figure 3.1 may better be thought of as projections of the observed variables onto the latent space.)

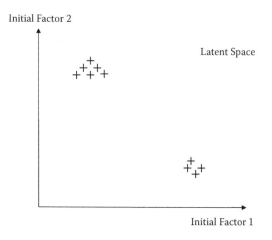

FIGURE 3.1
Geometric interpretation of factor rotation.

The graph in Figure 3.1 presents one of the simplest examples illustrating what rotation is about, viz., for the case of $m = 2$ factors. There is no simpler example, because if $m = 1$ the problem of rotation does not exist. In that case, there is only 1 factor, and it is not meaningful to talk about rotating it, because its direction is determined completely (for the aims of FA). Furthermore, we note in passing that the case $m = 0$ is actually not at all meaningful to consider. Indeed, if a set of p measures is not associated with any shared source of variance, then the only logical explanation of the situation would be that each variable is its own source of variance. In that case, one could just as well talk of there being $m = p$ 'common factors' that are each equal to an observed measure. Hence, for a given set of p observed measures, it makes sense to talk about only 1, 2, ..., or p latent factors. In the case of p factors, however, a FA model accomplishes no different representation than the collected data set itself, because there are as many common factors as there are observed variables. This is a clear case where the use of FA would not provide any meaningful results beyond the available data.

3.5.2 Types of Rotation

In the search of a substantively more interpretable solution, two types of rotation can be carried out, which are called orthogonal and oblique rotations. In orthogonal rotation, the axes of the original factor space are rotated while their perpendicularity is preserved throughout this activity. As a result, after such a rotation the latent factors are orthogonal to one another, as they usually are in an initial solution. Because of this feature, one may argue that orthogonal rotation may not often be attractive to a social or behavioral researcher. The reason is that latent constructs in the behavioral and social sciences tend to exhibit some interrelationship, at times considerable. This relationship cannot be captured, however, by orthogonal rotation, because its end result is uncorrelated factors that cannot reflect such construct relationships.

In oblique rotation, on the other hand, the new axes are allowed to cross at an angle that is possibly different from 90 degrees. That is, the latent factors are permitted to be correlated after rotation, if this may lead to a more meaningful (and easier) substantive interpretation of the factors. In the graphical example in Figure 3.1, it is clear that an oblique rotation will do much better than an orthogonal one. (With correlated factors, typically resulting after oblique rotation, a modification of Equation (3.5) is in order as pointed out before, and then factor loadings are more interpretable not as measure-factor correlations but only as weights of observed measures upon latent factors; more detail is presented in Section 3.7.)

3.5.3 Simple Structure and How Rotation Proceeds

In general terms, rotation—whether orthogonal or oblique—can be viewed as a process of accomplishing 'simple structure', i.e., reaching a substantively interpretable solution. The notion of simple structure is inextricably connected to the factor loading matrix $A = [a_{jk}]$. Specifically, to accomplish simple structure, such a rotation is sought that leads to a new factor solution with the matrix A having a pattern that would allow easy subject-matter interpretation. In particular, this would be facilitated if after rotation the matrix A fulfills, as closely as feasible, as many of the following criteria as possible (cf. Thurstone, 1947; for a related discussion, see also McDonald, 1999):

1. each row of the matrix A has at least one 0;
2. each column of A has at least m zeros;

3. for every pair of columns of A, there are at least *m* measures with a 0 loading in one column and a nonzero loading in the other;

4. if *m* > 3, for every pair of columns of A, there is a large proportion of observed variables with loadings of zeros in both columns; and

5. for every pair of columns of A, there is a small number of variables with nonzero loadings in both columns.

One of the most popular approaches aimed at approaching simple structure in case of orthogonal rotation is based on the so-called Kaiser's *V* index. Accordingly, an orthogonal rotation maximizes the following index *V*, often referred to as varimax criterion:

$$V = \frac{1}{p} \sum_{j=1}^{m} \left[\sum_{i=1}^{p} \frac{\tilde{a}_{ij}^4}{h_i^4} - \left(\sum_{i=1}^{p} \frac{\tilde{a}_{ij}^2}{h_i^2} \right)^2 \middle/ p \right]. \tag{3.6}$$

In Equation (3.6), $\tilde{a}_{ij}$ denote the factor loadings after rotation, and h_i^2 are the R²-indices when considering (conceptually) the regression of the *i*th observed measure on the common factors. (These indices are also called communalities and are alternatively defined formally further below in this section.) As can be seen from its definition, Kaiser's varimax criterion *V* aims at maximizing the sum of factor-specific variances of the squared scaled factor loadings (by h_i^2). Similarly, other rotation methods optimize alternative numerical criteria of this general type (e.g., Jennrich, 2007).

Once rotation is completed, interpretation of each factor is carried out in terms of the common features shared by measures that load highly on it. In addition to the analyzed data, interpretation also depends on the particular subject-matter domain, previous research, and accumulated knowledge in it (as well as the extent to which the researcher involved in this activity is familiar with them). In the next section, we will consider in more detail an example of FA, including interpretation of rotation outcome as well as of latent factors.

3.5.4 Oblique Rotation as a Matter of 'Routine' in Behavioral Research?

As indicated earlier in this section, it can be argued that oblique rotation tends to yield more meaningful results in behavioral and social research, because typically latent constructs in these sciences tend to be interrelated rather than unrelated. Thus, from a pragmatic viewpoint, it may be claimed that in an empirical study, one could set out for an oblique rotation and then examine whether the resulting correlation(s) between the latent factors are sizeable. If this is not the case, one could redo the analyses with an orthogonal rotation that would lead to a more parsimonious, and hence more desirable, solution. The reason is that unlike oblique rotation, orthogonal rotation will not be associated with any factor correlation parameters. As a result, an orthogonal rotation will generally tend to make the factor loading and unique variance estimates more precise (because of the fact that there are fewer parameters to be estimated then). However, an orthogonal rotation will frequently run against the substantive nature of underlying latent constructs that are typically interrelated. For this reason, it seems preferable to set out in principle for an oblique rotation in empirical research, with the option of redoing rotation using an orthogonal criterion if the resulting factor correlations are deemed to be fairly small.

In the next chapter, we will familiarize ourselves with a specific version of FA that will allow us to readily test whether the underlying factors are orthogonal (uncorrelated) in a studied population.

3.6 A Useful Diagrammatic Notation

How can we graphically represent a factor analysis model? Suppose we place the factors in circles (or ellipses) and the observed measures in squares (or rectangles) and denote by one-way arrows the assumption that a latent factor plays an explanatory role for a corresponding observed measure or indicator (cf. Raykov & Marcoulides, 2006a). In addition, if we add short one-way arrows for the unique factors (residual terms), then a single-factor model with five observed measures X_1 through X_5 as indicators of the common factor f, say, would look pictorially as in Figure 3.2.

Using this notation, a two-factor model with six observed measures, X_1 through X_6 that load on the factors f_1 and f_2, can be presented diagrammatically as in Figure 3.3, whereby a two-way arrow denotes correlation. (In this chapter, we will not be concerned with the issue of unique estimation of all model parameters; we attend to it in the next chapter.)

We can recommend that this graphical notation be used as often as possible by an empirical behavioral or social researcher, whenever he or she has an idea of (a) how many factors could be behind a given set of observed measures and (b) which of the observed variables load on which of the factors. This graphical notation is frequently referred to as path-diagram notation (e.g., Bollen, 1989) and is very often utilized when discussing latent variable models (see Chapter 4). A particular diagram resulting from using this notation to depict a model is commonly referred to as path-diagram of that model. We will employ this reference frequently throughout the rest of the book.

We stress that we used the path-diagram notation to represent a factor analysis model in a way equivalent to a set of equations between its variables. In particular, a path-diagram of a factor analysis model, like those in Figures 3.2 and 3.3, is equivalent to the set of equations relating observed and latent variables involved in it. Hence, when one adds to the path-diagram an appropriate set of distributional assumptions, one obtains a statistical

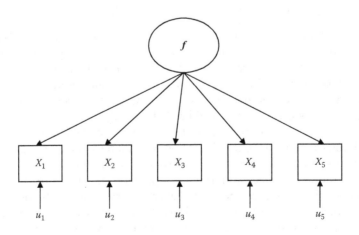

FIGURE 3.2
Diagram of a single-factor model.

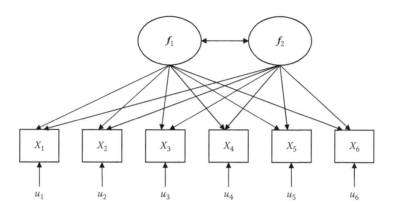

FIGURE 3.3
Diagram of a two-factor model.

model. That is, a factor analysis model depicted in a path-diagram is equivalent to (a) a set of equations relating each observed measure to the common and unique factors, like the above Equations (3.1), plus (b) the distributional assumptions discussed earlier in the chapter—including possibly the assumption of interrelated factors as in Figure 3.3. When one is also interested in statistical inference and hypothesis testing, a further added assumption could be that of normality for the observed variables.

   We similarly note that the important assumption of unrelated unique factors with common factors, mentioned earlier in this chapter, is readily seen from Figures 3.2 and 3.3. In particular, we notice that there are no two-way arrows connecting any of the unique factors, the *u*s, with any of the common factors, the *f*s. Moreover, the assumption of uncorrelated unique factors is reflected in these figures by the absence of two-way arrows connecting any pair of *u*s. (We will relax this assumption in the next chapter.)

3.7 Communality and Uniqueness

The earlier Equations (3.1) suggest an important decomposition of observed variable variances. Indeed, when we look at the right-hand sides of these equations, we see two types of variables: (a) common factors that are assumed to explain shared variance in an observed measure and (b) unique factors that represent unexplained variance by the common factors, which is specific to a corresponding observed variable.

   With this in mind, given the earlier assumption of uncorrelated unique and common factors, and using the formula for variance of a sum of random variables (see Chapter 2), we obtain for the jth observed variable X_j the following variance decomposition:

$$Var(X_j) = Var(a_{j1} f_1 + \cdots + a_{jm} f_m) + Var(u_j), \qquad (3.7)$$

$j = 1, \ldots, p$. We call the first variance on the right-hand side of Equation (3.7) communality of the measure X_j, as it depends on the variance of the common factors. The second variance term there is called uniqueness of X_j (or unique variance), because it is the variance of the unique factor specific to X_j. (Sometimes this variance is also referred to as residual or error variance.)

Much of the time when FA is applied, especially when used as a means for exploring the underlying structure of a given set of measures, one is interested in analyzing the correlation matrix of the observed variables. This is tantamount to assuming that each manifest measure has a variance of 1. In addition, as already assumed, and to contribute to making possible the estimation of unknown parameters of FA (which is discussed further in the next chapter), the common factors are also often assumed to have each variance of 1. Hence, from Equation (3.7) follows then that a given variable's communality, denoted h_j^2 for X_j, is

$$h_j^2 = a_{j1}^2 + \cdots + a_{jm}^2 + 2(a_{j1}a_{j2}\varphi_{12} + \cdots + a_{j,m-1}a_{jm}\varphi_{m,m-1}), \quad (3.8)$$

where φ_{sr} is the covariance (correlation) of the sth and rth common factors ($s, r = 1, \ldots, m$, $s \neq r$; $j = 1, \ldots, p$). When the common factors are uncorrelated, as in the orthogonal factor model, the following simplified version of Equation (3.8) results:

$$h_j^2 = a_{j1}^2 + \cdots + a_{jm}^2 \quad (3.9)$$

($j = 1, \ldots, p$). Either way, when the observed measure variance is 1—as usually assumed in traditional FA—it equals the sum of communality and uniqueness, denoted θ_j^2 (for X_j):

$$1 = h_j^2 + \theta_j^2, \quad (3.10)$$

or alternatively

$$\theta_j^2 = 1 - h_j^2 \quad (3.11)$$

($j = 1, \ldots, p$).

As we pointed out earlier in this chapter, the unique factors contain each (a) random measurement error plus (b) all sources of variance in the pertinent observed variable that are not accounted for by the common factors and are thus specific to that measure. The error of measurement in point (a) comprises all random effects that contribute to manifest performance and are unrelated to the common factors and thus can be thought of as being also unrelated to all those variable-specific, unaccounted variance sources mentioned in point (b). For this reason, we can actually split the unique factor further into the sum of the measurement error in (a), on the one hand, and the totality of the variable-specific sources of variance pointed out in (b), on the other hand. We call the latter part of the unique factor, for a given measure, specificity of that observed variable. Hence, if δ_j^2 denotes the variance of the measurement error and ω_j^2 the variance of the specificity term, it follows that

$$\theta_j^2 = \delta_j^2 + \omega_j^2 \quad (3.12)$$

holds ($j = 1, \ldots, p$). Therefore, Equation (3.10) entails that an observed measure's variance is the sum of three sources:

$$1 = h_j^2 + \delta_j^2 + \omega_j^2 \quad (3.13)$$

($j = 1, \ldots, p$). The last equation states that, according to the FA model, observed variance is decomposable into the sum of (a) communality, (b) specificity, and (c) random measurement error variance. In subsequent chapters, we will capitalize on this variance decomposition.

3.8 Exploring the Number of Factors

The developments so far in this chapter were based on the tacit assumption that we knew the number m of latent factors underlying individual performance on a given set of observed measures. In reality, this number is in general unknown, unless of course research is being carried out in a fairly advanced subject-matter domain where the number of factors has been justified by previous research and available body of accumulated substantive knowledge. The situation that is much more frequently encountered in behavioral and social research, however, is that prior empirical work in a particular area cannot support unambiguously a specific number m of factors. In those circumstances, which could be argued to be empirically more often the case than not, one needs some guidance as to how to find out this number of factors.

There is more than one criterion available that can guide the search for an appropriate number of factors. Often they may yield similar results that lead to a largely unambiguous conclusion about this number. Sometimes, however, they may be differing more notably in their suggestions about m, and additional substantive considerations would be called for in determining the number of factors. A main criterion then is substantive interpretability, as it is in any other situation where the number of latent factors underlying a given set of measures is under consideration.

As pointed out in our comparative discussion of PCA and FA, an essential part of the latter consists in interpretation of the latent factors. This is also valid when one is concerned with assessing the number of factors. If a preliminary value for m suggested by the 'rules of thumb' mentioned next is larger (smaller) than the number of latent dimensions that are substantively interpretable given the knowledge in a domain of application, then that number of factors m needs to be reconsidered.

Guidelines for Determining the Number of Factors

A suggested value of m can be obtained by using the so-called eigenvalue rule. An eigenvalue could be viewed as a counterpart of the concept 'explained variance' that is of special relevance within, say, the framework of regression analysis (cf., e.g., Raykov & Marcoulides, 2008). A large eigenvalue suggests (for the purposes of this chapter) the presence of a relatively strong source of variance that explains a large part of variability in a given set of observed variables and that (some of) these measures have possibly a marked proportion of shared variance along a pertinent latent continuum.

For a given set of analyzed data (i.e., a correlation matrix), there are as many eigenvalues as the number of observed variables, say p. Oftentimes, some eigenvalues will be relatively large, whereas the remaining ones may be considerably smaller. In fact, as is frequently the case in behavioral research, the clearer the latent structure behind a given set of observed measures, the larger the number of eigenvalues that are small, in particular close to 0.

An interesting relationship discussed in detail in many multivariate statistics texts is that the sum of all eigenvalues of a given correlation (or covariance) matrix equals the sum of the observed variable variances (e.g., Johnson & Wichern, 2002). When the correlation matrix is analyzed, as traditionally done in FA applications, this sum is obviously p, because each variable has a variance of 1. That is, the eigenvalues can be viewed as representing an alternative 'redistribution' of observed variance. Eigenvalues can be readily obtained in empirical research using specialized statistical software, in particular SPSS and M*plus*, which we will use later in this chapter and in the next chapters.

The 'eigenvalue rule' suggests that the number of factors would equal that of 'large' eigenvalues. When the correlation matrix is analyzed, for the above reasons one can consider as 'large' any eigenvalue that is higher than 1, i.e., higher than the average eigenvalue (which is obviously $p/p = 1$ then). We will use this eigenvalue rule throughout the remainder of the chapter.

A graphical guide related to this rule has become known as the 'scree-plot', which represents a plot of the eigenvalues against the successive numbers 1 through p. Using this plot, the number of suggested factors m is found as one fewer than that among these numbers, at which the plot of eigenvalues begins to trail off (i.e., obtains for the first time a nearly horizontal slope; an illustration is provided in Section 3.9. next).

A closely related guide, which, however, tends to have a more subjective flavor, is that of amount explained variance. As mentioned above an eigenvalue is analogous to explained variance, and so this rule suggests that the number of factors m be determined in such a way that the largest m eigenvalues contribute together to a sufficiently large amount of explained variance, say 70% or 80% of all variance in the analyzed variables. This joint contribution by those eigenvalues represents the amount of explained observed variance by the corresponding factors and is evaluated by specialized statistical software for each value of m from 1 through p. (Alternatively, according to the preceding discussion, this proportion explained variance can be obtained by dividing the sum of any considered number of the largest eigenvalues by the sum of all observed variable variances, i.e., by p when the correlation matrix is analyzed; for an example, see next chapter.)

When examining the percentage explained variance by the largest eigenvalues, the researcher decides on a specific 'cutoff value' for explained variance. This value usually is affected by substantive considerations as well as accumulated knowledge and possibly established practice in the substantive area of application. Then m is the smallest number at which the factors corresponding to the highest m eigenvalues together explain an amount of observed variance that is higher than that cutoff (see also Raykov & Marcoulides, 2010c).

The process of conducting factor analysis for examining the latent structure underlying a given set of measures is illustrated next on empirical data.

3.9 An Illustration of Factor Analysis

Here we will be interested in exploring whether a single latent factor can explain well the pattern of interrelationships among university freshmen scores on five intelligence tests. Three of these measures are meant to tap into one's ability to find out and use subsequently rules underlying series of symbols, figure parts, and letters and are denoted below 'test1' through 'test3'. The fourth test, referred to as 'test4', addresses the capability to mentally rotate figures in three-dimensional space (test4). The fifth measure is the popular Raven's progressive matrices test (e.g., Baltes, Dittmann-Kohli, & Kliegl, 1986), referred to as 'test5'. We assume that all five measures can be treated as (approximately) continuous random variables and are interested in finding out whether they could be considered indicative of a single latent factor that we could then call 'Fluid intelligence' (e.g., Horn, 1982). This type of intelligence comprises our innate abilities to solve problems that are content free and do not involve any particular knowledge that we may (or may not) have received throughout our lives, upbringing, socialization process, or schooling. The motivation for being interested in whether a single factor could explain performance on these five intelligence tests is our desire to develop a test battery of Fluid intelligence. From the preceding brief discussion in this section, it appears that each of the five tests listed could contribute important information with regard to one's Fluid intelligence.

This observation is not sufficient, however, for a decision to compile a test battery consisting of these five tests and claim that it measures Fluid intelligence. To develop such a test battery, we need additional evidence, as objective as possible, that these intelligence measures could be considered indicators of a single common factor that we would then like to call, for obvious reasons, Fluid intelligence.

As we will discuss in more detail later in this book, this type of query is quite characteristic of the process of constructing and developing behavioral tests (scales, test batteries), i.e., multiple-component measuring instruments that are highly popular in the behavioral, social, and educational sciences. Throughout this process, most of the time it would be meaningful to require that there be a single latent source of variability (shared variability) behind a set of components we are thinking of using as elements of an instrument supposed to accomplish measurement of a latent dimension of interest, such as ability, aptitude, attitude, opinion, or in general a behavioral trait.

Factor analysis provides a highly useful methodology for exploring whether the so-designed multiple-component instrument, test battery, or scale consisting of a proposed set of components is unidimensional, i.e., measures a single factor. Such instruments are also frequently referred to as homogeneous, or unidimensional. This unidimensionality requirement is relevant because, simply speaking, if our set of measures assesses more than a single latent trait, then a high, low, and, in particular, medium score on the whole battery could not be readily and unambiguously interpreted as indicative of a particular level (high, low, or medium) on any of these traits. We note parenthetically, however, that in general it is only the substantive researcher who, on the basis of all available knowledge and prior research in the pertinent substantive domain, would be in a position to decide whether, say, a two- or higher-dimensional test (instrument, scale) could be useful as a specific measurement device. This discussion means to provide only a relatively simple argument in favor of unidimensionality (rather than a strong argument against multidimensionality) of a test under consideration.

We illustrate next how one can use FA for purposes of exploring the latent structure of a given set of measures and in particular for examining whether from this explorative viewpoint there could be evidence for a single underlying latent factor behind subjects' performance on a given set of observed variables. To this end, we use a correlation matrix from $n = 161$ university freshmen, which is presented in Table 3.2. (This matrix is obtained after the original score, number correct responses, on each of the measures was transformed into percentage correct from maximal possible score, i.e., number of items in a test. In this way, a 'unit of measurement' was introduced that is somewhat more comparable across measures, viz., percentage correct answers.)

A widely circulated and popular software that can be routinely used to carry out factor analysis is SPSS (PASW; this is, however, not the only one available for this purpose—for instance, programs like SAS, STATA, or R could also be readily used). To invoke factor analysis using SPSS, once we read in the data we choose 'Analyze' from the main toolbar, in the then-opened vertical list of options choose 'Data Reduction', and then choose 'Factor'. In the newly created window, we highlight the measures to be analyzed (in this case all five tests) and move them into the 'Variable' window to the right. Next we select 'Descriptives' at the lower left end of the current window, then select 'Univariate descriptives' and 'Initial solution', and in the correlation matrix part choose 'Coefficients', 'Significance levels', and 'KMO and Bartlett's test of sphericity', before 'Continue'. After selecting 'Extraction' to the

Table 3.2. Correlation matrix of 5 intelligence tests (n = 161).

Measure:	test1	test2	test3	test4	test5
test1	1				
test2	.65	1			
test3	.83	.72	1		
test4	.68	.76	.76	1	
test5	.62	.64	.68	.64	1

Note: test1 = Induction reasoning with symbols; test2 = Induction reasoning with figure parts; test3 = Induction reasoning with letters; test4 = Figure rotations; test5 = Raven's advanced progressive matrices.

right of 'Descriptives', we select 'Unrotated factor solution' (which represents the initial factor solution) and 'Scree-plot', before 'Continue'. We choose then 'Rotation', 'Promax', 'Rotated solution', 'Loading plot(s)', and 'Continue'. In the 'Options' button window, we select 'Sorted by size' and 'Suppress size lower than .30', to use a traditional rule of thumb about 'small' factor loadings (see below in this section), followed by 'Continue'. We submit this analysis to SPSS by clicking 'OK'. The following output results from these menu choices. We insert clarifying comments after consecutive output sections presented next, unless a section is self-explanatory.

Factor Analysis

Notes

Comments		
Input	Data	D:\data\ex31.sav
	Filter	<none>
	Weight	<none>
	Split File	<none>
	N of Rows in Working Data File	161
Missing Value Handling	Definition of Missing	MISSING=EXCLUDE: User-defined missing values are treated as missing.
	Cases Used	LISTWISE: Statistics are based on cases with no missing values for any variable used.
Syntax		FACTOR /VARIABLES test1 test2 test3 test4 test5 /MISSING LISTWISE /ANALYSIS test1 test2 test3 test4 test5 /PRINT UNIVARIATE INITIAL CORRELATION SIG KMO EXTRACTION ROTATION /FORMAT SORT BLANK(.30) /PLOT EIGEN ROTATION /CRITERIA MINEIGEN(1) ITERATE(25) /EXTRACTION PC /CRITERIA ITERATE(25) /ROTATION PROMAX(4) /METHOD=CORRELATION.
Resources	Elapsed Time	0:00:00.53
	Maximum Memory Required	4100 (4.004K) bytes

The above is a list of 'technical' information pieces, including the echoed-back input (command) file that could be of relevance if one were to redo earlier analyses or provide a detailed account of specific analytic options chosen.

Warnings

Only one component was extracted. Component plots cannot be produced.

This warning is actually a desirable one here, because we are interested in exploring if there may be a single source of variance behind the five tests that we are considering putting together into a test battery of fluid intelligence.

Descriptive Statistics

	Mean	Std. Deviation	Analysis N
TEST1	30.8256	14.76676	161
TEST2	49.4834	16.14806	161
TEST3	37.4824	17.53457	161
TEST4	48.3907	12.62472	161
TEST5	37.5116	20.17669	161

Correlation Matrix

		TEST1	TEST2	TEST3	TEST4	TEST5
Correlation	TEST1	1.000	.651	.853	.681	.616
	TEST2	.651	1.000	.719	.761	.636
	TEST3	.853	.719	1.000	.765	.676
	TEST4	.681	.761	.765	1.000	.639
	TEST5	.616	.636	.676	.639	1.000
Sig. (1-tailed)	TEST1		.000	.000	.000	.000
	TEST2	.000		.000	.000	.000
	TEST3	.000	.000		.000	.000
	TEST4	.000	.000	.000		.000
	TEST5	.000	.000	.000	.000	

These are the descriptive statistics for the five observed variables, including their correlation matrix that is analyzed in this session.

KMO and Bartlett's Test

Kaiser-Meyer-Olkin Measure of Sampling Adequacy.		.859
Bartlett's Test of Sphericity	Approx. Chi-Square	614.146
	df	10
	Sig.	.000

Bartlett's test of sphericity is of particular relevance as an initial check of whether FA makes sense for a given matrix of variable interrelationships. (This test assumes multivariate normality of the analyzed variables.) If the test is not significant, at, say, a conventional level of .05—unlike in this example where it is significant—one could argue that FA would be meaningless to proceed with. The reason is that the null hypothesis this test examines is H_0: 'The analyzed correlation matrix consists of 1's on its main diagonal and 0's off it.' That is, the null hypothesis is that there are no (linear) relationships at all among the variables. If this is indeed the case, there cannot be a latent factor (or several of them but fewer than the number of variables) that could explain well the analyzed variable interrelationship indexes, as outlined within the framework of FA. Then attempting a FA would obviously be a futile exercise. Under those circumstances, one could talk of as many factors underlying the analyzed correlation matrix as there are observed variables, which is another way of expressing the fact that carrying out FA on that matrix would be a meaningless activity. We stress, however, that for the presently analyzed data, the null hypothesis underlying Bartlett's sphericity test is rejected. We can interpret this result as suggesting that FA could be used to explore the latent structure behind the correlation matrix in Table 3.2.

Communalities

	Initial	Extraction
TEST1	1.000	.765
TEST2	1.000	.746
TEST3	1.000	.854
TEST4	1.000	.781
TEST5	1.000	.659

Extraction Method: Principal Component Analysis.

This is the initial solution (see final column of the table for the associated communalities) before an attempt is in general undertaken to make it as interpretable as possible. In case more than one latent factor is found at this stage, rotation would have to be carried out in general, and then this initial solution would be of no special interest. If only one factor is found here, however, as in the present example, these communalities can be viewed as R^2-indices in a 'theoretical' regression of each observed variable upon that factor. High communalities are therefore indicative of a well-fitting solution, as one could argue for in the present example (see last column).

Total Variance Explained

Component	Initial Eigenvalues			Extraction Sums of Squared Loadings		
	Total	% of Variance	Cumulative %	Total	% of Variance	Cumulative %
1	3.805	76.096	76.096	3.805	76.096	76.096
2	.429	8.576	84.673			
3	.398	7.962	92.634			
4	.236	4.726	97.361			
5	.132	2.639	100.000			

Extraction Method: Principal Component Analysis.

This table indicates only 1 eigenvalue being larger than 1, with all remaining eigenvalues being considerably smaller than 1. Hence, it seems reasonable to suggest that there is only one latent factor underlying the pattern of interrelationships in Table 3.2. As it happens, this factor would explain more than three fourths of the total observed variance, a relatively large percentage, as we see from the top row of the previously presented table.

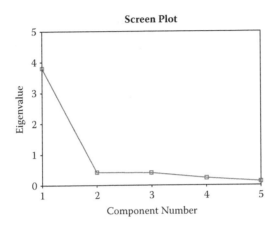

The scree-plot also supports the conclusion that only 1 factor could be found in (or alternatively expressed, 'extracted' from) the analyzed data. To interpret the scree-plot, as indicated above, we subtract 1 from the number where the lower part of the 'elbow' (scree) begins, which is here 2 (e.g., Raykov & Marcoulides, 2008).

Component Matrix[a]

	Component
	1
TEST3	.924
TEST4	.884
TEST1	.874
TEST2	.864
TEST5	.812

Extraction Method: Principal Component Analysis.
a.   1 components extracted.

These numbers are the weights with which the tests need to be each multiplied and then added to one another in order to produce a linear combination with the highest possible variance from all linear combinations of the five tests. On this linear combination (also referred to as 'component' here), subjects will be most differentiated from each other in terms of their observed scores. We will not pay special attention to this type of linear combination in the rest of this book (which in this example is the first principal component for the analyzed data; for more details on PCA, see, e.g., Johnson & Wichern, 2002, or Raykov & Marcoulides, 2008). However, we emphasize that the preceding results in this output allow us to conclude—within the limits of this explorative and hypothesis-generating approach (see also next section)—that the analyzed data are consistent with the assumption of there being a single latent factor underlying subject performance on the five Fluid intelligence tests of concern. We can thus also consider the weights in the last presented output section as informative about the relationships between the observed measures and that factor.

Rotated Component Matrix[a]

a. Only one component was extracted.
The solution cannot be rotated.

The last couple of sentences only restate the finding of a single factor, which as we know from the earlier discussion in this chapter cannot be rotated. (A rotation attempt for it, as pointed out earlier, would be meaningless.) In the next chapter, we present another illustrative example of FA with more than one latent factor, which will be used for the same purpose, viz., latent structure examination.

3.10 Factor Analysis as a Means of Data Exploration

In this concluding section of the chapter, we revisit some aspects of the way FA was utilized in it. In particular, we wish to emphasize that this FA application allowed us to explore only the latent structure of a given set of observed measures. In the FA we dealt with, we were not concerned with testing any hypothesis or a reasonably well-developed theory. Indeed, we were interested only in finding out what type of latent structure (factors and their relationships to observed measures) would be consistent with the analyzed data. For that reason, this type of FA is often called exploratory factor analysis and will be further discussed in the next chapter. For the example considered in the preceding Section 3.9, we found that the analyzed data there were suggestive of a single factor underlying subjects' performance on the five intelligence measures in question.

To what degree, however, can we state that this single factor explains well the structure of these observed measures in the population of interest? On the basis of the way we used FA in this chapter, we cannot claim that we have been able to confirm any found or suggested structure by the obtained results. Indeed, in the FA we discussed, we started with no preconceived idea as to what the latent structure looked like—we did not have a clue how many factors were operating at the latent level or which observed measures were indicative of which factor(s). This is the reason why we cannot be more assertive with regard to our findings, based only on the exploratory way in which FA was used in this chapter. In particular, the evidence found in the analysis presented in Section 3.9 does not allow us to confirm the suggested unidimensional structure, i.e., a single factor underlying (explaining well) the analyzed correlation matrix. This is because the analysis that we conducted does not provide enough information about the factorial structure pertaining to the five measures under consideration, which information we should rely on for the purpose of reaching such a conclusion.

If we were interested in being in a position to say more about the latent structure for a set of observed measures, and especially to confirm or disconfirm their unidimensionality, we need to carry out other analyses that would permit us to actually test the hypothesis that the measures are homogeneous, e.g., indicative of a single underlying factor. That type of study can also be conducted within the same conceptual framework of factor analysis but has a different analytic nature. We will discuss it in the next chapter, after introducing an increasingly popular and highly versatile latent variable modeling software, M*plus*. This program can also be used for the type of factor analysis we were concerned with in the present chapter, exploratory factor analysis. In addition, we can also employ factor analysis and this software for purposes of testing latent structures, an activity that is typically referred to as confirmatory factor analysis and is discussed in detail next. Furthermore, we can use the underlying comprehensive latent variable modeling methodology for more general purposes, viz., modeling correlative as well as explanatory relationships among observed and/or latent factors, which is the topic we now turn to.

4

Introduction to Latent Variable Modeling and Confirmatory Factor Analysis

In Chapter 1, we introduced the notion of a latent construct (latent variable) and discussed its relevance for behavioral, social, and educational research. The previous chapter used that concept in the context of factor analysis (FA), where latent constructs are typically referred to as 'common factors', 'latent factors', or simply 'factors'. We also discussed there the traditional model of FA. As was made clear, the FA model represents a set of equations relating in a linear fashion observed measures with one or more common factors, in addition to several distributional assumptions. The discussion in Chapter 3 was focused on a model concerned with orthogonal factors or alternatively with correlated factors but with no particular explanatory relationships being postulated between them. The latter type of relationships can be examined using a more general modeling approach, called latent variable modeling (LVM) that will be of concern in this chapter. The general framework of LVM will be of special relevance in the remainder of this book.

4.1 A Latent Variable Modeling Framework

The factor analysis (FA) model discussed in Chapter 3 is a special case of a more general modeling approach that can be employed in the behavioral and social sciences for the purpose of studying relationships between latent constructs evaluated by multiple indicators (proxies or measures). Being concerned with the relations between latent variables, this approach is typically referred to as latent variable modeling (LVM). Similarly to FA, models used in LVM involve latent variables and for this reason are referred to as latent variable models. To begin our discussion of LVM, we examine a widely applicable model that is utilized in much of the present book. This is the so-called linear structural relationships (LISREL) model.

The LISREL model goes back to the early and highly influential work by Jöreskog on factor analysis (e.g., Jöreskog, 1969, 1978) and represents a special type of a latent variable model that will be of particular relevance for the rest of this text. The version of the general LISREL model with observed and latent variables assumed to have zero means, the version that will be of importance in this chapter, is an extension of the FA model in Equations (3.1) in Chapter 3 and can be defined by the following two equations (using notation from earlier chapters):

$$\underline{X} = A\,\underline{f} + \underline{u} \qquad (4.1)$$

and

$$\underline{f} = B\,\underline{f} + \underline{v}.$$

In Equations (4.1), $\underline{X}$ denotes a vector of, say, p observed variables ($p > 1$), and $\underline{f}$ is a vector of m latent factors ($m \geq 1$, typically $m < p$), whereas $\underline{u}$ and $\underline{v}$ are residual terms associated with observed and latent variables, respectively. In these equations, A is the factor loading matrix, and B is the matrix containing all assumed explanatory relationships among the latent variables in $\underline{f}$. In addition, it is assumed that the components of the residual vectors $\underline{u}$ and $\underline{v}$ have means of 0 and are unrelated with any of the variables in $\underline{f}$, as well as with one another (the last assumption can be relaxed in certain circumstances). Typically, it is further assumed that the matrix (I − B) is invertible, which is a rather mild restriction in behavioral and social research. This assumption allows one to solve the second of Equations (4.1) in terms of the latent variables in $\underline{f}$, thus obtaining

$$\underline{f} = (I - B)^{-1} \underline{v}. \tag{4.2}$$

Equation (4.2) states that each dependent latent variable is expressed in terms of an assumed linear function of its explanatory latent variables. (In Equation (4.2), one could formally consider independent latent variables as corresponding elements of $\underline{v}$; e.g., Jöreskog and Sörbom [1996].)

We stress that the latent variable model defined by Equations (4.1) provides a very comprehensive modeling framework and allows one to consider, but does not require, regression-type relationships among latent variables (factors). As alluded to in Chapter 3, this possibility to include also explanatory relationships among latent variables was not available in the FA model considered there, where the latent factors could be only correlated (or alternatively uncorrelated, as in the orthogonal factor model). In addition, when B is the $m \times m$ matrix consisting of zeros only (i.e., $B = O_{m \times m}$, with $O_{m \times m}$ denoting that matrix), the FA model in Equations (3.1) of the preceding chapter results as a special case of that defined by Equations (4.1). That is, the LISREL model in (4.1) is more general than the FA model in the earlier Equations (3.1) (Chapter 3).

In this regard, and in analogy to the pertinent discussion in the preceding chapter, it is worthwhile stressing that the parameters of the general LISREL model in Equations (4.1) can be similarly found to be the following: (a) the parameters of the factor analysis model in the first of these equations, (b) the latent regression coefficients in B, and (c) the elements of the covariance matrix of the disturbance terms $\underline{v}$ (with this matrix being oftentimes assumed diagonal).

To illustrate this discussion, consider a model that aims at studying the relationships between the following three constructs: (a) Parental domination, denoted f_1 and assessed with three measures, X_1 through X_3; (b) Child ability, denoted f_2 and evaluated with two proxies, X_4 and X_5; and (c) Child aspiration, denoted f_3 and indicated by the three measures X_6 through X_8. The path-diagram of this model is presented in Figure 4.1 (see Chapter 3 for a discussion of the elements of the path-diagram notation used).

We notice from Figure 4.1 that this model contains two explanatory relationships between latent variables, which was not the case with the FA model of concern in Chapter 3 (see, e.g., Figure 3.2 there). For this reason there is a residual term, denoted v_3, which is attached to the latent dependent variable in the model, f_3 (Child aspiration), and bears the same subindex. We emphasize the qualifier 'explanatory' with regard to the latent variable relationships, rather than 'causal'. Latent variable models are not used in this book to necessarily imply causal relations between involved variables. We refer to causality literature for discussions of issues pertaining to causal analysis and interpretation, including possible use of structural equation modeling for similar purposes (e.g., Marcoulides, 2007a, 2007b; Pearl, 2001).

We stress at this point that the long one-way arrows in Figure 4.1 are representative of (a) appropriate elements of the matrix B, when they connect latent variables in assumed

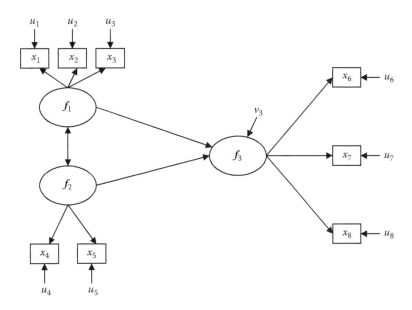

FIGURE 4.1
Example of a latent variable model of the relationships between Parental domination (f_1), Child ability (f_2), and Child aspiration (f_3).

explanatory relationships, or (b) factor loadings when they connect a latent variable with its indicators (viz., the observed measures used to evaluate it). Furthermore, the short one-way arrows attached to each observed variable or the latent variable f_3 are correspondingly representative of (a) the assumed effect of unique factors associated with these indicators (the us) or (b) the latent disturbance term belonging to its associated dependent latent variable. This disturbance term encompasses all sources of variance other than the variables in the model assumed to play an explanatory role for the pertinent dependent variable. At the same time, the two-way arrow connecting f_1 with f_2 stands for their covariance (correlation).

A more detailed, nontechnical discussion of LVM, and specifically of the structural equation modeling approach, can be found for example in Raykov and Marcoulides (2006a), and a more advanced discussion of LVM is provided by Muthén (2002). In this text, we will use special latent variable models, which can be represented as versions of the LISREL model (4.1) and will be well suited for the aims of instrument construction and development as relevant for the goals of this book. In order to handle these models at the empirical analytic level, we will use a popular LVM software, M*plus*, which is introduced next.

4.2 An Introduction to M*plus*, and Traditional Factor Analysis With This Software

As we discussed in the second part of Chapter 3, a main issue that a researcher using FA needs to resolve involves the determination of the number m of latent factors underlying subject performance on a given set of observed measures. We also mentioned several guides (or 'rules') that could be used in this endeavor. In the present section, we will be concerned with application of specialized software to achieve this aim, in the context of the more general goal of conducting factor analysis.

This software is the widely used LVM program M*plus* that provides a highly comprehensive tool for carrying out LVM (Muthén & Muthén, 2010). Because of the breadth of modeling that M*plus* can conduct, it is not possible to thoroughly introduce M*plus* and even most of its features and capabilities in a single chapter, perhaps not even in a single book. Here we will only scratch the surface of what this software can accomplish, specifically focusing on its applicability for purposes of conducting factor analysis. For a more extensive coverage of software capabilities and command structure, we refer the reader to the M*plus* user's guide manual (Muthén & Muthén, 2010; see also Raykov & Marcoulides, 2006a).

Like any software, M*plus* is based on a set of commands, each of which has a number of options that additionally specify particular sorts of analyses or details pertaining to the data or the intended modeling process or its outcome. In this book, we will use only a relatively limited set of commands and options that will specifically serve our purposes— measuring instrument construction and development as well as related modeling aims.

To introduce M*plus* for the purpose of factor analysis, consider the following study setting. A random sample of $n = 600$ university freshmen are administered 11 subtests of the Wechsler Adult Intelligence Scale (WAIS; e.g., Chapter 3; cf. Crocker & Algina, 1986), whereby their normality assumption is deemed plausible. A random subsample of $n_1 = 300$ students is drawn from the initial sample, and the correlation matrix associated with the students' scores on these 11 measures is presented in Table 4.1. (We will use the data from the remaining $n_2 = 300$ subjects in a later part of this chapter.)

We are interested here in examining the structure of the interrelationships among these 11 intelligence measures. Specifically, we would like to know how many latent factors could have been assessed by this test battery, and we use M*plus* to explore the underlying structure associated with the data in Table 4.1. (In the appendix to this chapter, we list some activities pertaining to initial creation of the data and input file associated with this application of M*plus*. The following discussion in this section assumes that an ASCII file, i.e., a plain text file, with all correlations in Table 4.1 has been previously saved following the instructions in the appendix and the name TABLE4_1.DAT was given to it. In the remainder of this book, we will assume that an ASCII file with the data to be analyzed has been made

Table 4.1. Correlation matrix of WAIS subtests ($n_1 = 300$)

Subtest:	1.	2.	3.	4.	5.	6.	7.	8.	9.	10.	11.
1.	1										
2.	.64	1									
3.	.66	.65	1								
4.	.62	.62	.65	1							
5.	.64	.66	.62	.64	1						
6.	.63	.67	.63	.66	.65	1					
7.	.17	.12	.15	.13	.12	.15	1				
8.	.13	.17	.15	.17	.16	.18	.55	1			
9.	.15	.13	.12	.14	.15	.12	.57	.52	1		
10.	.16	.15	.15	.16	.17	.15	.51	.57	.59	1	
11.	.13	.17	.16	.15	.15	.11	.60	.53	.55	.58	1

Note: 1. = *Information;* 2. = *Comprehension;* 3. = *Arithmetic;* 4. = *Similarities;*
      5. = *Digit Span;* 6. = *Vocabulary;* 7. = *Digit Symbol;* 8. = *Picture Completion;*
      9. = *Block Design;* 10. = *Picture Arrangement;* 11. = *Object Assembly;*
      n_1 = sample size.

available prior to the analysis to be conducted; the name of the file will typically be closely tied to the chapter and table or example to which the corresponding analysis pertains.)

To accomplish this latent structure exploration, there is a set of software commands and options that we will use. First, the command TITLE typically starts the modeling session with this software, regardless of the type of analysis to be performed. Even though it is optional, this command is highly recommendable to use. It can go for any number of lines needed for a succinct description of the goal of the following commands; with its exception, all remaining commands and options should end with a semicolon. (One can also use a semicolon at the end of the title command.) To start creating our M*plus* input file, we begin with the following TITLE line. (In the rest of this book, we will use a different font to present input and output from M*plus*.)

```
TITLE:        WAIS EXAMPLE
```

Next we need to direct the software to the data to be analyzed, which in our case is the correlation matrix in Table 4.1. (As mentioned in the previous chapter, traditionally the correlation matrix has been analyzed when exploring the structure of a given set of observed measures using factor analysis; see later in this chapter for other arrangements.) To achieve this, we have to give the name of the file where it is saved in (if necessary, with disk location path), then indicate what type of data they are and finally what the sample size is. This leads to the second command with its pertinent options (see also the appendix), which is as follows:

```
DATA:         FILE = TABLE4_1.DAT;
              TYPE = CORRELATION;
              NOBSERVATIONS = 300;
```

To enhance the interpretability of the output, it is desirable to assign names to the variables in the data file (here 'correlation matrix'; names should be assigned exactly in the order the variables appear in the data file). This is accomplished with the following command (see the note to Table 4.1):

```
VARIABLE:     NAMES = INFO COMPREH ARITH SIMIL DIGSPAN
              VOCAB DIGSYMB PICTCOMP BLOCKDES PICARRGE
              OBJASSEM;
```

We note that in the input file, if need be, we continue on to the next line when we finish one, without using any particular symbol to indicate wrapping over to the next line. (M*plus* keeps reading the contents of the next line, presuming they pertain to those of the preceding one, until it encounters a semicolon.) Thereby, the used variable names are abbreviations, consisting of up to eight letters, of these found in the note to Table 4.1.

At this time, we are ready to proceed with the instructions that M*plus* needs to receive in order to begin the intended modeling effort. To this end, we have to indicate what type of analysis we wish to be conducted. For the factor analysis of interest here, we use the following command:

```
ANALYSIS:     TYPE = EFA 1 3;
```

This command instructs the software to carry out factor analysis of the type we discussed in Chapter 3. As pointed out there, this is exploratory factor analysis (EFA), and it is further dealt with in this chapter. Specifically, with this ANALYSIS command, we ask M*plus* to conduct three different factor analyses—one with a single factor, another with two factors, and the last with three factors. This is because we do not really know how many factors are behind the individuals' performance on the 11 subtests of the WAIS battery, but assuming some knowledge of the substantive domain of intelligence research, one would not expect here more than three factors. (We mention in passing that at this stage the software could be asked for any positive number of factors up to that of observed variables.) We will compare the obtained results for each number of factors and will choose the one that is plausible for the analyzed data and permits meaningful substantive considerations in the subject-matter domain.

This ANALYSIS command is the last we need in order to complete the instructions to M*plus* for conducting the desired factor analysis of the data in Table 4.1. We present next the entire input in compact form, in which it needs to be provided to the software. (As we type this input file in the M*plus* operating window, the color of the discussed software commands becomes blue.)

```
TITLE:          WAIS EXAMPLE

DATA:           FILE = TABLE4_1.DAT;
                TYPE = CORRELATION;
                NOBSERVATIONS = 300;

VARIABLE:       NAMES = INFO COMPREH ARITH SIMIL
                DIGSPAN VOCAB DIGSYMB PICTCOMP
                BLOCKDES PICARRGE OBJASSEM;

ANALYSIS:       TYPE = EFA 1 3;
```

This input file yields the following results. (We are inserting clarifying comments after consecutive output sections and expound on specific issues. In addition, to save space, we dispense with output segments that display software-version-related information and details regarding execution time.)

```
INPUT INSTRUCTIONS
  TITLE:     WAIS EXAMPLE
  DATA:      FILE = TABLE4_1.DAT;
             TYPE=CORRELATION;
             NOBSERVATIONS=300;
  VARIABLE:  NAMES = INFO COMPREH ARITH SIMIL DIGSPAN VOCAB
             DIGSYMB PICTCOMP BLOCKDES PICARRGE OBJASSEM;
  ANALYSIS:  TYPE = EFA 1 3;
```

In this output section, the software echoes back the input. It is essential that we check this input to make sure that it is identical to the one we intended to submit to M*plus* in the first place (because typing errors or such of content can sometimes be easily made during the command file creation phase).

```
INPUT READING TERMINATED NORMALLY
```

The last line contains an important message. It states effectively that the software has not encountered any syntax errors. That is, the entire contents of the input file 'made sense' to the program, as far as its command language was concerned; in other words, this software-printed statement is a testament to the fact that we have used the language (syntax) of M*plus* correctly.

```
WAIS EXAMPLE

SUMMARY OF ANALYSIS

Number of groups                                                 1
Number of observations                                         300

Number of dependent variables                                   11
Number of independent variables                                  0
Number of continuous latent variables                            0

Observed dependent variables

  Continuous
    INFO        COMPREH      ARITH      SIMIL      DIGSPAN    VOCAB
    DIGSYMB     PICTCOMP     BLOCKDES   PICARRGE   OBJASSEM


Estimator                                                       ML
Rotation                                                    GEOMIN
Row standardization                                    CORRELATION
Type of rotation                                           OBLIQUE
Epsilon value                                               Varies
Information matrix                                         EXPECTED
Maximum number of iterations                                  1000
Convergence criterion                                   0.500D-04
Maximum number of steepest descent iterations                   20
Optimization Specifications for the Exploratory Factor Analysis
Rotation Algorithm
  Number of random starts                                       30
  Maximum number of iterations                               10000
  Derivative convergence criterion                       0.100D-04

Input data file(s)
  TABLE4_1.DAT

Input data format FREE
```

This part of the output contains a summary of the requested analysis and data specifics, as well as some 'technical' details pertaining to the underlying numerical procedure invoked by the software as a result of the above input submission (we note in particular the default oblique rotation). Specifically, after stating the first line of the title used—which the software will display at the beginning of each new page or section in the output—we are informed that we are dealing with a single group analysis (as we have data from only one group of subjects that are to be analyzed), with a sample size of 300. Furthermore, the data arise from 11 variables that are treated as dependent in our analysis, because they are presumed in factor analysis to be indicators of underlying factors (see also the definition of the FA model in Equations (3.1) in Chapter 3). We do not have latent regression-like relationships postulated in the FA model, so there are no dependent latent variables, as stated by the software. At this stage, i.e., before the actual factor extraction, we do not have any factors specifically included in the analysis, which is similarly recognized by the program that states here their number as 0. A list of the observed dependent variables with their names follows then, which are all variables from Table 4.1. When carrying out FA of the presently considered type, i.e., exploratory factor analysis, on the correlation matrix, M*plus* uses by default the method of maximum likelihood. When employing this method, of concern is the estimation of the FA model parameters in such a way that they would give rise to the highest likelihood ('probability') of the analyzed data. This principle of estimation has a distinct intuitive basis, is mathematically sound, is associated with optimal statistical properties with large samples, and is highly popular across many different modeling methodologies used in the behavioral and social sciences (e.g., log-linear modeling, multilevel modeling, the general linear model, etc.). Its application within the framework of factor analysis can also be rather revealing and can be recommended in cases with normality of observed variables and large samples (perhaps ranging from several hundred subjects to several thousand with increasing number of manifest measures). We now move on to the next output sections.

```
NO CONVERGENCE. NUMBER OF ITERATIONS EXCEEDED.
PROBLEM OCCURRED IN EXPLORATORY FACTOR ANALYSIS WITH 3 FACTOR(S).
```

This message of 'no convergence' can be expected for overspecified solutions in terms of number of factors, i.e., solutions attempting to extract too many factors than could be sustained by the analyzed data. This attempt is an explanation of why the software could not finalize its search for optimal values for the parameters of the three-factor model. It did, however, converge—i.e., finalize its search for optimal parameter values—in the two cases with fewer factors, which are presented below.

```
RESULTS FOR EXPLORATORY FACTOR ANALYSIS
        EIGENVALUES FOR SAMPLE CORRELATION MATRIX
            1              2              3          4          5
         _____        _____        _____    _____    _____
         4.667          2.776          0.517      0.495      0.456

        EIGENVALUES FOR SAMPLE CORRELATION MATRIX
            6              7              8          9          10
         _____        _____        _____    _____    _____
         0.397          0.386          0.363      0.347      0.312

        EIGENVALUES FOR SAMPLE CORRELATION MATRIX
           11
         _____
         0.285
```

In this output section, we are informed about the eigenvalues of the analyzed correlation matrix in Table 4.1. Because this matrix is based on 11 measures, there are 11 eigenvalues and their sum is 11 (since it is equal, as mentioned in Chapter 3, to the sum of variable variances that are all 1 here). They differ substantially from one another in their magnitude, however, with the largest eigenvalue being nearly 20 times the smallest. (This finding of considerable difference in eigenvalues is not infrequent in empirical behavioral and social research.) Looking at their magnitude, the eigenvalues suggest $m = 2$ as a possibly appropriate number of factors, because only two eigenvalues are larger than 1, and all remaining eigenvalues seem to be comparable among themselves yet much smaller in magnitude. The largest two eigenvalues account for over two thirds of the original variance. Indeed, because we have 11 observed variables with variance 1 each, we have a total of 11 units of variance—hence, the share of the first two eigenvalues is $(4.67 + 2.78)/11 = 68\%$. We nonetheless examine in detail also the FA solution with one factor, which is presented next.

```
EXPLORATORY FACTOR ANALYSIS WITH 1 FACTOR(S):


TESTS OF MODEL FIT


Chi-Square Test of Model Fit


            Value                         614.888
            Degrees of Freedom                 44
            P-Value                        0.0000
```

This output section pertaining to the single-factor solution contains a number of important pieces of information. The first three lines of the 'TEST OF MODEL FIT' part display the results evaluating the fit of the considered one-factor model. This is the first time in this book that we are faced with a hypothesis of a particular number of factors. Specifically, the underlying null hypothesis is that $m = 1$ factor is sufficient to account for the analyzed 11 measures' correlations, i.e., in symbols, H_0: $m = 1$. We must now assess how strong the evidence in the data against this null hypothesis is. Specifically, is there sufficient evidence—based on the fit indexes—to reject this hypothesis? This question is addressed by inspecting, along with other indexes, the chi-square value that represents a test statistic for this null hypothesis. To evaluate its significance, and thus test that hypothesis, we look at its degrees of freedom and corresponding p-value. When a model is a plausible means of data description and explanation, and the sample size is not very large (or fairly small), the chi-square value would be expected to have the magnitude of associated degrees of freedom, and the corresponding p-value would not be very small, e.g., above .05 (e.g., Raykov & Marcoulides, 2006a). In the present case, the chi-square value is much higher than the degrees of freedom, and as a result the pertinent p-value is very small, in fact the smallest possible. These results do not allow us to consider at this stage the null hypothesis of a single-factor retainable, and we will find further evidence against this hypothesis as we advance through the output.

```
Chi-Square Test of Model Fit for the Baseline Model


            Value                        1787.033
            Degrees of Freedom                 55
            P-Value                        0.0000
```

These three lines pertain to what one may often argue is a highly uninteresting model, at least in the current context. This model, referred to as the baseline model, stipulates no (linear) relationships at all among the 11 WAIS subtests and can be considered a counterpart of Bartlett's test of sphericity that we attended to in Chapter 3 when discussing the SPSS output on the illustration example (Section 3.8). Because the baseline model is fundamentally incorrect from a substantive viewpoint in this example (since the analyzed WAIS subtests are, as is well-known, notably intercorrelated), its fit indexes are far from accept-able, which thus comes as no surprise to us.

```
CFI/TLI
```

CFI	0.670
TLI	0.588

The comparative fit index (CFI) and Tucker-Lewis index (TLI) measure how far the current single-factor model is from that baseline model when one compares their lack of fit to the analyzed data. A finding of these indexes being close to 1 (or equal to 1) is indicative of a considered model fitting much better the data than that baseline model. In the present case, these indexes are considerably lower than 1, which finding cannot be interpreted in favor of plausibility of the single-factor model.

```
Loglikelihood
```

H0 Value	-4090.915
H1 Value	-3783.471

These two likelihood indexes represent the respective values of the maximized likelihood for the one-factor model and for a model that fits the data perfectly. The latter is a saturated model that has as many parameters as there are unique variances and covariances for the analyzed set of observed measures. More precisely, minus twice the difference in these two values equals the chi-square index of fit from the earlier discussed model output part.

```
Information Criteria
```

Number of Free Parameters	22
Akaike (AIC)	8225.831
Bayesian (BIC)	8307.314
Sample-Size Adjusted BIC	8237.543
(n* = (n + 2) / 24)	

The information criteria become relevant when we wish to compare several rival models fitted to the same data (on the same observed variables) and possibly select one of them. Then the model with the smallest such indexes would typically be considered preferable. Thus far, we have not seen the information criteria for the model with two factors in order to make use of these indexes here, and so we move on.

```
RMSEA (Root Mean Square Error Of Approximation)
```

Estimate	0.208	
90 Percent C.I.	0.194	0.223
Probability RMSEA <= .05	0.000	

The root mean square error of approximation (RMSEA) is a model fit index that is closely related to the chi-square value (index; for a nontechnical discussion of the RMSEA, see, e.g., Raykov & Marcoulides, 2006a). The RMSEA, however, does not share the chi-square value tendencies to be (a) spuriously high with very large samples, suggesting rejection of a model that may be only trivially incorrect (misspecified), or (b) spuriously low with small samples, when it would suggest retaining an apparently well-fitting model that may, however, be considerably misspecified (i.e., incorrect or deviating considerably from the 'true' model). The RMSEA is defined as misfit per degree of freedom, with the latter being an inverse measure of model complexity, and hence cannot be negative. Therefore, good or tenable models should have limited misfit and small values of RMSEA. A model may be considered tenable for a data set if its RMSEA is smaller than .05, or at least the left endpoint of its associated 90%-confidence interval is considerably lower than .05 (e.g., Browne & Cudeck, 1993). In addition, the length of this interval is indicative of precision of estimation of the model parameters, as well as of power associated with the underlying test of model fit and related tests of parameter significance. For the current example, the RMSEA index of .208 is unacceptably high, as is the left endpoint .194 of its confidence interval. This is another important piece of evidence against the single-factor model currently discussed.

```
SRMR (Standardized Root Mean Square Residual)

        Value                           0.198
```

The standardized root mean square residual (SRMR) is a descriptive statistic that represents an average index of the degree to which a single factor fails to explain the analyzed correlation matrix. Because the value of this index is fairly large, in particular compared to the entries of the sample correlations (see Table 4.1 and also below in this section), it seems that the single-factor solution leaves quite something to be desired in terms of fit. Next we see yet further deficiencies of this solution.

```
GEOMIN ROTATED LOADINGS
              1
          _____

  INFO         0.792
  COMPREH      0.808
  ARITH        0.797
  SIMIL        0.793
  DIGSPAN      0.799
  VOCAB        0.807
  DIGSYMB      0.222
  PICTCOMP     0.245
  BLOCKDES     0.216
  PICARRGE     0.242
  OBJASSEM     0.228


         GEOMIN FACTOR CORRELATIONS
              1
          _____
            1.000


         ESTIMATED RESIDUAL VARIANCES
            INFO        COMPREH      ARITH      SIMIL      DIGSPAN
          _____  _____  _____  _____  _____
            0.373       0.348       0.364      0.372       0.362
```

```
ESTIMATED RESIDUAL VARIANCES
     VOCAB         DIGSYMB        PICTCOMP  BLOCKDES  PICARRGE

   _____     _____       _____ _____ _____
     0.349         0.951           0.940     0.953     0.942


ESTIMATED RESIDUAL VARIANCES
     OBJASSEM

   _____
     0.948


  S.E. GEOMIN ROTATED LOADINGS
            1
        _____
INFO        0.025
COMPREH     0.023
ARITH       0.024
SIMIL       0.025
DIGSPAN     0.024
VOCAB       0.024
DIGSYMB     0.058
PICTCOMP    0.057
BLOCKDES    0.058
PICARRGE    0.057
OBJASSEM    0.057


  S.E. GEOMIN FACTOR CORRELATIONS
            1

        _____
          0.000


  S.E. ESTIMATED RESIDUAL VARIANCES
     INFO          COMPREH        ARITH     SIMIL     DIGSPAN

   _____     _____       _____ _____ _____
     0.039         0.038           0.039     0.039     0.039


  S.E. ESTIMATED RESIDUAL VARIANCES
     VOCAB         DIGSYMB        PICTCOMP  BLOCKDES  PICARRGE

   _____     _____       _____ _____ _____
     0.038         0.025           0.028     0.025     0.028


  S.E. ESTIMATED RESIDUAL VARIANCES
     OBJASSEM

   _____
     0.026
```

```
          Est./S.E.  GEOMIN ROTATED LOADINGS
                 1
               _____
INFO           31.981
COMPREH        34.521
ARITH          32.802
SIMIL          32.073
DIGSPAN        33.038
VOCAB          34.315
DIGSYMB         3.854
PICTCOMP        4.299
BLOCKDES        3.744
PICARRGE        4.243
OBJASSEM        3.984

          Est./S.E.  GEOMIN FACTOR CORRELATIONS
                 1

               _____
     1           0.000

          Est./S.E.  ESTIMATED RESIDUAL VARIANCES
              INFO          COMPREH         ARITH       SIMIL       DIGSPAN

            _____       _____        _____     _____     _____
     1        9.504         9.194          9.401       9.492       9.372

          Est./S.E.  ESTIMATED RESIDUAL VARIANCES
              VOCAB         DIGSYMB        PICTCOMP   BLOCKDES    PICARRGE

            _____       _____        _____     _____     _____
     1        9.218        37.307         33.782      38.312      34.186

          Est./S.E.  ESTIMATED RESIDUAL VARIANCES
              OBJASSEM

            _____
     1       36.189

          FACTOR DETERMINACIES
                 1

               _____
     1           0.957
```

The factor loading estimates and unique variance estimates (referred to as 'estimated residual variances') for this solution suggest that each of the manifest measures is associated with a fairly small communality. (M*plus* uses as a general heading the reference of rotated loadings that would be applicable in the general case of $m > 1$ factors; in case of $m = 1$, when rotation cannot be carried out, the same general heading is, however, still automatically used by the software without really conducting any rotation. Hence, the presented output in this section contains in fact the initial solution factor loadings and associated parameter estimates.) Because communality is the complement to 1 of residual term variance (see Chapter 3), the last printed output section shows it in the .60s for the verbal measures but not even in the .10s range for the performance measures. In particular, at least 37% of the variance in the Information score remains unexplained by this single-factor solution, and as much as 95% of the variance in the Object assembly score is unaccounted for (like for the remaining performance measures). In addition, the factor loadings of the performance measures are several times smaller than those of the verbal measures, which would, however, be very unusual for a reasonably well-fitting single-factor solution. We note in passing that all factor loadings appear significant (at a conventional significance level, say, of .05). This is observed by inspecting their ratios to corresponding standard errors, which could be treated with large samples and under the model as z-values; these are found in the column labeled 'EST/S.E. GEOMIN ROTATED LOADINGS' and are all larger here than the 5%-significance cutoff of 1.96 for the underlying large sample, standard normal distribution of these ratios. (Conversely, if a z-value is smaller than –1.96, it is also interpreted as significant. We note in passing that these z-values are not infrequently referred to as *t*-values in the literature.) We stress, however, that we cannot place much trust in these significance findings, because overall the single-factor model does not seem to fit the data well (see next paragraph).

All these noted deficiencies build a sufficiently strong case against the one-factor solution, and so we conclude that the single-factor model does not provide a plausible means of data description and explanation. We now move on to the two-factor solution.

```
EXPLORATORY FACTOR ANALYSIS WITH 2 FACTOR(S):

TESTS OF MODEL FIT

Chi-Square Test of Model Fit

            Value                           32.247
            Degrees of Freedom                  34
            P-Value                         0.5537

Chi-Square Test of Model Fit for the Baseline Model

            Value                         1787.033
            Degrees of Freedom                  55
            P-Value                         0.0000

CFI/TLI

            CFI                              1.000
            TLI                              1.002

Loglikelihood

            H0 Value                      -3799.595
            H1 Value                      -3783.471

Information Criteria

            Number of Free Parameters           32
            Akaike (AIC)                   7663.190
            Bayesian (BIC)                 7781.711
            Sample-Size Adjusted BIC       7680.226
               (n* = (n + 2) / 24)

RMSEA (Root Mean Square Error Of Approximation)

            Estimate                        0.000
            90 Percent C.I.                 0.000        0.039
            Probability RMSEA <= .05        0.992

SRMR (Standardized Root Mean Square Residual)

            Value                           0.016
```

As we can see from its goodness-of-fit indexes, the two-factor solution is associated with multiple pieces of evidence that it provides a plausible means of data description and explanation. First, its chi-square value is of the magnitude of corresponding degrees of freedom, and the associated *p*-value is fairly sizeable rather than significant (as was the case with the single-factor model). Furthermore, the TLI and CFI are very good, effectively at their highest possible values, and much higher than those fit indexes of the one-factor model. This suggests also that the currently considered two-factor model is far better fitting the data than the baseline model. The information criteria of the two-factor model are considerably lower than those indexes for the single-factor model, again indicating the superiority of the former to the latter model. The RMSEA is here as good as possible, viz., 0, and the SRMR is much lower than that index in the previously fitted model. All these indexes clearly show that the two-factor model is plausible for the analyzed data. With this in mind, we move on to interpreting the two-factor solution.

```
GEOMIN ROTATED LOADINGS
                    1                    2

                 _____             _____

   INFO           0.793                 0.003
   COMPREH        0.811                -0.002
   ARITH          0.800                -0.001
   SIMIL          0.793                 0.005
   DIGSPAN        0.800                 0.004
   VOCAB          0.813                -0.012
   DIGSYMB       -0.006                 0.748
   PICTCOMP       0.028                 0.713
   BLOCKDES      -0.013                 0.751
   PICARRGE       0.014                 0.752
   OBJASSEM      -0.003                 0.763
```

```
          GEOMIN FACTOR CORRELATIONS
                 1              2

              _____      _____

     1         1.000
     2         0.242          1.000
```

ESTIMATED RESIDUAL VARIANCES				
INFO	COMPREH	ARITH	SIMIL	DIGSPAN
_____	_____	_____	_____	_____
0.370	0.343	0.360	0.369	0.359

ESTIMATED RESIDUAL VARIANCES				
VOCAB	DIGSYMB	PICTCOMP	BLOCKDES	PICARRGE
_____	_____	_____	_____	_____
0.343	0.443	0.481	0.440	0.430

ESTIMATED RESIDUAL VARIANCES
OBJASSEM
_____
0.420

S.E. GEOMIN ROTATED LOADINGS

	1	2
INFO	0.026	0.035
COMPREH	0.025	0.033
ARITH	0.026	0.034
SIMIL	0.027	0.037
DIGSPAN	0.026	0.035
VOCAB	0.025	0.039
DIGSYMB	0.035	0.033
PICTCOMP	0.049	0.036
BLOCKDES	0.043	0.034
PICARRGE	0.044	0.033
OBJASSEM	0.026	0.031

S.E. GEOMIN FACTOR CORRELATIONS

	1	2
1	0.000	
2	0.064	0.000

S.E. ESTIMATED RESIDUAL VARIANCES

	INFO	COMPREH	ARITH	SIMIL	DIGSPAN
1	0.039	0.038	0.039	0.039	0.038

S.E. ESTIMATED RESIDUAL VARIANCES

	VOCAB	DIGSYMB	PICTCOMP	BLOCKDES	PICARRGE
1	0.038	0.047	0.048	0.047	0.047

S.E. ESTIMATED RESIDUAL VARIANCES

	OBJASSEM
1	0.046

Est./S.E. GEOMIN ROTATED LOADINGS

	1	2
INFO	29.986	0.097
COMPREH	32.661	-0.055
ARITH	31.042	-0.033
SIMIL	29.928	0.136
DIGSPAN	30.922	0.110
VOCAB	32.097	-0.303
DIGSYMB	-0.179	22.608
PICTCOMP	0.582	19.599
BLOCKDES	-0.304	22.328
PICARRGE	0.321	22.436
OBJASSEM	-0.121	24.241

```
      Est./S.E. GEOMIN FACTOR CORRELATIONS
           1                  2
        _____          _____
   1      0.000
   2      3.758             0.000
```

Est./S.E. ESTIMATED RESIDUAL VARIANCES				
INFO	COMPREH	ARITH	SIMIL	DIGSPAN
9.458	9.120	9.338	9.447	9.322

Est./S.E. ESTIMATED RESIDUAL VARIANCES				
VOCAB	DIGSYMB	PICTCOMP	BLOCKDES	PICARRGE
9.110	9.391	10.010	9.343	9.233

Est./S.E. ESTIMATED RESIDUAL VARIANCES
OBJASSEM
9.053

```
      FACTOR STRUCTURE
           1                  2
        _____          _____
INFO      0.794             0.195
COMPREH   0.811             0.194
ARITH     0.800             0.192
SIMIL     0.794             0.197
DIGSPAN   0.801             0.197
VOCAB     0.811             0.185
DIGSYMB   0.175             0.747
PICTCOMP  0.201             0.720
BLOCKDES  0.168             0.748
PICARRGE  0.196             0.755
OBJASSEM  0.181             0.762
```

```
      FACTOR DETERMINACIES
           1                  2
        _____          _____
   1      0.957             0.930
```

As mentioned in Chapter 3, in order to interpret substantively each factor, we look at those observed measures that load highly on it and then find out what features they have or share in common. With respect to Factor 1, we see that the first six measures load highly on it (see sections 'GEOMIN ROTATED FACTOR LOADINGS' and 'EST./SE GEOMIN ROTATED FACTOR LOADINGS'). At the same time, the remaining five measures load nonsignificantly on the first factor. In the section 'FACTOR STRUCTURE' that contains the correlations of observed measures and underlying factors, we see that the first factor correlates markedly with the first six measures but weakly with the next five observed variables. Given that, as known from the intelligence literature, the first six measures evaluate verbal abilities (e.g., Wechsler, 1958), it makes sense to interpret or label Factor 1 'Verbal intelligence'. With regard to Factor 2, we notice in the same way that the last five measures load highly on it and are correlated markedly with it, whereas the first six load nonsignificantly on this factor and correlate weakly with it. What the last five measures have in common is that they are performance measures, as known from the intelligence literature (Wechsler, 1958). Hence, we can interpret or label Factor 2 'Performance intelligence'.

What factor loading can be considered large, and what small, when we are attempting factor interpretation, as we just did? A long-standing 'rule of thumb' is that when the correlation matrix is analyzed (as in this example), loadings lower than .3 could be considered small. The rationale behind it is based on the observation that when a factor loading is no larger than .3, the part of observed variance explained by that factor (on its own) in the pertinent measure can be seen as being under 10% (indeed, $.3^2 = .09$). Loadings higher than .3, according to that rule of thumb, would thus usually be considered as generally contributing to factor interpretation, as opposed to those lower than .3. As we have just seen while interpreting the two-factor solution, the used software also provides standard errors for factor loadings as well as associated z-values (see output section 'EST./SE GEOMIN ROTATED FACTOR LOADINGS'). These z-values can similarly be quite helpful in accomplishing this aim by permitting one to test loadings for significance. (We reiterate that as is well-known from introductory statistics courses, a loading with a z-value larger than 1.96 in absolute value would be significant, at the conventional significance level of .05, and not significant if the z-value is in absolute value smaller than 1.96.)

From the section 'ESTIMATED RESIDUAL VARIANCES' we see by subtraction from 1 that the communalities of all measures in this two-factor solution are in the .50s and .60s and thus on average much higher than their counterparts in the single-factor solution. In the section 'EST./S.E. GEOMIN FACTOR CORRELATIONS', we also observe that the factor correlation is significant (its z-value is 3.758, i.e., higher than 1.96). In the 'FACTOR DETERMINACIES' section, we note that these coefficients are quite high for both factors. The factor determinacy coefficient can be considered an analog to the R^2-coefficient if trying to predict the pertinent factor using its indicators (cf. McDonald, 1967a). For both factors, this index is fairly high, indicating another aspect in which the present two-factor solution can be viewed as fitting quite well the analyzed data.

Because the three-factor solution was not really obtained, due to the underlying numerical procedure not having converged, our discussion of the output associated with the requested EFA for the 11 WAIS subtests is finished. We conclude that according to this exploratory analysis, the two-factor solution provides a plausible means of description and explanation of the analyzed data.

We finalize this section by presenting in Figure 4.2 the conceptual diagram of the preferred two-factor solution for the data in Table 4.1. (For ease of presentation, the triple of

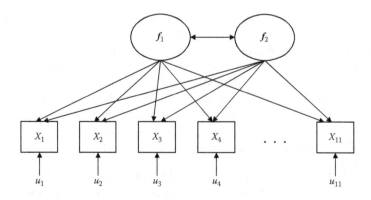

FIGURE 4.2
Conceptual diagram of preferred two-factor solution (see Table 4.1).

points between X_4 and X_{11} denote the intervening six measures, X_5 through X_{10}, which share the same features of loading on both factors of this solution, as the explicitly depicted measures X_1 through X_4 and X_{11}.) We stress that in it all observed variables load on all common factors, a characteristic property of exploratory factor analysis models. Thereby, we can look at this conceptual diagram as representing any of the infinitely many EFA solutions (as opposed to a single one) that fit the analyzed data equally well, as mentioned in Chapter 3. (We will address this issue pertaining to unique estimability of model parameters later in the chapter.) In addition, we point out that there are no relationships allowed in the model between unique and common factors as well as between the unique factors (residual or error terms). The first of these two restrictions is typical for regression analysis approaches, which factor analysis may be viewed as analogous to (up to the fact that predictors are unobserved here); the second is specific to the particular exploratory mode in which we have been using FA so far. This restriction can be relaxed when we 'shift' to another mode of utilizing FA, which is represented by confirmatory factor analysis that allows also addressing the general problem of unique estimability of model parameters.

4.3 Exploratory Versus Confirmatory Factor Analysis

The factor analysis discussed in Chapter 3 and up to this point in the present one is referred to as exploratory factor analysis (EFA), as mentioned earlier. The reason is that before we started it, we did not have any idea about the number of factors as well as how they related to the observed measures, in particular which measure loaded markedly on which factor. This situation is typical for most behavioral and social research domains where there is limited knowledge available from past research with respect to the structure of a studied phenomenon. This is also often the case with somewhat underdeveloped substantive areas. Under such circumstances, which are not rare in empirical research, it is appropriate to carry out EFA. The essence of an application of EFA then is to generate a hypothesis about the structure of the studied phenomenon, specifically in terms of the number of underlying factors and their relationships to observed measures.

A generated hypothesis regarding the structure of a set of variables under consideration, as obtained from an EFA, is, however, not a hypothesis that can be relied on. In order to consider it trustworthy, additional evidence in favor of it needs to be provided. This can be accomplished using a different mode of application of FA, which is confirmatory factor analysis (CFA). CFA is well-suited for testing hypotheses (theories) about relationships between latent factors and their indicators. Therefore, CFA can be utilized only when there is a relatively well-formulated theory, or hypothesis, about how many factors underlie subjects' performance on a given set of measures and how the latter are related to each of the factors. In particular, the specific relationships between measures and factors are of special relevance when conducting CFA, because with their postulation one resolves the serious problem of infinitely many solutions in EFA.

Hence CFA is applicable, and called for, when one is interested in testing a theory or hypothesis about the structure of a studied phenomenon. This theory or hypothesis needs to be expressed specifically in terms of the number of latent factors and which observed measures load on which of them. This implies that in order to be in a position to apply CFA, knowledge must be available beforehand or a hypothesis must be advanced that is to be tested with CFA, according to which (a) the number of factors is stated, rather than to be determined from the analyzed data, and (b) for each member of a given set of observed measures, it is stipulated which of its loadings on which factor are 0, with the remaining factor loadings being parameters of the CFA model. This knowledge or hypothesis is reflected in a postulated model that underlies a CFA application.

With this in mind, CFA is a method of testing (sufficiently well-developed) hypotheses or theories about the latent structure of studied sets of observed measures, rather than a procedure for generating hypotheses about their structure, as EFA is. We stress that CFA is not affected by the problem of infinity of solutions that is characteristic of EFA (see pertinent discussion in Chapter 3). The reason is that there is typically a multitude of factor loadings that are fixed at 0 in a CFA model, rendering a unique solution (i.e., unique estimability of the model parameters). (We also note that the common use of EFA is to explore the structure behind a given set of observed variables, where the verb 'explore' is used with the distinct connotation of 'generating a hypothesis about the latent/factor structure'.) As a consequence of these features of CFA, it becomes possible to test (a) how well the assumed FA model fits the analyzed data and (b) whether any of its unknown parameters that could be of particular interest are significant. Furthermore, unlike the situation in EFA, it is possible to include as model parameters error term covariances within a CFA application.

In particular, the earlier question whether a factor loading is large or small can also be addressed now using a statistical testing approach that allows one to test for significance any factor loading or another parameter of the CFA model, such as a factor correlation—the latter being of interest when the relationship between two factors is of concern. In more advanced applications of CFA, it is also possible to test hypotheses about specific relations among model parameters, such as linear or nonlinear relationships among them.

A special, highly beneficial application of CFA is as a follow-up to EFA on the same set of observed variables (but different data set/sample; see below). Although EFA generates only a hypothesis about the structure of these variables, a subsequent application of CFA can test this hypothesis. However, we stress that the CFA needs to be conducted on a data set that is different from the one on which the EFA was carried out in the first instance— the typical recommendation in this regard is to conduct CFA on a sample of subjects from the same studied population, which sample is independent of the one used for EFA. When this is not the case, the p-values obtained with the CFA may not be trustworthy, because capitalization on chance may have occurred. When such an independent sample is available, CFA can test the hypothesis obtained with EFA, or the most favorably considered among several hypotheses generated in a preceding EFA session. We demonstrate in the next section how one can carry out CFA as a follow-up to EFA, and at the same time we illustrate an application of CFA using the popular software M*plus*.

In conclusion of this section, we stress that in order for CFA to be a meaningful analytic approach in a given empirical situation, one does not need to first carry out EFA and only then use CFA to test subsequently the hypothesis(-es) generated by the former. As long as there is a theory or hypothesis about the latent structure of a studied set of observed variables, irrespective of where that hypothesis comes from (assuming of course that it is meaningful substantively and not obtained from the same data set/sample on which the CFA is to be conducted), one can carry out CFA to test it. This is because, as indicated, all one needs in order to proceed with CFA is knowledge of or a hypothesis about the number of factors and which observed variable loads on which factor. Typically, all remaining possible loadings of a measure upon a factor are assumed 0, thus achieving unique parameter estimation (identification) and resolving the issue of rotation, which is no more applicable to CFA, as pointed out earlier.

4.4 Confirmatory Factor Analysis Using M*plus*

At the software level, conducting CFA with M*plus* is similar (though not identical) to carrying out EFA. In particular, we need to communicate to the program the number of latent factors and which variables load on which of them, i.e., which variables 'define' which factor. We accomplish this using a new command, MODEL. This command describes the CFA model in such a way that the software unambiguously can interpret the number of factors and the measures that define in this sense each one of them.

For the purpose of CFA illustration, we return to the setting of our previously considered example in Section 4.2, in which college freshmen were administered the WAIS test battery. A main feature of CFA is that in general it is to be conducted on the covariance matrix rather than correlation matrix. The reason is that the statistical theory needed for CFA application has been most completely developed and implemented for the case of covariance structures (matrices). In fact, with more general CFA models, particularly those containing parameter restrictions, analysis of the correlation matrix can yield misleading results unless specialized software is used (such as RAMONA or SEPATH; see Browne & Mels, 2005; Steiger, 2003). A more detailed discussion of this theoretically and empirically important issue can be found in Cudeck (1989).

The covariance matrix on the 11 WAIS subtests for the unused, holdout sample of 300 subjects that were not in the subsample employed for EFA earlier in this chapter is presented in Table 4.2.

Using these data, we wish to test the hypothesis that there are two factors underlying subjects' performance on the 11 measures, with the first 6 loading (only) on one of the factors and the remaining 5 loading (only) on the second factor. We note that this hypothesis corresponds in terms of latent structure to the preferred two-factor solution we obtained with EFA earlier in this chapter. At the same time, however, this hypothesis is slightly more specialized because it assumes that the last 5 measures have zero loadings on the first factor, whereas the first 6 measures have zero loadings on the second factor. With this in mind, in this section we wish to test, on a different sample from the same population,

Table 4.2. Covariance matrix of WAIS subtests for hold-out freshmen subsample ($n_2 = 300$ subjects, not used for EFA)

Subtest:	1.	2.	3.	4.	5.	6.	7.	8.	9.	10.	11.
1.	1.6										
2.	.67	1.5									
3.	.68	.65	1.3								
4.	.63	.61	.65	1.4							
5.	.65	.67	.63	.64	1.3						
6.	.63	.68	.64	.67	.65	1.1					
7.	.17	.12	.15	.14	.12	.15	1.2				
8.	.25	.13	.15	.16	.26	.18	.54	1.1			
9.	.12	.15	.11	.17	.15	.12	.55	.52	.94		
10.	.23	.26	.13	.24	.17	.15	.58	.61	.58	.99	
11.	.13	.17	.26	.15	.15	.11	.60	.57	.56	.59	.99

Note: 1. = Information; 2. = Comprehension; 3. = Arithmetic; 4. = Similarities; 5. = Digit Span; 6. = Vocabulary; 7. = Digit Symbol; 8. = Picture Completion; 9. = Block Design; 10. = Picture Arrangement; 11. = Object Assembly.

this two-factor hypothesis generated by those earlier analyses (Sections 4.2 and 4.3). (We stress that none of the observed variables loads here on both factors, according to the hypothesis to be tested.)

We emphasize that in order to start a CFA session, we need a fully specified model. This requirement is not valid when conducting EFA because in that case all we can do is explore what kind of latent structure could best describe a given set of observed measure correlations. As pointed out before, the fully specified model required for an application of CFA can come from (a) an earlier EFA (developed, though, on a different sample) or (b) an earlier theory in a given subject-matter domain or can alternatively represent (c) a hypothesis we wish to test with CFA. By way of contrast, an application of EFA can be initiated in general as soon as we have access to the data for a set of observed variables (for which an application of EFA would be meaningful; see Chapter 3). That is, in a sense EFA requires far less than CFA in order to be invoked (and thus may deliver difficult to interpret solutions).

In order to communicate to M*plus* that we wish to fit the two-factor model under consideration, we need to tell the software which observed variables load on which factor, i.e., which measures define which factor; in other words, we need to communicate how each of the two factors is defined in terms of observed measures having nonzero loadings on it. This is accomplished within the command MODEL, as mentioned above, whose further specifications describe in detail the model to be fitted to the data. In our case, we achieve this model description as follows (we discuss each of the following lines immediately after stating them):

```
MODEL:    F1 BY INFO*1 COMPREH-VOCAB;
          F2 BY DIGSYMB*1 PICTCOMP-OBJASSEM;
          F1-F2@1;
```

The first of these three lines defines the latent factor F1 as being measured by the first six subtests, Information through Vocabulary. (We note that the dash symbol is used to save writing out the names of all measures stated in the earlier VARIABLE command as positioned between those named COMPREH and VOCAB.) To this end, the name of the latent factor is stated first, followed by the keyword BY (for 'measured by') and the observed variables that load on that factor are then stated. Thereby, the implication for the software is that any of the remaining observed measures has a zero loading on this factor, because none of those measures are mentioned in this line, which is precisely what the CFA model under consideration posits, as indicated above. Similarly, the second line defines the second factor, F2, as measured by the remaining five variables from the original list of variables, i.e., by Digit Symbol through Object Assembly. (The implication for the software from this second line is also that the remaining six observed variables have loadings of 0 on this second factor.) The third line defines the variances of the two factors as set at 1, in order for their correlation to become uniquely estimable (and associated with a standard error) in their covariance parameter. We use the asterisk after the first factor indicator to define its loading on the factor as a model parameter and thus override an otherwise useful default in M*plus*, which we discuss next.

If we dispense with this third MODEL section line, F1-F2@1, and do not attach an asterisk after the name of the first stated observed variable after the BY keyword in the first two lines of this section, then M*plus* will invoke an important default feature. Accordingly, the software will assume the two factor variances as model parameters to be estimated but will fix at 1 the loading of the first appearing variable after the BY keyword in the lines defining each of the two factors. This fixing at 1, of either a loading or a factor variance, is required for obtaining uniquely estimable, or identifiable, model parameters. Otherwise, a factor loading and variance will be unidentified model parameters, i.e., it will not be possible to uniquely estimate them from the data. (For a nontechnical discussion of this important issue of parameter and model identification, see, e.g., Raykov and Marcoulides [2006a].) A model with at least one nonidentifiable parameter, called unidentified model, is associated with (a) multiplicity of possible solutions that are equally consistent with the analyzed data and (b) output that cannot be trusted. In this case, one should not interpret parameter estimates that may be produced by software. We note that the used LVM program, M*plus*, has defaults ensuring identifiability for all models and cases we will be interested in this book.

By freeing the loadings for all observed indicators of a given factor, while fixing the latent variances at 1 as we do in the currently considered command file, we ensure that the factor covariance equals the factor correlation (see Chapter 2). In this way, we can estimate the factor correlation, viz., in the factor covariance, and obtain at the same time a standard error for it. (If we use the M*plus* defaults mentioned above, we would obtain only a standard error for the factor covariance.)

All remaining lines of the earlier M*plus* input file used for EFA in this chapter remain valid for this example, except of course the line requesting EFA and the fact that we now analyze the covariance matrix (as we are carrying out CFA; see above in this section). The complete CFA input file needed here looks as follows (we note the use of a comment in the second line, which is preceded by an exclamation mark; we will occasionally use comments in this way in the remainder of the book):

```
TITLE:      WAIS CFA EXAMPLE USING THE SECOND, HOLD-OUT
            SUBSAMPLE (HALF) OF ORIGINAL FRESHMEN SAMPLE.
            NOTE THAT ANALYZED IS THE COVARIANCE MATRIX.


DATA:       FILE = TABLE4_2.DAT; ! see Table 4.2
            TYPE = COVARIANCE;
            NOBSERVATIONS = 300;


VARIABLE:   NAMES = INFO COMPREH ARITH SIMIL DIGSPAN VOCAB
            DIGSYMB PICTCOMP BLOCKDES PICARRGE OBJASSEM;

MODEL:      F1 BY INFO* COMPREH-VOCAB;
            F2 BY DIGSYMB* PICTCOMP-OBJASSEM;
            F1-F2@1;
```

The following output results when submitting this command file to M*plus*. We are commenting only on output sections that have not been discussed previously in this chapter.

```
INPUT READING TERMINATED NORMALLY

WAIS CFA EXAMPLE USING SECOND, HOLD-OUT
SUBSAMPLE OF ORIGINAL FRESHMEN SAMPLE.
NOTE THAT ANALYZED IS THE COVARIANCE MATRIX
```

```
SUMMARY OF ANALYSIS

Number of groups                                                    1
Number of observations                                           300

Number of dependent variables                                     11
Number of independent variables                                    0
Number of continuous latent variables                              2

Observed dependent variables

   Continuous
    INFO        COMPREH      ARITH       SIMIL       DIGSPAN      VOCAB
    DIGSYMB     PICTCOMP     BLOCKDES    PICARRGE    OBJASSEM

Continuous latent variables
    F1          F2

Estimator                                                         ML
Information matrix                                           EXPECTED
Maximum number of iterations                                    1000
Convergence criterion                                     0.500D-04
Maximum number of steepest descent iterations                     20

Input data file(s)
    table4_2.dat

Input data format FREE

THE MODEL ESTIMATION TERMINATED NORMALLY

TESTS OF MODEL FIT

Chi-Square Test of Model Fit

              Value                          52.918
              Degrees of Freedom                 43
              P-Value                        0.1429

Chi-Square Test of Model Fit for the Baseline Model

              Value                        1311.378
              Degrees of Freedom                 55
              P-Value                        0.0000

CFI/TLI
              CFI                             0.992
              TLI                             0.990

Loglikelihood
              H0 Value                    -4351.903
              H1 Value                    -4325.444
```

```
Information Criteria

        Number of Free Parameters            23
        Akaike (AIC)                    8749.807
        Bayesian (BIC)                  8834.994
        Sample-Size Adjusted BIC        8762.051
          (n* = (n + 2) / 24)

RMSEA (Root Mean Square Error Of Approximation)

        Estimate                           0.028
        90 Percent C.I.                    0.000      0.050
        Probability RMSEA <= .05           0.948

SRMR (Standardized Root Mean Square Residual)

        Value                              0.027
```

The first several lines of the TESTS OF MODEL FIT output section indicate a well-fitting model. Specifically, we take a look at the chi-square value that as mentioned before is an inferential index of fit. This value is approximately of the same magnitude as the model degrees of freedom. The chi-square value represents here a test statistic of a particular null hypothesis, viz., H_0: 'The model fits the population covariance matrix perfectly'. We also note the *p*-value pertaining to this statistic, which is satisfactory (rather than significant). In addition, the RMSEA index is within an acceptable range. In particular, its value .028 is well below the threshold of .05, and the left endpoint of its confidence interval is as low as it could be, viz., 0 (e.g., Raykov & Marcoulides, 2006a). Overall, this is clearly a well-fitting model, and hence we can interpret its following parameter estimates with confidence.

```
MODEL RESULTS
                                                        Two-Tailed
                  Estimate      S.E.     Est./S.E.      P-Value

F1       BY
   INFO            0.805       0.070      11.506         0.000
   COMPREH         0.818       0.067      12.235         0.000
   ARITH           0.800       0.061      13.042         0.000
   SIMIL           0.798       0.064      12.382         0.000
   DIGSPAN         0.801       0.061      13.067         0.000
   VOCAB           0.809       0.055      14.834         0.000

F2       BY
   DIGSYMB         0.749       0.059      12.698         0.000
   PICTCOMP        0.743       0.056      13.307         0.000
   BLOCKDES        0.723       0.051      14.278         0.000
   PICARRGE        0.790       0.051      15.571         0.000
   OBJASSEM        0.765       0.051      14.897         0.000
```

The presented model results here are the estimates of the loadings (in column 'Estimate') of each observed measure upon each of the factors, followed by standard error (S.E.), *z*-value (ratio of the two, per measure), and associated *p*-value of the null hypothesis that in the studied population the pertinent factor loading is 0. Thereby, loadings not mentioned explicitly in the input file statements are set equal to 0 to begin with, as mentioned before, in accordance with the CFA model fitted. For example, the loading of the subtest Information on F2 is set at 0, because according to the tested hypothesis about the structure of the 11 WAIS tests, the Information measure loads only on F1 (and thus has a zero loading on the latent variable F2).

		Estimate	S.E.	Est./S.E.	Two-Tailed P-Value
F2	WITH				
	F1	0.268	0.063	4.231	0.000

This is the factor correlation, estimated at .27 with S.E. = .06, and is thus significant (see *p*-value in the last column of this output section). This correlation is similar to the one we have obtained in the EFA earlier in this chapter, but we stress that here we are analyzing different subjects' data (though from the same population and on the same observed variables).

	Estimate	S.E.	Est./S.E.	Two-Tailed P-Value
Variances				
F1	1.000	0.000	999.000	999.000
F2	1.000	0.000	999.000	999.000

As mentioned before, we fixed the variances of both factors at 1 to obtain their correlation in their covariance parameter. In this way, we ensured model identification and hence a unique solution for this CFA model that therefore—like any identified CFA model—does not suffer from the problem of infinitely many equally well-fitting solutions typical for EFA. Because these variances are fixed rather than estimated (free) parameters, the following numbers in their lines are meaningless values—thus we can just ignore the last three numbers within each of these two rows.

	Estimate	S.E.	Est./S.E.	Two-Tailed P-Value
Residual Variances				
INFO	0.946	0.088	10.789	0.000
COMPREH	0.826	0.078	10.518	0.000
ARITH	0.656	0.065	10.161	0.000
SIMIL	0.759	0.073	10.457	0.000
DIGSPAN	0.654	0.064	10.149	0.000
VOCAB	0.442	0.049	9.068	0.000
DIGSYMB	0.635	0.060	10.524	0.000
PICTCOMP	0.545	0.053	10.263	0.000
BLOCKDES	0.414	0.042	9.759	0.000
PICARRGE	0.363	0.041	8.851	0.000
OBJASSEM	0.401	0.043	9.363	0.000

These are the unique factor variance estimates. We note that none of them is negative, as is expected in any admissible solution.

By way of summary, this application of factor analysis in its confirmatory mode allowed us to test the two-factor hypothesis we generated using exploratory factor analysis earlier in the chapter, while using a different, independent sample from the same population. The CFA model fitted in this section was found to be tenable as a means of data description and explanation, and the two postulated factors were found to be notably correlated. These results may be seen as supportive of the two-factor hypothesis regarding the 11 subtests of WAIS (according to the analyzed data), with the first 6 loading on the Verbal factor, the last 5 loading on the Performance factor, and none of the 11 measures loading on both factors. We emphasize that in order to be in a position to come to such a conclusion, we carried out the two analyses—EFA and CFA—on two independent samples of subjects from a studied population, a strategy that has a lot to recommend in empirical behavioral and social research.

4.5 Application of Confirmatory Factor Analysis in Test Construction: An Introduction

In Chapter 3, we mentioned that most of the time when we are interested in developing a behavioral test or measuring instrument based on a given set of components, it is desirable that the latter be unidimensional. Also there, we used EFA to explore the latent structure of a prespecified set of components (subtests in a possible test battery). As pointed out earlier in this chapter, however, even though an EFA may have suggested a single factor behind a set of components considered for inclusion into an instrument under development, it is essential that we confirm the pertinent unidimensionality hypothesis before deciding to have the instrument indeed be based on these components. CFA is a methodology that allows us to accomplish this goal, and now we can use the software M*plus* for this purpose.

4.5.1 Continuous Instrument Components

In this subsection, we will assume that the components of an instrument under consideration, such as a tentative scale, self-report, inventory, questionnaire, or test, are continuous or approximately so. (We relax this assumption in Subsection 4.5.2.) This will be the case when each component exhibits a multitude of scores taken by examined subjects in an empirical study. For example, subtests in a test battery (such as, say, the WAIS) or subscales within a larger scale or inventory oftentimes yield a relatively large number of possible scores that individuals demonstrate on them and thus can be considered approximately continuous variables (see also below). For measuring instruments with such components, the CFA approach underlying the preceding developments in this chapter is directly applicable when the goal is to examine their unidimensionality. This is accomplished by fitting and testing the fit of a unidimensional (i.e., single-factor) confirmatory factor analysis model, as discussed earlier, which is most of the time desirable to hold for an instrument under consideration.

To demonstrate a CFA application for these aims, we assume we are interested in testing unidimensionality of four mathematics anxiety measures that we are considering for inclusion into a test for mathematics test-taking anxiety, with the normality assumption deemed plausible for them. Their covariance matrix, based on $n = 250$ students, is presented in Table 4.3.

The M*plus* input file we need for testing unidimensionality of these four measures via CFA resembles in most features the M*plus* command files used in the preceding section. The important difference is, however, that here we are interested in testing the hypothesis

Table 4.3. Covariance matrix of four mathematics anxiety measures
(denoted 1. through 4.; n = 250)

Measure:	1.	2.	3.	4.
1.	1.10			
2.	.58	1.05		
3.	.49	.45	1.16	
4.	.41	.36	.38	.99

that not two but a single factor accounts sufficiently well for the data on the measures. Hence, the pertinent M*plus* input looks as follows.

```
TITLE:    TESTING UNIDIMENSIONALITY OF A TENTATIVE INSTRUMENT VERSION

DATA:     FILE = TABLE4_3.DAT;
          TYPE = COVARIANCE;
          NOBSERVATIONS = 250;

VARIABLE: NAMES = MATHANX1 MATHANX2 MATHANX3 MATHANX4;

MODEL:    F1 BY MATHANX1-MATHANX4;
```

The first six lines of this input do not need discussion, as their contents adhere precisely to the above guidelines for title and references to analyzed data and variables. The only 'new' input line is the last one, which describes the tested hypothesis of unidimensionality. Specifically, all four observed measures are stated here as loading on a single latent construct denoted for simplicity F1. (Another name is also possible; this remark is valid for any latent variable model fit with M*plus*.) This command file yields the following output. (Again, as in the rest of this book, we are commenting only on new sections and those that are not directly explainable based on our earlier output discussions.)

```
INPUT READING TERMINATED NORMALLY

TESTING UNIDIMENSIONALITY

SUMMARY OF ANALYSIS

Number of groups                                    1
Number of observations                            250

Number of dependent variables                       4
Number of independent variables                     0
Number of continuous latent variables               1

Observed dependent variables

  Continuous
    MATHANX1    MATHANX2    MATHANX3    MATHANX4

Continuous latent variables
    F1
```

```
Estimator                                                ML
Information matrix                                  EXPECTED
Maximum number of iterations                           1000
Convergence criterion                             0.500D-04
Maximum number of steepest descent iterations            20


Input data file(s)
  TABLE4_3.DAT


Input data format FREE


THE MODEL ESTIMATION TERMINATED NORMALLY


Chi-Square Test of Model Fit

          Value                          1.459
          Degrees of Freedom                 2
          P-Value                       0.4821
```

The fit of the model is satisfactory, as judged by the chi-square value (see below for further evidence of a well-fitting model).

```
Chi-Square Test of Model Fit for the Baseline Model

          Value                        211.052
          Degrees of Freedom                 6
          P-Value                       0.0000


CFI/TLI

          CFI                            1.000
          TLI                            1.008


Loglikelihood

          H0 Value                   -1347.447
          H1 Value                   -1346.717


Information Criteria

          Number of Free Parameters          8
          Akaike (AIC)                2710.893
          Bayesian (BIC)              2739.065
          Sample-Size Adjusted BIC    2713.704
             (n* = (n + 2) / 24)


RMSEA (Root Mean Square Error Of Approximation)

          Estimate                       0.000
          90 Percent C.I.                0.000      0.114
          Probability RMSEA <= .05       0.663
```

```
SRMR (Standardized Root Mean Square Residual)

        Value                              0.015
```

The RMSEA is also acceptably low (in fact, it cannot be any lower, as it is a measure of misfit). This result corroborates our earlier suggestion that the single-factor model is fitting well the data. Hence, we can view the unidimensionality hypothesis as plausible for the considered mathematics test-taking anxiety scale consisting of the four components in question, named MATHANX1 through MATHANX4 in this analysis.

```
MODEL RESULTS

                                                        Two-Tailed
                  Estimate    S.E.    Est./S.E.          P-Value

F1        BY
   MATHANX1        1.000     0.000     999.000           999.000
   MATHANX2        0.909     0.111       8.200             0.000
   MATHANX3        0.806     0.107       7.498             0.000
   MATHANX4        0.668     0.097       6.872             0.000
```

As pointed out before, by default *Mplus* fixes at 1 the first measure loading listed in the input line defining the pertinent factor, in this case, F1. We note in passing that the remaining loadings are significant (see their associated *p*-values in the last column).

```
Variances
   F1               0.622     0.109       5.732            0.000

Residual Variances
   MATHANX1         0.473     0.076       6.236            0.000
   MATHANX2         0.532     0.071       7.446            0.000
   MATHANX3         0.751     0.082       9.203            0.000
   MATHANX4         0.709     0.073       9.766            0.000
```

With these results, we can also answer the question how well the underlying factor explains observed variance in each of the manifest measures. To this end, we subtract from 1 the ratio of each residual variance to the corresponding observed variable's variance on the diagonal of Table 4.3. In this way, we find out that the first two measures are associated with percentage explained variance well into the .50s and .60s, whereas the last two measures with such in the .30s. Although these are not very high percentages, especially the latter pair of them, we can conclude that the underlying latent construct captures a marked shared part of variance in the four analyzed measures. In case, however, we can identify in this output section instrument components that have markedly lower communality relative to the remaining ones, it may be suggested that those components may be evaluating a dimension(s) that is distinct from the one the remaining measures in the scale tap into. Such a suggestion may be additionally reinforced in some settings when the fit of the single-factor model is not satisfactory. In the latter cases, the unidimensionality hypothesis cannot be considered plausible for the entire multiple-component measuring instrument under consideration. We discuss this issue further in a later chapter.

To finalize this discussion, we note that its approach is best used for examining the hypothesis of unidimensionality for instrument components with at least, say, 15 scores taken by subjects in a study and that exhibit up to minor deviations from normality. (We hasten to add that there is nothing 'written in stone' or magic about the number 15, which we use here only to give an idea of the range of optimal applicability of the discussed testing procedure.) Although extensive and conclusive research is lacking at this moment, it may be argued that the same modeling approach could be used in a largely credible way with scale components having at least 5 to 7 possible scores and more serious deviations from normality that do not result, however, from piling of cases at their minimal or maximal score or considerable clustering effects, provided one utilizes the so-called robust maximum likelihood method (MLR; e.g., Muthén & Muthén, 2010; see also DiStefano, 2002; Johnson & Creech, 1983). This method introduces corrections for such nonnormality in the overall goodness-of-fit indexes as well as standard errors of parameter estimates and can also be used with minor and negligible clustering effects (as in hierarchical data, e.g., students nested within classes, patients within doctors, clients within counselors, employees within firms, managers within industries). To invoke this robust method, all one needs to do additionally in the last M*plus* input file for CFA is include the command ANALYSIS: ESTIMATOR = MLR; (with the latter being the abbreviation of 'maximum likelihood robust'). We return to this robustness-related issue later in the book (Chapter 7).

In conclusion of this section, via an application of CFA we were in a position to test the hypothesis that the four continuous measures of mathematics anxiety were unidimensional, and we found it to be retainable. There was no (sufficient) evidence in the analyzed data that they assess more than a single construct, and in fact the obtained results suggested that they share a marked proportion of variance. How well they measure the putative construct of mathematics test-taking anxiety, as a set of test components, is an issue that needs further attention. We address aspects of it in the following chapters.

4.5.2 Discrete Components

In empirical behavioral and social research, it is often the case that components of a given instrument cannot be considered approximately continuous. This will obviously occur when a test is based on binary items or a scale consists of components exhibiting a very small number of possible scores, e.g., 3 or 4, say (cf. Raykov & Mels, 2009). In more general empirical situations, this type of measurement results from the lack of capability in a subject-matter domain to measure in a fine-graded way an individual characteristic of interest. Rather, there may be only the possibility to 'coarsely' evaluate the characteristic with a scale rendering a fairly limited number of scores that a subject could obtain. For example, a particular aspect of ability (e.g., number addition) could be assessed only rather coarsely with a pertinent item in an achievement test. Alternatively, certain kinds of mathematics test-taking anxiety may be possible to evaluate not directly but only with the response (say on a Likert scale) on an appropriate question. A special intelligence subability may not lend itself to evaluation any other way than with a correct–false response on a given task, which is similarly a fairly coarse—as opposed to fine-graded—way of assessing it. In such situations, treating the observed components as continuous and applying the modeling approach in the preceding subsection may well yield seriously misleading results and subsequent decisions in relation to instrument construction and development. A different approach is therefore needed, when one cannot assume that the instrument components are approximately continuous, which is the subject of this subsection. Throughout the remainder of this chapter, we assume that a discrete item or instrument component under consideration provides measurement at an ordinal scale, i.e., a scale with at least two ordered categories.

Such a modeling approach has become popular in the social and behavioral sciences over the past quarter of a century (e.g., Muthén, 1984; Skrondal & Rabe-Hesketh, 2004). It is based on the assumption of an underlying, normally distributed variable behind each discrete item or instrument component. This variable is of actual interest to the researcher but cannot be measured in any fine-graded way that would render approximately continuous observed scores on it. Rather, that variable can be evaluated only coarsely by a corresponding item or scale component. This assumption is plausible in many substantive settings in the social, behavioral, and educational sciences. In the case of a binary item as test component, for instance, this underlying variable could in general be interpreted as the individual propensity to provide the 'correct', 'yes', or 'endorsing (present)' answer on it (e.g., Lord, 1980). We stress that this is an assumption about individual performance and is thus made at the individual subject level rather than at the population level. We will refer to it as the underlying normal variable (UNV) assumption and note that by virtue of normality this latent variable is also presumed to be continuous.

To discuss the UNV assumption more formally, suppose a multiple-component measuring instrument consists of a set of ordinal items denoted, say, $X_1, X_2, ..., X_p$ ($p > 2$; cf. Raykov & Mels, 2009; such items will often be referred to in this book as categorical items). Following the UNV assumption, denote by $X_1^*, X_2^*, ..., X_p^*$ their corresponding underlying normal variables. Let further $X = (X_1, X_2, ..., X_p)'$ and $X^* = (X_1^*, X_2^*, ..., X_p^*)'$ be the $p \times 1$ vectors, respectively, collecting them. As discussed in detail in the literature, observed subject responses on a particular item, say ith, result from the relationship of their underlying variable realizations to an associated set of thresholds that are population parameters (e.g., Skrondal & Rabe-Hesketh, 2004; $i = 1, ..., p$). Specifically, if there are k possible values (responses) that a study participant can provide on this item ($k \geq 2$), denote these thresholds by $\tau_{i1}, \tau_{i2}, ..., \tau_{i,k-1}$ ($i = 1, ..., p$); then this relationship is as follows (suppressing individual subindex for simplicity):

$$X_i = 0, \text{ if } -\infty < X_i^* \leq \tau_{i1},$$

$$1, \text{ if } \tau_{i1} < X_i^* \leq \tau_{i2},$$

$$...$$

$$k\text{-}1, \text{ if } \tau_{i,k-1} < X_i^* < \infty \qquad (i = 1, 2, ..., p). \qquad (4.3)$$

That is, depending on the magnitude of the underlying normal variable, X_i^*, the actually observed response on the ith item is correspondingly $0, 1, ..., k-1$. More specifically, the higher an individual realization of the underlying variable X_i^* is in terms of interval between thresholds that it falls into, the higher is his or her recorded score on the ith component ($i = 1, 2, ..., p$). The special case of $k = 2$, i.e., the ith item being binary, is of particular relevance in many test and scale construction and development contexts. In that case, the UNV assumption for this item is tantamount to that of existence of a threshold τ_{i1}, such that the observed score X_i on this item is 1 when the associated individual value on the underlying variable X_i^* is no smaller than τ_{i1} and 0 otherwise. (Note that because of the continuity of X_i^*, it is immaterial how the observed score is defined in case $X_i^* = \tau_{i1}$, since the latter occurring is an event that is associated with probability of 0; e.g., Roussas, 1997.) That is, if the ith item is binary,

$$X_i = 0, \quad \text{if } -\infty < X_i^* \leq \tau_{i1},$$

$$1, \quad \text{if } \tau_{i1} < X_i^* < \infty \qquad (i = 1, 2, \ldots, p). \qquad (4.4)$$

Once the UNV assumption is made for the observed variables X, conceptual access is accomplished to the normal variables X^* underlying each discrete instrument component. Then modeling of the relationships among the observed scale components X can be seen as achieved by modeling those among their underlying normal variables, X^* (e.g., Skrondal & Rabe-Hesketh, 2004). In particular, the confirmatory factor analysis model

$$\underline{X}^* = A\underline{f} + \underline{u}, \qquad (4.5)$$

where the same notation is used as in the right-hand side of Equations (4.1), can be fitted to data, and if it is found to be tenable, one can consider it a plausible means of data description and explanation. As a special case, the query if a set of discrete components is unidimensional can be addressed by fitting the single-factor model

$$\underline{X}^* = Af + \underline{u}, \qquad (4.6)$$

where f denotes now a single factor (i.e., the earlier vector $\underline{f}$ is unidimensional in this case). Then, if model (4.6) is found tenable, the unidimensionality hypothesis can be considered plausible for the analyzed data on a test with discrete (binary) items that is under consideration.

The CFA model (4.5) can be fitted to data via a three-step estimation procedure (e.g., Muthén, 1984), which is implemented in the LVM software *Mplus* (see also Skrondal & Rabe-Hesketh, 2004). In the first phase, based on the observed frequencies for each discrete test component (item), the threshold parameters are estimated. These parameters can be viewed as nuisance parameters in the single-group, single-assessment occasion setting of concern in this section. That is, their estimates per se are of little interest if any, but their inclusion in the estimation process—and in particular in the model fitted—are essential for ensuring that the estimates of the remaining model parameters possess optimal large-sample properties, such as unbiasedness, consistency, normality, and efficiency. In the second step, the correlation matrix of the underlying normal variables $\underline{X}^*$ is estimated, which is also referred to as polychoric correlation matrix associated with the observed variables $\underline{X}$ (see also next section). In the third phase, the model (4.5) is fitted to the polychoric correlation matrix using the method of weighted least squares (WLS). This can be considered the most general, distribution-free method for fitting confirmatory factor analysis and structural equation models with large samples (e.g., Muthén & Muthén, 2010; a nontechnical discussion of this method can be found in Raykov & Marcoulides, 2006a).

To illustrate this discussion, we will use as an example a data set stemming from a scale of college aspiration administered to $n = 823$ juniors in high school. On each of its six Likert-type items, there were four possible answers ranging from *strongly disagree* to *strongly agree*, via *disagree* and *agree*. To fit a CFA model to these items, in terms of software use, we can formally proceed as before in this chapter when analyzing continuous components but accounting for their particular nature (viz., ordinal scale). This is achieved by communicating to *Mplus* that these items are categorical and otherwise using the same instructions as in the earlier-considered continuous component case. In this way, the needed WLS method of model fitting and testing will be invoked by the software (as will the UNV assumption and fitting of model (4.5)). To test specifically the unidimensionality hypothesis for the six items of concern here, denoted ITEM_1 through ITEM_6, the following *Mplus* input file is needed; we emphasize that in order to make this analysis possible, we need to provide the raw data (in free format, say, for simplicity), which is a requirement of the WLS method.

```
TITLE:          EXAMINING UNIDIMENSIONALITY OF A SCALE WITH
                CATEGORICAL (ORDINAL) ITEMS.
DATA:           FILE = CHAPTER_4.DAT;
VARIABLE:       NAMES = ITEM_1-ITEM_6;
                CATEGORICAL = ITEM_1-ITEM_6;
MODEL:          F1 BY ITEM_1-ITEM_6;
```

We observe that this command file is very similar to the earlier ones used in this chapter, with the only exception that now we have an added line (the second last) that declares the observed variables as categorical. (This, as mentioned above, is needed because otherwise *Mplus* assumes by default it is dealing with continuous observed variables.) This input file leads to the following output.

```
INPUT READING TERMINATED NORMALLY

EXAMINING UNIDIMENSIONALITY OF A SCALE WITH
CATEGORICAL (ORDINAL) ITEMS.

SUMMARY OF ANALYSIS

Number of groups                                  1
Number of observations                          823

Number of dependent variables                     6
Number of independent variables                   0
Number of continuous latent variables             1
```

We notice that in this analysis we are dealing with a continuous latent variable. Even though our observed variables are categorical, this does not automatically change the nature of the latent variable (unless of course we conduct more complicated modeling, such as latent class analysis, which is not of concern to us here; e.g., Muthén & Muthén, 2010).

```
Observed dependent variables
  Binary and ordered categorical (ordinal)
    ITEM_1      ITEM_2      ITEM_3      ITEM_4      ITEM_5    ITEM_6
```

This section is important to check, because it ensures that the software is treating the observed variables as categorical, as they are.

```
Continuous latent variables
        F1
Estimator      WLSMV
Maximum number of iterations        1000
Convergence criterion        0.500D-04
```

```
Maximum number of steepest descent iterations  20
Parameterization     DELTA

Input data file(s)
       CHAPTER4.DAT

Input data format FREE

SUMMARY OF CATEGORICAL DATA PROPORTIONS

     ITEM_1
        Category 1     0.160
        Category 2     0.231
        Category 3     0.286
        Category 4     0.323
     ITEM_2
        Category 1     0.461
        Category 2     0.045
        Category 3     0.264
        Category 4     0.231
     ITEM_3
        Category 1     0.419
        Category 2     0.055
        Category 3     0.244
        Category 4     0.282
     ITEM_4
        Category 1     0.452
        Category 2     0.055
        Category 3     0.213
        Category 4     0.281
     ITEM_5
        Category 1     0.471
        Category 2     0.039
        Category 3     0.213
        Category 4     0.277
     ITEM_6
        Category 1     0.485
        Category 2     0.038
        Category 3     0.200
        Category 4     0.277
```

This part of the output, after indicating the appropriate estimation procedure (weighted least squares, which is implemented as default in the software if analyzed items are declared as categorical in the input), provides an account of the frequency distribution of each categorical item.

```
THE MODEL ESTIMATION TERMINATED NORMALLY

TESTS OF MODEL FIT

Chi-Square Test of Model Fit

              Value                        9.057*
              Degrees of Freedom              9**
              P-Value                       0.4321
```

* The chi-square value for MLM, MLMV, MLR, ULSMV, WLSM and WLSMV cannot
   be used for chi-square difference tests. MLM, MLR and WLSM chi-square
   difference testing is described in the Mplus Technical Appendices at
   www.statmodel.com. See chi-square difference testing in the index of
   the Mplus User's Guide.

** The degrees of freedom for MLMV, ULSMV and WLSMV are estimated
   according to a formula given in the Mplus Technical Appendices at www.
   statmodel.com. See degrees of freedom in the index of the Mplus User's
   Guide.

   These results suggest that the fit of this unidimensional model is satisfactory (see also the RMSEA below), and so we can conclude that the hypothesis of homogeneous items is plausible for the six college aspiration items under consideration. Hence, we can now move on to interpreting the associated parameter estimates. (The starred statements by the software pertain to a situation where one would be willing to work with nested models, which we are not here.) If model fit is found at this point not to be tenable, however, one could look next to see which items might be considered for possible deletion in the search of a unidimensional instrument version. With lack of model fit, one should not overrely on the following parameter estimates and standard errors, however. The better situation to be then in is to have available a large sample that is randomly split into two parts. In one of them it can be explored which items, if deleted, could lead to a unidimensional instrument version; on the other part, one can test for unidimensionality—as here—in the suggested revised scale version(s) by the analyses of the first sample part.

```
Chi-Square Test of Model Fit for the Baseline Model

              Value                      3162.726
              Degrees of Freedom              6
              P-Value                       0.0000

CFI/TLI

              CFI                          1.000
              TLI                          1.000

Number of Free Parameters                   24

RMSEA (Root Mean Square Error Of Approximation)

              Estimate                     0.003

WRMR (Weighted Root Mean Square Residual)

              Value                        0.349
```

MODEL RESULTS

	Estimate	S.E.	Est./S.E.	Two-Tailed P-Value
F1 BY				
ITEM_1	1.000	0.000	999.000	999.000
ITEM_2	0.995	0.032	31.327	0.000
ITEM_3	1.017	0.029	34.530	0.000
ITEM_4	1.040	0.029	35.721	0.000
ITEM_5	0.943	0.032	29.490	0.000
ITEM_6	0.904	0.033	27.553	0.000
Thresholds				
ITEM_1$1	-0.993	0.052	-18.915	0.000
ITEM_1$2	-0.276	0.044	-6.232	0.000
ITEM_1$3	0.459	0.045	10.105	0.000
ITEM_2$1	-0.099	0.044	-2.265	0.023
ITEM_2$2	0.014	0.044	0.314	0.754
ITEM_2$3	0.736	0.048	15.247	0.000
ITEM_3$1	-0.204	0.044	-4.633	0.000
ITEM_3$2	-0.066	0.044	-1.499	0.134
ITEM_3$3	0.577	0.046	12.430	0.000
ITEM_4$1	-0.121	0.044	-2.753	0.006
ITEM_4$2	0.017	0.044	0.383	0.701
ITEM_4$3	0.581	0.046	12.498	0.000
ITEM_5$1	-0.072	0.044	-1.638	0.101
ITEM_5$2	0.026	0.044	0.593	0.553
ITEM_5$3	0.592	0.047	12.701	0.000
ITEM_6$1	-0.038	0.044	-0.871	0.384
ITEM_6$2	0.056	0.044	1.290	0.197
ITEM_6$3	0.592	0.047	12.701	0.000
Variances				
F1	0.668	0.029	22.730	0.000

We see that all items are associated with quite similar loadings in magnitude, which are all significant. Their pertinent standard errors are also very similar. We further notice the lack of an output section containing residual variances. The reason is that the fitted model would not be identified if these were also to be considered parameters, in addition to the thresholds that are such. Therefore, one further assumption needs to be made when fitting model (4.5) to data, viz., that the residual term variances are all set equal to 1 (e.g., Muthén & Muthén, 2010). We stress that the currently considered setting of discrete observed variables is in fact one where there is very limited information about individual differences (because subjects can give rise to very few distinct scores). This implies the necessity of the additional fixing of residual variances in order to achieve model identification. (We reiterate that the threshold estimates are not of real relevance in the current setting. They become important indeed with multiple-group or longitudinal models with latent variables measured by multiple categorical indicators.) We note in passing that there are three thresholds per item, as we discussed before, because each item has four categories. All considered, given the earlier-found plausibility of the fitted single-factor model and model parameter estimates, it is suggested that the six Likert-type items in question represent a homogeneous measuring instrument. We will have more to say about its psychometric properties in a later chapter (Chapter 7), where we will revisit this example in the context of a discussion of the concept of instrument reliability.

4.6 Point and Interval Estimation of Classical Item Analysis Indexes Using Latent Variable Modeling

Behavioral, social, and educational scientists become frequently involved in constructing, revising, and developing multiple-component measuring instruments. This is usually a multistage process, during which researchers often are interested in revisions of tentative test or scale versions that are intended to be of higher quality than initially considered ones. In the preceding section of this chapter, we discussed ways in which one could test for unidimensionality of a set of components (items) under consideration, whereby the latter need not necessarily be approximately continuous but could as well be discrete (e.g., binary). We emphasized that when examining the results obtained with the fitted single-factor model, one may be in a position to identify items that may be evaluating a dimension(s) other than the one tapped into by the remainder of the items. This may be possible to achieve when inspecting loading estimates and their standard errors, with items exhibiting markedly lower loadings—possibly even nonsignificant and/or associated with large error variances—being suspicious of not really strengthening the intended scale (e.g., McDonald, 1999). These items may in particular be measuring predominantly a construct distinct from the one that the original instrument was designed to capture.

Over the past century, empirical social and behavioral researchers have frequently utilized for related aims in instrument construction and development—especially in its early phases—what may be referred to as classical item analysis. Within the framework of this analytic approach, interest was usually centered on (a) item difficulty parameters (see Chapter 2) as well as (b) inter-item and (c) item-total score interrelationships. For a given item, this difficulty parameter was defined as the probability of correct response in a studied population (i.e., the frequency of 'correct' answer or 'yes', 'endorse', 'present' response were the entire population to be observed; for simplicity, we will refer to such a response as 'correct' in the remainder of this chapter). In addition, of main concern in classical item analysis have been the indexes of interrelationship between items, frequently referred to as inter-item correlations, as well as between items and the overall sum (scale) score. A statistic that has been frequently used thereby is that reflecting the relationship between an item and the total score on the scale. In particular, the so-called adjusted item-total correlation that represents the degree to which an item relates to the sum of the remaining components of the instrument furnishes possibly important information about the contribution of the item to the total score (e.g., Crocker & Algina, 1986).

Applications of inter-item and item-total relationship indexes during the past century very often used Pearson product–moment correlations between involved variables. When the items cannot be considered approximately continuous, however, this approach effectively treats them incorrectly as continuous components, yielding potentially misleading correlations that have been frequently referred to as phi-correlations. Since the 1980s, an alternative approach leading to more appropriate evaluation of inter-item relationship indexes when the items are discrete (ordinal) has been made widely available by popular structural equation modeling software, such as LISREL (Jöreskog & Sörbom, 1996), EQS

(Bentler, 2004), and M*plus* (Muthén & Muthén, 2010). Although their point estimation is relatively direct, obtaining standard error and confidence interval estimates for them has received less attention by empirical researchers.

In the remainder of this section, we outline a direct procedure for point and interval estimation of indexes of main interest in classical item analysis—item difficulty, inter-item correlations, and item-total correlations—for instruments consisting of categorical items. (The rest of this section draws substantially from Raykov and Marcoulides [2010a].) Unlike a recent alternative approach (Raykov & Mels, 2009), the following procedure does not use dummy latent variables and is readily applied by the general researcher involved in scale construction and development. In addition, this method allows as a by-product examination of the latent structure underlying a tentative scale version by providing a test of its unidimensionality. Last but not least, the present procedure is easily implemented in practice using M*plus* (Muthén & Muthén, 2010), and the software R if desired by the researcher, with a fraction of the effort needed for that earlier approach. With this feature, the method outlined next may be used on an essentially routine basis in the early phases, as well as later ones if need be, of instrument development.

4.6.1 Estimation of Item Difficulty

When an instrument under consideration consists of binary items, or of items scored using a binary format (e.g., assigning a score of 1 for a correct answer and 0 for any other possible answer), the item difficulty parameter is an informative quantity that may be useful in the process of scale revision and development. In such a case, suppose one were interested in evaluation of the classical difficulty parameters for each of a set of p ($p > 2$) dichotomous items denoted X_1, X_2, ..., X_p, which comprise a scale under consideration that may have an unconstrained latent structure. In particular, we do not assume this instrument to be unidimensional, but we can test this hypothesis as a by-product of the following method. (The latter is also applicable with fewer than three items, provided sufficient constraints are imposed in order to achieve identification of the formal model used in its second step.) For the ith item—which will be under consideration in the remainder of this section—we designate its difficulty parameter by π_i ($1 \leq i \leq q$; we assume throughout $0 < \pi_i < 1$, to avoid triviality considerations; $i = 1, ..., p$). That is, in a studied population, π_i is the probability of correct response on the ith item. In a given sample from the population, the item difficulty parameter is usually estimated by the relative frequency of correct response, $\hat{\pi}_i$ (e.g., Chapter 2).

As we discussed in Chapter 1, oftentimes scholars choose items to be initially included into a measuring instrument depending on the goals for which it is to be used (e.g., Crocker & Algina, 1986). In particular, they may select items that (a) are relatively easy, i.e., are associated with high proportion of correct response or high 'item difficulty', if developing an instrument for identifying underachievers; (b) possess medium 'item difficulty', when concerned with measuring an ability across a wide spectrum; or (c) have low 'item difficulty', if constructing a test for screening high achievers, for instance, from among applicants for prestigious university fellowships. Over the past century, empirical researchers have nearly routinely used the sample estimates of item difficulty, $\hat{\pi}_i$, for such purposes. However, these point estimates have a number of consequential limitations (e.g., King & Minium, 2003). Although they represent 'best' numerical guesses about corresponding population parameters, they do not contain any information as to how far they could be from the latter. Also, sample estimates are affected by sampling error and are thus associated with a certain lack of stability across repeated sampling from a given population. In contrast with them, interval estimates (confidence intervals) of item difficulty provide additional information that can be of special value to the scientist. Specifically, these intervals offer ranges of plausible values for the population item difficulties and thus permit one to make more informed choices of items if need be with respect to difficulty. Despite these potentially serious concerns about point estimates of item difficulty parameters that have been often used in applications, in previous research there has been little interest in interval estimation of these parameters. In particular, no procedure seems to have been made available that could be readily and routinely employed to point and interval estimate classical item difficulty for a set of binary scored items under consideration. Whereas their point estimates are easily rendered via frequency analysis using widely circulated statistical software, such as SPSS, SAS, STATA, or R, the remainder of this section outlines a readily applicable procedure for their interval estimation.

To accomplish this aim, we observe first that for a binary item with probability π_i of correct response, the variance of its estimator—i.e., of the relative frequency $\hat{\pi}_i$ of correct answer—is

$$Var(\hat{\pi}_i) = \sqrt{\frac{\pi_i(1-\pi_i)}{n}},$$

where n is sample size (e.g., Agresti & Finlay, 2009). This variance can be estimated in empirical research by

$$V\hat{a}r(\hat{\pi}_i) = \sqrt{\frac{\hat{\pi}_i(1-\hat{\pi}_i)}{n}} = v_i^2, \tag{4.7}$$

say, where a positive square root is taken ($i = 1, \ldots, p$). Next we make an important observation that will often have relevance for interval estimation of parameters in later sections and chapters. The item difficulty parameter π_i, being a probability is bounded from below and above: $0 < \pi_i < 1$ ($i = 1, \ldots, p$; see above in this section). For this reason, a confidence interval (CI) for π_i must completely reside in the interval (0, 1) because otherwise the CI would contain meaningless values. One can ensure enclosure of the CI within this interval by initially obtaining a confidence interval of a suitable monotone increasing transformation of π_i, the result of which is unbounded (e.g., Browne, 1982). Given that we are dealing with a probability here, viz., π_i, such a transformation is the familiar logit function

$$\kappa_i = \ln(\pi_i/(1 - \pi_i)), \tag{4.8}$$

where ln(.) denotes natural logarithm (e.g., Agresti & Finlay, 2009). Then a useful estimator of the transformed item difficulty parameter is

$$\hat{\kappa}_i = \ln(\hat{\pi}_i/(1-\hat{\pi}_i)) \qquad\qquad (i = 1, \ldots, q). \tag{4.9}$$

A standard error associated with this estimator can be obtained using the popular delta-method (see also Browne, 1982) and is as follows:

$$S.E.(\hat{\kappa}_i) = v_i/[\hat{\pi}_i(1-\hat{\pi}_i)], \tag{4.10}$$

where S.E.(.) denotes standard error ($i = 1, \ldots, p$).

Our next observation relates to the statistical properties of this logit-transformed difficulty parameter. First, we recall that the frequency of correct response, $\hat{\pi}_i$, is a maximum likelihood (ML) estimator of the probability of correct response on the ith item (e.g., Lord & Novick, 1968). Yet, as is well-known, ML estimators possess a highly useful property, called invariance. Accordingly, a function of them is also an ML estimator of the same function of the population parameters involved in it (e.g., Roussas, 1997). Therefore, the logit in Equation (4.9) is in fact the ML estimator of the logit-transformed item difficulty in Equation (4.8). For this reason, $\hat{\kappa}_i = \ln(\hat{\pi}_i/(1-\hat{\pi}_i))$ possesses all large-sample properties of ML estimators and in particular their asymptotic normality. Thus, with large samples, one can treat the ML estimator $\hat{\kappa}_i = \ln(\hat{\pi}_i/(1-\hat{\pi}_i))$ as approximately normally distributed, with mean being the true logit-transformed item difficulty in (4.8) and variance estimated by the square of the right-hand side of Equation (4.10) (e.g., Roussas, 1997). Hence, from Equation (4.10) a large-sample $100(1-\alpha)\%$-confidence interval ($0 < \alpha < 1$) for the logit-transformed item difficulty parameter κ_i is furnished as

$$(\hat{\kappa}_i - z_{\alpha/2}S.E.(\hat{\kappa}_i), \hat{\kappa}_i + z_{\alpha/2}S.E.(\hat{\kappa}_i)), \tag{4.11}$$

where $z_{\alpha/2}$ denotes the $(1-\alpha/2)$th quantile of the standard normal distribution ($i = 1, ..., p$).

Having now this CI of the transformed parameter κ_i, a large-sample $100(1-\alpha)\%$-confidence interval for the item difficulty parameter π_i of actual interest is rendered via use of the inverse of the logit function. This inverse is, as is well-known, the logistic function (e.g., Lord, 1980; see also Chapters 10 and 11):

$$\pi_i = 1/(1+e^{-\kappa_i}) \tag{4.12}$$

($i = 1, ..., p$). Specifically, denoting by $\kappa_{i,lo}$ and $\kappa_{i,up}$ the lower and upper endpoints of the confidence interval (4.11), respectively, using Equation (4.12) a large-sample $100(1-\alpha)\%$-confidence interval for the item difficulty of concern follows as (Raykov & Marcoulides, 2010a):

$$(1/(1+e^{-\kappa_{i,lo}}), 1/(1+e^{-\kappa_{i,up}})) \quad (i = 1, ..., p). \tag{4.13}$$

We next address the issue of evaluating the classical item difficulty confidence interval (4.13) in empirical behavioral and social research.

4.6.1.1 *Using* M*plus* *for Interval Estimation of Item Difficulty*

The lower and upper endpoints of the CI in (4.13), for a given confidence level and item, are readily calculated using M*plus*. To accomplish this, we can proceed in two steps. In the first, referred to as Step 1 below, we request basic analysis using the command 'ANALYSIS: TYPE = BASIC;'. The corresponding M*plus* input file is as follows.

```
TITLE:     POINT AND INTERVAL ESTIMATION OF CLASSICAL ITEM DIFFICULTY
           (STEP 1).

DATA:      FILE = <name of raw data file>;

VARIABLE: NAMES = X1-XP; ! ENTER NUMBER OF ITEMS FOR P HERE AND NEXT.
           CATEGORICAL = X1-XP;

ANALYSIS: TYPE = BASIC;
```

In the resulting output we obtain a given item's difficulty estimate from the section 'FIRST ORDER SAMPLE PROPORTIONS', which concludes this first step of analysis. In the second step, referred to as Step 2 below, we substitute this estimate into Equations (4.7) and (4.9) through (4.11) and (4.13) to furnish the sought CI for the difficulty of the item under consideration. This can be achieved with the following M*plus* input file.

```
TITLE:      POINT AND INTERVAL ESTIMATION OF CLASSICAL ITEM DIFFICULTY
            (STEP 2). (DIFFICULTY ESTIMATE, DENOTED D BELOW, OBTAINED
            FROM PRECEDING STEP 1.)

DATA:       FILE = <name of raw data file>;

VARIABLE:   NAMES = X1-XP; ! ENTER NUMBER OF ITEMS FOR P HERE AND BELOW.
            CATEGORICAL = X1-XP;

MODEL:      F1 BY X1-XP;

MODEL CONSTRAINT:
    NEW(D, SE, L, SEL, CI_L_LO, CI_L_UP, CI_D_LO, CI_D_UP);
    D = #; ! ENTER ESTIMATE OBTAINED IN STEP 1 (FOR ITEM OF INTEREST)
    SE = (D*(1-D)/N)**.5; ! EQUATION (4.7) (N = SAMPLE SIZE);
    L = LOG(D/(1-D)); ! EQUATION (4.8) - LOGIT TRANFORM
    SEL = SE/(D*(1-D)); ! EQUATION (4.10) - S.E. FOR TRANSFORM
    CI_L_LO = L-1.96*SEL; ! SEE CI IN (4.11) - CI OF LOGIT TRANSFORM
    CI_L_UP = L+1.96*SEL;
    CI_D_LO = 1/(1+EXP(-CI_L_LO); ! SEE CI IN (4.13) - THIS IS THE CI
    CI_D_UP = 1/(1+EXP(-CI_L_UP)); ! OF THE ITEM DIFFICULTY PARAMETER.
```

In this command file, a formal MODEL section is used that provides a test of the unidimensionality hypothesis if of interest. (We stress that the present method does not assume unidimensionality, or depend on it in any way, but the latter hypothesis can be tested as a by-product of this procedure if desired. We use this MODEL section in the M*plus* command file in order to be in a position to compute the confidence interval as requested in its remainder.)

The new features of the last input file, relative to those used in the preceding sections and chapters, are in the MODEL CONSTRAINT section. In it, we first define 'place-holders' for a number of quantities that participate in the above formulas (4.7) through (4.12) leading up to the item difficulty CI (4.13) of ultimate interest. We accomplish this by introducing initially as new parameters (i.e., entities that are not model parameters themselves but functions of such) all these needed quantities, using the command NEW. Specifically, we denote (a) by D the item difficulty parameter estimate (obtained from Step 1 and to be substituted in the next line of this input section), (b) by SE its standard error (see Equation (4.7)), (c) by L the logit-transformed item difficulty parameter (see (4.8)), (d) by SEL its standard error (see (4.10)), (e) by CI_L_LO and CI_L_UP the endpoints of the CI of the transformed parameter (see (4.11)), and (f) by CI_D_LO and CI_D_UP these for the CI of the item difficulty parameter of actual interest (see (4.13)). Once submitting this input file to the software, we obtain in the last two quantities the lower and upper limits of the 95%-CI (4.13) for the given item's difficulty. (If a CI at another confidence level is sought, the multiplier 1.96 used in the third- and fourth-last lines of the above M*plus* command file is correspondingly modified—e.g., for a 99%-CI use 2.58 rather than 1.96 and for a 90%-CI use 1.645 instead.)

We illustrate this point and interval estimation procedure with the following example (cf. Raykov & Marcoulides, 2010a). In it, $n = 498$ high school juniors were administered a test for algebra knowledge consisting of $p = 6$ binary scored items. (This file is called CHAPTER_4_IA.DAT on the Web page associated with the book.) To obtain point estimates of their difficulty parameters, we use the first command file in this subsection for Step 1. The following relevant output section results thereby.

```
RESULTS FOR BASIC ANALYSIS

    ESTIMATED SAMPLE STATISTICS

        FIRST ORDER SAMPLE PROPORTIONS :
          X1              X2            X3          X4          X5
        _____        _____      _____    _____    _____
         0.576           0.588         0.566       0.562       0.588

        FIRST ORDER SAMPLE PROPORTIONS :
          X6
        _____
         0.602
```

That is, the six-item difficulty parameter estimates are as follows: $\hat{\pi}_1 = 0.576$, $\hat{\pi}_2 = 0.588$, $\hat{\pi}_3 = 0.566$, $\hat{\pi}_4 = 0.562$, $\hat{\pi}_5 = 0.588$, and $\hat{\pi}_6 = .602$. If one were interested in interval estimation of, say, the last item's difficulty (e.g., at the 95% confidence level), we employ the second M*plus* input file given in this Subsection 4.6.1.1, for Step 2, entering in it D = .602, as found in Step 1. This leads to the following relevant output parts, which allow us at the same time to examine the unidimensionality hypothesis.

```
THE MODEL ESTIMATION TERMINATED NORMALLY

TESTS OF MODEL FIT

Chi-Square Test of Model Fit

          Value                           18.945*
          Degrees of Freedom                   9**
          P-Value                          0.0257
```

*The chi-square value for MLM, MLMV, MLR, ULSMV, WLSM and WLSMV cannot be used for chi-square difference tests. MLM, MLR and WLSM chi-square difference testing is described in the Mplus Technical Appendices at www. statmodel.com. See chi-square difference testing in the index of the Mplus User's Guide.

**The degrees of freedom for MLMV, ULSMV and WLSMV are estimated according to a formula given in the Mplus Technical Appendices at www.statmodel. com. See degrees of freedom in the index of the Mplus User's Guide.

```
Chi-Square Test of Model Fit for the Baseline Model

          Value                                210.219
          Degrees of Freedom                        13
          P-Value                               0.0000


CFI/TLI

          CFI                                    0.950
          TLI                                    0.927


Number of Free Parameters                          12


RMSEA (Root Mean Square Error Of Approximation)

          Estimate                               0.047


WRMR (Weighted Root Mean Square Residual)

          Value                                  0.815
```

These indexes (in particular the RMSEA) suggest that the single-factor model is tenable. That is, the hypothesis of unidimensionality of the six items in question is tenable. (We reiterate that unidimensionality is not an assumption of the procedure outlined in this section but can be tested as a by-product if desired.) The starred statements immediately following the section titled 'Chi-square Test of Model Fit' are relevant, e.g., when one is additionally concerned with models resulting by imposing restrictions upon parameters in the model of unidimensionality that is fitted here. Because here we are not interested in such models with restrictions, we do not concern ourselves with this part of the output. (We will attend to this output part in later chapters.)

```
MODEL RESULTS
                                                  Two-Tailed
                    Estimate    S.E.   Est./S.E.   P-Value


F1          BY
      X1          1.000      0.000    999.000     999.000
      X2          0.987      0.173      5.700       0.000
      X3          0.938      0.167      5.615       0.000
      X4          0.844      0.156      5.400       0.000
      X5          0.803      0.153      5.244       0.000
      X6          0.466      0.138      3.380       0.001


Thresholds
      X1$1       -0.192      0.057     -3.404       0.001
      X2$1       -0.223      0.057     -3.940       0.000
      X3$1       -0.167      0.056     -2.956       0.003
      X4$1       -0.157      0.056     -2.777       0.005
      X5$1       -0.223      0.057     -3.940       0.000
      X6$1       -0.260      0.057     -4.566       0.000
```

```
Variances
      F1                 0.357    0.082      4.326          0.000


New/Additional Parameters
      D                  0.602    0.000      0.000          1.000
      SE                 0.022    0.000      0.000          1.000
      L                  0.414    0.000      0.000          1.000
      SEL                0.092    0.000      0.000          1.000
      CI_L_LO            0.234    0.000      0.000          1.000
      CI_L_UP            0.593    0.000      0.000          1.000
      CI_D_LO            0.558    0.000      0.000          1.000
      CI_D_UP            0.644    0.000      0.000          1.000
```

As seen from the last output section titled 'New/Additional Parameters', the approximate standard error for the difficulty parameter of the sixth item of interest here is S.E. $(\hat{\pi}_6) = .022$ (see second line). Furthermore, its 95%-confidence interval is (.558, .644), as seen from the last two lines of this section (see specifically the numbers in the first column). We note that this is not a symmetric interval around the parameter estimate, .602. This asymmetry feature follows from the nonlinearity of the logit transformation involved in furnishing the confidence interval in question (see preceding section).

In conclusion of this Subsection 4.6.1.1, we note that as an alternative method for obtaining a confidence interval for the classical item difficulty, one could invoke the normality approximation with large samples, thus adding and subtracting to its estimate 1.96 times the estimated S.E. of .022. We do not consider this to be in general an optimal method, however. The reason is that it can produce confidence intervals that extend either below 0 or beyond 1 for sufficiently small or alternatively sufficiently large population difficulty parameters (or sufficiently small samples and/or large confidence levels), which, however, are not infrequent in empirical research on scale construction and development. Even if one were then to truncate those CIs correspondingly at 0 or 1, they can still contain in general implausible values, including those very close to 0 or 1.

4.6.1.2 Employing R for Interval Estimation of Item Difficulty

The statistical analysis software R can be alternatively used to obtain the lower and upper limits of the confidence interval (4.13) of item difficulty, via application of specifically defined devices called functions. These are very convenient objects that need to be first programmed in R and then can be called subsequently to produce estimates of interest. A function is a linear or nonlinear expression of certain quantities, which are referred to as 'arguments' of the function. For example, the lower and upper limits of (4.13) of a given item's difficulty parameter are each a function correspondingly of the lower or upper limit of the CI (4.11) of its logit, with the latter two limits being themselves functions of the estimate of the logit and its standard error in (4.9) and (4.10). That is, the lower and upper limit of the CI (4.13) for a given item's difficulty (say, of the ith item) is a function of two arguments: (a) the estimate of the logit of the item difficulty, $\hat{\kappa}_i$, and (b) its standard error, $S.E.(\hat{\kappa}_i)$; thereby, (4.13) coupled with (4.11) provides this particular function ($i = 1, ..., p$). Hence, if we define an appropriate function producing the limits of the CI (4.13), calling it subsequently by providing the empirical values of two appropriate arguments will furnish the endpoints of the CI (4.13).

The function to produce the endpoints of the CI (4.13) of interest here is defined as follows (its consecutive lines are discussed subsequently):

```
ci.id = function(d, n){
  se = sqrt(d*(1-d)/n)
  l = log(d/(1-d))
  sel = se/(d*(1-d))
  ci_l_lo = l-1.96*sel
  ci_l_up = l+1.96*sel
  ci_lo = 1/(1+exp(-ci_l_lo))
  ci_up = 1/(1+exp(-ci_l_up))
  ci = c(ci_lo, ci_up)
ci
}
```

We thus commence by stating the name of the function, here 'ci.id' for 'confidence interval for item difficulty'. We assign to this 'object', ci.id, the status of a function by stating the latter word, followed by parentheses in which we give the item difficulty estimate, denoted d, and sample size, n. (These are the two arguments of the function ci.id, as mentioned above.) The open curved parenthesis at the end of the first line signals to the software that following are the computational activities, which need to be performed. The next seven lines are identical in meaning to their corresponding ones in the MODEL CONSTRAINT section of the last discussed *Mplus* file (for Step 2 in the preceding Subsection 4.6.1.1) and work out successively (a) the S.E. of item difficulty, the logit of the latter (denoted 'l'); (b) the S.E. of the logit (denoted 'sel'); and (c) the lower and upper limits of the CI (4.11) followed by those of the CI (4.13). Once the two endpoints of (4.13) are calculated, we concatenate them into a vector denoted 'ci', viz., by stating ci = c(ci_lo, ci_up) (see Section 2.8 in Chapter 2). In the second-last line, we state just the name of this vector, which requests the function (actually R) to print to the computer screen the elements of this vector—first the lower limit and then the upper one of the CI (4.13). The definition of the function ci.id is finalized with a closing curved parenthesis in its last line. At times it may be simpler to have this function written outside of R, e.g., in a plain text editor (such as, say, WordPad or NotePad), and then pasted at the R prompt. Once the latter reappears after the pasted text of the function, we obtain the lower and upper endpoints of the CI (4.13) of concern in this section by just 'calling' the function, which is achieved as follows:

```
> ci.id(d,n)
```

where we now enter for 'd' the previously estimated difficulty of an item under consideration (Step 1 in the preceding Subsection 4.6.1.1) and for 'n' the sample size of the study in question.

To illustrate this discussion, let us return to the last example in the preceding Subsection 4.6.1.1, where the software *Mplus* was used in Step 2 to compute the lower and upper limits of the CI (4.13). In that example we were interested, among other things, in interval estimation of the difficulty parameter for the sixth item from a study with $n = 498$ subjects—this parameter was estimated at .602 in Step 1 there. To obtain the CI of this item's difficulty parameter with R, we call the above-created function 'ci.id' as follows:

```
> ci.id(.602, 498)
```

where we stress that we substitute (a) for d this parameter's estimate of .602 and (b) 498 for sample size n in the originally defined function 'ci.id' (of which d and n are arguments as mentioned). This call of the function 'ci.id' produces the R output

```
[1] 0.5583264 0.6441078
```

That is, the sought 95%-CI of the item difficulty parameter of the sixth item under consideration is (.558, .644), which when rounded off to the third decimal is identical to the CI for this parameter that was obtained in Step 2 with M*plus* in the preceding Subsection 4.6.1.1.

4.6.2 Estimation of Inter-Item and Item-Total Interrelationship Indexes

In addition to item difficulty parameters, inter-item and item-total correlations have been traditionally of special interest in classical item analysis. The reason is that they contain information about the extent to which items in a scale (test, multiple-component instrument) under consideration relate to another item as well as to the overall sum score (cf. Raykov & Marcoulides, 2010a). In particular, one might expect that if a set of items evaluates a common underlying attribute, the interrelationships among them will be pronounced as will the relationships of each of them with the total score (possibly adjusted for the item by not including it in this overall sum). As discussed at length in the literature over the past couple of decades, however, when interested in inter-item relationships, it would be in general more appropriate to be concerned with the polychoric correlation coefficient (called tetrachoric correlation in case of binary items; e.g., Jöreskog & Sörbom, 1996; see also McDonald, 1999). Similarly, if one considers in addition a (approximately) continuous variable, such as possibly the sum score of certain items, it would be generally more appropriate to be interested in the corresponding polyserial correlation coefficient (called biserial correlation when the other involved variable is binary).

The polychoric and polyserial correlation coefficients have been developed based on the assumption of an underlying normal variable (UNV) behind each categorical item (e.g., Muthén, 1984; in the rest of this Section 4.6.2, the items are not necessarily assumed to be binary but assumed in general to be categorical, e.g., Likert-type measures). As we indicated earlier in this chapter, it is this underlying variable that is of actual interest to measure for a social or behavioral scientist. However, because of various reasons—including in particular its nature—that variable cannot be directly evaluated but instead only coarsely measured. More formally, for a given set of categorical items, say, $X_1, X_2, ..., X_p$ ($p > 2$), denote by $X_1^*, X_2^*, ..., X_p^*$ their corresponding underlying normal variables. (If any of the variables $X_1, X_2, ..., X_p$ are continuous, or are to be treated as such, then one sets $X_i^* = X_i$; $1 \le i \le p$.) Then, as pointed out earlier in the chapter, the observed responses on an item, say ith, result from the relationship of their underlying variable realization to an associated set of thresholds (e.g., Muthén, 1984).

The degree to which the underlying normal variables are interrelated is of particular interest when studying the psychometric properties of a scale with categorical items. This is reflected in their polychoric and polyserial correlations, which are the correlation coefficients between the underlying latent variables X^* for two or more of the X measures or of the former variables with the overall (adjusted) sum score. Specifically, the polychoric correlations are the elements of the correlation matrix of the variables $X_1^*, X_2^*, ..., X_p^*$, whereas the polyserial correlations are those among each of the underlying variables $X_1^*, X_2^*, ..., X_p^*$ and the total sum score $X = X_1 + X_2 + \cdots + X_p$ (possibly adjusted for an item in question by subtracting it from X; e.g., Jöreskog, 1994).

The point estimation of polychoric and polyserial correlations has been already discussed in detail in the methodological literature (e.g., Jöreskog, 1994; Muthén, 1984). This estimation is typically carried out using the so-called weighted least square (WLS) method that is implemented in widely available structural equation modeling programs like EQS and LISREL (Bentler, 2004; Jöreskog & Sörbom, 1996) as well as M*plus* (Muthén & Muthén, 2010). Interval estimation of these correlations has received substantially less attention in the past, however. Fortunately, it can be accomplished along lines similar to those pursued in the preceding Section 4.6.1 of this chapter. To outline the pertinent procedure, denote generically by ρ a polychoric or polyserial correlation of concern. As described, e.g., in Raykov and Mels (2009), first a large-sample $100(1 - \alpha)\%$-confidence interval $(0 < \alpha < 1)$ for the Fisher-transform $z(\rho)$ of ρ can be obtained as

$$(z(\hat{\rho}) - z_{\alpha/2}\, S.E.(\hat{\rho})/(1 - \hat{\rho}^2), z(\hat{\rho}) + z_{\alpha/2}\, S.E.(\hat{\rho})/(1 - \hat{\rho}^2)), \qquad (4.14)$$

where

$$z(\rho) = .5\ln[(1 + \rho)/(1 - \rho)] \qquad (4.15)$$

is the Fisher z-transform (e.g., King & Minium, 2003) and $S.E.(\hat{\rho})$ denotes the standard error of the polychoric/polyserial correlation estimator (cf. Browne, 1982). Then the following large-sample $100(1 - \alpha)\%$-confidence interval $(0 < \alpha < 1)$ for the correlation ρ of concern is obtained via the inverse of Fisher's z-transform:

$$((\exp(2z_{\rho,lo}) - 1)/(\exp(2z_{\rho,lo}) + 1), (\exp(2z_{\rho,up}) - 1)/(\exp(2z_{\rho,up}) + 1)), \qquad (4.16)$$

with exp(.) standing for exponent and $z_{\rho,lo}$ and $z_{\rho,up}$ denoting the lower and upper limits of the interval in (4.14). We turn next to the question of how to obtain the limits of the confidence interval (4.16) in an empirical study.

4.6.2.1 Using Mplus for Estimation of Inter-Item and Item-Total Correlations

The polychoric correlation estimates, with standard errors, can be obtained with the software M*plus* using the command file for the basic analysis discussed in the preceding Subsection 4.6.1.1 (Step 1). Specifically, to furnish polyserial correlation estimates, one includes in that basic analysis input the command DEFINE: X = X1 + X2 + ⋯ + XP, which is used to introduce into the analysis the total score X (overall sum score; P being the number of instrument components). Thereby, if one is interested in adjusted item-total correlations, the sum score should be defined in the last command as the sum of all items but the one in question. For example, if we are interested in the adjusted item-total correlation for the second item, we use the following command: DEFINE: X = X1 + X3 + ⋯ + XP; with P being the number of scale items. This activity is accomplished with the following M*plus* input file (referred to as Step 3 below; we present next the case when one is interested in the adjusted item-total correlation with respect to the second item, say, with corresponding modifications in the sum score X if of concern is this correlation with regard to another item).

```
TITLE:     POINT AND INTERVAL ESTIMATION OF INTER-ITEM AND ITEM-TOTAL
           CORRELATIONS (STEP 3).
```

```
DATA:       FILE = <name of raw data file>;

VARIABLE: NAMES = X1-XP;
          CATEGORICAL = X1-XP;
          USEVARIABLE = X1-XP X; ! THIS LINE ENABLES OBTAINING
          ! POLYSERIAL CORRELATION ESTIMATES WITH STANDARD ERRORS

DEFINE:     X = X1+X3+...+XP; ! USE THIS IF INTERESTED IN THE ADJUSTED
            ! ITEM-TOTAL CORRELATION FOR THE 2nd ITEM SAY

ANALYSIS: TYPE = BASIC;
```

With the estimates of the correlation(s) and standard error(s) of concern that are obtained thereby, one uses in the second M*plus* command file of the earlier Subsection 4.6.1.1 (Step 2) a modified MODEL CONSTRAINT section that evaluates the lower and upper limits of the confidence interval of the polychoric or polyserial correlation of concern via (4.16). This is achieved with the following M*plus* input file (referred to as Step 4 below; when used in an empirical study, enter in the second and third line of the MODEL CONSTRAINT section the estimate and associated standard error from Step 3 for the correlation coefficient that is to be interval estimated).

```
TITLE:      POINT AND INTERVAL ESTIMATION OF INTER-ITEM AND ITEM-TOTAL
            CORRELATIONS (STEP 4).

DATA:       FILE = <name of raw data file>;

MODEL:      F1 BY X1-XP; ! INVOKES A TEST OF UNIDIMENSIONALITY OF SCALE.

MODEL CONSTRAINT:
            NEW(C, SE, Z, SEZ, CI_Z_LO, CI_Z_UP, CI_C_LO, CI_C_UP);
            C = #; ! ENTER THE CORRELATION ESTIMATE ρ̂ FROM STEP 3.
            SE = #; ! ENTER ITS ASSSOCIATED S.E., FROM STEP 3.
            Z = .5*LOG((1+C)/(1-C)); ! FISHER'S Z-TRANSFORM OF C.
            SEZ = SE/(1-C**2); ! THIS IS ITS PERTINENT S.E.
            CI_Z_LO = Z-1.96*SEZ; ! CI FOR FISHER'S Z-TRANSFORM OF C.
            CI_Z_UP = Z+1.96*SEZ; ! (SEE EQUATION (4.14)).
            CI_C_LO = (EXP(2*CI_Z_LO)-1)/(EXP(2*CI_Z_LO)+1); ! EQ. (4.15)
            CI_C_UP = (EXP(2*CI_Z_UP)-1)/(EXP(2*CI_Z_UP)+1);
```

As seen from this command file, its MODEL CONSTRAINT section precisely follows Equations (4.14) through (4.16) and is otherwise developed in full analogy to the same section in the second M*plus* command file from the earlier Subsection 4.6.1.1 (see Step 2 there).

We illustrate this discussion using the example employed in Subsection 4.6.1. In order to estimate the 21 inter-item correlations for the set of items used there, we utilize the above command file for Step 3 (dispensing with the DEFINE and USEVARIABLE command lines, as we are not dealing here with item-total correlations). This leads to the following relevant output sections.

```
INPUT READING TERMINATED NORMALLY

POINT AND INTERVAL ESTIMATION OF INTER-ITEM AND ITEM-TOTAL CORRELATIONS
(STEP 3).
```

```
SUMMARY OF ANALYSIS

Number of groups                                                    1
Number of observations                                           498

Number of dependent variables                                     6
Number of independent variables                                   0
Number of continuous latent variables                             0

Observed dependent variables

  Binary and ordered categorical (ordinal)
  X1           X2           X3           X4          X5          X6

Estimator                                                     WLSMV
Maximum number of iterations                                   1000
Convergence criterion                                    0.500D-04
Maximum number of steepest descent iterations                   20
Parameterization                                             DELTA

Input data file(s)

Input data format FREE
```

We note that the default estimator is weighted least squares (with mean and variance correction for improved performance; Muthén & Muthén, 2010). This estimator is precisely the one that is needed in order to furnish in an empirical study the sought polychoric and polyserial correlation estimates, as discussed in detail in Muthén (1984).

```
SUMMARY OF CATEGORICAL DATA PROPORTIONS
    X1
       Category 1       0.424
       Category 2       0.576
    X2
       Category 1       0.412
       Category 2       0.588
    X3
       Category 1       0.434
       Category 2       0.566
    X4
       Category 1       0.438
       Category 2       0.562
    X5
       Category 1       0.412
       Category 2       0.588
    X6
       Category 1       0.398
       Category 2       0.602


RESULTS FOR BASIC ANALYSIS
      ESTIMATED SAMPLE STATISTICS
            FIRST ORDER SAMPLE PROPORTIONS :
```

X1	X2	X3	X4	X5
0.576	0.588	0.566	0.562	0.588

FIRST ORDER SAMPLE PROPORTIONS :

X6
0.602

As mentioned in the preceding section, these are the item difficulty estimates, which are not of concern to us now.

SECOND ORDER SAMPLE PROPORTIONS

	X1	X2	X3	X4	X5
X1					
X2	0.406				
X3	0.390	0.369			
X4	0.359	0.386	0.351		
X5	0.373	0.380	0.386	0.382	
X6	0.359	0.384	0.373	0.365	0.369

These are estimates of the frequencies of correct response on pairs of items, which are similarly not of interest to us in this discussion.

SAMPLE THRESHOLDS

X1$1	X2$1	X3$1	X4$1	X5$1
-0.192	-0.223	-0.167	-0.157	-0.223

SAMPLE THRESHOLDS

X6$1
-0.260

The last are the estimates of the item thresholds. As mentioned earlier, they are not of interest in a single-group study or such with a single assessment occasion—like the one under consideration here. For these reasons, we can view them as nuisance parameters, because we are not really interested in them but need to estimate them along with the parameters of actual interest in order for the latter to be optimally estimated.

SAMPLE TETRACHORIC CORRELATIONS

	X1	X2	X3	X4	X5
X1					
X2	0.420				
X3	0.397	0.234			
X4	0.227	0.348	0.211		
X5	0.223	0.218	0.334	0.323	
X6	0.081	0.192	0.211	0.175	0.100

These are the sought estimates of the polychoric correlations (in fact, tetrachoric correlations here, because of binary items being involved). They will tend to be higher than the

Pearson product–moment correlation coefficients, as discussed in detail in the literature (e.g., Jöreskog & Sörbom, 1996).

STANDARD DEVIATIONS FOR SAMPLE TETRACHORIC CORRELATIONS

	X1	X2	X3	X4	X5
X1					
X2	0.062				
X3	0.063	0.069			
X4	0.069	0.065	0.069		
X5	0.069	0.069	0.066	0.066	
X6	0.071	0.070	0.069	0.070	0.071

The entries of this matrix are the indexes of instability of the correlations from the preceding table, across repeated sampling from a studied population. As pointed out earlier in this section, they are needed in the process of construction of confidence intervals for these correlations (in particular, in (4.14)).

Suppose we were now interested in interval estimation of the degree to which the third and fifth items were interrelated. To this end, we find in the above output the estimate of .334 for the pertinent tetrachoric correlation and then from the last presented output section its associated standard error as .066. Entering these two quantities correspondingly in the last presented M*plus* command file (Step 4), we obtain (.199, .457) as the 95%-confidence interval of this correlation for these two items. We stress that the latter interval is not symmetric around the parameter estimate, because of the nonlinearity of Fisher's z-transform involved in rendering it (see preceding subsection).

As another example, in case one were interested in the correlation of the second item, X_2, and the adjusted (for it) sum score, from the output of Step 3 we find that this polyserial correlation is estimated at .394, with a standard error of .047. (To this end, as mentioned earlier we use the command DEFINE: X = X1+X3+X4+X5+X6; in the M*plus* command file for Step 3.) With these two quantities, the M*plus* command file for Step 4 yields a 95%-confidence interval (.298, .482) for this item-total correlation, which is similarly nonsymmetric.

4.6.2.2 Employing R for Interval Estimation of Polychoric Correlations

As an alternative to an application of M*plus* for obtaining the endpoints of the confidence intervals of polychoric correlations (including tetrachoric and polyserial correlations as special cases), we can utilize the software R like we did earlier in this Section 4.6.1. To this end, we need a correspondingly developed function. As before, to furnish the CI (4.16) of concern here, we use the same computational steps as in the MODEL CONSTRAINT section of the M*plus* command file in Subsection 4.6.2.1:

```
ci.pc <- function(c, se){
 z=.5*log((1+c)/(1-c))
 sez = se/((1-c^2))
 ci_z_lo = z-1.96*sez
 ci_z_up = z+1.96*sez
 ci_lo = (exp(2*ci_z_lo)-1)/(exp(2*ci_z_lo)+1)
 ci_up = (exp(2*ci_z_up)-1)/(exp(2*ci_z_up)+1)
 ci = c(ci_lo, ci_up)
ci
}
```

To illustrate, let us revisit the polychoric correlation example discussed in Subsection 4.6.2.1. In it, we were interested in obtaining the CI (4.16) for the correlation between Items 3 and 5, which was estimated there at .334 with a standard error .066. (These quantities are denoted 'c' and 'se', respectively, in the last-presented function and are the arguments of the latter.) To this end, we call the last-defined R function as follows:

```
> ci.pc(.334, .066)
```

using the relevant estimates .334 and .066 as its corresponding argument values. This call of the function yields

```
[1] 0.1990286 0.4565362
```

That is, the sought 95%-CI is (.199, .456), which is identical to the CI obtained previously with M*plus* (after rounding-off to the third decimal). Using the same R function, 'ci.pc', we can also obtain a CI for an item-total correlation, namely, by entering its corresponding (earlier-obtained) estimate and standard error in the call of this function.

By way of summary, we have (at least) two possibilities—one with M*plus* and the other with R—of obtaining confidence intervals for classical item analysis indices when of interest, such as item difficulty and polychoric, tetrachoric and polyserial correlations, including in particular adjusted item-total correlations. These parameters and their estimates, especially confidence intervals, may be quite informative in early stages of empirical research involving scale construction and development in the behavioral and social sciences. These confidence intervals can be of particular importance when a scholar is interested in ranges of plausible values for population item difficulty and polychoric–polyserial correlation parameters under consideration. Another possible application of these interval estimates could occur prior to, or along, a utilization of a procedure for item (component) selection into a multiple-component instrument, which is based on the relationships between pertinent factor loadings and error variances in case of unidimensionality and is described in detail in McDonald (1999, Chap. 7).

In conclusion of the present Section 4.6, we note that a distinct possibility for interval estimation of classical item analysis indexes is via use of the bootstrap methodology (e.g., Efron & Tibshiriani, 1993). Such an application would be in general quite computer intensive at present, however, and would need initially evidence that the bootstrap distribution of these parameter estimates (i.e., item difficulty and polychoric–polyserial correlation estimates) indeed approaches with increasing sample size and number of resamples the sampling distribution of their corresponding parameters (cf., e.g., Bollen & Stine, 1993, for counterexamples in a more general setting). We thus leave to future studies a more thorough examination of the properties of the resulting bootstrap confidence intervals and corresponding recommendations with regard to interval estimation of classical item analysis indexes when of interest in empirical behavioral and social research.

Appendix: Initial Activities Facilitating Use of M*plus*

After opening either M*plus* or a plain text processing editor, such as NotePad or WordPad, one types in the correlation matrix in Table 4.1 (as a lower-triangular matrix) in the opened window and saves the file. If this is done in M*plus*, the suffix '.inp' may be automatically appended. (One should therefore refer later to this data file with the name first given to it but extended by the '.inp' suffix. If one created the correlation matrix using a simple plain text processing editor, such as NotePad or WordPad, one needs to refer later to that file using the file name given to it when saving it in that editor.) We note that current versions of M*plus* will not accept word processing files, like those from Word or WordPerfect, with data to be analyzed, e.g., any matrix of variable interrelationship indices, but accept only ASCII (plain text) files.

Once the data to be analyzed are saved, one starts M*plus* and types in it the entire command file. After one saves it and gives it a name of one's choice (and notices that M*plus* automatically appends to it the suffix '.inp'), a click on the running icon in the toolbar submits it to the software. Thereby the data file, created as above, is assumed to be in the same directory as the M*plus* input file constructed in this way.

Last but not least, if one has the raw data file—which as mentioned earlier is the most preferable analytically option—one need not create a new data file as described in the previous two paragraphs but only to point within the M*plus* command file to the name (and location, if not in the current directory) of that data file. This is accomplished by the command

```
DATA:  FILE = <NAME OF RAW DATA FILE>;
```

No further subcommands are needed with this DATA command, because M*plus* by default assumes raw data are being analyzed, in which case it also works out the sample size.

5

Classical Test Theory

Throughout the first four chapters, we repeatedly mentioned a major problem associated with measurement in the behavioral and social sciences—the ubiquitous error of measurement. Most measuring instruments used in these disciplines suffer from this serious problem. In fact, the majority of measurements we can obtain (currently) in these sciences contain a sizeable error. This is not the case to a similar degree with measurements routinely carried out in the 'hard' sciences, most notably physics, chemistry, engineering, and the technical disciplines. Although they are also concerned with error of measurement, its magnitude seems far more limited and not comparable to that typically committed in behavioral and social research. This chapter focuses on a classical approach to accounting for measurement error in these sciences. This approach is commonly referred to as classical test theory and exhibits important relationships with factor analysis that was the topic of the two preceding chapters.

5.1 The Nature of Measurement Error

Measurement error in the social, behavioral, and educational sciences can be broadly categorized as (a) systematic and (b) random. We discuss these two error types in turn next.

5.1.1 Systematic Error

Systematic error affects measurement in a consistent, i.e., regular or repeatable, manner but has nothing to do with the construct of actual interest (cf. Crocker & Algina, 1986). One way in which such error may occur is when a particular person consistently gives rise to lower scores on a test that are below his or her level of the attribute, trait, or ability being measured. This may be due to some special characteristics of that subject, e.g., being distracted by a recent event specific to him or her or a physiological state he or she is in at the time of measurement, such as fatigue resulting from preceding activities, sickness, etc. As another example, a person may have a tendency to endorse a particular answer when lacking knowledge pertaining to a given question, e.g., consistently selecting to check the response 'disagree' when an item appears ambiguous to him or her. These two examples show how systematic error can affect individual performance.

Alternatively, systematic error may affect performance of most, if not all, examined subjects on a given test because of some peculiarities of the measuring instrument or procedure of its utilization. For instance, when administering a reading test to elementary school children, the instructor may pronounce incorrectly a word that is not well understood by the students or use an unfamiliar term. In this case, systematic error affects group performance, because all examinees possibly perform below their ability. In a similar testing situation, a hearing-impaired child may misunderstand a word or whole passage of the test instructions because of incorrect pronunciation by the instructor, in which case systematic error potentially affects only this child's performance.

The common features underlying all these situations are (a) that the resulting measurement error has nothing to do with the construct being measured, such as a particular ability in the above examples, and (b) that this error occurs in a systematic manner. As a consequence, systematic error biases the measurement of the studied construct either in the positive or negative direction. This bias may be individual specific, as in two of the examples considered, or alternatively may have validity for more than a single person, perhaps even for an entire group. Either way, the systematic error is such that it will occur in general any time the measurement is conducted with the same instrument under the same conditions for the same subject(s). In other words, this type of error persists across repeated testing (at approximately the same point in time) with the same instrument. To put it differently, systematic error is repeatable if one measures again the same subjects with the same instrument. Hence, across these repeated measurements, the systematic error has a nonzero average that may be positive or alternatively negative; in the former case the systematic error leads to a spuriously enhanced (inflated) average performance, whereas in the latter case it leads to a spuriously depressed (deflated) average performance. This spuriousness of the effect on observed score(s) results regardless whether systematic error is in effect for a given subject or for a group of individuals. (The average mentioned above is taken in the former case with respect to repeated testing of the same subject with the same instrument; in the latter case, it is taken with respect to repeated testing with the same instrument of the same group of individuals.)

Because of resulting biased measurement, systematic error can lead to seriously misleading conclusions and in particular such decisions based on obtained test scores. Hence, systematic measurement error must be eliminated, or informed arguments in favor of it not being present in tests under consideration must be justified, before one can place trust in given instruments and recommend them for use. In fact, lack of systematic error of measurement is an essential requirement for any measuring instrument. Without this requirement being fulfilled, it cannot be claimed that a particular instrument is a really trustworthy device of behavioral measurement.

5.1.2 Random Error of Measurement

Random error of measurement affects an individual's score because of pure chance effects that are momentary and have nothing to do with the construct being measured. That is, random measurement error represents the combined effect of particular, transient, unrepeatable, and nonsystematic factors on manifest performance that are unrelated to the attribute of concern. These could be momentary feelings, moods, distractions, environmental effects, or fluctuations in an examinee's physiological state, which are at work only at the moment of testing. Furthermore, uninformed guessing and relatively minor administration or scoring errors can also lead to random errors. As a result, random error of measurement—being the totality of such random effects on the performance of a given subject on a measure under consideration—biases his or her observed performance on it, bringing the observed score at a given testing occasion either above or below his or her actual level of a studied attribute.

Random and systematic measurement errors have one property in common, viz., that they have nothing to do with the construct of interest to evaluate. However, unlike systematic error, this random error occurs only at the moment of measurement. If administration of the same test were to be repeated to the same subject (at approximately the same point in time), the random effects that in their totality represent the random error at the first measurement need not occur, although it is quite likely that other random effects may operate at the repeated measurement(s), however. Another distinction between the two types of error is that unlike systematic error, whose average is not zero, random error is on average zero for any given subject (and on any prespecified instrument of interest; see next section).

Both systematic error and random error adversely affect observed performance and limit substantially the utility of resulting test scores. Thus, it is desirable that measurement procedures be developed that minimize the effect of measurement error on recorded scores. In general, however, because of the nature of behavioral and social measurement and its object, it is not possible to entirely eliminate measurement error.

With this in mind, it is highly desirable to be in a position to evaluate the degree to which measurement error impacts observed scores, so as to take it into account when using these scores further. Evaluation of the extent to which observed scores are affected by measurement error can be carried out within the framework of the so-called classical test theory, to which we turn next. As we will see later, it is closely related to the factor analysis approach we discussed in the two preceding chapters.

5.2 Foundations of Classical Test Theory

Classical test theory (CTT) may be seen as having its beginnings in the work of Spearman (1904). Its subsequent development culminated in the highly instructive work by Zimmerman (1975). The foundations of CTT are also described in Lord and Novick (1968; see also Steyer & Eid, 2001). The discussion of CTT in this chapter aims to present its basis at a relatively introductory level.

5.2.1 The Classical Test Theory Equation

CTT is based on our intuitive understanding that a given test score, which in general contains error of measurement as discussed in the preceding section, can be thought of as consisting of two parts. One of them is the error of measurement, and the other is the actual individual score on the studied latent dimension that is of interest to evaluate. This latter part of the observed score is called 'true score'. (We will define the concept of true score more formally later in this section.) Hence, according to CTT, a given test score, X, is decomposed into the sum of true score, denoted T, and error score, symbolized by E:

$$X = T + E. \tag{5.1}$$

Specifically, for a given individual—say the ith in a population under consideration—his or her score on a prespecified test is

$$X_i = T_i + E_i, \tag{5.2}$$

where the subindex i denotes individual (see also below; $i = 1, ..., N$, with N being population size). In order to emphasize the dependence also on an instrument in question, Equation (5.2) is more comprehensively written as

$$X_{ki} = T_{ki} + E_{ki}, \tag{5.3}$$

where the subindex k stands to remind us of the fact that we are talking about a score on a given test or measure, say the kth. Hence, for a given group of N subjects and a set of p tests ($p \geq 1$), CTT asserts that

$$X_{ki} = T_{ki} + E_{ki} \tag{5.4}$$

($1 \leq k \leq p$; $i = 1, ..., N$). We call Equation (5.4) the classical test theory equation or classical test theory decomposition. We note that (5.4) is actually a set of equations, in fact Np such, but for simplicity of reference it is called the CTT equation. Equation (5.4) is a detailed representation of the generic Equation (5.1), which will often be of particular relevance in the rest of this book. Equation (5.1) states that an observed score is decomposable into the sum of true score and error score, represents formally this decomposition, and reflects the conceptual idea behind CTT.

We emphasize that according to Equation (5.4), every individual's observed score on any of a set of administered tests (measures, items, scale components) is the sum of (a) a true score of that subject on the test and (b) an error score of that individual on the test. A given subject has possibly different true scores on different tests, as well as different error scores on them. Furthermore, different individuals have different (in general) true scores for any given test or across tests, like they have different error scores. Also, different tests (measuring instruments) generally have different components of the decomposition (5.4) of their observed scores into true score and error score that also differ across subjects.

5.2.2 A Definition of True Score and Error Score

The preceding discussion was concerned with more of an intuitive presentation of the CTT equation and its components. A formal development of CTT is possible by first defining the concept of true score. A rigorous definition of true score is provided in Zimmerman (1975). For our purposes in this book, we can define the true score for a given test and individual less formally as follows.

Suppose a test (instrument) is administered many times to the same individual in a way ensuring a large number of resulting statistically independent and identically distributed measurements of this person; assume thereby that these measurements occur within a very short period of time, so that no underlying development or change of the construct of actual interest occurs (Lord & Novick, 1968). The average of all measurements obtained then is defined as the true score of this individual on this test (instrument). This is the definition of the true score T_{ki} in the above Equation (5.4) ($1 \leq k \leq p$; $i = 1, ..., N$). We define then the error score E_{ki} of this individual on this test (instrument) as the complement of his or her true score to his or her observed score on that test: $E_{ki} = X_{ki} - T_{ki}$ ($1 \leq k \leq p$; $i = 1, ..., N$). That is, if X_{kij} is the observed score at the jth of these measurements of the ith individual with the kth test (instrument), where $j = 1, ..., J$, with J being a very large number, then one can define for our goals in this book the true score for that subject and test as

$$T_{ki} = \bar{X}_{ki.} \tag{5.5}$$

where $\bar{X}_{ki.}$ denotes the average of the J measurements ($1 \leq k \leq p$; $i = 1, ..., N$).

More formally, the true score is defined as the expectation of the distribution of very many (i.e., 'practically all possible') statistically independent and identically distributed measurements made on a given subject with a prespecified test (instrument; cf.

Lord & Novick, 1968). This distribution is called propensity distribution and is obviously both test and subject specific. As such, this distribution generally differs across tests and subjects. The definition of the concept of true score implies that the only impact on the scores observed during the repeated measurements described above, other than the true score itself, is by random error of measurement. In this sense, the process of taking the mean (expectation) of the propensity distribution 'cancels out' the effect of random error of measurement. Across the repeated measurements, the only variable that is allowed to differ from one measurement to another is random error of measurement (but not systematic error of measurement, as the latter is repeatable; see its definition in the preceding subsection).

An important point in the definition of true score that we wish to stress is that during these repeated measurements, the construct being measured remains the same, or constant, i.e., does not undergo any changes or development. This definition does not imply, however, that the true score is (assumed) the same across different time points at which the construct may be planned beforehand to be evaluated, as in longitudinal (repeated measure or panel) studies say. We note that the above definition of true score does not involve time, because in it time is supposed to be fixed (in a sense, stopped). In fact, the definition of true score is completely compatible with its change in the context of a longitudinal study where multiple successive assessments are conducted at different measurement occasions (points in time). This is seen by considering the notion of true score at each given point in time at which the construct under consideration is evaluated, e.g., at each measurement occasion of a longitudinal investigation.

As indicated above, formally the concept of true score is defined as the mathematical expectation of the propensity distribution for a given test and subject. It is thereby assumed of course that this mathematical expectation exists, as we do in the rest of this book, yet its existence can be seen as ensured in essentially all practical applications in behavioral and social research (except in cases of 'pathological' nature that will not be of interest in this book; cf. Lord & Novick, 1968). An alternative expression for this definition is to say that the true score is the conditional expectation of a prespecified test's (instrument's) score, whereby the conditioning is taken with respect to the subject (for a more rigorous treatment of this issue, see Zimmerman, 1975). That is, if one were interested in obtaining a given individual's true score on a measuring instrument of concern, one needs (a) to condition with regard to the subject (i.e., consider it 'fixed') and then (b) to take the mean of all his or her measurements possible to obtain with the test. This leads to taking in the end the expectation of the pertinent propensity distribution, which we reiterate is individual and test specific.

The true score can also be defined using advanced notions of measure theory and probability theory, specifically probability spaces, sigma algebras, and probability measures, as well as projections of appropriately defined vectors on such spaces. This is rigorously carried out and extensively discussed in Zimmerman (1975; see also Steyer & Eid, 2001). For the purposes of this book, the above definition provided in Equation (5.5) will be sufficient.

We emphasize that in this entire Section 5.2, we are concerned with true score and error score at the population level.

5.2.3 Interpretation of the True Score

What does the notion of true score actually mean? Given that it is an expectation (of a corresponding propensity distribution), obviously it does not depend on a random effect, which has zero mean. Hence, the true score does not depend on the random error of measurement, because this error is the totality of particular random effects on observed performance as discussed earlier in this chapter. This can also be realized by recalling that the random error of measurement has a mean of zero. Therefore, there is no impact of random error of measurement on the mean of observed score, i.e., random measurement error does not affect the true score.

This is not the case with systematic error of measurement, however, which is also part of measurement error as discussed above. Because its mean is not zero (at least in general), and this error is consistently occurring, systematic error affects the true score. In fact, any effect that systematically biases observed score, in either a positive or a negative direction (and regardless whether that's the case for a single individual or a group), affects in exactly the same way the true score. That is, the mean systematic effect is part of the true score. Keeping this in mind and revisiting the CTT Equation (5.4), we see that the error score in CTT, E_{ki}, is in fact equal to the random measurement error ($k = 1, ..., p, i = 1, ..., N$).

How do we interpret substantively the true score? Because it is an average performance (in the sense defined above in this Section 5.2), it captures all enduring individual examinee's characteristics, as opposed to momentary chance effects, which are of relevance in his or her performance on a given test. We note that random measurement error is not observed and hence cannot be separated from true score in a given observed score. The reason is that all we have really measured, recorded, or evaluated is the actual test performance; that is, all we have available is the observed score X_{ki} on the left-hand side of the CTT Equation (5.4) ($k = 1, ..., p, i = 1, ..., N$). The interpretation of the true score is therefore as a latent, unobserved score on the underlying dimension of actual interest, which is free from random measurement error.

To exemplify this interpretation empirically, suppose we were interested in measuring the writing ability of elementary school children. Assume we happen to measure it with a given test under fairly noisy conditions. As implied from the above discussion, the true score for each child on this test will be affected by these conditions. Hence, this true score will likely be lower than each child's real writing ability because of the systematic measurement error resulting from the noisy conditions. If we administer, however, this test under normal conditions, i.e., conditions that are not noisy (and correspond precisely to those required in the instructions for test administration), the true score on the same test for the same children will be different and most likely higher.

Assuming no systematic measurement error, the true score is interpretable as the score of a given individual on the latent dimension of actual interest, i.e., the latent score or, in other words, the individual score on the attitude, trait, or ability under investigation. Hence, the true score is then the score on the 'true' dimension of real interest, i.e., on the construct one is willing to measure (attempting to measure). With no systematic measurement error, the true score is the score that one is interested in obtaining anytime a test is administered to individuals. However, the true score cannot be obtained directly because it is not measured directly, being entangled (i.e., confounded) with error score in the observed score. Conversely, with systematic error of measurement, the true score is the correspondingly biased score (positively or negatively, depending on that error) on the underlying latent dimension of interest, whereby the bias equals the mean systematic effect. (The latter mean effect could be obtained if one could get the mean of the systematic error across repeated measurements of the same individual with the same instrument, as outlined earlier in the chapter.)

The above empirical example illustrates that in order to be in a position to capture what we want to really measure, we must ensure that there is no systematic error of measurement (see also Section 5.1). This requires advanced knowledge of the pertinent subject-matter domain as well as experience with measuring activities in it. Both are instrumental in identifying all possible sources of systematic measurement error and taking effective measures aimed at their elimination. With regard to test application in empirical situations, one therefore needs to ensure that test administration instructions are exactly followed. These and further related specific matters pertain to more applied aspects of utilization of test theory, mostly covered within the field of behavioral assessment, and as mentioned in Chapter 1, we will not be concerned with them in this book.

5.2.4 Misconceptions About Classical Test Theory

In a considerable part of the literature dealing with test theory (in particular, on other approaches to test theory), the version of Equation (5.1) for a given test is occasionally incorrectly referred to as the 'CTT model'. There is, however, no CTT model (cf. Steyer & Eid, 2001; Zimmerman, 1975). In fact, for a given test, the CTT decomposition (5.1) of observed score as the sum of true score and error score can always be made (of course as long as the underlying mathematical expectation of observed score—to yield the true score—exists, as mentioned above). Hence, Equation (5.1) is always true. Logically and scientifically, any model is a set of assumptions that is made about certain objects (scores here). These assumptions must, however, be falsifiable in order to speak of a model. In circumstances where no falsifiable assumptions are made, there is also no model present. Therefore, one can speak of a model only when a set of assumptions is made that can in principle be wrong (but need not be so in an empirical setting). Because Equation (5.1) is always true, however, it cannot be disconfirmed or falsified. For this reason, Equation (5.1) is not an assumption but rather a tautology. Therefore, Equation (5.1)—which is frequently incorrectly referred to in the literature as 'CTT model'—cannot in fact represent a model. Hence, contrary to statements made in many other sources, CTT is not based on a model, and in actual fact, as mentioned earlier, there is no CTT model.

A related misconception about CTT, similarly to be found in literature on other approaches to test theory, asserts that CTT is based on certain assumptions, e.g., of 'unrelated errors' or 'unrelated true score and error score' (cf. Zimmerman, 1975, for a rigorous clarification of this issue). As was the case with the above misconception about a CTT model, we emphasize that there is no assumption made in CTT that the true score and error score are unrelated to one another (or, alternatively, that they are related to one another). Instead, the fact that the error score and true score are always uncorrelated follows logically from the definition of true score and that of error score as being random error of measurement (see also Zimmerman, 1975). That is, the uncorrelatedness of true and error score is already 'contained' in the definition of true score (and that of error score, as its complement to observed score). For this reason, their uncorrelatedness cannot be wrong or disproved (falsified) and hence cannot be an assumption by any law of logic. Rather, true score and error score for a given individual and test are always uncorrelated, and their uncorrelatedness is always true, follows from their very construction (definition), and cannot be wrong.

A third misconception about CTT asserts that CTT assumes error scores on different tests (measures) to be uncorrelated. There is no such assumption in CTT per se (cf. Zimmerman, 1975). In fact, it is up to a researcher using CTT with more than a single test (measure) to assume pertinent errors as correlated or alternatively as uncorrelated. Lack of error correlation is in fact assumed any time one considers at least two tests for which he or she does not stipulate their errors as correlated and vice versa. Unlike the CTT equation, lack of error correlation is a hypothesis (i.e., an assumption) that can be tested with appropriately developed models and procedures in certain settings, and we will return to this issue later in the book.

A fourth misconception about CTT, also found in alternative measuring-theory-related literature, relates to the issue of the 'scale' underlying observed score. Specifically, one can find claims there for an assumption in CTT that the observed score X (for which the decomposition $X = T + E$ is valid) is continuous. There is neither such an assumption in CTT nor a requirement nor a need for the observed score X to be a continuous measure. In particular, all that is required from X within the CTT framework is that the mean of its propensity distribution exists, i.e., the associated true score T exists. A sufficient condition for this to be the case is that the variance of this distribution exists. In most social and behavioral research, however, this condition is fulfilled (e.g., Lord & Novick, 1968). Hence the observed score X can be discrete (e.g., binary), or alternatively continuous (as opposed to discrete), and all that is needed for CTT to function then is that the associated with X true score T be well defined. For the true score T to be well defined, it suffices that the propensity distribution of X is with finite variance. This is a rather mild if at all restrictive condition, and it is one that is essentially routinely fulfilled when measurement is conducted in the behavioral, social, and educational disciplines. (This is not to imply that a pathological example could never be constructed where this condition could be violated, but the present authors are not aware of such an example with practical relevance, and it seems likely that an example of this kind would be exceptional and not representative of the vast majority of meaningful current settings of measurement in these sciences.)

This discussion on misconceptions about CTT leads us also to a related point. Even though CTT is not based on a model, it is possible to develop models of behavioral tests or measuring instruments that are based on CTT. In particular, if one posits assumptions about true scores and possibly error scores for a given set of tests (observed measures), which assumptions can be falsified, then one obtains models. These models will be referred to as CTT-based models in this and later chapters. As an example, readily obtained models within the CTT framework can postulate, say, linear relationships among the true scores of a given set of tests (measures), as we will discuss below (e.g., Jöreskog, 1971). These models, unlike the CTT Equation (5.1), can be tested against data. We will see how this can be done later in this chapter, in particular using formally a modeling and testing approach that we know from our discussion of confirmatory factor analysis in the preceding chapter.

5.2.5 Relationships Between True Score and Error Score

Following our discussion of the misconceptions about CTT, a revisit is worthwhile of the above definition of (a) true score as the mathematical expectation of the propensity distribution and (b) error score as the remainder of observed score (see Equation (5.1)). From these two definitions, it follows that the true score and error score are uncorrelated (e.g., Zimmerman, 1975), that is,

$$Corr(T, E) = 0 \tag{5.6}$$

always holds (and hence true and error scores are independent when they are bivariate normal; e.g., Roussas, 1997). Equation (5.6) can be considered a counterpart, within the framework of CTT, of the well-known lack of relationship between predictors and residuals in linear models, e.g., conventional linear regression or factor analysis models.

In fact, it can be more generally shown (e.g., Zimmerman, 1975) that the true score on a given test is unrelated to the error score on any other test or the same one, i.e.,

$$Corr(T_k, E_{k'}) = 0, \tag{5.7}$$

where T_k is the true score on the kth test and $E_{k'}$ is the error score on test k', with $1 \le k, k' \le p$. (We emphasize that Equation (5.7) holds also when $k = k'$.)

Equation (5.7) has no consequence, however, for the relationships among true scores associated with different tests (measures). In fact, true scores on different tests can have *any* type of relationships among themselves. In particular, they may or may not be correlated with one another. Most of the time in informed behavioral research, true scores on tests evaluating related (or common) latent dimensions will likely be related to one another. As we will see later in this chapter, a particular type of relationships among true scores—specifically, identity or more general linear relationships—will be of special interest in test construction and development efforts. We will in fact consider models that assume such relationships in the next section. These models will be conceptualized within the CTT framework.

Similar to true scores, error scores can also have *any* relationship to one another (i.e., covary with one another or alternatively not covary), as we already mentioned earlier in this section. We will consider in the next section models that make the assumption of uncorrelated error scores and point out that there can be models that make the assumption of correlated error scores. We will also indicate later ways in which one can test such assumptions. At this moment, we emphasize that unlike Equations (5.6) and (5.7), either of these statements (related or unrelated error scores) is indeed an assumption as it can be wrong and is in fact falsifiable, because it can be at least in principle empirically tested.

5.3 Models Based on Classical Test Theory

Suppose we administer a set of p tests (measures, items, scale components) to a group of individuals ($p \ge 3$). As discussed previously in this chapter, for each of these tests, any of the subjects has a true score. This assumes of course the existence of the pertinent mathematical expectation used to define it, but as indicated earlier we will presume it in the rest of this book. As mentioned before, this assumption does not impose any practical restrictions and technically will be fulfilled if the variance of the observed score is finite. This is a rather mild assumption if any of practically restrictive nature (e.g., Lord & Novick, 1968).

To emphasize the presence of these p true scores, we may specialize Equation (5.1) to stress that we are concerned with a set of tests rather than a single one:

$$X_k = T_k + E_k, \tag{5.8}$$

where k is a subindex for test ($k = 1, \ldots, p$). (Equation (5.8) is obtained from (5.4) by suppressing the individual subindex, for the purposes of the current discussion; we will follow this practice in the rest of this chapter and the next chapters and deviate from it if confusion may arise or if we wish to emphasize individual scores.)

How do these p true scores, T_1 through T_p, relate to one another? When we are dealing with tests that at least on substantive reasons may be expected to be related to each other, one may also expect that their true scores could be correlated. Perhaps there is even a strong relationship between them? If so, one could benefit from it in developing batteries of tests, in general comprehensive measuring instruments consisting of more than just one component (test, measure).

As we indicated in an earlier chapter, of particular relevance when developing such sets of tests (measures) is that they be homogeneous, i.e., unidimensional, since they frequently tend to be used as elements of multiple-component measuring instruments in social and behavioral research. This type of relationship among sets of tests can actually be examined using specific models developed within the framework of CTT and that capitalize on the preceding discussion in this chapter (cf. Jöreskog, 1971). We turn to these models next. All of them assume that the error terms $E_1, ..., E_k$ are uncorrelated. (We reiterate that this is an assumption.)

5.3.1 Model of Parallel Tests

Based on the CTT Equation (5.8), viz., $X_k = T_k + E_k$ ($k = 1, ..., p$), the model of parallel tests asserts that all p tests (measures) X_1 through X_p share the same true score; thereby, all differences among their observed scores come from differences in their error scores that are also assumed to be equally varied, i.e., have the same variance. That is, the model of parallel tests (MPT) assumes that

$$X_k = T + E_k \qquad (5.9)$$

and

$$Var(E_k) = Var(E_{k'})$$

($k = 1, ..., p; k \neq k'$; T can be taken to denote the true score of any of the tests, e.g., the first: $T = T_1$). We stress the lack of subindex attached to the true score in the right-hand side of the first of Equations (5.9). In fact, the missing k there is an essential feature of the MPT, as is the second of these equations. That is, the MPT assumes that the p tests measure the same true score, denoted T, with the same precision—as reflected in the associated error variance.

We emphasize three points here. One, the first of Equations (5.9) is not the 'CTT model' or the CTT equation, because there are two further statements made in (5.9) that are not so in the CTT decomposition of an observed score (see, e.g., Equation (5.4)). These additional statements are of (a) the same true score and (b) the same error variances for the set of p measures under consideration. Second, unlike the CTT equation, these of (5.9) are based on two assumptions, viz., (a) and (b) in the preceding sentence, which may be false and in fact are falsifiable because they are empirically testable, as shown below. Third, because Equations (5.9) are based on assumptions, unlike the CTT Equation (5.4), say, the set of Equations (5.9) does represent a model, viz., the model of parallel tests (measures).

To see that the assumptions underlying the MPT are testable, we note that there are consequences, i.e., logical implications, from Equations (5.9) for the variances and covariances of the observed scores on the tests X_1 through X_p. Specifically, if the MPT were to be correct as a model, direct use of the variance and covariance rules in Chapter 2 for linear combinations of random variables—which the observed, true, and error scores obviously are—yields the following structure for the covariance matrix of these

p tests, denoted Σ_{XX}:

$$\Sigma_{XX} = \begin{bmatrix} \sigma_T^2 + \sigma_E^2 & & & \\ \sigma_T^2 & \sigma_T^2 + \sigma_E^2 & & \\ \cdot & \cdot & \cdot & \cdot \\ \sigma_T^2 & \sigma_T^2 & \cdots & \sigma_T^2 + \sigma_E^2 \end{bmatrix}. \tag{5.10}$$

where $\sigma_T^2 = Var(T)$ and $\sigma_E^2 = Var(E_k)$ $(k = 1, \ldots, p$; see the second of Equations (5.9)). (Similarly, the observed variable means are implied as equal among themselves in the general case). Therefore, the MPT cannot be true for a given set of tests, $X_1, X_2, \ldots, X_p$, unless there exist two real numbers, σ_T^2 and σ_E^2, with which Equation (5.10) is fulfilled. That is, the postulation of the MPT is tantamount to the claim of existence of such two real numbers σ_T^2 and σ_E^2, which have the property that when they are substituted into the right-hand side of Equation (5.10), the resulting covariance matrix with numerical entries equals the population covariance matrix of these p observed variables (i.e., Σ_{XX} is structured exactly as prescribed by (5.10)). Whether two such numbers exist (σ_T^2 and σ_E^2), however, is empirically testable. We will see how this can be done in the next section. For this reason, Equation (5.8) defines a model, which as mentioned is commonly referred to as the model of parallel tests (measures).

5.3.2 Model of True Score Equivalent Tests (Tau-Equivalent Tests)

The assumptions made in the MPT—that the p tests measure the same true score with the same precision (error variances)—are often quite strong and restrictive in behavioral and social research. According to this model, it is required not only that the same true score be measured in the same units of measurement with the given set of tests but also that they all are equally error prone (meaning, with identical error variances). Both of these assumptions are limiting substantially the range of applicability of the MPT in empirical work, making it rather difficult for substantive scholars to construct measures that fulfill it. It is therefore desirable to have available alternatives that do not make these strong assumptions.

In fact, it is possible to relax the second assumption of identical error variances and obtain another popular model for tests evaluating the same underlying construct (true score). This relaxation is accomplished in the so-called true score equivalence model (TSEM), also frequently referred to as the tau-equivalent test model. The TSEM assumes only the first of Equations (5.9), i.e.,

$$X_k = T + E_k \tag{5.11}$$

$(k = 1, \ldots, p)$. In other words, the TSEM assumes that the set of p given tests evaluates the same true score, T, in the same units of measurement but with possibly different precision (i.e., error variances; again, T in (5.11) can be taken to denote the true score associated with any of the tests, e.g., the first: $T = T_1$).

Formally the TSEM assumes only that the true score of any test equals the true score of any other test: $T_k = T_{k'}$ $(k, k' = 1, \ldots, p, k \neq k')$, which is identical to the assumption in the first of Equations (5.9) for the MPT. Thus, as can be seen directly from its definition, the TSEM is a more general model than the MPT. In fact, the MPT is such a special case of the TSEM, which is obtained when one imposes in the TSEM the additional restriction of equal error variances (i.e., the second of Equations (5.9)).

Imposing a constraint to obtain one model from another, as here to yield the MPT from the TSEM, is in general an approach often used in many areas of applied statistics and in particular in latent variable modeling (LVM). This approach is typically employed when one wants to obtain a special case of a more general model. Introducing a restriction in a given model to render another one leads to obtaining in the latter a model that is referred to as nested in the former. This notion of nested models is of fundamental relevance in applied statistics, and especially in LVM, and we will soon use it in a more instrumental way. For the moment, we stress that the MPT is nested in the TSEM.

Like the MPT, the TSEM implies a specific structuring of the covariance matrix of the given set of p measures, X_1 through X_p. In particular, should the TSEM be correct, their covariance structure ought to look as follows (see Equation (5.11) and the rules for variances and covariances in Chapter 2):

$$\Sigma_{XX} = \begin{bmatrix} \sigma_T^2 + \sigma_{E_1}^2 & & & \\ \sigma_T^2 & \sigma_T^2 + \sigma_{E_2}^2 & & \\ . & . & . & . \\ \sigma_T^2 & \sigma_T^2 & ... & \sigma_T^2 + \sigma_{E_p}^2 \end{bmatrix}, \tag{5.12}$$

where now the error variances added in the main diagonal to the true score variance may differ from test to test (i.e., $\sigma_{E_1}^2$ through $\sigma_{E_p}^2$ need not be equal among themselves). Hence, if the TSEM is correct, there should exist $p + 1$ real numbers—one for each of the p error variances and one for the true score variance—which when substituted correspondingly into the covariance matrix in the right-hand side of Equation (5.12) will render it numerically equal to the population covariance matrix of the p observed variables X_1 through X_p.

These implications of Equation (5.11), viz., the particular structuring of the observed measure covariance matrix Σ_{XX} in (5.12) are empirically testable, as we will demonstrate later in this chapter. We note that similarly to the MPT, the TSEM is also developed based on the p CTT equations in (5.11) for the set of observed measures under consideration, X_1 through X_p. Thereby, the TSEM does make assumptions about the relationships of the underlying true scores, which assumptions are testable, unlike any single CTT equation for a given test X_k (k being a fixed number between 1 and p). This fact makes the TSEM, like the MPT, a model indeed, contrary to a CTT equation for a particular observed measure (see discussion in the preceding Section 5.2).

5.3.3 Model of Congeneric Tests

The assumption of the same true score being evaluated with the same units of measurement by a set of given tests, which underlies both the MPT and TSEM, is rather strong and restrictive in the behavioral and social sciences. It requires not only that the same latent continuum be evaluated by all tests (measures) but in addition that they all should be based on the same units of measurement. In behavioral and social research, however, units of measurement are quite often lacking particular meaning, arbitrary or perhaps even irrelevant, in addition to being specific to different tests and therefore likely to be distinct across tests. This assumption of equality of measurement units does indeed strike one as fairly strong, because it requires what seems to be in general far too much from these arbitrary units that cannot be typically meaningfully interpreted.

The assumption of identical units of measurement that is made in both the MPT and the TSEM is relaxed in the most general model that can be conceptualized within the framework of CTT for purposes of measuring the same underlying latent continuum, the model of congeneric tests (MCT; Jöreskog, 1971). This model assumes only that the true scores pertaining to different tests (measures) are linearly related to one another:

$$X_k = d_k + b_k T + E_k, \tag{5.13}$$

where d_k and b_k are test-specific constants (i.e., the same across subjects), and T can again be taken to be the true score associated with any of the tests, e.g., the first (i.e., $T = T_1$; $k = 1, ..., p$). Hence, the true scores of congeneric measures are perfectly correlated, because (5.13) implies $T_k = d_k + b_k T$ ($k = 1, ..., p$). From the last p equations follows that in the MCT, any test's true score can be expressed as a linear combination of any other test's true score using an appropriate pair of d and b parameters ($k = 1, ..., p$). We stress, however, that perfect correlation is an assumption at the true score level, not at the observed score level. Even though the true scores are perfectly correlated according to the MCT, because of the added effect of error, the observed scores are in general not perfectly correlated. Nonetheless, like the TSEM and MPT, the MCT defined by Equation (5.13) implies a certain structuring of the covariance matrix of observed measures. Specifically, if the MCT is correct, the covariance matrix of the given set of p observed measures X_1 through X_p should look as follows:

$$\Sigma_{XX} = \begin{bmatrix} b_1^2 \sigma_T^2 + \sigma_{E_1}^2 & & & \\ b_1 b_2 \sigma_T^2 & b_2^2 \sigma_T^2 + \sigma_{E_2}^2 & & \\ \cdot & \cdot & \cdot & \cdot \\ b_1 b_p \sigma_T^2 & b_2 b_p \sigma_T^2 & ... & b_p^2 \sigma_T^2 + \sigma_{E_p}^2 \end{bmatrix}. \tag{5.14}$$

Hence, if the MCT is correct, there should exist $3p + 1$ real numbers (p ds, p bs, p error variances, and one true score variance), with which the right-hand side of Equation (5.14) equals the population covariance matrix of the p measures, X_1 through X_p. (Preempting some of the following discussion, as mentioned further below, we will need to make an additional assumption about one of the b parameters or the true score variance in order to be in a position to uniquely estimate, given data, all these unknown numbers. This requirement applies to each of the three CTT-based models considered in this Section 5.3.) Because the MCT has implications for the covariance structure of the given set of p tests, its assumptions are testable and thus Equation (5.13) does define a model, unlike the CTT decomposition (equation) for any given test, say X_j ($1 \leq j \leq p$). How this testing is conducted is discussed in the next section. We also note that the MCT is more general than the TSEM and hence also more general than the MPT, because the assumption of identical units of measurement that is characteristic of the MPT and TSEM is relaxed in the MCT. That is, the MPT and the TSEM are each a special case of the MCT and are obtained from the latter by imposing in it additional restrictions on some of its parameters (viz., equality of units of measurement for the TSEM and also that of error variances in the MPT).

We emphasize that the MPT, TSEM, and MCT are all models assuming a single underlying latent dimension that is assessed with the set of measures $X_1, ..., X_p$ under consideration. For this reason, we will also use the term 'unidimensional' or 'homogeneous' for such a set of tests, $X_1, ..., X_p$, as long as any of these three models is correct (plausible) for them. That is, according to the MPT, TSEM, or MCT model, the used set of p tests (observed measures) $X_1, ..., X_p$ is homogeneous or unidimensional.

By way of summary of much of the discussion in this section, we can state that (a) the TSEM is nested in the MCT, (b) the MPT is nested in the TSEM, and hence (c) the MPT is also nested in the MCT. That is, all CTT-based models considered so far are nested, with the MPT being the most restrictive model and the MCT being the least restrictive model. Hence, if one uses the symbol "<" to denote the relation of nestedness (of the model to its left, in that to its right), one can state

$$\text{MPT "<" TSEM "<" MCT.}$$

More specifically, the TSEM follows from the MCT when the assumption $b_1 = b_2 = ... = b_p$ is adopted in the latter model, and the MPT follows from the TSEM when in addition the assumption $Var(E_1) = Var(E_2) = ... = Var(E_p)$ is introduced in the TSEM.

We turn next to a useful relationship between CTT-based models and factor analysis models, which we will capitalize on in a subsequent section.

5.4 Relationship Between Factor Analysis and CTT-Based Models

If we look once again at Equation (5.13) defining the most general of the CTT-based models considered, the model for congeneric tests (MCT), we will notice a close resemblance to the traditional factor analysis (FA) model (3.1) (see Chapter 3), in particular in case of a single common factor. To examine more thoroughly the relationship between these two models, first we note that we can disregard in the rest of this chapter the intercepts d_k in the MCT by assuming we are dealing with zero-mean observed variables. Indeed, we can assume without limitation of generality, for the purposes of this and the next three chapters, that $d_k = 0$ ($k = 1, ..., p$; if this was not the case, we could subtract the mean from each observed variable, leading to $d_k = 0$ in the MCT equations for the resulting measures of interest then). Given the formal resemblance of the CTT-based and FA models, the question that naturally arises is what the distinction is between them.

This question is answered by revisiting the definition of the terms in the FA model and in particular the unique factors (residual terms) in it. As we recall from Chapter 3, the unique factor variance in the FA model comprises both random measurement error variance and systematic variance that is specific to each observed variable considered. Hence, based on our discussion earlier in this chapter, the difference between the FA model with a single factor and the most general of the three considered CTT-based models, the MCT, is the fact that the residual term in that FA model is 'bigger' than the error term in the MCT for a given observed measure. This is because in addition to random measurement error, which is all that the error score in the MCT (or any other CTT-based model) consists of, the residual term in the FA model also comprises measure specificity. Hence, the FA model with a single latent factor (called for simplicity 'single-factor' model) is more general than the MCT model and thus more general than any of the three CTT-based models considered in this chapter, as they are all special cases of the MCT. In other words, the MCT is a special case of the FA model, which results from the latter model under the additional assumptions of (a) unidimensionality and (b) no variable specificity. This is due to the random measurement error being identical in the FA model and any of the discussed CTT-based models.

As an aside for this discussion, we mention in passing that this relation of inclusion of the CTT-based models into counterpart factor models is also valid for any model conceptualized in terms of CTT, not only the MPT, TSEM, and MCT. That is, for any model developed within the framework of CTT, there is a corresponding more general model that can be developed within the framework of FA, with the former model being a special case of the latter—viz., obtained in case of no specificity in each observed variable.

The discussed relationship between the two classes of models—CTT-based and FA models—allows us to obtain the true score for each observed variable from the traditional FA model. To this end, we first revisit the equation for the kth observed variable in that FA model (see Chapter 3):

$$X_k = a_{k1}f_1 + a_{k2}f_2 + \dots + a_{km}f_m + s_k + e_k,$$

where s_k is its specificity and e_k its random measurement error. In this equation for X_k, s_k is that part of the observed measure X_k (other than e_k) that is not explainable in terms of the common factors $f_1, \dots, f_k$, i.e., the part of X_k not shared with the other observed measures in the given set of tests $X_1, \dots, X_p$ ($k = 1, \dots, p$). Because as mentioned earlier in this section $e_k = E_k$, where E_k is the error score of the CTT equation for X_k (viz., $X_k = T_k + E_k$), it follows that

$$T_k = a_{k1}f_1 + a_{k2}f_2 + \cdots + a_{km}f_m + s_k \tag{5.15}$$

($k = 1, \dots, p$). We note from Equation (5.15) that even though we are speaking of one true score per observed variable, in the context of FA that true score is made up of several common factors, in general, plus a variable specificity term. That is, apart from measure specificity, there is a linear relationship between true score and common factors. However, the presence of measure specificity is essential for the relationship between common factors and true score to be completely described, as seen from Equation (5.15).

From Equation (5.15), it might seem that there could be a simple statistical test whether one is dealing with a CTT-based model or an FA model in a given empirical situation, especially in the unidimensionality context of interest in most of this book. Specifically, one might think that this test would be equivalent to that of whether for all observed variables their specificity term vanishes. Hence, it might appear that such a test would be accomplished by testing whether for each variable the specificity variance equals zero, i.e., by testing a particular restriction in the FA model (and using the typical assumption that the specificity mean is 0, which is also implied by the above assumption of zero mean for the observed variables X_1 through X_p; see also Chapter 3).

The problem with pursuing this direction is that one cannot get access to variable specificity (unless very restrictive assumptions are made). The reason is that variable specificity is not an observed entity and is in fact entangled in the observed score with the random error of measurement as well as the combined effect of possible latent factors on observed performance (score). In certain cases of repeated measure designs, however, specifically multiwave, multiple-indicator models (discussed in alternative sources; e.g., Bollen & Curran, 2006), such a statistical test may become possible to carry out. Under those circumstances, with a plausible appropriately constructed FA model, one can examine whether in addition the corresponding true score model as its special case is a plausible means of data description and explanation (e.g., Raykov, 2007c).

5.5 Testing and Evaluation of CTT-Based Models

CTT-based models can be tested using the same analytic approach employed for testing FA models in Chapter 4, in particular utilizing the same software, M*plus*. What is involved in testing these CTT-based and FA models is the statistical examination of whether their implications are consistent with the analyzed data. Strictly speaking, one evaluates whether there is sufficient evidence in the analyzed data that indicates the model implications as being inconsistent with the data. If there is no such evidence, the model can be considered retainable, i.e., the tested model can be viewed as a plausible means of data description and explanation.

Indeed, if one uses the rules of variances and covariances for linear combinations of random variables (see Chapter 2), one will see that any of the considered CTT-based models in this chapter have the same implications for the covariance structure as a corresponding unidimensional (i.e., single-factor) FA model in which one formally

1. considers the common factor as 'playing the role' of the true score T in any of the MPT, TSEM, and MCT models in question (note that the definition equations of all three latter models are expressed in terms of one and the same underlying, common true score T),

2. considers the unique factor per observed measure as 'playing the role' of its error score in a CTT-based model under consideration, and then

3. imposes restrictions for identical factor loadings when the TSEM is to be considered and, additionally, equality of error variances when the MPT is to be considered.

With this formal identity of the resulting covariance structure for the single-factor model (with appropriate restrictions if needed), on the one hand, and a corresponding CTT-based model on the other, one can use the same approach to estimation and testing of the MPT, TSEM, and MCT models as for the corresponding confirmatory factor analysis models (cf., e.g., Jöreskog, 1971). One can thereby simply start by testing the MCT model, which is the most general of the three, and with 1. and 2. above can be treated analytically (i.e., in terms of model testing and parameter estimation) in the same way as a single-factor model. We illustrate this approach in the next section.

Within this approach to model testing and estimation, one can use the generally applicable method of the likelihood ratio test (LRT) to evaluate parameter restrictions. This method is based on the ratio of the maximal 'probability' (actually, likelihood) of observing the given data set if the restrictions were correct to the maximal 'probability' (likelihood) if they were not correct (e.g., Raykov & Marcoulides, 2008). If the restrictions are valid in the studied population, one would expect this ratio to be close to 1; if they are not, the ratio would be expected to be considerably smaller than 1. It can be shown mathematically that after multiplying by (-2), the logarithm of this ratio follows a chi-square distribution with large samples and observed variable normality, if the restrictions were true, with degrees of freedom being equal to the number of nonredundant parameter restrictions imposed (e.g., Roussas, 1997). Hence, parameter restrictions can be tested then by comparing the maximized log-likelihoods associated with the corresponding pair of restricted and unrestricted models.

Returning to our concern with CTT-based models, as we already know from earlier discussions in this book (e.g., Chapter 4), each of these log-likelihoods is closely related to the chi-square value, a goodness-of-fit index associated with the pertinent latent variable model (confirmatory factor analysis model), and hence with each fitted CTT-based model. Specifically, to test the validity of a set of parameter restrictions under consideration in such a model, with multinormality of the observed variables, all one needs to do is subtract the chi-square value for the model without the restrictions from that value for the model with the restrictions imposed. The resulting difference in chi-square values is to be judged for significance by referring it to the chi-square distribution with as many degrees of freedom as there are additional independent parameters in the more general of the two nested models (i.e., number of nonredundant restrictions). Therefore, if the MCT model (i.e., single-factor model; see above) is found plausible when tested as outlined earlier, using this LRT-based approach one can test also whether the TSEM model is plausible. This is accomplished by imposing the restrictions of equal units of measurement in the MCT (i.e., the restrictions of equal factor loadings in the pertinent single-factor model). If these restrictions are found plausible with the LRT approach, one can test also the fit of the MPT model. That is, in case the TSEM model is found plausible for the analyzed data set, one can add in this model the restrictions of equal error variances (i.e., identity of variances of unique factors in the pertinent single-factor model) and test their validity with the same approach. A relatively minor modification to this approach, from the point of view of its empirical application, is needed with violations of the observed measure multivariate assumption that do not result from some of the dependent variables being highly discrete or exhibiting piling of cases at their maximal or minimal values (or pronounced nesting/clustering effects). This modification is based on use of robust maximum likelihood estimation and a corrected chi-square difference statistic and is implemented as well as readily invoked when using M*plus* (e.g., Muthén & Muthén, 2010; see later in this chapter and in following chapters).

In this way, for a given set of observed measures, one can test if they are unidimensional (homogeneous) by testing the MCT model. If they are unidimensional, one can further test if the measures are in fact complying with the TSEM, as outlined above. If they are so, then one can test if they adhere to the MPT model. Proceeding in this manner, one ends with a most parsimonious, tenable model along this multistep procedure—which model may be the MCT if the TSEM is found not to be plausible for the analyzed data, the TSEM if the MPT is not plausible, and the MPT if plausible for the data.

The benefit of obtaining a most parsimonious, tenable model is that its parameters are most precisely estimated. As seen from the above developments in this chapter (or alternatively in Chapter 3), the parameters of the CTT-based models are the following: (a) the (relative) units of measurement, viz., the *b*s in the MCT model if tenable and most parsimonious; (b) the true score variance; and (c) the error variances. However, the parameters in (b) cannot be estimated uniquely together with those of (a), as indicated in Chapter 4, because if one tries to do this, one will end up with too many parameters to estimate (e.g., Raykov & Marcoulides, 2006a). The resolution of this problem, also referred to as parameter identification (model identification), is, as mentioned, to either set the parameter in (b) equal to a constant—e.g., 1—or set one parameter from those in (a) equal to a constant (say 1). We will use either of these two ways of model identification later in this chapter and in following chapters.

In conclusion of this section, we would like to note that its underlying procedure involves possibly multiple testing on the same data set. For this reason, in order to avoid capitalization on chance (e.g., MacCallum, 1986), it is recommended that one carries out a replication study on an independent sample from the same population before placing more trust in the CTT-based model found preferable with this procedure. We illustrate next the discussion in this section with an empirical example, where we will again use the software M*plus* as the analytic tool.

5.6 Empirical Illustration of Model Testing and Evaluation

We employ in this section the last example we considered in Chapter 4. Accordingly, four mathematics anxiety tests administered to elementary school children were associated with the covariance matrix provided in Table 4.3 there. We are interested now in finding out whether these four tests are only congeneric, or perhaps true score equivalent, or possibly even parallel.

5.6.1 Searching for the Most Restrictive, Tenable Model

To use the testing approach outlined in the preceding Section 5.5, we start with the least restrictive model, that of congeneric tests (MCT). As indicated there, for the purposes of the present analysis, this model is equivalent to the already-fitted unidimensional factor analysis (single-factor) model in Chapter 4. Hence, all results obtained in Chapter 4 with that factor model pertain to our test of MCT. In particular, because the goodness-of-fit indexes (chi-square value, *p*-value, RMSEA, and its confidence interval) were all acceptable for the single-factor model as found in Chapter 4, it follows that the MCT is plausible for the four mathematics anxiety tests under consideration here. Thus, we can conclude that these tests are at least congeneric.

To examine if they are in addition true score equivalent (tau equivalent), we add in the MCT the restrictions of equal factor loadings, as discussed in Section 5.5. These restrictions, as mentioned there, are for our purposes equivalent to the restrictions of identical units of measurement that characterize the TSEM. To this end, all we need to alter in the M*plus* input file for the single-factor model (MCT) fitted in Chapter 4 is the following modification of its MODEL command, which pertains to the definition of the common factor through its indicators and specifically its factor loadings:

```
MODEL:   F1 BY MATHANX1* MATHANX2-MATHANX4 (1);
         F1@1;
```

Note that, as mentioned in Section 5.5, for model identification purposes we need to fix either one factor loading to 1 or the factor variance to 1 (see also Chapter 4). Here, it is appropriate to fix the factor variance in order to be in a position to restrain all four factor loadings to be the same. (If we do not fix that variance, the M*plus* default will keep it free and instead will fix at 1 the loading of MATHANX1, yet this is not really what we want, because this loading should be set equal to all remaining three factor loadings and estimated at an optimal value along with them, which need not necessarily be 1.) Furthermore, once the factor variance is fixed, we need to free the first factor loading, which we do in the first line of the MODEL command by adding the asterisk immediately after the name of the pertinent measure, MATHANX1, and then set equal all four factor loadings. We accomplish this loading equality setting by adding '(1)' at the end of the first line of this command, which one may simply interpret as requesting the same single estimated value for all four factor loadings involved. Hence, the complete M*plus* input file needed for the TSEM model is compactly presented as follows (note the use of the dash notation when assigning names, to save space and time when creating the needed source code):

```
TITLE:      TESTING THE TSEM MODEL
DATA:       FILE = TABLE4_3.DAT; ! SEE TABLE 4.3
            TYPE = COVARIANCE;
            NOBSERVATIONS = 250;
VARIABLE:   NAMES = MATHANX1-MATHANX4;
MODEL:      F1 BY MATHANX1* MATHANX2-MATHANX4 (1);
            F1@1;
```

This command file yields the following results. (For space considerations, we are commenting only on the output part pertaining to our concern with testing parameter restrictions here.)

```
THE MODEL ESTIMATION TERMINATED NORMALLY

Chi-Square Test of Model Fit

            Value                        10.461
            Degrees of Freedom                5
            P-Value                      0.0632
```

In order to test the TSEM now, given the plausibility of the MCT, as indicated above, we need to test the restrictions of identical units of measurement, i.e., the equality of the loadings of the four tests on the underlying latent factor. This test is accomplished as mentioned by subtracting from the chi-square value of the present restricted model (TSEM), viz., 10.461, that of the unrestricted model (MCT), viz., 1.459; see the pertinent output section for the first empirical example in Section 4.5 of Chapter 4. The resulting difference is $10.461 - 1.459 = 9.002$, which needs to be now judged for significance. To this end, as pointed out earlier, this difference is referred to as the chi-square distribution with $5 - 2 = 3$ degrees of freedom (the degrees of freedom for the MCT, i.e., single-factor model, are 2; see Chapter 4). This is because the imposed restrictions $b_1 = b_2 = b_3 = b_4$ on the four parameters in question (see the MCT definition earlier in this chapter) in fact involve only three nonredundant restrictions, e.g., $b_1 = b_2$, $b_2 = b_3$, and $b_3 = b_4$. That is, the restricted (TSEM) and unrestricted (MCT) models differ only in the added three parameters in the latter model, which are the unrestricted factor loadings beyond, say, that of the first measure (i.e., a free parameter in both models). Because the cutoff value of the chi-square distribution with 3 degrees of freedom is 7.81 (e.g., King & Minium, 2003), which is smaller than the above-found difference of 9.002, we conclude that the tested restrictions are not plausible. Hence, the TSEM model is not plausible either, because an integral part of it—the restriction $b_1 = b_2 = b_3 = b_4$—is sufficiently inconsistent with the analyzed data. Given this finding, we conclude that the MPT model is not plausible either, because it makes this empirically falsified assumption as well. We now present the remainder of the output for the TSEM model.

```
Chi-Square Test of Model Fit for the Baseline Model

            Value                       211.052
            Degrees of Freedom                6
            P-Value                      0.0000
```

```
CFI/TLI
              CFI                              0.973
              TLI                              0.968
Loglikelihood
              H0 Value                       -1351.948
              H1 Value                       -1346.717
Information Criteria
              Number of Free Parameters            5
              Akaike (AIC)                   2713.895
              Bayesian (BIC)                 2731.503
              Sample-Size Adjusted BIC       2715.652
              (n* = (n + 2) / 24)
RMSEA (Root Mean Square Error Of Approximation)
              Estimate                         0.066
              90 Percent C.I.                  0.000      0.123
              Probability RMSEA <= .05         0.264
SRMR (Standardized Root Mean Square Residual)
              Value                            0.072
MODEL RESULTS
                                                          Two-Tailed
                     Estimate      S.E.      Est./S.E.     P-Value
  F1        BY
     MATHANX1          0.671        0.041       16.466       0.000
     MATHANX2          0.671        0.041       16.466       0.000
     MATHANX3          0.671        0.041       16.466       0.000
     MATHANX4          0.671        0.041       16.466       0.000

  Variances
     F1                1.000        0.000      999.000     999.000

  Residual Variances
     MATHANX1          0.562        0.064        8.823       0.000
     MATHANX2          0.563        0.064        8.829       0.000
     MATHANX3          0.721        0.077        9.354       0.000
     MATHANX4          0.656        0.072        9.168       0.000
```

We conclude this Subsection 5.6.1 by noting that for the given data on the four mathematics anxiety tests (Table 4.3 in Chapter 4), the tenable model among the three CTT-based models discussed in this chapter is that of congeneric tests. Therefore, we can now say that it is plausible to assume the four tests to be measuring the same true score in different units of measurement.

5.6.2 Model Testing Through Restriction Testing

We note that if we had tested only the TSEM overall, because its chi-square value, pertinent *p*-value and RMSEA with its 90%-confidence interval were acceptable one might be willing to conclude that the TSEM was plausible. However, this would not be really a correct conclusion, as we have just found using the above more specialized approach—viz., testing the particular restrictions $b_1 = b_2 = b_3 = b_4$ that are characteristic of the TSEM and were found not to be plausible. The reason for these apparently contradictory results is that the test of fit of the TSEM is an overall (omnibus) test. That is, it gives information only about whether the entire true score equivalence model is plausible and not whether particular parts of it (like these restrictions) are so. However, our concern was with whether the restrictions themselves were correct—we already knew that the MCT was plausible. Hence, the correct testing approach was to test those restrictions rather than examine only the overall fit of the TSEM.

We also wish to stress a more general point here. Specifically, it is possible that an entire model is associated with plausible overall fit indexes and yet a part of it is incorrect (cf. Raykov & Marcoulides, 2006a). This would happen when the model fits very well in all remaining parts so that its overall fit indexes suggest it as a plausible means of data description and explanation. The example in the preceding Section 5.6.1 is very instructive in this respect. This is because it highlights the need to be concerned also with examining specific parts of an initially considered model. In some settings, these can be special restrictions—like those examined in the previous subsection—that are part of the overall model. Our discussion emphasizes the necessity to be concerned with evaluating for plausibility also parts of a model (i.e., local model fit), even when the whole model is found possible, not only to evaluate its overall fit to the analyzed data. In particular, we stress that if a part of a model under consideration is found not to be plausible (e.g., a set of parameter restrictions), then the entire model cannot be considered tenable for an analyzed data set, even if all its overall fit indexes may be deemed as acceptable (i.e., suggestive of 'good' overall fit).

5.6.3 Testing Error Variance Equality

If we now wish to test for equality the error variances of the four mathematics anxiety measures under consideration, in the unrestricted, plausible model—viz., the MCT (see Subsection 5.6.1)—we need only to add the restraint of these variances being equal to one another. To this end, we merely introduce as last the following line in the M*plus* input file for the MCT model:

```
MATHANX1-MATHANX4(1);
```

The effect of this line is setting the error variances of the four observed variables equal to one another, which is formally achieved by assigning to all of them the same parameter number symbol. Thus, the needed complete M*plus* file is as follows:

```
TITLE:       TESTING EQUAL ERROR VARIANCES
DATA:        FILE = TABLE4_3.DAT;
             TYPE = COVARIANCE;
             NOBSERVATIONS = 250;
VARIABLE:    NAMES = MATHANX1-MATHANX4;
MODEL:       F1 BY MATHANX1* MATHANX2-MATHANX4;
             F1@1;
             MATHANX1-MATHANX4(1);
```

We stress that one accomplishes setting the equality of error variances by stating the name of the observed variables they pertain to and adding the symbols '(1)' at the end of that line. This ensures that all four error variances are constrained to be the same. With this feature, the last command file furnishes the following results:

```
THE MODEL ESTIMATION TERMINATED NORMALLY

TESTS OF MODEL FIT

Chi-Square Test of Model Fit
            Value                          9.284
            Degrees of Freedom                 5
            P-Value                       0.0983
```

With the LRT approach used above, the test statistic for the hypothesis of equal error variances is the difference in the chi-square values of this model and of the MCT, i.e., $9.284 - 1.459 = 7.824$, and the corresponding associated degrees of freedom are $5 - 2 = 3$. Thus, the test statistic for the equality of error variances is significant (as mentioned above, the relevant cutoff value is 7.81). We conclude that there is evidence in the analyzed data that warrants rejection of the claim that the four tests are associated with equal precision (error variances). Because with this our concerns here are responded to, we do not present the remainder of the output associated with the last-fitted model (the MCT with equal error variances).

We note in passing that if we had found earlier that the TSEM was plausible, we would have had to add in it—rather than in the MCT model as in this subsection—the restriction of equal error variances when testing the latter constraint. Software-wise, we would have had to do that by adding the line MATHANX1—MATHANX4 (2) as a last line in the TSEM command file. Given the already-imposed restriction in that model on the b parameters, we would have had to assign a different parameter symbol or number at the end of this command line, e.g., 2, to the error variances (which obviously need not be equal to the factor loadings that are constrained for equality in the TSEM).

By way of summary of all analyses conducted in this Section 5.6, the most parsimonious, tenable model for the four mathematics anxiety tests considered is the model of congeneric tests. Accordingly, these four tests measure a single construct with different units of measurement and precision (error variances).

In conclusion of this chapter, we note that it is also possible to consider slightly more general CTT-based models than the ones we were concerned with here. Those are the so-called model of *essentially parallel measures* and model of *essentially tau-equivalent measures* (e.g., Lord & Novick, 1968). They differ from the corresponding ones in this chapter by additionally considering the d parameters (intercept parameters) of the MPT and similarly introducing them in the TSEM. Those slightly more general models will not be of concern to us, however, until we start discussing item response theory (Chapters 10 and 11). The reason is that, until then, without limitation of generality for the aims of the pertinent discussions, these d parameters can be assumed to be zero and in addition will not be of relevance for us. Hence, at this point, we limit our discussion of those more general models merely to their mentioning.

6

Reliability

In the previous chapter, we discussed issues pertaining to measurement error in the behavioral and social sciences. However, none of our discussion was focused on means of quantifying its impact on observed scores. We will address this important problem in the present chapter that draws substantially on classical test theory (CTT) as well as the developments and notation introduced in Chapter 5. Before we commence, we note that the entire discussion in the present chapter will be at the population level, whereas matters pertaining to estimation of involved parameters will be addressed in the next chapter.

6.1 Reliability Index and Reliability Coefficient

Whenever conducting measurement in social and behavioral research, we are typically interested in the true score but have available only the observed score in which the former is entangled with the error score, as is seen from the familiar CTT equation $X = T + E$ (see Chapter 5). Thereby, we have (in general) no way of disconfounding true score from error score, and the observed individual scores are all we have at our disposal with regard to information about the true scores.

6.1.1 Definitions and Implications

Given our interest in the true score, T, the natural question is how much information about it is indeed contained in the observed score X? More specifically, how strongly (or weakly) are observed scores related to the true scores of a group of individuals on a given test? This question is addressed by the so-called reliability index. For a measure under consideration, we can define the reliability index as the correlation between its true score, T, and observed score, X, i.e., as the correlation coefficient $\rho_{X,T}$.

We emphasize that because a correlation coefficient is defined only when each of the two involved variables has nonzero variance (see Chapter 2), we can speak of a reliability index only if there are individual differences both in the observed scores and in the true scores on a measure of concern. (As mentioned before, we use in this book the notion of individual differences as synonymous with variance; e.g., Chapter 2.) Hence, whenever we use this definition of reliability index as a correlation coefficient, we will presume that both observed score and true score have nonvanishing variances, i.e., $\sigma_T \neq 0$ and $\sigma_X \neq 0$. (We note that this is a fairly mild assumption in empirical research, and we will extend this definition shortly to cover the case $\sigma_T = 0$.)

From the formal definition of correlation coefficient as the ratio of covariance to the product of the standard deviations of the variables participating in it—in this case X and T—and our discussion of CTT in Chapter 5, it follows that when the reliability index exists, it can be reexpressed as

$$\rho_{X,T} = Corr(X,T) = \frac{Cov(X,T)}{\sqrt{Var(X)Var(T)}} = \frac{Cov(T+E,T)}{\sqrt{Var(X)Var(T)}}$$

$$= \frac{Var(T)}{\sqrt{Var(X)Var(T)}} = \sqrt{\frac{Var(T)}{Var(X)}} = \sqrt{\frac{\sigma_T^2}{\sigma_X^2}} = \frac{\sigma_T}{\sigma_X}, \tag{6.1}$$

whereby as usual positive square roots are taken (see notation used in Chapter 5 and recall that $\sigma_T \neq 0$ is assumed in order for $\rho_{X,T}$ to exist, hence σ_T can be canceled from the numerator and denominator at the beginning of the second line of (6.1)). That is, the reliability index is then equal to the ratio of the true score to observed score standard deviations. We can now formally extend the definition of reliability index by setting the latter in addition equal to 0 if there are no true individual differences, i.e., when $\sigma_T = 0$ or, in other words, when all subjects have the same true score.

When it comes to interpreting a correlation coefficient, in this case the reliability index, it is best done by examining its square; this is because in order to interpret readily the magnitude of a correlation, one typically squares it (e.g., King & Minium, 2003). This observation leads us to another important psychometric index, the reliability coefficient, denoted ρ_X. We can define the reliability coefficient as the squared reliability index, i.e.,

$$\rho_X = \rho_{X,T}^2. \tag{6.2}$$

(As an aside, in a considerable part of the literature related to psychometric theory and its applications, the notation ρ_{XX} is frequently found; e.g., Allen and Yen [1979]. However, we see no reason for using the latter notation here in lieu of ρ_X.)

Equation (6.2) defines the reliability coefficient in case there are individual differences on both the true score and the observed score, i.e., when $\sigma_T \neq 0$ and $\sigma_X \neq 0$. With Equation (6.1) in mind, it is readily seen that when $\sigma_T \neq 0$ also

$$\rho_X = \frac{\sigma_T^2}{\sigma_X^2} \tag{6.3}$$

holds, i.e., the reliability coefficient equals the ratio of true variance to observed variance. We can extend the definition in Equation (6.2) also to the case of no true individual differences, i.e., when $\sigma_T = 0$, by defining the reliability coefficient then as $\rho_X = 0$. We stress that although with these extensions the reliability index and coefficient are defined also when there are no true individual differences, none of them is defined in case there are no observed individual differences, i.e., when $\sigma_X = 0$. For this reason, and to avoid trivial situations (that would be very rare if at all to be found in common empirical social or behavioral research in meaningful settings), we will assume throughout the rest of this book that $\sigma_X \neq 0$ on any given observed measure X of interest.

In the remainder of this text, we will adopt this extended definition of the reliability coefficient in Equation (6.3) as the ratio of true score variance to observed score variance. Furthermore, because the concept of reliability index is relatively rarely used in the literature, whereas its square—the reliability coefficient—is mostly meant when reference to 'reliability' is made, we will employ the term 'reliability' whenever talking about the reliability coefficient.

From Equation (6.2) we see that reliability equals the R^2-index when predicting true score from observed score (cf., e.g., Bollen, 1989). This is a particularly relevant interpretation of reliability and one that we find to be rather revealing, because it shows reliability as an important and useful index of the strength of (linear) relationship between true score and observed score. A closely related interpretation of reliability follows from Equation (6.3), viz., as the percentage of observed variance that is due to true individual differences (variance; this interpretation holds after multiplying reliability by 100%). That is, reliability gives us the degree to which observed individual differences are indicative of true individual differences. In other words, reliability tells us how much of the differences in observed scores for a given measure are due to differences on the latent dimension of actual interest. Equation (6.2) also implies that reliability is the R^2-index associated with the regression using observed score as dependent variable and true score as predictor, which, as is well-known, is the same R^2-index as that associated with the regression model where true score is regressed on observed score (e.g., King & Minium, 2003).

From this discussion, it follows that reliability bears a distinct relationship to the predictive power with which one can predict observed score from true score. As is well-known from introductory statistics textbooks, error of prediction incurred thereby is the product of dependent variable variance and the square-rooted complement to 1 of the squared correlation between the two variables involved (e.g., Agresti & Finlay, 2009). Hence, the prediction error is here $\sigma_X\sqrt{1-\rho_{X,T}^2} = \sigma_X\sqrt{1-\rho_X}$. Therefore, this prediction error increases with diminishing reliability, and conversely decreases with increasing reliability, for fixed observed variance. We will return to this issue later in the chapter. Before we move on, however, let us also note that by definition, reliability is an 'overall' measure and thus does not tell how well one measures given individuals, for example, those with particular true scores (e.g., high, low, or medium true scores).

6.1.2 Reliability and Relationships Between Parallel Tests

Consider two parallel tests (measures) whose observed scores are denoted X_1 and X_2. The CTT equation for either of them provides their decomposition into true scores and error scores: $X_1 = T_1 + E_1$ and $X_2 = T_2 + E_2$. According to the pertinent definition in Chapter 5, the parallelism of these measures means that (a) $T_1 = T_2 = T$, say (for the sake of notation), and (b) $Var(E_1) = Var(E_2)$. Let us denote this common variance by σ_E^2, say. Hence, given the uncorrelatedness of true score and error score (Chapter 5), it follows that the variance of the two tests is

$$Var(X_1) = Var(T) + \sigma_E^2 = Var(X_2) = \sigma_X^2, \tag{6.4}$$

that is, the observed variance of two parallel tests is the same, just like their true variance is the same and their error variance is the same (for the two measures). Hence, the reliability of each of these two parallel tests is

$$\frac{Var(T_i)}{Var(X_i)} = \frac{\sigma_{T_i}^2}{\sigma_{X_i}^2} = \frac{\sigma_T^2}{\sigma_X^2} = \rho, \tag{6.5}$$

that is, two parallel tests have the same reliability. Therefore, their correlation is (see Chapter 2)

$$\rho_{X_1,X_2} = \frac{Cov(X_1, X_2)}{\sqrt{Var(X_1)Var(X_2)}} = \frac{Cov(T + E_1, T + E_2)}{\sqrt{Var(T + E_1)Var(T + E_2)}}$$

$$= \frac{Var(T)}{Var(X_1)} = \frac{Var(T)}{Var(X_2)} = \frac{\sigma_T^2}{\sigma_X^2} = \rho. \tag{6.6}$$

Hence, the correlation of a pair of parallel tests (measures) equals the reliability of either of them. Because the square of this correlation, ρ_{X_1,X_2}^2, is the R^2-index associated with the linear regression of any of these tests on the other (e.g., King & Minium, 2003), it follows that the squared reliability, ρ_X^2, is the proportion of variance in any of a pair of parallel tests that is explained then in terms of the variance in the other test.

We reiterate that all developments so far in this chapter have been at the population level and in particular also of theoretical nature. Therefore, because the definition of reliability is given in terms of population quantities, with the true variance σ_T^2 in particular being unknown, it follows that we cannot really determine reliability in a given empirical setting, as we do not know these quantities. (This is of course because we do not have observations of the individual true scores, even if an entire population were to be available for study.) In the next chapter, we will be concerned with procedures for estimation of reliability from empirical data sets.

6.2 Reliability of a Composite

As we indicated already in Chapter 1, most of the time in behavioral and social research, we are interested in composites, e.g., tests, scales, self-reports, questionnaires, or inventories consisting of several components. The reason is that these components are constructed so as to provide multiple converging pieces of information about the underlying latent construct being studied. Thereby, we are frequently concerned with sum scores (composite scores) on a set of components, often called scale scores or test scores, which accumulate or integrate these pieces of information. How can we evaluate that scale's reliability, also frequently referred to as composite reliability (test reliability)? Perhaps there is a relationship between composite reliability and the reliability coefficients of its components? Before we consider this issue in a more general context, we will look at a relatively simple setting that was first attended to in detail almost a century ago.

6.2.1 The Spearman-Brown Formula

Suppose a researcher has administered two parallel tests X_1 and X_2 to individuals from a population under investigation. The researcher computes then a composite score for each subject, denoted $X = X_1 + X_2$, in an attempt to obtain a more informative measure of an underlying latent dimension evaluated by X_1 and X_2. (For notational simplicity, the individual subindex that could be attached to these measures is dropped.) How reliable is this composite X, and how does its reliability relate to that of the components X_1 and X_2? This question can be answered with the so-called Spearman-Brown formula. We note in passing that although we know that the reliability of either X_1 or X_2 is just the correlation between them, $Corr(X_1, X_2)$, the previous query is about the reliability of their sum, not the individual measures.

Why would this composite score X, and in general a composite (sum score) of more than two measures, be of interest? As we know, each of these measures is only a fallible proxy of their common underlying true score that we are actually interested in. Thus, by combining the information about that common true score, e.g., by adding the measures, we are hoping to obtain a more dependable score informing about that true score of interest.

From a more general perspective, assume that the researcher has access to $p \geq 2$ parallel tests $X_1, X_2, ..., X_p$ and forms the composite $X = X_1 + X_2 + \cdots + X_p$. As discussed in the previous section, all these tests have the same reliability. If we knew the reliability of any of these p components, how could we determine the reliability of their composite X? To answer this question, first we recall from Chapter 2 that the variance of the composite score relates to that of the components and their covariances as follows:

$$Var(X) = Var(X_1) + \cdots + Var(X_p) + 2\sum_{i<j} Cov(X_i, X_j).$$

Furthermore, as we saw in the preceding section, each test in a set of parallel measures has the same variance that we can denote here by σ^2. In addition, in that section we also saw that the covariance of any two parallel tests equals the variance of the true score of either of them and hence is also constant across tests (as they are parallel); let us denote this variance σ_t^2. If ρ stands for the reliability of any of the parallel tests, obviously the equality $\sigma_t^2 = \rho\,\sigma^2$ holds, which follows from the definition of reliability as the ratio of true to observed variance. Then the previous composite variance equation entails (e.g., Crocker & Algina, 1986)

$$Var(X) = p\sigma^2 + p(p-1)\rho\,\sigma^2 = p\sigma^2[1 + (p-1)\rho].$$

Next, if T denotes the true score of the composite X, then in the same way one can show that

$$Var(T) = p\sigma_t^2 + p(p-1)\sigma_t^2 = p^2\sigma_t^2.$$

Therefore, dividing the expression in the right-hand side of the previous equation by that of the one preceding it, we obtain that

$$\rho_X = \frac{Var(T)}{Var(X)} = \frac{p\rho}{1 + (p-1)\rho} \tag{6.7}$$

is the reliability of the composite $X = X_1 + X_2 + \cdots + X_p$.

Equation (6.7) represents the so-called Spearman-Brown prophecy formula. It expresses the reliability of a composite of a set of p ($p > 1$) parallel tests as a nonlinear function of the reliability of any of them (that have all the same reliability, ρ, as noted earlier). Thus, if we knew the reliability of any member of a set of parallel tests, and their number, Equation (6.7) furnishes the reliability of the sum of these tests and hence an answer to our earlier question about their composite reliability.

We stress that Equation (6.7) provides composite reliability only for the case of parallel tests. Whether a set of p measures is parallel can be tested in the way we described in Chapter 5, if $p > 2$. The test of parallelism then involves comparing the fit indices of the parallel measure and congeneric measure models. If $p = 3$, this congeneric model is saturated, and one can test in this way each of the two assumptions underlying the model for parallel measures, viz., (a) identity of factor loadings and (b) identity of error variances. (In case $p = 1$, the question about parallel tests is obviously meaningless.)

6.2.2 Coefficient Alpha

The Spearman-Brown formula (6.7) requires that the components $X_1, X_2, ..., X_p$ be parallel. In many empirical settings in various behavioral and social research areas, however, it is very difficult to construct even two parallel measures, let alone a larger number of such tests. Instead of parallel tests, one may have access to components with a more general relationship to one another, which are not parallel. How could one then estimate the reliability of their composite $X = X_1 + X_2 + \cdots + X_p$?

If the components X_i ($i = 1, ..., p$) are at least true score equivalent (if not parallel), a popular index that allows one to evaluate reliability is Cronbach's coefficient alpha (referred to as 'alpha', or just α, in the rest of this and following chapters):

$$\alpha = \frac{p}{p-1}\left[1 - \frac{\sum_{i=1}^{p} Var(X_i)}{Var(X)}\right]. \tag{6.8}$$

Simple algebra using relationships from Chapter 2 leads from Equation (6.8) to the following expression for alpha:

$$\alpha = \frac{p}{p-1} \cdot \frac{\sum_{i \neq j} Cov(X_i, X_j)}{Var(X)}. \tag{6.9}$$

From Equation (6.9), one sees that α can be approximately interpreted as 'average' inter-item covariance, whereby 'average' means 'per unit of composite variance'. Coefficient alpha goes back at least to work by Cronbach (1951) and bears a distinct relationship to that by Guttman (1945; cf. McDonald, 1999).

The basis of the popularity of α across the behavioral and social disciplines is the fact that if (a) the set of components $X_1, X_2, ..., X_p$ are true score equivalent (or even parallel) and (b) the error scores $E_1, E_2, ..., E_p$ are uncorrelated, i.e., $Cov(E_i, E_j) = 0$ for $i \neq j$ ($1 \leq i, j \leq p$), then

$$\alpha = \rho_X \tag{6.10}$$

(e.g., Novick & Lewis, 1967). Because α equals reliability of a composite (overall sum score) for a set of true score equivalent tests with unrelated error scores, use of alpha in those cases allows one through only a single administration of the components $X_1, X_2, ..., X_p$ to determine composite reliability, i.e., the reliability of the composite or test consisting of these components. Thus, in such empirical settings, it is very convenient to apply α for purposes of reliability estimation for the composite. We stress that Equation (6.10) is valid only under certain conditions—at least true score equivalent components (or parallel components) and no error correlations. Hence, (6.10) does not really represent the general relationship between α and composite reliability. We turn next to this important topic for purposes of test construction.

6.3 Relationships of Coefficient Alpha to Composite Reliability

In the general case, the relationship of alpha to composite reliability (scale, test reliability) is more complex and requires considering two complementary situations—correlated errors versus uncorrelated error scores of the scale or test components—that are also exhaustive.

6.3.1 Uncorrelated Errors

When component errors are unrelated to one another (uncorrelated), coefficient alpha cannot be higher than composite reliability, as shown in Novick and Lewis (1967). This feature is frequently referred to as alpha being a 'lower bound of reliability'. We stress that this property holds only with uncorrelated errors. In those cases, however, alpha can markedly underestimate composite reliability (for further discussion of the underpinnings of this relationship, see, e.g., Raykov, 1997, 2001a).

When the set of components (a) is unidimensional (i.e., congeneric), (b) is with uncorrelated errors, and (c) has uniformly high loadings on the underlying true score (say, in excess of .6 on a 0-1 metric), then α is not underestimating by much composite reliability. Specifically, under those circumstances (a) through (c), in many practical settings α can be fairly close to composite reliability (Raykov, 1997). Settings with uniformly high loadings are typical primarily of advanced stages in the process of test construction and development, however, and not likely in its early phases. In these phases, α can markedly underestimate composite reliability (e.g., Raykov, 2001b). Then interval estimation (standard error and confidence interval for α) obtained with existing methods cannot be generally trusted, because they are interval estimates of a parameter, α, that is possibly quite far from the one of actual concern, ρ_X. In particular, in those same cases, confidence intervals of alpha will not have the required (nominal) coverage rate with respect to the reliability coefficient of relevance and thus may be seriously misleading.

More generally, the qualitative relationship between alpha and composite reliability was studied in detail in Novick and Lewis (1967). Accordingly, with uncorrelated error scores—whether the components are unidimensional or not (i.e., whether one or more true scores underlie performance on them)—important relationships were demonstrated in their instructive paper. As shown in that paper, (a) alpha is never larger than composite reliability, and (b) alpha equals composite reliability if and only if the components are true score equivalent, i.e., measure the same underlying true score in the same units of measurement (see Chapter 5). Novick and Lewis (1967) did not quantify, however, the relationship between alpha and composite reliability (with uncorrelated errors). Their quantitative relationship, in the unidimensionality case with uncorrelated errors, was dealt with in Raykov (1997). A summary of the developments in the latter paper was presented in the preceding paragraph. This concludes our consideration of the case of uncorrelated measurement errors for a set of considered scale (test, instrument) components, and we now move on to the case of correlated errors.

6.3.2 Correlated Errors

In such settings, according to a considerable body of research that goes back at least to the early 1970s (e.g., Zimmerman, 1972; see also Maxwell, 1968), alpha can be higher, or alternatively lower, than composite reliability. Which of the two would apply depends on underlying parameter relationships. This statement covers both unidimensional and multidimensional tests or composites, i.e., single as well as at least two true scores (latent factors) underlying subject performance on the composite (e.g., Raykov, 1998b, 2001a).

We stress that with correlated errors the underestimation feature of alpha does not generally hold. Hence, alpha can safely be considered a lower bound of composite reliability only when error scores are uncorrelated. If they are correlated, however, alpha may or may not be a lower bound of composite reliability, regardless of the number of underlying true scores, i.e., irrespective of the dimensionality of the multiple-component measuring instrument under consideration. In fact, under those circumstances alpha may as well be an 'upper bound of reliability'. Thus, the widely circulated reference to coefficient alpha as a lower bound of reliability is not correct if to be interpreted as implying to hold also in the correlated error case (see the preceding Subsection 6.3.1 for a discussion of when it holds). We will be concerned in the next chapter with further aspects of the relationship between alpha and test (scale, composite) reliability, specifically as they pertain to the process of instrument development and construction.

6.4 The Standard Error of Measurement

We emphasized earlier in this book that the true score is in general confounded with error score in the observed score on a given test or measure. Hence, looking at the observed score, X, we cannot determine either the true score T or the error score E, even in cases when one may have measured an entire population under study (and even if all subjects had the same true, error, and observed scores, i.e., if there were no individual differences on any of these three scores). However, we could describe the variability of observed score around the true score, and we could do this for each studied person, within the CTT framework.

To this end, we recall the definition of true score for a given test and individual as the mean (i.e., expectation) of the associated propensity distribution—the distribution of very many measurements of the same individual with the same test under the same conditions (including fixed time). This distribution, like any other (for which, strictly speaking, variance exists), has a standard deviation. This standard deviation is closely related to a useful index of quality of measurement, the so-called standard error of measurement (SEM). We define the SEM as the average, across persons, of the standard deviations of the individual propensity distributions on a measure under consideration.

If we assume that the standard deviation of the individual propensity distributions is the same across subjects, we can obtain a useful result about the SEM. (We make this assumption for the rest of the current Section 6.4, unless otherwise indicated.) To this end, first we note that based on the CTT decomposition $X = T + E$ for a given subject and measure, it follows that SEM $= \sqrt{Var(E)}$, i.e., SEM $= \sigma_E$ in the alternative (simpler symbolically) nota-tion. This is because for that person the propensity distribution on the measure is the error distribution shifted by T units to the right or left (depending on the sign of T) from the zero mean of the latter distribution. Furthermore, we note that from the CTT equation $X = T + E$ it follows that

$$Var(X) = Var(T) + Var(E), \qquad (6.11)$$

or in the alternative (simpler) notation

$$\sigma_X^2 = \sigma_T^2 + \sigma_E^2; \qquad (6.12)$$

that is, observed individual differences are the sum of true individual differences and those in the error scores. Moreover, with (6.12), the definition of reliability entails

$$\rho_X = \frac{\sigma_T^2}{\sigma_X^2} = \frac{\sigma_X^2 - \sigma_E^2}{\sigma_X^2} = 1 - \frac{\sigma_E^2}{\sigma_X^2}. \qquad (6.13)$$

Equation (6.13) shows that reliability is the complement to 1 of the ratio of error variance to observed variance. From the beginning and last part of Equation (6.13), simple algebra leads to

$$\sigma_E = \sigma_X \sqrt{1 - \rho_X} \qquad (6.14)$$

(whereby the positive root is taken). Hence, the standard error of measurement depends on (a) observed variability (standard deviation of recorded or manifest score) and (b) reli-ability. At the same time, Equation (6.14) also expresses the error involved in predicting the observed score from the true score (prediction error), as mentioned earlier in this chapter, which results from simple linear regression considerations (e.g., Agresti & Finlay, 2009).

In many empirical settings, it will be possible to assume that the error score (i.e., the random error of measurement) is normally distributed. This may be justified by the obser-vation that the random error of measurement is the combined effect of many impacts unrelated to the underlying construct of interest and use of the central limit theorem (e.g., King & Minium, 2003; cf. McDonald, 1999). Then from the properties of the normal distribution, considering the true scores as given, it follows that approximately two thirds of subjects' observed scores in a studied group can be expected to lie within one SEM from their true score, which represents the means of the individual propensity distributions; similarly, approximately 95% of them can be expected to lie within two SEMs from their true score. (One obviously cannot say which two thirds and which 95%, respectively, these are from the studied group of subjects.) This statement can also be 'reversed', con-sidering the individuals' observed scores as given (after they have been observed), to say that approximately two thirds of the individual true scores can be expected to lie within one SEM from their observed score, and roughly 95% of these true scores to lie within two SEMs from their observed score (again, not knowing which these proportions actually are, in terms of individuals included in them). This is clearly not a very precise statement about a true score, unless of course the SEM is very small, which in practice will probably rarely be the case.

The discussion in the previous paragraph also serves to remind us that the observed score is only a fallible and imprecise indicator of the true score. Furthermore, we note that this discussion was based on the assumption of normality of observed scores as well as of identical standard deviations of the individual propensity distributions. Even though SEM can also be informative when this identity assumption is not fulfilled, it will be then not as good a descriptor of error-induced variability in an arbitrarily chosen observed score (but will instead be much better in this regard for an 'average' individual's observed score).

In conclusion of this section and chapter, we would like to note that the assumption of identical standard deviation of the individual propensity distributions has received unduly strong criticism in some literature on alternative approaches to test theory. In actual fact, this assumption is at least akin to the conventional assumption of equal variability of the individual error terms in the general linear model $\underline{y} = Z\,\beta + \underline{\varepsilon}$ for a given measure administered to a group of, say, N subjects, regardless of the value of the predictor(s) collected in the 'design' matrix Z (e.g., Agresti & Finlay, 2009). Specifically, the classical regression (ordinary least squares, or OLS, regression) assumes that the individual random variables of error terms, ε_i (whose vector is ε in the equation of the general linear model), have all the same variance ($i = 1, \ldots, N$). The assumption of identical error standard deviation across individuals is restrictive, like any assumption is, yet this is due to the particular parameterization pursued in CTT applications when discussing error-related concepts. In some sense, therefore, one can say that this assumption is the price one pays in such applications for adopting the CTT decomposition that is effectively assumption free (for a given test or measure). We emphasize that the fundamental CTT decomposition/equation (5.1) (see Chapter 5) does not make the assumption of equal error variances across subjects but instead only assumes the existence of the propensity distribution mean (which can be viewed as fulfilled in most if not all behavioral and social research; e.g., Lord & Novick, 1968).

From a more general perspective, analytic approaches based on statistical methods usually make some assumptions in order to make headway, and so this can be expected to be the case also with any test theory framework. Unlike other measurement frameworks that make assumptions to 'get started', e.g., of a particular model for a given measure (such as the logistic or probit models; see Chapters 10 and 11), within the framework of CTT one needs only to make the assumption of identity of error standard deviation (in addition to that of existence of the propensity distribution mean for a measure under consideration) when discussing issues pertaining to reliability or standard error of measurement. That is, an assumption needs to be adopted in order to make headway then, and when using CTT for these aims, it is done at this junction (for the purpose of discussing error-related concepts like reliability and SEM). In a similar way, in some alternative test theories, another assumption is in fact adopted at the moment a particular item characteristic curve—e.g., logistic or probit curve—is assumed.

7

Procedures for Estimating Reliability

The preceding chapter discussed a psychometric quality index quantifying the impact of error on obtained test scores, the reliability coefficient. Having defined it as the ratio of true score to observed score variance (assuming the latter being nonzero), one readily sees that in empirical research we cannot determine reliability precisely even if we have studied an entire population of interest. This is because of the fact that unlike observed variability, the variance of the true scores is not obtainable then. Alternatively, because the correlation between two parallel measures equals reliability, one could determine their common reliability through correlating them (if, of course, population data were available). However, the problem then is that constructing equivalent measures is in general a rather difficult task in empirical behavioral and social research, as indicated earlier, and in fact it is very difficult to ensure that two given measures are truly parallel.

Rather than attempting to determine reliability, we can instead estimate it using data from a representative sample of individuals from a population under investigation. This chapter deals with both traditional and more recent approaches to reliability estimation. Throughout the chapter, we will place a caret on the estimated reliability coefficient from a given sample and/or related parameters or quantities to emphasize that they are not the population quantities that were of primary concern in the preceding chapter but rather their empirical estimators (estimates).

7.1 Traditional Methods for Reliability Estimation

These methods were first developed several decades ago and can be classified into two groups depending on the number of measure administrations needed (cf. Crocker & Algina, 1986).

7.1.1 Procedures With Two Test Administrations

7.1.1.1 Alternate Form Method

This approach requires constructing two similar forms of a test or measure, denoted A and B, and administering both of them to the same sample, typically within a short period of time. Thereby, to counterbalance order of presentation, half of the sample receives the forms in the order first A then B, whereas the other half receives them in the order first B and then A. The correlation between the scores on form A and form B is called coefficient of equivalence. The higher the coefficient of equivalence, the more confident a researcher can be that scores from the different forms can be used interchangeably. It is usually required that any test with multiple forms should be associated with some evidence of their equivalence. Although there are no rules of thumb, coefficients in excess of at least .80, and preferably .90, would be viewed as needed before one could place trust in interchangeably using scores from two or more forms.

In empirical research the coefficient of equivalence may be interpreted as an estimate of reliability, if it is high and the observed means, standard deviations, and standard errors of measurement are very close on both forms. That is, under these assumptions, a reliability estimate may be obtained with the alternate form method as

$$\hat{\rho}_{X,af} = Corr(X_A, X_B),$$ (7.1)

where X_A and X_B denote the individual scores on form A and form B, respectively, and the second subindex 'af' that is attached to the reliability symbol signals that this estimate results from using the alternate form method. (In this chapter, we often use a second subscript to the reliability estimate to designate the method it is obtained with.)

How good is the coefficient of equivalence as an index (estimate) informing about reliability, and what are the factors that affect its quality in this regard? Sources of error that affect the coefficient of equivalence are primarily those resulting from differences in content of the test forms. Hence, this method of reliability estimation is mostly sensitive to (in the sense of being adversely impacted by) effects of differences in what makes up the test forms. For this reason, the alternate form reliability estimate is more trustworthy when there are fewer discrepancies in content across the two forms and could generally be better used as a coefficient of equivalence.

7.1.1.2 Test–Retest Method

In some situations, a single form of a test of interest may be deemed sufficient, but one is interested in the degree to which subjects' performance is repeatable, i.e., how consistent their test scores are. This consistency is indexed by the correlation coefficient of two assessments carried out with the test, which are typically referred to as test and retest. Obviously the measurement errors of primary relevance and adversely affecting this coefficient are the fluctuations of subjects' observed scores around their true scores due to temporary changes in their state. The correlation of the two assessments may then be considered an estimate of test (instrument, scale) reliability and is—perhaps more appropriately—also called coefficient of stability. That is, a reliability estimate that could be obtained with the test–retest method is

$$\hat{\rho}_{X,tr} = Corr(X_t, X_r),$$ (7.2)

where the subindex 'tr' in the left-hand side signals that this estimate results with the test–retest method, whereas the subindexes in the right-hand side indicate test scores at first ('test') and second ('retest') assessment.

Critical factors contributing to the magnitude of this coefficient of stability are usually the length of time elapsing between the two assessments, sometimes the subject's age, and in particular the nature of the underlying attribute being evaluated. Regarding time interval, there is no single answer as to what is its optimal length in order to obtain a 'good' reliability estimate in the coefficient of stability. Evidently, the interval needs to be long enough in order to minimize memory, practice, or learning effects, yet on the other hand it should not be so long as to allow maturational developments or historical changes to affect subjects' true scores. In general, different time periods may lead to different test–retest (stability) coefficient estimates.

This brings us to a related point that needs to be stressed. If a researcher suspects that the studied trait (attitude, ability, construct) changes with time, and specifically across the time interval between planned test and retest assessments, the so-obtained correlation coefficient (stability coefficient) cannot in general be considered a dependable estimate of reliability of the instrument in question. In addition, effects of memory, practice, learning, boredom, sensitization, or any other consequences of the measurement at first assessment may deflate the critical correlation coefficient of test and retest, thus leading to an inaccurate estimate of reliability as obtained in this coefficient. Therefore, when the test–retest method is considered for use as a means of reliability estimation, lack of these types of adverse effects on it should be justified before one can place some trust in the resulting reliability estimate, which in general could be better used as a coefficient of stability of the pertinent scale score over time.

7.1.1.3 Test–Retest With Alternate Forms

It is possible to combine the reliability estimation procedures outlined so far, whereby at test assessment one of the forms is administered while at retest its alternate form is used. In addition, it will be desirable to counterbalance the order of presentation—e.g., administer form A first then form B to a random half of the sample and administer the two forms in reverse order to the other half of the sample. The correlation coefficient between the two forms, which is called coefficient of stability and equivalence, may then be considered an estimate of reliability of any of these test forms (instrument in question):

$$\hat{\rho}_{X,traf} = Corr(X_{tA}, X_{rB}),$$
(7.3)

where the subindex 'traf' signals that this is a reliability estimate resulting from the test–retest method with an alternate form used at retest.

This discussion suggests that the magnitude of the estimated coefficient in Equation (7.3) can be adversely affected by (a) errors of measurement due to content discrepancies of the two forms (differences in content) as well as (b) all above indicated changes in subjects' performance over the time period elapsed between the two assessments. That is, the quality of the resulting reliability estimate is affected by all types of error indicated earlier in this section that pertain to the alternate form and test–retest procedures (see Subsections 7.1.1.1 and 7.1.1.2), which could thus be better used in general as a coefficient of equivalence or stability over time of the observed test score.

We would like to stress that the left-hand sides of Equations (7.1) through (7.3) are in general different and hence furnish different reliability estimates because different scores participate in their right-hand sides and in addition different periods of time may elapse between the assessments involved. These differences result in the way these procedures are defined. Furthermore, any estimate in Equations (7.1) through (7.3) is only as good as the extent to which the errors have been minimized, which it is sensitive to and adversely affected by. Hence, in some situations only one or two of these estimates may be trustworthy (to a certain degree); in others possibly none is trustworthy.

We similarly wish to underscore that for none of the three reliability estimates (methods) covered so far is there a readily applicable procedure available that would allow one to obtain a confidence interval for reliability. Hence, this interval estimation—which in its own right is at least as important as point estimation (e.g., Wilkinson & The Task Force on Statistical Inference, 1999)—is not easily available with any of these three methods requiring two test administrations. Furthermore, each procedure furnishes a coefficient that is an approximation to reliability even if an entire population were to be available for study. Thus, in empirical research each coefficient discussed above presents an estimate of an approximation of reliability to begin with, which estimate in addition is affected by the sampling error in the analyzed data that is in effect during its actual empirical estimation.

In conclusion of this section, we emphasize that each of the three methods discussed so far yields in the end a 'good' reliability estimate only under practically very restrictive conditions in order to minimize if not eliminate the sources of bias that it is sensitive to, as pointed out above. Similarly, for none of these three methods has there been a demonstration that it yields statistically optimal estimates of reliability, a rather important issue that we attend to later in this chapter. Moreover, as indicated, the discussed methods yield in general different estimates of reliability, with no hint as to which could be preferable if at all and on what grounds. All these limitations decrease substantially the utility and value in contemporary empirical research of the discussed traditional reliability estimation procedures with two test administrations (cf. McDonald, 1999). These limitations also indirectly contribute to enhancing the popularity of some of the alternative reliability estimation methods that we discuss in the remainder of this chapter.

7.1.2 Procedures Requiring a Single Test Administration

In many empirical situations, a researcher may have access only to results from a single administration of a given test or scale. In a majority of diagnostic or academic aptitude measurement settings, for example, only one administration is envisaged, meaningful, relevant, or possible. A particular mental state that needs to be evaluated in a clinical context may be of interest only at a given instance. Also, knowledge in a certain school curriculum subject may need to be evaluated only at a given point in the teaching process in the academic year.

Most measuring instruments in these and many similar settings consist of multiple components that each highlight a particular side (aspect) of a focused, usually multifaceted ability, attribute, trait, or attitude. These instruments, such as tests, scales, inventories, questionnaires, self-reports, or test batteries, are typically developed with the intention to yield an overall assessment (overall score) of an underlying latent dimension by accumulating information about various aspects of it across their components, typically via summation. (More complex arrangements are also possible, as mentioned earlier, but currently not often used in applications and will not be of concern in this chapter.) In such situations, procedures for reliability estimation that capitalize on the interrelationships among the instrument components are used. There are two classes of methods that allow reliability estimation then, which we discuss next.

7.1.2.1 Split-Half Method

With this method, a researcher administers first the multiple-component instrument (test, scale) to a given group of individuals, but before proceeding further he or she splits the set of its components (items) into two groups, called subtests or split halves. This splitting can be done for instance in a random fashion, with the intention to create two halves of the original test that are as similar as possible. As another possibility, one can assign all odd-numbered components into half 1 and all even-numbered ones into half 2. Alternatively, one can do this after first rank ordering the items in terms of difficulty (frequency of correct response; Chapter 4) and then picking every other into one of the halves and the remaining items into the other half or by assigning components so that the resulting halves are 'matched' in content as well as possible. (More sophisticated methods for obtaining split halves are also possible, but we will not be concerned with them because of a consequential limitation of the general approach using split halves, which is highlighted below.)

Once this split is done, the two halves are separately scored for each subject, and their correlation is obtained. This coefficient could then be considered an estimate of reliability but at least as appropriately can be viewed as a coefficient of equivalence for the two halves. On the assumption that the halves are (close to) parallel, a better estimate of reliability may result using Spearman-Brown's prophecy formula (Chapter 6), where one formally substitutes the correlation coefficient of the two halves for their 'reliability coefficient':

$$\hat{\rho}_{X,sh} = \frac{2Corr(half\_1, half\_2)}{1 + Corr(half\_1, half\_2)},$$ (7.4)

with X denoting the score on the original test (that is split into two halves), and 'half_1' and 'half_2' standing for the sum scores on the two corresponding halves (split halves). Obviously, the greater the violation of the assumption of parallelism of the two halves, the more biased (7.4) will be as a reliability estimate, even if data on an entire studied population were to be available.

An alternative method for estimating reliability from split-half test scores goes back to Rulon (1939) and circumvents application of the Spearman-Brown formula. With Rulon's method one estimates reliability as follows:

$$\hat{\rho}_{X,Rulon} = 1 - \frac{\hat{\sigma}_D^2}{\hat{\sigma}_X^2},$$ (7.5a)

where D is the difference score between the two halves. It has been argued that as long as the ratio of the standard deviations of the two halves is close to 1 (in particular between .9 and 1.1), the first discussed method based on the Spearman-Brown formula and Rulon's method yield very similar results (reliability estimates; Cronbach, 1951). As the two standard deviations become less similar, so do the reliability estimates they furnish. Guttman (1945) also offered a method for estimating reliability from split-half test scores that is equivalent to Rulon's method. With Guttman's method one estimates reliability as follows:

$$\hat{\rho}_{X,Guttman} = 2\left[1 - \frac{\hat{\sigma}_A^2 + \hat{\sigma}_B^2}{\hat{\sigma}_X^2}\right],$$ (7.5b)

where $\hat{\sigma}_A^2$ and $\hat{\sigma}_B^2$ are, respectively, the variances of the two created halves.

A major limitation of the split-half methods of reliability estimation, including Rulon's and Guttman's, is the fact that the resulting estimate is in principle not unique but instead depends on how exactly the split was carried out. Indeed, different splits into halves of an initial multiple-component instrument (and there can be very many possible splits, e.g., Crocker & Algina, 1986; Leite, Huang, & Marcoulides, 2008) can well yield different reliability estimates. This holds even though one and the same sample of data, or even population data set, is analyzed with these methods (and thereby all of that data are observed as opposed to some potentially missing). The resulting multitude of possible estimates is a serious if not critical drawback of all these methods, because one would expect that for a given set of observed data a meaningful estimation procedure will yield a single final result. This is obviously not the case with any split-half procedure discussed in the current section (or possible to devise within the split-half approach).

In addition, as a main assumption of all split-half methods, one should consider in our view that of unidimensionality. Indeed, if homogeneity does not hold for the original scale (before splitting), obviously the estimate of reliability obtained with any of the methods discussed in this section (including Rulon's and Guttman's) can well be meaningless. The reason is that two halves may contain items that disproportionately represent two or more underlying constructs (even if they are closely interrelated), leading to an estimate that may be hard to interpret meaningfully if at all possible. Even in the case of unidimensionality, in our view the assumption of parallel components needs to be advanced as well as examined prior to using a split-half method (see Chapter 6 for the relationship between reliability and correlation of parallel measures, of relevance for a split-half method). This assumption is, however, very hard to satisfy because of the empirical difficulty with developing several such tests, as we indicated in the preceding chapter. Last but not least, all split-half methods are not readily used for purposes of interval estimation of reliability. An application of the bootstrap approach is possible (e.g., Efron & Tibshiriani, 1993), but future research needs to establish possible resample distribution convergence, whether the so-obtained confidence interval will have the required coverage, and if so under which conditions.

In conclusion, despite their apparent intuitive appeal, we find that the split-half methods discussed in this section have serious limitations that in general preclude them from leading to dependable reliability estimates in empirical social and behavioral research. Use of alternative approaches is therefore desirable then, like the ones we next turn to.

7.1.2.2 Methods Based on Item Covariances

These procedures accomplish the goal of reliability estimation following a different approach, viz., capitalization on the interrelationships between the instrument components and specifically their covariances. We discuss several procedures of reliability estimation based on the covariances between the elements $X_1, X_2, ..., X_p$ of a given composite $X = X_1 + X_2 + \cdots + X_p$.

Coefficient Alpha: We familiarized ourselves with coefficient alpha (α) in Chapter 6, where we provided its population definition, along with a detailed discussion of the conditions when it could be used as a dependable index of instrument reliability. For this reason, we present here only the resulting empirical estimate of composite reliability with it, when those conditions are fulfilled:

$$\hat{\rho}_X = \hat{\alpha} = \frac{p}{p-1}\left[1 - \frac{\sum\limits_{k=1}^{p} \hat{\sigma}^2_{X_k}}{\hat{\sigma}^2_X}\right]. \tag{7.6}$$

The estimate (7.6) of α is then available in widespread statistical packages, such as SPSS or SAS, and can be readily obtained with them in an empirical setting. In particular, using the interactive mode in SPSS, one can consecutively select the menus 'Analyze', 'Scale', and 'Reliability Analysis' to furnish this estimate. (Alternatively, the estimate can be readily obtained using the batch mode and the syntax editor in this software.)

As indicated in the preceding chapter, dependable reliability estimates can be obtained using coefficient alpha with true score equivalent instrument components. With normally distributed components, there is also a substantial body of earlier research that can be utilized to furnish interval estimates of coefficient alpha, which will also be interval estimates of reliability for instruments with true score equivalent components (e.g., Feldt, 1969). As discussed earlier in this book, alpha will be fairly close to composite reliability also with unidimensional tests with uncorrelated errors, which have uniformly high loadings of their components on the underlying construct (see details of pertinent discussion in Chapter 6; Raykov, 1997).

Kuder-Richardson Formulas: Coefficient alpha is just as applicable when the components of a given instrument are dichotomous or polytomous, and it represents a generalization of the so-called Kuder-Richardson formulas (often simply referred to as KR-20 and KR-21). The latter, being special cases of α, are nowadays of limited relevance on their own, because in all cases when they could be of concern, a direct application of α renders the empirical values of these formulas. We find it useful, however, to include them here, because their structure is instructive as a means toward understanding reliability estimation via inter-item covariances.

The first of these formulas, the so-called Kuder-Richardson formula 20 (KR-20), is applicable in case of dichotomous items (components) and yields the reliability estimate

$$\hat{\rho}_{X,20} = \frac{p}{p-1}\left[1 - \frac{\sum_{k=1}^{p}\hat{r}_k(1-\hat{r}_k)}{\hat{\sigma}_X}\right], \tag{7.7}$$

where r_k is a symbol for difficulty (strictly speaking, 'easiness') of the kth component, i.e., the relative frequency of correct response on it ($k = 1, \ldots, p$; e.g., Chapter 2). We stress that Equation (7.7) is a special case of (7.6), i.e., of α, which results when all components are associated with only two possible values—e.g., yes or no, present or absent, true or false, agree or disagree, endorse or not endorse. This relationship is readily seen by realizing that $r_k(1 - r_k)$ is the variance of a dichotomous item (e.g., King & Minium, 2003) and a comparison of Equation (7.7) with (7.6).

If these instrument components are in addition all of equal difficulty, the right-hand side of Equation (7.7) further specializes to what is called Kuder-Richardson formula 21 (KR-21):

$$\hat{\rho}_{X,21} = \frac{p}{p-1}\left[1 - \frac{\hat{\mu}(p-\hat{\mu})}{p\hat{\sigma}_X}\right], \tag{7.8}$$

where $\hat{\mu}$ is the average total score (test, scale, or composite score) in the available sample. Because Equation (7.8) is a special case of (7.7), it is also a special case of coefficient alpha, viz., when all items are binary and with the same difficulty. Conversely, coefficient alpha can be seen as a generalization of both Kuder-Richardson formulas that also preceded it historically by several decades.

Hoyt's Method: At a computational level, this procedure differs conceptually from the approaches discussed so far in this section. Hoyt's method is based on an analysis of variance (ANOVA) approach that within the context of classical test theory views persons and components (items) as sources of variability in observed scores (see below for assumptions of this method). By considering these two sources, one could pool over items—a common activity with this analytic approach when interested in the other factor's main effect (in this case persons). Then, treating error score variance as analogous here to residual variance, the resulting reliability estimate is

$$\hat{\rho}_{X,Hoyt} = \frac{\frac{SS_{persons}}{df_{persons}} - \frac{SS_{residual}}{df_{residual}}}{\frac{SS_{persons}}{df_{persons}}} = \frac{MS_{persons} - MS_{residual}}{MS_{persons}} = 1 - \frac{MS_{residual}}{MS_{persons}}. \tag{7.9}$$

With the analogy noted in the preceding paragraph, one could view the mean square due to persons as an estimate of observed variability on the sum score X and the mean square due to residual as an estimate of error variance:

$$MS_{persons} = \hat{\sigma}_X^2 \quad \text{and} \quad MS_{residual} = \hat{\sigma}_E^2, \tag{7.10}$$

where the caret is used to symbolize these particular mean squares as corresponding variance estimates. With Equation (7.10) in mind, (7.9) would precisely equal the estimated reliability coefficient as the complement to 1 of the ratio of error to observed variance (see Chapter 6). Hence, in a given sample one obtains the reliability estimate based on Hoyt's method by substituting in Equation (7.9) the variance component estimates for the person and residual effects, as provided by an application of the ANOVA procedure. (As we will see in Chapter 9, this strategy forms the basis of an estimation approach used in generalizability theory, discussed extensively there.)

Because the ANOVA procedure is implemented in widespread statistical packages, estimation of reliability using Hoyt's method is readily carried out in empirical settings (as long as the underlying ANOVA assumptions are fulfilled; e.g., King & Minium, 2003).

We stress that Hoyt's method assumes no person by component interaction, which may not be a plausible assumption in some settings. This assumption is not testable, however, in the present context, as there is a single observation per cell of the pertinent two-way ANOVA design, and thus the lack of replications renders a test for interaction being associated with 0 degrees of freedom and as such impossible to conduct (e.g., Agresti & Finlay, 2009). We note in passing that this assumption of no subject by item interaction is not needed in the reliability estimation methods discussed later in this chapter (Section 7.4).

7.2 What Coefficient Alpha Is, and What It Is Not

The multitude of reliability estimates covered in the preceding section naturally leads to the question as to what kind of relationships hold among them. The present section deals with aspects of this query, highlighting several points that emerged from earlier research related to coefficient alpha, which is at present still one of the most frequently used psychometric indices. The following discussion relates to several widely circulated 'myths' about coefficient alpha and has borrowed considerably from earlier work by McDonald (1981, 1999; see also Bentler, 2009; Crocker & Algina, 1986; Green & Yang, 2009a, 2009b; Raykov, 1997, 1998b, 2001a; Revelle & Zinbarg, 2009; Sijtsma, 2009a, 2009b).

1. Alpha is an index of internal consistency, i.e., the degree to which a set of components is interrelated, in the sense of inter-item covariance per unit of overall sum variance. The higher (smaller) this covariance, the higher (smaller) alpha, and conversely. We stress that this does not imply unidimensionality of the set of components of a considered instrument (see also point 5 below). In fact, there is a tendency in the measurement-related literature to use the term 'internal consistency' as synonymous to coefficient alpha. In those cases, the utility and value of the concept of 'internal consistency' is the same as those of alpha. That is, the notion of internal consistency is useful and informative with respect to composite reliability only in those cases when coefficient alpha is—for a detailed discussion of them, see Chapter 6 as well as further below in this section.

2. Alpha is not in general a lower bound of reliability, unlike statements to the opposite that are frequently found in empirical research and related literature. Alpha is a lower bound of reliability only under certain circumstances that we have discussed in detail in Chapter 6 (see also point 6 below).

3. The relationship of alpha to composite reliability is further complicated by the fact that typically an empirical researcher has access to only sample data and then can only estimate parameters of interest as opposed to determine their population values. Thus, in a particular sample, alpha can actually overestimate (or alternatively underestimate or even equal) population reliability, but one has no way of knowing whether this is indeed the case or not, because that reliability is unknown. (If the population reliability of the instrument under consideration were known, there is no need to even look at alpha or an estimate of reliability.)

4. Alpha is the mean of all possible split-half coefficients calculated via Rulon's method (see Crocker & Algina, 1986). As we discussed in the preceding section, there is, however, generally up to limited value in the split-half reliability estimation methods, because they do not yield a unique estimate of reliability for any given set of observed data.

5. Alpha is not an index of unidimensionality, contrary to what may still be the view among some applied behavioral and social researchers (see Green, Lissitz, & Mulaik, 1977, for an insightful discussion and counterexamples; see also McDonald, 1981). Alpha is only a measure of inter-item covariance per unit composite variance (see point 1 above) and a reasonably good index of reliability only under certain restrictive conditions (see point 6 next). If one is interested in unidimensionality, there is no need to use or refer to alpha, as it can be misleading, but instead it is required to examine the unidimensionality hypothesis itself. For this aim, use of exploratory factor analysis and especially confirmatory factor analysis (on another sample) is recommended (see Chapters 3 and 4). With the latter approach, one tests statistically this hypothesis and evaluates the extent to which it may be viewed as 'supported' (actually, disconfirmed) in a given data set.

6. Alpha is a good estimate of reliability for congeneric measures (test or scale components) if (a) they are true score equivalent and errors of measurement are uncorrelated or (b) errors are uncorrelated and the components load uniformly highly

on the common latent dimension (for specific details, see Raykov, 1997; see also Chapter 6). With correlated errors, whether for congeneric measures or such with more than a single source of latent variability (i.e., more than a single underlying factor), coefficient alpha can overestimate or alternatively underestimate instrument reliability—depending on parameter constellation—even when data on these measures are available from an entire studied population (e.g., Raykov, 1998b, 2001a, and references therein). Even with uncorrelated errors and a unidimensional instrument, alpha is not going to be a good index of reliability in general, unless the components load equally or uniformly highly on their common latent dimension (Raykov, 1997).

Interrater Reliability: This is a relatively commonly used notion in situations where a single set of items (components) is administered to a set of persons, and multiple observations are obtained for each individual, e.g., using several raters or occasions and/or on multiple dimensions. The notion of interrater reliability then refers to the extent to which raters' judgments are consistent with one another. To evaluate this degree, a recommendable approach is the use of generalizability theory (at times also referred to as G theory), which is the topic of Chapter 9. We mention it here only for the sake of completeness of the present discussion, and we deal with this and related topics in that chapter.

7.3 Factors Affecting Reliability Coefficients and Their Estimates

Reliability was defined in Chapter 6 as the ratio of (a) true variance to (b) observed variance (assuming the latter was nonzero). There is a multitude of factors that affect at least one of the two quantities (a) and (b), thus impacting also the reliability coefficient in a studied population and in a sample from it. We discuss these factors in turn next.

7.3.1 Group Homogeneity

Homogeneity is the flip side of variance and generally refers to the lack of (or limited) individual differences. The more homogeneous a studied group is on the true scores, other things being equal, the smaller the reliability. This follows directly from the reliability definition as the ratio of the quantities in (a) and (b) of the preceding paragraph. For this reason, low reliability may be consistent with (a) large error variance and/or (b) small true variance. Hence, a finding of low reliability does not necessarily mean that there is plenty of error in a measure but also or instead that there is little variability in the studied group on the true latent dimension of interest. In fact, in two groups differing on true variance but with same error variances, reliability will be lower in the group where subjects are more homogeneous on the latent dimension.

This observation suggests that reliability is such a property of observed scores obtained on a given test, scale, or instrument, which depends on the particular group studied. Even when we are talking in terms of instrument reliability, we should keep in mind that one and the same instrument may have different reliability in different groups (samples, populations), precisely for this group dependence. This property has been often referred to as population (or group) dependence of reliability and represents an important limitation of the latter.

If we consider reliability as a parameter, which is quite legitimate, this dependency on the population studied should not be striking. This is because many important parameters are population dependent, for instance, means, variances, correlation coefficients, etc. In particular, for a given set of observed scores obtained with a given instrument, looking at their distribution one could ask the question what the relationship of the variance of their true scores is to the variance of the recorded score distribution. This is an entirely meaningful question that obviously need not have the same answer in different populations, like there is no need to expect that distinct populations would have the same means on a given measure, such as, say, an intelligence test, or the same variance on it for that matter. This shows that it is meaningful to consider reliability as a parameter associated with variable distributions in a population, viz., those of the observed and true scores on a given instrument. Hence, there should be no wonder realizing that this parameter depends on the population (just as the mean or variance of the observed score distribution does), and expectations of the parameter being a characteristic of the measuring instrument alone are unwarranted. Rather, the reliability coefficient (and index) can instead be viewed as a characteristic of both an instrument in question and a population of concern (see also McDonald, 1999).

This population dependency of reliability has important implications for instrument use and application. The reason is that it implies researchers should use only tests with high reliability found for populations (groups) that are very similar in composition to the group that they plan to study. Otherwise a researcher should not rely on reported reliability estimates in the instrument documentation. Therefore, when looking up reliability of a published instrument, test, measure, or scale, one needs to check also which population has been used to obtain its reported estimate. The latter is to be treated as the reliability estimate for that population, rather than any other, in the general case. Hence, with regard to reliability considerations, one should use a given test only on a group coming from a population that is as close as possible to the one that its estimate reported in the test documentation stems from.

7.3.2 Time Limit

When time limit is imposed on test completion, reliability estimates obtained with most methods discussed in this section must be interpreted with great caution, as they may be misleading. This is in particular the case whenever one is interested in reliability of the test had all subjects finished it but has data only when the time limit was imposed. The reason for this caution is that under time limits, in general, differences in individual speed of task processing are confounded with the ability being evaluated by the test. It has been argued that introducing time limits is likely to yield artificially inflated estimates of reliability and that the 'best' methods to accomplish reliability estimation then may be test–retest or alternate (equivalent) form methods. The rationale behind our caution when interpreting reliability estimates under time limit constraints is also seen by recalling how the true score was defined—we did not use any reference to time then and not in particular to a time limit under which an instrument in question is administered. Hence, the concept of reliability, as defined in the preceding chapter (see also earlier in this chapter), may not be well suited for examining error effect on scores obtained in situations when time limit accompanies administration of psychometric measures.

7.3.3 Test Length

The Spearman-Brown formula (Chapter 6) can be used to work out reliability of a test resulting from adding components parallel to those already in an instrument, all being parallel among themselves, or alternatively removing some of a set of parallel components in an original test consisting of such. Revisiting that formula in Chapter 6, we see that under those circumstances composite reliability increases with increasing length (other things being the same). Conversely, shortening a test then leads to lower reliability. To give a simple example, if a 10-item test with reliability of .50 were to be increased by adding another test of 10 items that is parallel to it, Equation (6.7) can be readily used to work out the reliability of the resulting 20-item test as $2 \times .5/[1 + (2 - 1) \times .5] = .67$ (with '×' denoting multiplication).

Another highly useful feature of the Spearman-Brown formula is the fact that it is applicable (under its assumptions) with p being other than a whole number. That is, the formal 'number' of components (subtests) used in this formula, p, can be smaller than 1, larger than 1, or a fractional number (e.g., $p = 1.33$ or $p = .75$). This property of the formula can be used when it is of interest to work out how much a given instrument needs to be extended (by parallel measures as mentioned above) in order to reach a given level or reliability or what reliability a test will possess if a certain number of its components are removed. For example, by how much would we have to extend in this way the previously considered 10-item test with reliability of .50 in order to reach a reliability of say .90? Using Equation (6.7), by algebraic reexpression, we can readily determine that the test would have to be increased to $p = \frac{\rho_X(1-\rho)}{\rho(1-\rho_X)} = \frac{.9(1-.5)}{.5(1-.9)} = 9$ parallel sets of the same length, which corresponds to 90 items or components for the final test (in this equation, ρ_X denotes the desired reliability whereas ρ stands for the one of the initially available test).

The latter type of question may also be of relevance when one is concerned with revising an existing test consisting of parallel components, which happens to have reliability higher than what could be considered sufficient in a given empirical setting. Then the analytic query could be how much shorter that test could be made while still maintaining a level of reliability that is prespecified (e.g., .80, as may be often considered satisfactory in applied research). We stress that the premise of any use of Spearman-Brown's formula is the assumption of parallel tests (instrument components), which as mentioned earlier is in general rather hard to satisfy in empirical behavioral and social research. This assumption will be also seriously challenged in empirical settings with relatively long tests, where practice effects, fatigue, boredom, and related circumstances are likely to adversely affect the likelihood of the parallelism presumption being plausible.

7.4 Estimating True Scores

As we indicated in the last chapter, the true score for a given subject on a particular test, instrument, or scale cannot be determined precisely (even if data on an entire studied population were to be available on the measure in question). However, an estimate of that true score can be obtained based on observed scores of a given sample of subjects, which is sometimes referred to as predicted score (or predicted/estimated true score). To this end, one can use the regression analysis framework (e.g., Agresti & Finlay, 2009; see also Chapter 2) to obtain what is commonly referred to as a regression estimate of true score. With it, symbolizing for simplicity in this section estimated or predicted score by priming, we obtain

$$T_i' = \rho_{X,T} \frac{\sigma_T}{\sigma_X}(X_i - \bar{X}) + \bar{T}, \tag{7.11}$$

where the subindex i is used to denote subject ($i = 1, ..., N$). Because the reliability index is the correlation of observed and true scores, and also the ratio of standard deviations of true to observed scores, as we saw in Chapter 6 (as long as there are individual observed differences), from Equation (7.11) it follows that

$$T_i' = \rho_{X,T}^2(X_i - \bar{X}) + \bar{T} = \rho_X(X_i - \bar{X}) + \bar{T} = \rho_X(X_i - \bar{X}) + \bar{X}. \tag{7.12}$$

The expression in the right-hand side of Equation (7.12) follows from the realization that the classical test theory (CTT) equation (e.g., Equation (5.1) in Chapter 5) implies the mean across subjects of the true score, T, as equal to the mean of the observed score X (because of the mean of the error score E being 0). Another way of reexpressing the last part of Equation (7.12) is

$$T_i' - \bar{X} = \rho_X(X_i - \bar{X}). \tag{7.13}$$

Hence, the estimated true individual score is typically closer to the mean of observed scores (which is the same as the true score mean) than the original observed score is, owing to reliability being typically smaller than 1. In other words, the estimated true score is 'shrunken' toward the observed mean. The degree of this shrinkage depends on reliability: The higher the reliability, the smaller this shrinkage, whereas the lower the reliability, the stronger the shrinkage. In extreme cases, with perfect reliability (i.e., $\rho_X = 1$) the estimated true score is the observed score itself, which then also obviously equals the actual true score. With worst possible reliability (i.e., $\rho_X = 0$), the predicted true score is the mean of observed score. For intermediate reliability, the predicted true score lies between the observed mean and the original observed score. For example, if in an empirical setting an individual observed score is $X = 20$, the observed mean is $\bar{X} = 16$, and reliability is $\rho_X = .7$, then the predicted true score would be $T_i' = 18.8$, whereas with reliability $\rho_X = .9$ the predicted true score for the same observed score $X = 20$ would be $T_i' = 19.6$.

We stress that the result of an application of Equation (7.13) is a true score estimate only, which is in general not equal to the 'real' true score that is unknown (compare with the concept of factor score estimate; e.g., Raykov & Marcoulides, 2008). Furthermore, the same rank ordering is preserved on the true score estimates as on the observed scores, as well as with respect to observed mean, and only the variance of these estimates is smaller (typically) than observed score variance. This fact, in addition to the realization that there is usually no inherent scale underlying the observed scores, suggests that the estimates (7.13) of the true scores, in and of themselves, are of limited value in test applications. We also note that true score estimates depend on which group the data come from, because the right-hand side of Equation (7.13) depends on reliability and observed mean, and obviously these are population-dependent quantities (in addition to being sample dependent). In general, data from studied groups rather than subgroups should be used for true score estimation, if at all to be proceeded with. The reason for this recommendation is the fact that if subgroups are used for this purpose, then estimation tends to be less stable because of their generally being of much smaller size.

7.5 Factor-Analysis-Based Estimation of Measuring Instrument Reliability

The preceding discussion in this chapter pointed out the widespread use of coefficient alpha in empirical research as an index supposed to inform about test (composite) reliability. As we have elaborated on, however, there are situations in which reliance on alpha can be misleading. The natural question is then whether there are other means of estimating composite reliability that (a) could be readily applicable in behavioral and social research (especially when there is only a single administration of an instrument under consideration) and (b) do not share alpha's limitations discussed in detail earlier (see Chapter 6 and above in the present chapter).

To respond to this query, we adopt in the rest of this chapter the logical principle that if a question asks about reliability, it must be given an answer in terms of reliability itself. Hence, if we ask what the estimate of reliability is in a given situation, we must search for an estimate of the reliability coefficient rather than for an estimate of another quantity, even if the latter may equal reliability under some restrictive conditions.

7.5.1 Point Estimation

As we indicated earlier in this book, many times when measurement carried out in the behavioral and social sciences leads to a composite, scale, or test score, the set of components used thereby is homogeneous, i.e., it evaluates the same underlying construct. The most general case then is that of congeneric measures (within the conventional factor analytic tradition used so far in this book). This unidimensionality hypothesis is testable using the method of confirmatory factor analysis, as discussed in Chapter 4. (We address in the last section of this chapter the case when this hypothesis is incorrect.)

According to the congeneric test model, if one denotes by $X_1, ..., X_p$ these components and by T their underlying common true score, their CTT decomposition into true and error scores is

$$X_i = b_i T + E_i, \tag{7.14}$$

where E_i is the pertinent error score ($i = 1, ..., p$; as indicated in Chapter 5, we can assume for the purpose of reliability estimation in this discussion that for the associated intercept parameters, $d_i = 0$ holds). Then the composite is $X = X_1 + \cdots + X_p = (b_1 + \cdots + b_p) T + E_1 + \cdots + E_p$, with $(b_1 + \cdots + b_p) T$ being its true score and $E_1 + \cdots + E_p$ its error score. Because reliability is the ratio of true variance to observed variance, using pertinent results from Chapter 4 it follows that (e.g., Bollen, 1989; see also McDonald, 1999)

$$
\begin{aligned}
\rho_X &= \frac{Var[(b_1 + \cdots + b_p)T]}{Var[(b_1 + \cdots + b_p)T + E_1 + \cdots + E_p]} \\[2mm]
&= \frac{(b_1 + \cdots + b_p)^2 Var(T)}{Var[(b_1 + \cdots + b_p)T] + Var(E_1 + \cdots + E_p)} \\[2mm]
&= \frac{(b_1 + \cdots + b_p)^2 Var(T)}{(b_1 + \cdots + b_p)^2 Var(T) + Var(E_1) + \cdots + Var(E_p)} \\[2mm]
&= \frac{(b_1 + \cdots + b_p)^2 Var(T)}{(b_1 + \cdots + b_p)^2 Var(T) + \theta_1 + \cdots + \theta_p},
\end{aligned}
\tag{7.15}
$$

where $\theta_i = Var(E_i)$ denote the error variances ($i = 1, ..., p$). Therefore, if we could get good estimates of $b_1, ..., b_p$, $Var(T)$, and $\theta_1, ..., \theta_p$, we would obtain by substitution into Equation (7.15) an estimator of composite reliability as

$$\hat{\rho}_X = \frac{(\hat{b}_1 + ... + \hat{b}_p)^2 \hat{V}ar(T)}{(\hat{b}_1 + ... + \hat{b}_p)^2 \hat{V}ar(T) + \hat{\theta}_1 + ... + \hat{\theta}_p}. \qquad (7.16)$$

How could we obtain 'good' estimates of all parameters appearing in the right-hand side of Equation (7.16)? We discussed previously in this book that if we are given a data set with subjects' performance on all p components, we can fit the congeneric test model (7.14), and if found plausible that model will provide us with estimates of its parameters. In the congeneric test model, as defined in Equation (7.14), not all parameters are uniquely estimable, however. In particular, we cannot estimate all construct loadings $b_1, ..., b_p$ and its variance, $Var(T)$. That is, as given in (7.14), the congeneric test model is not identified (cf., e.g., Raykov & Marcoulides, 2006a; see also Chapter 5). In order to identify this model, i.e., in order to be in a position to uniquely estimate all its parameters, as indicated on a few occasions in Chapter 5, we need to fix one of the loadings $b_1, ..., b_p$ or alternatively the variance of the construct, $Var(T)$, to 1. For simplicity reasons, we choose here the latter option, after which the reliability estimator in Equation (7.16) becomes

$$\hat{\rho}_X = \frac{(\hat{b}_1 + \cdots + \hat{b}_p)^2}{(\hat{b}_1 + \cdots + \hat{b}_p)^2 + \hat{\theta}_1 + \cdots + \hat{\theta}_p}, \qquad (7.17)$$

which has been also referred to as omega coefficient (see McDonald, 1999, also for a further discussion of this coefficient; see also Bollen, 1989).

Hence, once we fit the above identified congeneric test model (7.14) to a given data set and make sure that it is plausible as a means of its description and explanation, we can substitute into the right-hand side of Equation (7.17) the estimates of the loadings and error variances furnished by that model. This will render an estimate of reliability of the composite score X. This point estimation process of composite reliability can be automated using the software M*plus* that we introduced earlier in the book, and we attend to this matter in the next section.

7.5.2 Interval Estimation

The latent variable modeling (LVM) program M*plus*, which we very often use throughout this book, can also readily produce an approximate standard error for reliability and confidence intervals for it at both the 95%- and the 99%-confidence levels. These standard error and intervals are based on an application of the popular delta method (e.g., Raykov & Marcoulides, 2004; cf. Raykov, 2009a). They can in fact be obtained as a by-product of the point estimation procedure outlined in Subsection 7.5.1. To implement that procedure in the software, and obtain thereby an approximate standard error and confidence intervals for composite reliability, we need to communicate to M*plus* our data, the model defined by Equation (7.14), and the reliability estimator formula (7.17). In addition, we need to request evaluation of the approximate standard error of reliability to be used subsequently for obtaining a confidence interval for scale reliability. We describe the details of how this is achieved further below, after discussing next the way in which we inform the software of the particular form of the reliability coefficient as a function of model parameters.

To accomplish this aim, we observe that we already know how to communicate to M*plus* the specifications of the congeneric test model that is relevant in this respect—we attended to this matter already in Chapter 4. In order to be in a position to submit within its framework also a request for a particular estimator formula computation to the software, like that in Equation (7.17), we need to make use of additional features about constraint evaluation (e.g., Muthén & Muthén, 2010). We list next a few symbolic descriptions that permit one to communicate to M*plus* parametric expressions of the type found in the right-hand side of Equation (7.17):

1. Addition and subtraction are symbolized, as usual, by '+' and '−', respectively.
2. Multiplication is signaled by '*' and division by '/'.
3. Exponentiation can be symbolized by '**' followed by the relevant power.
4. Parentheses are used to denote operations that need to be performed in a particular order.
5. Operations within parentheses are performed first, then raising to power, then division and multiplication (in the order they appear, from left to right), and finally addition and subtraction (in their order of appearance).
6. A simple rule to watch out for is that within a single series of arithmetic operations, the number of opening and closing parentheses should be the same (M*plus* is checking this equality, so unless correct usage is made of parentheses, it will print a warning message).
7. M*plus* can point and interval estimate linear and nonlinear expressions of model parameters, if each of the latter is assigned a symbol; in this book, most of the time when needed we will assign to a parameter of concern the symbol 'P#', where '#' will be a number uniquely corresponding to that parameter.

The following are a few examples of how to use this simple symbolic language for mathematical operations in order to communicate to the software estimator formulas or expressions:

- 2×3, where '×' denotes multiplication, is communicated as 2 * 3.
- 3^2 can be represented by 3**2.
- (3 + 4)/7 results in 1 with M*plus*, because first the within-parentheses operation is performed (addition) and then that following it to the right (division by 7 of the obtained result).
- (3 + 5)**2 results in 64, whereas 3 + 5**2 yields 28.
- Suppose we were interested in point and interval estimation of the sum of a given parameter plus the squared product of two other parameters. We assign first the symbols P1, P2, and P3 to these three parameters; introduce next as a new parameter that defined as the above sum (in a way described in the following paragraph); and then define the sum as follows:

```
P4 = P1+(P2*P3)**2;
```

As a simple example of improper use of parentheses, the following symbolic statement

```
P4 = (P1 + (P2*P3))**2;
```

will result in an error message, because the number of opening parentheses (viz., two) is smaller than that of closing parentheses (namely, three).

   If we are interested in estimation of a parameter that is not part of a fitted model, like in the last example where we wanted to estimate P4, we need to create a 'placeholder' for that new parameter itself. This is achieved by using the following two command lines at the end of the MODEL section of the input file, which define the 'new' parameter P4 (sometimes also referred to as 'external', 'auxiliary', or 'additional' parameter, because it is not one of the actual model parameters):

```
MODEL CONSTRAINT;
NEW(P4);
```

   This descriptive discussion equips us with what we need for the moment to conduct point and interval estimation of multiple-component instrument (composite) reliability using M*plus* in the unidimensional instrument case. To illustrate it, consider a test of abstract thinking ability administered to $n = 400$ high school seniors. Its components are a measure of algebra knowledge (X_1), geometry (X_2), trigonometry (X_3), and logical reasoning (X_4); suppose normality could be viewed as plausible for the resulting data that are associated with the covariance matrix in the table below.

Covariance matrix of four components of a test of abstract thinking from n = 400 seniors

Measure:	1.	2.	3.	4.
1.	1.10			
2.	.62	1.05		
3.	.59	.65	1.16	
4.	.61	.59	.61	.99

   The M*plus* input file we need for the purpose of (a) testing unidimensionality of the four measures, (b) point estimation of reliability of the composite consisting of them (i.e., of their sum score), and (c) initiating this reliability interval estimation is given next. For the commands and options that have not been discussed earlier, we describe their meaning subsequently (cf. Raykov, 2008, 2009a).

```
TITLE:        ESTIMATION OF RELIABILITY OF A TEST OF ABSTRACT
              THINKING ABILITY
DATA:         FILE = TABLE7_1.DAT;
              TYPE = COVARIANCE;
              NOBSERVATIONS = 400;
VARIABLE:     NAMES = ABSTHIN1-ABSTHIN4;
MODEL:        F1 BY ABSTHIN1*(P1)
              ABSTHIN2-ABSTHIN4 (P2-P4);
              ABSTHIN1-ABSTHIN4 (P5-P8);
              F1@1;
MODEL CONSTRAINT:
              NEW(COMP_REL);
              COMP_REL =(P1+P2+P3+P4)**2/
              ((P1+P2+P3+P4)**2+P5+P6+P7+P8);
OUTPUT:       CINTERVAL;
```

The part of this input file appearing before the MODEL command is self-explanatory, given our detailed discussion in Chapter 5 of the commands involved. For this reason, we do not dwell on them here. The first line of the MODEL command makes the loading of the first listed component on the underlying true score (latent factor) a free parameter, as we pointed out in the preceding chapter and earlier in this section. This is because we wish to fix the latent variance at 1 in order to use Equation (7.17) for reliability estimation purposes. We do this variance fixing in the fourth MODEL line in order also to accomplish model identification. In this MODEL section, we also assign to each loading and to each error variance a separate parameter symbol and number, which will soon be of particular relevance for achieving our goals. Specifically, we assign the symbols P1 through P4 to the loadings b_1 through b_4 and P5 through P9 to the error term variances, respectively. We use these parametric symbols in the following MODEL CONSTRAINT part. In it, we first introduce the new parameter COMP_REL, for 'composite reliability', by using the NEW command. This new/additional parameter is defined in the next line as equal to the expression in the right-hand side of Equation (7.17), i.e., as the scale reliability coefficient of concern (for a unidimensional composite of concern in this section). In that equation, the composite reliability of the sum score $X = X_1 + X_2 + X_3 + X_4$ was represented as a particular nonlinear function of loading and error variance parameters (X_k denote for simplicity here the consecutive abstract thinking measures, named earlier ABSTHIN1 through ABSTHIN4; $k = 1, ..., 4$); this function is identical to the one defined in the MODEL CONSTRAINT section. Finally, the last line of the input file requests as part of the output also confidence intervals for all model parameters and in particular a large-sample standard error for composite reliability, which are obtained with the delta method internally invoked by the software after this command. This standard error is used subsequently to furnish a confidence interval for scale reliability, as discussed in detail below.

The above input file yields the following output:

```
THE MODEL ESTIMATION TERMINATED NORMALLY
TESTS OF MODEL FIT
Chi-Square Test of Model Fit


   Value                                 3.056
   Degrees of Freedom                        2
   P-Value                              0.2169
```

These results show that the congeneric model fits the analyzed data well (see also its RMSEA below, corroborating this suggestion). Hence, the unidimensionality (homogeneity) hypothesis can be considered plausible for the four abstract thinking measures under consideration.

```
Chi-Square Test of Model Fit for the Baseline Model

   Value                               619.112
   Degrees of Freedom                        6
   P-Value                              0.0000

CFI/TLI

   CFI                                   0.998
   TLI                                   0.995
```

```
Loglikelihood

  H0 Value                              -2016.765
  H1 Value                              -2015.237

Information Criteria

  Number of Free Parameters                     8
  Akaike (AIC)                           4049.531
  Bayesian (BIC)                         4081.462
  Sample-Size Adjusted BIC               4056.078
   (n* = (n+2)/24)

RMSEA (Root Mean Square Error Of Approximation)

  Estimate                                  0.036
  90 Percent C.I.                     0.000 0.112
  Probability RMSEA <= .05                  0.505

SRMR (Standardized Root Mean Square Residual)

  Value                                     0.012
```

With this finding of a tenable, unidimensional model, we can place trust in the following parameter estimates and standard errors. We are particularly interested in the reliability estimate of the overall sum score, as well as in its associated standard error.

```
MODEL RESULTS
                                                     Two-Tailed
                    Estimate      S.E.     Est./S.E.   P-Value
F1      BY
  ABSTHIN1           0.775        0.049      15.949     0.000
  ABSTHIN2           0.794        0.047      17.001     0.000
  ABSTHIN3           0.794        0.050      15.897     0.000
  ABSTHIN4           0.763        0.046      16.748     0.000

Variances
  F1                 1.000        0.000     999.000   999.000

Residual Variances
  ABSTHIN1           0.497        0.046      10.809     0.000
  ABSTHIN2           0.417        0.042       9.936     0.000
  ABSTHIN3           0.527        0.049      10.847     0.000
  ABSTHIN4           0.406        0.040      10.167     0.000

New/Additional Parameters
  COMP_REL           0.841        0.013      64.713     0.000
```

The last line of this output section shows the composite reliability coefficient estimated in the new parameter denoted COMP_REL as .841, with a standard error of .013 and z-value of 64.713 (and hence it is significant as seen in the last row of the final line in this output section, but this latter finding is not unexpected for us).

To obtain next a 95%- or 99%-confidence interval of composite reliability, we first make the following important observation (see Chapter 4). Because the population reliability coefficient is a parameter that is bounded between 0 and 1, it can be expected that its sampling distribution will not be symmetric in general. Especially when reliability is fairly high or alternatively fairly low, one may expect that an appropriately constructed nonsymmetric confidence interval (CI) would be desirable. Such a CI for reliability can be constructed using the corresponding approach employed earlier in this book. Specifically, as outlined in Chapter 4, when interval estimating item difficulty parameters, because of reliability being bound by 0 and 1, we can utilize first the logit transformation on the reliability estimate, then render a CI for the transformed reliability, and finally use the inverse—i.e., logistic transformation—to furnish the lower and upper limits of the sought CI for reliability (e.g., Browne, 1982; cf. Raykov, 2010b). That is, denoting by $\hat{\rho}_X$ the scale reliability estimate obtained as in the preceding section, we render its logit $\hat{\lambda}_X$, which is defined as

$$\hat{\lambda}_X = \ln[\hat{\rho}_X/(1-\hat{\rho}_X)]. \tag{7.18}$$

Its approximate standard error is (see Chapter 4; Browne, 1982)

$$S.E.(\hat{\lambda}_X) = S.E.(\hat{\rho}_X)/[\hat{\rho}_X(1-\hat{\rho}_X)], \tag{7.19}$$

where $S.E.(\hat{\rho}_X)$ denotes the standard error of the reliability coefficient obtained with the delta method, as earlier in the current section (see last-used M*plus* input file that yields $S.E.(\hat{\rho}_X) = .013$ in its final presented output section line for the example considered there). Adding and subtracting 1.96 times this standard error $S.E.(\hat{\lambda}_X)$ to the logit-transformed reliability estimate, $\hat{\lambda}_X$, renders a 95%-CI for the population logit reliability $\lambda_X = \ln[\rho_X/(1-\rho_X)]$ as follows:

$$(\hat{\lambda}_X - 1.96\ S.E.(\hat{\lambda}_X), \hat{\lambda}_X + 1.96\ S.E.(\hat{\lambda}_X)). \tag{7.20}$$

Finally, applying the inverse to the logit transformation, i.e., the logistic transformation, on the lower and upper endpoints of the CI in (7.19), we obtain the following CI for scale reliability:

$$(1/[1+\exp(-\hat{\lambda}_X + 1.96\ S.E.(\hat{\lambda}_X)], 1/[1+\exp(-\hat{\lambda}_X - 1.96\ S.E.(\hat{\lambda}_X)]). \tag{7.21}$$

In (7.20), one would use as multiplier 2.58 instead of 1.96, or an appropriate alternative cutoff of the standard normal distribution, if one wanted to obtain a 99%-CI or such at another, corresponding confidence level. (Alternatively, 1.645 would be used as a multiplier there instead of 1.96, if a 90%-CI is desirable.)

This procedure for constructing a CI of composite reliability is readily implemented with the LVM program M*plus*. To this end, as in Chapter 4, all we need to do is add the corresponding parametric expressions for the lower and upper endpoints in (7.21) in a MODEL CONSTRAINT section. In this way, in complete analogy to the developments in Section 4.6, the needed M*plus* command file here is the same as the last one used in this Subsection 7.5.2, but with a correspondingly modified model constraint section (see also clarifying comments added to its command lines):

```
TITLE:    POINT AND INTERVAL ESTIMATION OF
          RELIABILITY OF A TEST OF ABSTRACT
          THINKING ABILITY IN ELEMENTARY SCHOOL CHILDREN.
          OBTAINING A NON-SYMMETRIC CONFIDENCE INTERVAL
          FOR SCALE RELIABILITY (USING THE LOGIT TRANSF'N).

DATA:     FILE = TABLE7_1.DAT;
          TYPE = COVARIANCE;
          NOBSERVATIONS = 400;
```

```
VARIABLE:  NAMES = ABSTHIN1-ABSTHIN4;

MODEL:     F1 BY ABSTHIN1*(P1)
           ABSTHIN2-ABSTHIN4 (P2-P4);
           ABSTHIN1-ABSTHIN4 (P5-P8);
           F1@1;

MODEL CONSTRAINT:
           NEW(R, SE, L, SEL, CI_L_LO, CI_L_UP, CI_R_LO, CI_R_UP);
           R = .841; ! ENTER HERE THE RELIABILITY ESTIMATE,
           SE = .013; ! AND HERE ITS S.E. OBTAINED FROM LAST MPLUS RUN.
           L = LOG(R/(1-R)); ! EQUATION (7.18) - LOGIT TRANFORM/
           SEL = SE/(R*(1-R)); ! EQUATION (7.19) - S.E. FOR TRANSFORM.
           CI_L_LO = L-1.96*SEL; ! SEE CI IN (7.20) - CI OF LOGIT TRANSFORM
           CI_L_UP = L+1.96*SEL;
           CI_R_LO = 1/(1+EXP(-CI_L_LO)); ! SEE CI IN (7.21) - THIS IS THE SOUGHT
           CI_R_UP = 1/(1+EXP(-CI_L_UP)); ! CI OF COMPOSITE RELIABILITY.
```

As indicated in the last section of this input file (titled MODEL CONSTRAINT), one needs to enter in its third and fourth lines the composite reliability estimate and standard error obtained with the preceding M*plus* input file in this subsection. For the example used in it, with reliability estimate of .841 and associated standard error of .013, we obtain in this way the 95%-confidence interval for reliability as (.814, .865). We note that it is not symmetric around the estimate of .841, because of the earlier-mentioned fact that the sampling distribution of the reliability coefficient cannot be expected to be symmetric in general.

As an alternative computational approach for obtaining a CI for composite reliability, we can use the R function given next, which follows in its lines precisely the discussion so far in this subsection (cf. Section 4.6 in Chapter 4):

```
ci.rel = function(r, se){
 l = log(r/(1-r))
 sel = se/(r*(1-r))
 ci_l_lo = l-1.96*sel
 ci_l_up = l+1.96*sel
 ci_lo = 1/(1+exp(-ci_l_lo))
 ci_up = 1/(1+exp(-ci_l_up))
 ci = c(ci_lo, ci_up)
 ci
}
```

Employing (i.e., calling) this function with the above reliability estimate of .841 and standard error of .013—which are the values of its two arguments here—furnishes the 95%-confidence interval for reliability as (.814, .865) that is identical to the one just obtained with M*plus* (obviously, because of the same calculations being performed by both software).

We note, as in the end of Subsection 4.6.1.1 (Chapter 4), that one may obtain a confidence interval for reliability by invoking the normality approximation with large samples, thus adding and subtracting to its estimate 1.96 times the reported by the software standard error (for a 95%-CI and correspondingly for other confidence levels). This is in fact the CI for reliability that can be found in the section titled 'CONFIDENCE INTERVALS OF MODEL RESULTS' in the software output associated with the last-presented command file. As indicated earlier, this symmetric CI is constructed internally by the software using the delta method. We do not consider this CI to be in general optimal, however. The reason is, as mentioned in Chapter 4, that this CI for reliability can have endpoints that extend either below 0 or beyond 1 for sufficiently small or alternatively sufficiently large population reliability coefficients (or sufficiently small samples and/or large confidence levels), which coefficients are, however, not infrequent in empirical research on scale construction and development. Even if one were then to truncate those CIs correspondingly at 0 or 1, they can still contain in general implausible values, including those very close to 0 or 1. (In our pertinent discussions in the remainder of this book, this recommendation not to use in general a delta-method-based symmetric CI will be similarly applicable when of interest will be to obtain a CI for a bounded parameter that is not a function of at least two other parameters.)

Another analytic approach that can be used to obtain a CI for reliability is the bootstrap (e.g., Raykov, 1998a; cf. Chapter 4). As discussed in detail in the literature (e.g., Efron & Tibshiriani, 1993), an application of this approach here would entail first obtaining B resamples with replacements from the original sample of studied individuals and then estimating composite reliability in each one of them (with B being a large number, e.g., $B = 2,000$). We stress that in order to use this method, the software needs the raw data, regardless of measure distribution, unlike earlier in this section where the covariance matrix suffices, given multinormality of the instrument components. To employ this method in empirical research, what one needs to do is exchange the last line of the M*plus* command file in the preceding Subsection 7.5.2 with the following command: OUTPUT: CINTERVAL(BCBOOTSTRAP);. This command leads to construction of the so-called bias-corrected bootstrap interval, which has certain optimality features discussed in detail in the bootstrap-related literature (e.g., Mooney & Duval, 1993). In addition, the line ANALYSIS: BOOTSTRAP = 2000; should also be added before the MODEL command in the same input file. The resulting confidence interval may be expected to be nonsymmetric, especially when the population reliability is close to 0 or 1.

At present, no guidelines are available for selecting as preferable a particular method for CI construction from the two discussed in this section. However, it may be conjectured that when using large samples, these two methods would furnish fairly similar confidence intervals. Future research can examine this issue in detail, and perhaps extensive simulation studies may then provide guidelines for choosing a CI construction approach under specific circumstances.

In conclusion of this Section 7.5, we note that the discussed reliability point and interval estimation approach associated with the used M*plus* command files (and/or above R function) is applicable with (a) approximately continuous components $X_1, ..., X_p$ that can be viewed as having (b) a multinormal distribution. The method is also applicable with nonnormal, approximately continuous components that do not exhibit piling of cases (e.g., ceiling or floor effects) or pronounced clustering effect. In that case, application of the robust maximum likelihood method (MLR) can be made. For this to be possible, access to the raw data is required. (When that data are available, as mentioned earlier in this book, one need only provide the name of the file in the DATA command, via the subcommand FILE = <name of raw data>;.) To accomplish point and interval estimation of composite reliability in such empirical situations, we use the same last-presented M*plus* command file (which is applicable directly in case (a) and (b) hold), but with one important modification. Specifically, we add the command ANALYSIS: ESTIMATOR = MLR;. This command will invoke the robust ML estimation method that 'accounts' for the nonnormality of the analyzed data. In particular, this method corrects accordingly the overall goodness-of-fit indexes as well as parameter standard errors (e.g., Satorra & Bentler, 2001). We revisit this issue later in the chapter.

7.6 Instrument Revision and Development Satisfying Reliability Requirements

Oftentimes behavioral and social researchers start the process of developing measuring instruments with a preliminary version that does not have known psychometric properties, in particular reliability. This is typically the case when an instrument is being developed in a previously little-researched area. In such cases, it may also be unknown whether all considered components function appropriately as informative indicators of a presumed latent construct. At such early stages of test, scale, or instrument development, it is essential that a researcher examine the structure of the set of components under consideration, including evaluation of their unidimensionality. As we discussed earlier in this book, the confirmatory factor analysis approach represents a well-suited means for accomplishing this goal, and we illustrated its application for this purpose in Chapter 4 using M*plus*.

In this regard, we find it important to emphasize that unidimensionality, although typically desirable (and for some purposes required), is not a sufficient condition for a multiple-component measuring instrument to be of high psychometric quality, in particular with respect to its reliability. Specifically, it is possible that a set of components is homogeneous, and yet its sum score does not possess what may be considered sufficiently high reliability, e.g., .80 or higher as seems conventionally agreed on in much empirical work in the social and behavioral sciences. In those cases, the question is what activities may be undertaken to revise, i.e., further develop, the instrument so as to enhance its reliability. This may be achievable by revisiting its components and in particular considering removal of those of them that possibly contribute to lower reliability, an activity we turn to next. (A discussion on an automated algorithm for such activities is presented in Leite et al. [2008].) In essentially the same way, as outlined in the following two subsections, one can address the possibility of adding components to an initial instrument, which are congeneric with the ones already in it (see below). In this section and the next sections (7.6 and 7.7), we will assume that unidimensionality is a required property for a multiple-component measuring instrument under consideration. In Section 7.8, we discuss the case of instruments with general structure, i.e., with more than a single underlying latent source of variability.

7.6.1 Point and Interval Estimation of Reliability Following Revision

A widely adhered to approach in applied research is the repeated evaluation of coefficient alpha for an initial composite (test, scale, instrument) and revised versions of it, which result when each of its components is in turn considered for removal. This approach is readily available in popular statistical analysis software, such as SPSS and SAS, and the pertinent statistic that is currently nearly routinely used for these aims is called 'Alpha if item deleted'. However, as one can suspect from the discussion in the last chapter, this statistic is potentially misleading because alpha is in general unequal to reliability even if the scores on the components in question are available from an entire studied population. Unfortunately, although alpha's limitations have received a considerable amount of attention by methodologists and some substantive scholars over a number of decades—perhaps beginning with the instructive work by Novick and Lewis (1967) and Maxwell (1968)—the index 'Alpha if item deleted' has not been the focus of nearly as much interest and scrutiny. Recently, Raykov (2007b; see also Raykov, 1997) demonstrated that this index can suggest deletion of components that enhance markedly alpha yet at the same time lead to substantial loss in reliability. Similarly, Raykov (2008) showed that the same can happen with respect to validity as well (the topic of the next chapter). Specifically, deleting a component so as to enhance coefficient alpha may in fact entail considerable loss in what is referred to as criterion validity, the correlation between overall sum score and a criterion variable. This possible loss in reliability and/or validity as a result of adopting a revision that enhances coefficient alpha can be explained with the observation that, as we already know, in certain circumstances alpha can greatly underestimate reliability. Then deletion of an appropriately chosen component may cause alpha to move (increase) much closer to the actual reliability coefficient that is, however, decreased through that component's deletion.

Rather than examine the potentially misleading index 'Alpha if item deleted', which in addition is reported only in the form of a point estimate from a given sample by widely circulated software like SPSS and SAS (while one would be interested in making conclusions about revision effect in an entire studied population), we can make use of the developments in the preceding Section 7.5 in this chapter. To this end, one can simply point and interval estimate reliability before and after deletion of one or more particular components and compare these reliability estimates. Such candidate components for deletion can be those associated with (a) a relatively small loading(s) on the latent dimension evaluated by the initial composite and/or (b) a large residual variance(s) (e.g., McDonald, 1999). These components can be found based on the results (loading and residual variance estimates, standard errors, respective z-values) of a preceding confirmatory factor analysis aimed at testing unidimensionality of the instrument under consideration or from exploratory factor analysis examining the latent structure of this instrument. Applying then the techniques discussed in Section 7.5, based on the resulting point and interval estimates of reliability before and after component deletion, one can make a more informed conclusion whether the revision consisting in this component(s) removal is worthwhile carrying out. As indicated earlier, in essentially the same way, one can point and interval estimate reliability before and after one or more components are added to an initial instrument, which are congeneric (unidimensional, homogeneous) with the ones already in it (Raykov, 2007b; see also Raykov, 2008, 2009b).

We illustrate this discussion with the following example. Suppose one were interested in constructing a scale (test) of aggression in elementary school children and originally intended to use five components developed to tap into different aspects of this attribute. In a sample of $n = 350$ students, assume the resulting data on these measures were associated with the covariance matrix provided in the table below and fulfilled approximately the normality assumption.

Covariance matrix of five components of a test of aggressiveness from $n = 350$ elementary school students

Measure:	1.	2.	3.	4.	5.
1.	1.11				
2.	.61	1.04			
3.	.57	.64	1.15		
4.	.60	.60	.62	.98	
5.	.24	.32	.33	.32	1.02

We wish to examine (a) whether this five-component instrument is unidimensional and how well its components are functioning as presumed sources of information about the putative underlying construct of aggression, (b) how high the reliability is of this initial scale, as well as (c) how one could revise this tentative instrument in order to enhance its reliability, if need be. We address query (a) by fitting the congeneric test model (see Chapter 5) and inspecting the resulting loading and error variance estimates as well as their standard errors—checking in particular whether there may be some fairly small loadings (that may perhaps be even nonsignificant) and large residual variances (McDonald, 1999). We accomplish (b) by using the procedure outlined in the preceding Subsection 7.5.2 and achieve (c) by extending that procedure to point and interval estimate any version of the initial scale of five components, which could be of substantive interest and consist of four or fewer measures (cf. Raykov, 2007b, 2008). Goals (a) through (c) are accomplished with the *Mplus* command file used in Section 7.5.2, where the only necessary changes are now in the title, names of measures, their number, and sample size. For completeness of the present discussion, we include next the needed input file:

```
TITLE:          POINT AND INTERVAL ESTIMATION OF
                RELIABILITY OF AN AGGRESSION COMPOSITE,
                WITH A VIEW OF POSSIBLE REVISION.

DATA:           FILE = TABLE7_2.DAT;
                TYPE = COVARIANCE;
                NOBSERVATIONS = 350;

VARIABLE:       NAMES = AGGRESS1-AGGRESS5;

MODEL:          F1 BY AGGRESS1*(P1)
                AGGRESS2-AGGRESS5(P2-P5);
                AGGRESS1-AGGRESS5(P6-P10);
                F1@1;

MODEL CONSTRAINT:
                NEW(COMP_REL);
                COMP_REL =(P1+P2+P3+P4+P5)**2/
                ((P1+P2+P3+P4+P5)**2+P6+P7+P8+P9+P10);

OUTPUT:         CINTERVAL;
```

This command file furnishes the following output:

```
THE MODEL ESTIMATION TERMINATED NORMALLY
TESTS OF MODEL FIT
Chi-Square Test of Model Fit
  Value                            6.076
  Degrees of Freedom               5
  P-Value                          0.2989
```

This result suggests that the fitted congeneric model is tenable (see also its RMSEA below that is similarly within the acceptable range). Hence, we can view the initial set of five aggression measures to be homogeneous, i.e., unidimensional.

```
Chi-Square Test of Model Fit for the Baseline Model
  Value                                        675.734
  Degrees of Freedom                           10
  P-Value                                      0.0000
```

```
CFI/TLI
  CFI                                             0.998
  TLI                                             0.997
Loglikelihood
  H0 Value                                       -2557.134
  H1 Value                                       -2554.096
Information Criteria
  Number of Free Parameters                       10
  Akaike (AIC)                                    5134.268
  Bayesian (BIC)                                  5174.182
  Sample-Size Adjusted BIC                        5142.452
  (n*=(n+2)/24)
RMSEA (Root Mean Square Error Of Approximation)
  Estimate                                        0.023
  90 Percent C.I.                                 0.000 0.076
  Probability RMSEA <= .05                        0.740
SRMR (Standardized Root Mean Square Residual)
  Value                                           0.017
```

Given the plausibility of the congeneric (unidimensional) model, we can now move on to examining the associated model results, specifically inspecting the point and interval estimates of reliability of this five-component scale and, as mentioned earlier, the loading estimates, standard errors, and residual variances.

```
MODEL  RESULTS
                                                        Two-Tailed
                  Estimate      S.E.      Est./S.E.      P-Value
  F1     BY
   AGGRESS1        0.749        0.049       15.232        0.000
   AGGRESS2        0.794        0.046       17.195        0.000
   AGGRESS3        0.792        0.049       16.028        0.000
   AGGRESS4        0.777        0.045       17.372        0.000
   AGGRESS5        0.392        0.053        7.463        0.000

Variances
  F1               1.000        0.000      999.000      999.000
   Residual Variances
   AGGRESS1        0.546        0.048       11.443        0.000
   AGGRESS2        0.407        0.041       10.020        0.000
   AGGRESS3        0.520        0.047       10.948        0.000
   AGGRESS4        0.375        0.038        9.856        0.000
   AGGRESS5        0.864        0.063       13.688        0.000
   New/Additional Parameters
   COMP_REL        0.819        0.014       57.523        0.000
```

The last line of this output section shows the reliability of the overall sum of the five aggression measures as estimated at .819, with a standard error of .014. Using the R function 'ci.rel' from the preceding Section 7.5, by stating ci.rel(.819, .014) at the R prompt '>'

(after pasting first of course the text of this function after starting R), we obtain a 95%-confidence interval (.790, .845) for the reliability of this scale. This result indicates that values under .80 are also plausible, at the used confidence level of .95, for the reliability of the composite consisting of all five components. (We use this example only for didactic purposes here rather than to suggest that the left endpoint of this confidence interval is lower than .80 to a degree that will be meaningful in any subject-matter domain.) It therefore seems worthwhile to examine if a revision of the original scale of five components could lead to higher reliability so that its confidence interval lies perhaps entirely above .80 and thus indicates only values above .80 as plausible for the population scale reliability (at the used confidence level of 95%). To search for a revised version of this scale that may be associated with enhanced reliability, from the last output we notice that the loading of the last aggression measure, AGRESS5, on the underlying construct is fairly low (although significant). This loading is nearly twice smaller than that of the remaining measures, and its associated standard error is somewhat higher than theirs. In addition, the residual variance of this measure is largest among those of all components. On the basis of these observations, one may suggest that it would be of interest to examine the reliability of the composite resulting by removing that measure from the original instrument (see below for additional criteria about whether to remove a component from a tentative scale, test, or measuring instrument).

To point and interval estimate reliability of the revised composite score $X = X_1 + X_2 + X_3 + X_4$ under consideration, all we need to do is correspondingly alter the model constraint section in the last M*plus* input file. Specifically, we just need to delete the parameters P5 and P10 from the reliability formula implemented in that constraint section, because they pertain to the last aggression measure that does not participate in the revised scale in question here. The following command file results thereby (see Equation (7.17)):

```
TITLE:          POINT AND INTERVAL ESTIMATION OF
                RELIABILITY OF A REVISED AGGRESSION COMPOSITE
                CONSISTING OF THE FIRST 4 COMPONENTS

DATA:           FILE = TABLE7_2.DAT;
                TYPE = COVARIANCE;
                NOBSERVATIONS = 350;

VARIABLE:       NAMES = AGGRESS1-AGGRESS5;

MODEL:          F1 BY AGGRESS1*(P1)
                AGGRESS2-AGGRESS5 (P2-P5);
                AGGRESS1-AGGRESS5 (P6-P10);
                F1@1;

MODEL CONSTRAINT:
                NEW(COMP_REL);
                COMP_REL =(P1+P2+P3+P4)**2/
                ((P1+P2+P3+P4)**2+P6+P7+P8+P9); ! SEE EQ. (7.17) FOR p = 4

OUTPUT:         CINTERVAL;
```

We stress that we still fit the five-component model but estimate in the MODEL CONSTRAINT section the reliability of the scale consisting only of the first four components currently of interest. The 'bigger', five-component model is fitted here, because it is based on all available interrelated measures of aggression, and thus we utilize more relevant information when estimating the revised scale reliability. This additional information is available for this analysis, because of keeping the last aggression measure in the model fitting process, which measure is correlated with the four measures of concern at this stage. In this way, we utilize information in the last measure that is over and above that contained in those four measures.

The last input file leads to the following results, whereby we present only the revised scale reliability estimates because all remaining parts of the output are identical to the corresponding parts in the output associated with the immediately preceding analysis we conducted. (The effect of estimating a different 'new' parameter is only on its own estimates rather than on any other parameters or parts of the output, because the same model is fitted as earlier in this subsection.)

```
MODEL RESULTS

                                                              Two-Tailed
                         Estimate        S.E.       Est./S.E.    P-Value
        F1      BY
        AGGRESS1          0.749         0.049        15.232       0.000
        AGGRESS2          0.794         0.046        17.195       0.000
        AGGRESS3          0.792         0.049        16.028       0.000
        AGGRESS4          0.777         0.045        17.372       0.000
        AGGRESS5          0.392         0.053         7.463       0.000

        Variances
        F1                1.000         0.000       999.000     999.000

        Residual Variances
        AGGRESS1          0.546         0.048        11.443       0.000
        AGGRESS2          0.407         0.041        10.020       0.000
        AGGRESS3          0.520         0.047        10.948       0.000
        AGGRESS4          0.375         0.038         9.856       0.000
        AGGRESS5          0.864         0.063        13.688       0.000

        New/Additional Parameters
        COMP_REL          0.840         0.013        64.147       0.000
```

According to these analyses, the reliability estimate for the revised test is .840, with a standard error .013 and z-value 64.147. Using again the above R function 'ci.rel' with these estimate and standard error, we obtain the 95%-confidence interval for this reliability coefficient as (.811, .866), which is now completely within the often considered 'acceptable' range of .80 and above. Because the first four aggression measures load approximately uniformly high on the underlying latent construct, which we can perhaps refer to as aggression (and their standard errors are also of comparable magnitude), we may consider the attained reliability of the scale consisting of them as satisfactory at this point. This alone does not allow us to view this unidimensional, four-component scale of aggression as possessing overall satisfactory psychometric quality, however. In order to be in a position to make such a claim, we need to address also its validity. The pertinent issues of relevance then will be attended to, in a general context, in the next chapter.

This example demonstrates how one can conduct multiple-component instrument revision by (a) evaluating first unidimensionality of an initial version and, if found plausible, (b) point and interval estimating both its reliability and that of a revised version of it that may be of interest. Such a version may be obtained by deleting one or more 'weak' components—those loading relatively weakly on the underlying construct and/or associated with large residual variances (or possibly loading on another construct not of primary interest, as found during the activities in (a); McDonald, 1999). We emphasize that we have thereby never used 'Alpha if item deleted', a currently widely applied index that can, however, be seriously misleading (Raykov, 2007b, 2008). In addition, we were concerned throughout with reliability itself, rather than coefficient alpha, because our question was about reliability to begin with, and thus logically we had to evaluate the reliability coefficient rather than another quantity. Moreover, in the focus of our developments were the population reliability coefficients of the instrument versions involved rather than their sample versions (as would be the case with regard to alpha, if 'Alpha if item deleted' would be consulted instead). We also stress that in exactly the same manner one can address issues (a) and (b) when adding one or more components that are homogeneous with those in an initially considered instrument (for further details and related issues, see, e.g., Raykov, 2009b). Last but not least, we mention that one could use for the same goals pursued in this subsection also the earlier-mentioned bootstrap-based confidence intervals (see Section 7.5.2), for which access to the raw data is, however, essential.

7.6.2 Limitations of Approach

The discussed method of multiple-component measuring instrument revision has several limitations that need to be emphasized. One, as seen above, the method requires analyzing the same data set twice (and possibly more than twice, if the first revision is deemed not having yielded satisfactory reliability). At the same time, conclusions about population parameters are involved in each stage. Repeated analysis of the same data set, whereby specifics of subsequent analyses are decided based on (inferential) results of preceding steps, may lead to capitalization on chance as discussed at length in the literature (e.g., MacCallum, 1986). This phenomenon entails the possibility of obtaining 'spurious results' that are hard to replicate (or rarely replicate). In particular, p-values and confidence intervals obtained for the revised instrument need to be interpreted with caution. (One may then consider use of the confidence intervals obtained at confidence levels corresponding to a Bonferroni-protected significance level, in a given study; e.g., Johnson & Wichern, 2002). For this reason, one can rely on a suggestion for instrument improvement due to a particular component(s) removal, as indicated by such analyses, only if the result is replicated in a subsequent study with the same components on an independent sample from the same population.

We also note that the process of scale development we discussed in this section was concerned merely with one feature of a 'good' scale, reliability. Although opinions differ, one might consider reliability in excess of .80 as satisfactory, but we stress that this is a conventional number and there is no magic to be sought in it. As we will discuss in detail in the next chapter, however, there is another very important aspect of instrument quality that needs to be evaluated for each considered composite and revised version of it, namely, validity. In fact, it is not reliability but validity that is the bottom line of measurement. Therefore, in general terms, it is essential for a decision for component removal from a tentative scale (test, instrument) that the consequences of this action be assessed from all possible sides. Hence, an informed decision regarding component removal can be made only based on validity and related substantive considerations.

In conclusion of this section, we emphasize that the method of instrument development discussed in it is applicable (a) when considering deletion of one or more components from an initial instrument version and (b) when contemplating addition of one or more components to it that are congeneric (homogeneous, unidimensional) with those already in the instrument.

7.7 Reliability Evaluation With Categorical Items

So far in this chapter we have tacitly made the assumption that the components of an instrument under consideration are (at least) approximately continuous. However, as emphasized in Chapter 4 (Section 4.6 in particular), oftentimes in behavioral and social research one is dealing with categorical items as components of a test or scale in question. For example, some of its items may be responded to in only one of two possible ways, e.g., correct or false, yes or no, present or absent, agree or disagree. Other components may not be dichotomous (binary) like these but still may have only three or four possible ordinal responses. The preceding methods of reliability evaluation discussed in this chapter are not really applicable with categorical items of this kind. How one can handle this case is the topic of the present section.

With discrete categorical items, as discussed in Chapter 4, one may need to ascertain first that they are unidimensional—this can be done using confirmatory factor analysis (CFA) but accounting for the categorical nature of the instrument components as outlined in Section 4.5. In the affirmative case, a naturally arising question may be how reliable the overall test score is, i.e., what the reliability of the overall sum score of its components is. Returning for a moment to the empirical example used in Chapter 4, with the six-item college aspiration scale that we found to be unidimensional there, this query asks what proportion of error variance is contained in that of their sum. As mentioned, we cannot apply the method used in the preceding two sections, because these items are not continuous (not even approximately so).

A procedure for point and interval estimation of reliability for scales with binary items, which specifically utilizes the categorical nature on the original components, is presented in Raykov, Dimitrov, and Asparouhov (2010; see also Green & Yang, 2009b, for a discussion in the more general case). That approach becomes currently rather tedious to apply, however, with more than about 8 to 10 items. As a conceivable alternative to consider, the preceding developments in this chapter allow outlining the following approximate (and somewhat simplistic) method for estimation of reliability for instruments consisting of a larger number of items or such that have more than two possible scores. To this end, we first note that we can take the scale component sum any way we like, for the purpose of overall sum score reliability estimation. For instance, we can group items into parcels in a particular way, and then the sum of the parcels will equal the original test score (i.e., the original overall sum; the following discussion assumes that the model fitted to the parcels is itself identified). This is because the sum score is evidently the same regardless of the order in which we add the items. In other words, the population reliability of the scale of college aspiration that we discussed in Chapter 4 (Section 4.5) is the same as the population reliability of the sum of parcels built with its items. However, each of the parcels of two items has data ranging from 0 to 6, i.e., nearly twice as wide the range of the initial items. One could then proceed with the robust maximum likelihood method applied on the data from the parcels, which has been found to have considerable robustness against some deviations from normality (other than piling of cases at any scale end) and minor clustering effect, including categorical items with a number of categories like we would have for the parcels (viz., five, say, and above). This method is invoked in M*plus* by using the added command ANALYSIS: ESTIMATOR = MLR, as we indicated in the preceding section.

With this in mind, for the previously considered college aspiration example in Chapter 4, we can build three parcels of two items each, by adding, say, first and fourth items into the first parcel, second and fifth items into the second parcel, and third and sixth items into the third parcel. (We attach these three new variables to the earlier six items and name the resulting data file CHAPTER7_1.DAT that is needed next.) On the so-created data set with the three 'new' items (whereby there is no piling of cases at their minimal or maximal score of 0 or 6), we apply the earlier method for point and interval estimation of test reliability, using robust maximum likelihood (MLR) for parameter estimation purposes. We employ for this aim the following M*plus* input file:

```
TITLE:          RELIABILITY ESTIMATION AFTER PARCELING, FOR COMPOSITE WITH
                ORIGINAL CATEGORICAL ITEMS.

DATA:           FILE = CHAPTER7_1.DAT;
VARIABLE:       NAMES = ITEM_1-ITEM_6 NEWI1-NEWI3;
                USEVARIABLES = NEWI1-NEWI3;

ANALYSIS:       ESTIMATOR = MLR;

MODEL:          F1 BY NEWI1*(P1)
                NEWI2-NEWI3 (P2-P3);
                NEWI1-NEWI3 (P4-P6);
                F1@1;

MODEL CONSTRAINT:
                NEW(COMP_REL);
                COMP_REL = (P1+P2+P3)**2/((P1+P2+P3)**2+P4+P5+P6);

OUTPUT:         CINTERVAL;
```

We stress that we analyze only the 'new' items, which is accomplished by including the VARIABLE option USEVARIABLES = NEWI1-NEWI3 to select these 3 observed variables. This input leads to the following results:

```
INPUT READING TERMINATED NORMALLY

RELIABILITY ESTIMATION AFTER PARCELING FOR A COMPOSITE WITH
ORIGINAL CATEGORICAL ITEMS.

SUMMARY OF ANALYSIS

Number of groups                                        1
Number of observations                                823
Number of dependent variables                           3
Number of independent variables                         0
Number of continuous latent variables                   2

Observed dependent variables
  Continuous
  NEWI1  NEWI2  NEWI3

Continuous latent variables
  F1

Estimator                                             MLR
Information matrix                               EXPECTED
Maximum number of iterations                         1000
Convergence criterion                           0.500D-04
Maximum number of steepest descent iterations          20
```

```
Input data file(s)
 CHAPTER7_1.dat
Input data format FREE

THE MODEL ESTIMATION TERMINATED NORMALLY
TESTS OF MODEL FIT

Chi-Square Test of Model Fit

 Value                                                0.000
 Degrees of Freedom                                       0
 P-Value                                              0.0000
```

This model fits the data perfectly because of its particular construction, viz., being based on three observed variables. The reason is that it has as many parameters as there are variances and covariances pertaining to the three parcels analyzed, and thus it is saturated (e.g., Raykov & Marcoulides, 2006a; we stress that the present reliability estimation procedure is directly applicable also with more than three parcels). We move on to evaluation of reliability for the overall sum score of the original six categorical items, which equals the sum of these three parcels.

```
Chi-Square Test of Model Fit for the Baseline Model

 Value                                              387.507
 Degrees of Freedom                                       3
 P-Value                                             0.0000
CFI/TLI

 CFI                                                  1.000
 TLI                                                  1.000
Loglikelihood

 H0 Value                                         −1833.633
 H1 Value                                         −1833.633

Information Criteria

 Number of Free Parameters                               6
 Akaike (AIC)                                      3679.266
 Bayesian (BIC)                                    3702.006
 Sample-Size Adjusted BIC                          3682.974
 (n* = (n + 2) / 24)

RMSEA (Root Mean Square Error Of Approximation)

 Estimate                                             0.000
 90 Percent C.I.                             0.000   0.000
 Probability RMSEA <= .05                             0.000

SRMR (Standardized Root Mean Square Residual)

 Value                                                0.000

MODEL RESULTS

 Estimates S.E. Est./S.E.
 F1    BY

    NEWI1      1.371         0.089      15.393
    NEWI2      1.541         0.100      15.469
    NEWI3      1.661         0.103      16.092
```

```
Variances

    F1           1.000          0.000          0.000

Residual Variances
    NEWI1        1.178          0.140          8.444
    NEWI2        1.454          0.174          8.339
    NEWI3        1.404          0.189          7.435

New/Additional Parameters
    COMP_REL     0.839          0.016         52.439
```

According to these results, the composite under consideration—the sum score of the original six Likert items (ITEM_1 through ITEM_6)—is associated with a reliability of .838, with a standard error of .016 and a z-value 52.439. Using the R function 'ci.rel' from Section 7.5 of the present chapter, (.804, .867) results as a 95%-confidence interval for the scale's reliability, which lies entirely within a desirable range of .80 and above.

We recommend, however, that the results obtained with the approximate procedure outlined in this Section 7.7 be interpreted with caution, because of possible discrepancies with results obtained under different parceling than the one used here. In particular, one could have more trust in the results with a particular set of parcels when they are very similar (in particular, when the resulting confidence intervals are very similar, at the same confidence level) across different ways in which parcels could be built from a given set of highly discrete components under consideration.

7.8 Reliability Estimation for Measuring Instruments With General Structure

We have mentioned repeatedly in this book that unidimensionality of a given measuring instrument is a very useful feature in social and behavioral research. However, in some empirical situations there may be important reasons, e.g., in relation to validity (see Chapter 8), that may lead a scholar to decide to use an instrument with a more general structure than that of unidimensionality (e.g., McDonald, 1970, 1978, 1981, 1985, 1999; Raykov & Shrout, 2002; Zinbarg, Revelle, Yovel, & Li, 2005). Such instruments may be associated with two or even more sources of latent variability and may be especially attractive to scientists in particular substantive areas (e.g., potentially in depression or self-esteem research). In those cases, the question that naturally arises is how to evaluate reliability of multidimensional scales of this kind.

To discuss a latent-variable-modeling-based procedure accomplishing this aim, consider a set of continuous instrument components, denoted $X_1, X_2, ..., X_p$ $(p > 2$; cf. McDonald, 1999; Raykov & Shrout, 2002, and pertinent references therein; see also Chapter 6 and Raykov, 1998b, 2001a, regarding limitations of coefficient alpha for scales with general structure). Like them, their true scores $T_1, T_2, ..., T_p$ are random variables as well. Suppose that the scale with these components is not unidimensional. This implies that there are at least two sources of interindividual variability behind the set of their true scores, $T_1, T_2, ..., T_p$. Denote by $\underline{f}$ the $q \times 1$ vector of factors that are assumed to be underlying the interrelationships among $T_1, T_2, ..., T_p$ $(2 \leq q \leq p)$. That is, this model for the true scores is

$$\underline{T} = \underline{d} + A\underline{f} + \underline{u}, \tag{7.22}$$

where $\underline{T}$ is the $p \times 1$ vector of true scores, A is the associated $p \times q$ loading matrix relating true scores to underlying factors, and $\underline{u}$ is the pertinent $p \times 1$ vector of unique factors (residual terms; $\underline{d}$ is a vector of intercepts, which can be assumed for convenience to equal 0 as they do not affect the reliability of the composite under consideration). Then the observed scores on the instrument components satisfy the model

$$\underline{X} = \underline{T} + \underline{E} = A\underline{f} + \underline{u} + \underline{E}, \tag{7.23}$$

where $\underline{X}$ denotes the $p \times 1$ vector of recorded scores, and $\underline{E}$ is the $p \times 1$ vector of their error scores. Because the overall sum score X of the original scale components is

$$X = X_1 + X_2 + \cdots + X_p = T_1 + T_2 + \cdots + T_p + E_1 + E_2 + \cdots + E_p \tag{7.24}$$

(see Section 7.5), its true score is $T = T_1 + T_2 + \cdots + T_p = \mathbf{1}' \underline{T}$, where $\mathbf{1}'$ is the vector consisting of 1s only (p of them; see Chapter 2). Similarly, the error score associated with the total score $X = \mathbf{1}' \underline{X}$, is $E = E_1 + E_2 + \ldots + E_p = \mathbf{1}' \underline{E}$. Given that the reliability of the composite X is

$$\rho_X = Var(T)/Var(X) \tag{7.25}$$

(see Chapter 6), using the rules for obtaining covariance matrix of a random vector (i.e., a vector whose components are random variables; Chapter 2), via Equation (7.23), this reliability is expressed as

$$\rho_X = (\mathbf{1}'A\Phi A'\mathbf{1} + \mathbf{1}'\Omega'\mathbf{1})/(\mathbf{1}'A\Phi A'\mathbf{1} + \mathbf{1}'\Omega'\mathbf{1} + \mathbf{1}'\Theta'\mathbf{1}), \tag{7.26}$$

where Φ is the covariance matrix of the common factors $\underline{f}$ in Equation (7.23), that of the unique factors $\underline{u}$ there, and Θ is the covariance matrix of the error score (often assumed diagonal).

The expression in the right-hand side of equation (7.26) can be obtained also along the lines of the development of the omega coefficient (McDonald, 1999). A procedure for point and interval estimation of general structure scale reliability, for an identified model representable in the form of the right-hand side of Equation (7.23), is discussed, e.g., in Raykov and Shrout (2002; see also McDonald, 1970, 1978, 1981, 1985, 1999). Point estimation of reliability of such a multidimensional scale with nonnormal continuous components is accomplished along the same lines using the robust maximum likelihood method indicated earlier in this chapter. The latter method would also lead to (largely) trustworthy results with components having at least five to seven scores that individuals can take on them, as long as there is no piling of cases at their minimal or maximal value, as well as in cases with minor clustering (nesting) effect. In situations with hierarchical data, the approach in Raykov and du Toit (2005) can be used to point and interval estimate reliability for unidimensional instruments. That approach is directly extended, along the lines of this section, to the case of a multidimensional scale with hierarchical data. An application of the method in Raykov and Shrout (2002) to a general structure scale undergoing revision is also possible, when components are deleted or added to tentative versions of that instrument. This application renders point and interval estimates of reliability for any of its versions of interest.

Last but not least, a particular form of lack of unidimensionality is found in hierarchical scales (e.g., McDonald, 1999; Zinbarg et al., 2005). In these instruments, a set of interrelated factors account for the interrelationships between a set of observed test components, whereas these factors draw part of their variability from a second-order factor, frequently referred to as a general (hierarchical) factor. The degree to which this factor accounts for variability in the overall sum score can provide important information about instrument score interpretability (e.g., Uliaszek et al., in press; Zinbarg et al., 2009; Zinbarg, Yovel, Revelle, & McDonald, 2006). A latent-variable-modeling-based procedure for point and interval estimation of the proportion of general factor variance in a hierarchical scale of this type is outlined in Raykov and Zinbarg (2010) and of reliability and criterion validity of such scales in Raykov and Marcoulides (2010c). These procedures can be readily employed in empirical behavioral and social research settings, along the lines of the discussion in the last three sections.

7.9 Outlook

In this chapter, we discussed a number of procedures for estimation of composite reliability (test, scale, or instrument reliability). These included both traditional and more recent methods. We stressed a number of limitations of traditional methods. In our view, in the general case these limitations make those methods substantially less attractive than more recent ones.

We also provided important information that is helpful to behavioral and social researchers for ascertaining in a given empirical setting whether use of the popular coefficient alpha would be appropriate as opposed to potentially misleading. In addition, we outlined a readily and widely applicable approach to examining effect of instrument revision (deletion or addition of components) upon composite reliability, in particular for point and interval estimation of the reliability coefficient(s) after revision. This approach is not developed in terms of the still-popular index 'Alpha if item deleted' that can be, however, misleading as well and, unlike the latter, is concerned with population reliability and its change following of revision (rather than only with the sample values of alpha for possible revisions as that earlier index is).

We further discussed estimation of reliability of instruments that are not unidimensional but can be considered by social and behavioral scientists on substantive and/or validity grounds. Such instruments can be particularly attractive in situations where unidimensionality may be achieved by removing certain components from a scale under consideration, which, however, may entail nonnegligible loss of validity, the bottom line of measurement that we turn to in the next chapter.

8

Validity

In the preceding chapters of this book, we have discussed a number of topics that are of relevance to the process of developing measuring instruments in the behavioral and social sciences. In particular, we have spent a considerable amount of time on a major problem of measurement in these and cognate disciplines—the presence of measurement error when evaluating latent constructs that represent entities of major interest. In earlier chapters we were mainly concerned, however, with random error of measurement as well as its effect on observed scores, and we discussed relatively briefly the issue of systematic error. What we have not addressed yet in the needed detail is what may well be viewed as the bottom line of measurement, viz., whether an instrument is indeed measuring what it purports to evaluate, that is, the construct of actual interest. In this sense, we have not posed so far the question of how good the recorded scores with an instrument under consideration are in this particular respect. This issue is of paramount importance for measurement in the social and behavioral sciences, as well as outside them, and is the subject of the present chapter.

8.1 Introduction

In the last two chapters, we were concerned with issues pertaining to reliability of measurement. Accordingly, a test or measurement device was considered 'good', i.e., possessing high reliability, if it produced consistent results. These are results that are not affected by more than perhaps negligible error. The natural question that arises now is if this is all we want from the scores on an instrument of concern.

To motivate the need for examining related yet distinct aspects of behavioral measurement, consider the following example that someone might wish to claim represented a test of intelligence. This test consists of the following questions:

1. What is your birthday?
2. What is your last name?
3. What is your first name?
4. How old are you?
5. Who is the president of the USA?

It is conceivable that there will be very limited amount of error associated with this test if it were to be presented to a sample of subjects from a population of interest. One could perhaps reasonably argue that it is a highly reliable measuring instrument. Yet evidently the more important question is how good this is as an intelligence test. Clearly, very few would argue that the above set of five questions would represent a good measure of intelligence.

This simple example brings us to another aspect of quality of behavioral measuring instruments, which we have alluded to earlier but not discussed yet in the detail it deserves. This aspect reflects the 'goodness' of the instrument specifically with regard to the purposes for which it has been developed. It relates to the question of how good inferences, i.e., how veridical conclusions, can be drawn from a given test's individual scores. These inferences would typically be concerned with individuals' behavior beyond the testing situation, which behavior pertains to a trait or latent dimension (construct) the instrument has been developed to measure. If these inferences are correct, or essentially correct, then one can claim that the instrument has high quality. In the above example, this question translates into how good that five-item scale is as a measuring device for intelligence. Many would agree that it is not at all good in that sense. The serious doubts one would have pertain not to reliability but to the degree to which this test indeed measures intelligence. In particular, one could convincingly argue that the above is not a valid instrument for measuring intelligence, i.e., not a valid intelligence test.

We can thus give at this point the following relatively informal definition of validity, which we will make more specific and precise as we advance through the chapter. Accordingly, validity is the extent to which an instrument indeed measures the latent dimension or construct it was developed to evaluate in the first place. In our earlier example, the validity of the five-component test is the degree to which it indeed measures intelligence. That example also provides a demonstration of the fact that high reliability does not imply high validity of an instrument as a device for measuring a particular behavioral trait or ability. That is, high reliability is a feature of relevance by itself, but it does not necessarily go with high validity. A test may be lacking validity, or have very low validity, and still be a highly reliable measuring instrument. Hence, reliability is not all we need to look for. In terms of logic, high reliability is not a sufficient condition for high validity but only a necessary one. (In Section 8.6 below, we demonstrate this relationship formally.) Because in the behavioral and social sciences the question of paramount relevance is what actually is being evaluated and assessed with a given instrument, validity is the bottom line of measurement. This is also illustrated with our above example of an 'intelligence test'.

Studies of validity of a given behavioral measuring instrument amount to collection of evidence in support of the types of inferences that are to be drawn from its scores with respect to behavior outside of the specific measurement situation (e.g., Messick, 1989, 1995). There is, however, rarely if ever 'enough' evidence to claim with complete certainty that an instrument indeed evaluates what it is supposed or purports to measure. Rather, validity is an evolving property, and instrument validation is a continuing process, one with which we could perhaps never be done. Hence, the question of validity cannot typically be answered with absolute certainty, at least not in most areas of current behavioral and social science. That is, validity is a matter of degree, not an all or none situation, for most practical purposes. What we could do when addressing the question of validity is develop a 'strong case' for validity of a given instrument by accumulating evidence in support of the inferences to be drawn from scores obtained with it.

This discussion allows us to give now a more specific definition of validity. Accordingly, for a given measuring instrument, validity is an integrated evaluative judgment of the extent to which empirical evidence and theoretical rationales support the adequacy and appropriateness of inferences drawn from, and actions based on, scores obtained with that instrument (Messick, 1989, 1995). That is, validity is the degree to which evidence and theory support the interpretations of test scores entailed by proposed uses of the tests (measuring instruments; e.g., *Standards for Educational and Psychological Testing*, 1999). From this perspective, one can also claim that it is the inferences derived from the instrument scores that need to be validated. Therefore, to validate these inferences one needs (a) to ascertain the degree to which multiple lines of evidence are in agreement with the drawn inferences as well as (b) to establish that alternative inferences are less well supported. At the same time, we need to bear in mind that these inferences are based on use of a particular measuring instrument under consideration, so they are not independent of it or devoid of relationship to it.

As we see from this section, the concept of validity is multifaceted and cannot be comprehensively discussed in a single chapter. In the present one, we discuss in turn three main types of validity and address their evaluation in empirical behavioral and social research. For a more thorough discussion of validity and a number of additional closely related matters of theoretical and empirical relevance, we refer to Crocker and Algina (1986), McDonald (1999), Messick (1989, 1995), and Borsboom (2006). (The first cited source has considerably influenced the discussion in the next several sections.)

8.2 Types of Validity

The preceding section highlighted the multifaceted nature of the concept of validity of measurement. Although this is a single and unified notion, different aspects of it can become especially important under certain circumstances in behavioral and social research. Traditionally, scholars in these disciplines have considered three main types of validity. These are content, criterion, and construct validity. As we discuss them next in turn, we will also mention other related types of validity that can be of particular rather than general relevance. Our goal is not to provide an exhaustive coverage of all kinds of validity that have been considered in the literature and could become important in some empirical situations, but rather to provide a discussion of a more general framework within which these validity types can be viewed as contained.

A type of validity that is particularly important when developing instruments for measuring achievement, especially academic achievement tests, is content validity. This is the degree to which one can draw correct inferences from test scores to performance on a larger domain of similar items to those included in a test under consideration. Content validation is thus the process where a scholar accumulates evidence in favor of a claim that correct conclusions can be drawn from scores on the test, which conclusions refer to how well examined subjects would fare if they were given a relatively large set of items pertaining to the behavioral domain addressed by the instrument (oftentimes a particular ability).

Another type of validity that becomes of special relevance when performance on another measurement occasion is of concern is criterion validity. For a given instrument, this is the extent to which one can predict subject scores on another variable or criterion of interest from the scores on that instrument. A measure has high criterion validity if the prediction error is small when predicting with it performance on a criterion variable. Criterion validity is relevant when we wish to draw inferences, using a given test's scores, about performance on some behavioral variable of practical importance, which variable in some circumstances may be evaluated in the future—e.g., college grade, on the job performance, or clinical measure(s).

A third type of validity of major concern in social and behavioral research is construct validity. This validity is the degree to which (a) certain explanatory concepts or constructs account for performance on an instrument under consideration and (b) its scores are indicative of behavior that integrates (fits) well into an already existing net of relationships among constructs in a given substantive domain. Construct validity of a test is demonstrated to the extent to which performance on it is (a) related to such on indicators of constructs to which the claimed latent dimension behind the test is supposed to be correlated with, and (b) unrelated to indicators of constructs with which that dimension is expected not to be correlated with. Construct validity is thus a rather comprehensive type of validity and one that is intrinsically related to available theories in a given substantive area.

   The three discussed types of validity focus on specific aspects of the degree to which inferences drawn from an instrument's scores are trustworthy. Hence, more than one kind of validation may and often will be of interest in a particular study. Conversely, in order to claim validity for a given instrument, one may need to demonstrate more than one type of validity as being high. Furthermore, because of the fact that validity is such a multifaceted feature, unlike the case with reliability, there is actually no single index that represents how high a given measuring instrument's validity is. Only in the particular case of criterion validity can we provide an index, as we will see later in the chapter. We discuss next in more detail each of these three main types of validity.

8.3 Content Validity

This type of validity is concerned with the degree to which test components represent adequately a performance domain or construct of interest. For example, when developing a test of arithmetic proficiency, a main question is whether the particular items in the test adequately represent the domain of possible items one could construct, which would cover the ability to perform arithmetic operations. The extent to which they do is the content validity of the test. Hence, content validity represents a 'conceptual test' whether a given instrument evaluates what it is presumed to measure, i.e., what it was developed to measure in the first instance. In order to be in a position to evaluate content validity, first the substantive domain pertaining to the concept to be measured needs to be made clear. The extent to which the components of a test indeed represent that domain is the content validity of this instrument.

   Therefore, content validity is a qualitative type of validity that depends on the theoretical definition of a concept (construct) being studied and reflects the degree to which the components of the instrument represent that construct. Thus, the extent to which a test lacks content validity, i.e., does not represent the domain of concern, is the extent to which this measuring instrument could be misleading. The reason is that then the latter only taps into part of the concept of interest, and inferences based on its results or scores may be incorrect. We note that this relationship between test and domain parallels that of sample to population from which the former is drawn. Hence, to study a concept we need to use measures (test or instrument components) that fully represent its aspects or underlying dimension(s). If these measures do not accomplish this aim, then the researcher must further explicate the concept aspects that they reflect and perhaps restrict his or her study to these only.

   Evaluation of content validity is an involved process. A typical procedure is to recruit a panel of independent experts who have not been involved in item or test component development (item writing). The experts need to judge then whether the items on a given test or scale adequately sample the domain of concern. This procedure is invoked after an initial form of the instrument has been developed, and it is to be performed by persons not having participated in the test construction process. Content validation is most often conducted for achievement tests and is not the same as the notion of face validity. The latter is the degree to which items, or test components, appear to measure a construct that is meaningful to a layperson or typical examinee. Content validity obviously is a far deeper concept, in that it reflects the degree to which a set of components is representative of a subject-matter domain.

A main limitation of the notion of content validity is that it critically depends on the theoretical definition of a concept under study. Yet for many concepts of interest in the behavioral and social disciplines, no consensus exists on their theoretical definitions. The reason is that the substantive domain pertaining to a concept may not be very well defined and perhaps at times may even be ambiguous. In fact, the theoretical understanding of many concepts of importance in a substantive field evolves together with their study. As a result, at a given point in time, its domain may not be well delineated. This may create serious difficulties with developing instruments possessing high content validity.

8.4 Criterion Validity

In many empirical situations, one is interested in using a given instrument's scores to obtain an idea about individual performance on another measure that oftentimes has not been administered yet but is hoped to be related, possibly closely, to the instrument in question (cf. Crocker & Algina, 1986). For instance, can we draw trustworthy inferences, based on the scores on a particular test, regarding individuals' behavior with respect to some performance criterion (standard) that has not been measured before or for certain reasons cannot be measured at the same time as the test is administered? To the extent we can draw such veridical conclusions, we can claim the test has criterion validity. That is, criterion validity is the degree to which there is a relationship between a given test's scores and performance on another measure of particular relevance, typically referred to as criterion. For example, if one considers a college admission test, a natural question to ask is how good it is as a predictor of academic achievement at university level. That is, the query asks about the criterion validity of this college admission test. Similarly, when one is looking at an aptitude test, such as one of the SAT parts, a question that quickly comes to mind is about its validity as a predictor of success in college. In other words, this question asks about the criterion validity of that aptitude test.

Upon a closer inspection of the notion of criterion validity, it is useful to distinguish between two kinds of it, predictive and concurrent criterion validity. (Often they are correspondingly referred to, for short, as predictive and concurrent validity.) Predictive validity is the extent to which test scores predict criterion measurements to be made in the future, e.g., after a period of schooling or training. For instance, the second example from the last pair asks how closely related that SAT part scores are with college GPA. To the extent they are, one can claim that those SAT scores have predictive validity and that perhaps their use could be justified in making decisions about college admission. Conversely, concurrent validity reflects the strength of relationship between test scores and criterion measurements made at the time of test administration or shortly thereafter. For instance, consider the question of how high the concurrent validity of SAT scores is as predictors of academic success for the same semester in high school. We typically speak of concurrent validity for a given test when the criterion scores are available at the same time, at least approximately, as we obtain the test measurements.

Both types of criterion validity can be assessed with evidence for a relationship between test and criterion. To this end, denoting correspondingly by X and Y these measures, one can use the (absolute value of the) correlation $\rho_{X,Y}$ between test scores and criterion performance scores. (The discussion in the remainder of this chapter assumes that any correlation coefficient referred to is well defined—e.g., Chapter 2—and frequently uses the symbol ρ for correlation usually subindexed by the variables involved.) This correlation $\rho_{X,Y}$ is often referred to as validity coefficient, viz., of the test X with regard to the criterion Y. A criterion validation study aims at gathering evidence in favor of a relationship between the measure of interest and a criterion or against such a relationship.

There are a number of potential problems that may affect the outcome of this type of validation studies, which we mention next (e.g., Crocker & Algina, 1986).

Criterion Problem: As a criterion (reference) variable, one could take immediate, intermediate, or ultimate measures. The immediate measures are readily available and easy to evaluate but may not be completely informative in their role as criterion variables. An example of such measures is a teacher rating of students having taken a particular test whose criterion validity is to be evaluated. Conversely, ultimate criteria are typically of substantial importance but may be hard to define operationally and assess on their own. Such criteria tend to be constructs of relevance in relation to subject performance on the test in question. For instance, classroom effectiveness of teachers can be an ultimate criterion with respect to an instrument evaluating teacher quality that is administered at the beginning of a school year. Given these limitations of immediate and ultimate measures when used as criteria, one might consider utilizing instead an intermediate criterion. For instance, in the context of the last example, one could use ratings by a supervising teacher as an intermediate criterion.

Sample Size: Small samples are associated with marked if not large sampling error, so validity coefficients (being correlation coefficients) should be treated with caution, as their estimates are likely to be unstable (e.g., King & Minium, 2003). This is of particular relevance when test scores are used for purposes of subsequent decision making.

Criterion Contamination: In a given empirical setting, there are frequently other variables that impact the criterion beyond the construct underlying a test score under consideration. The total effect of their influences upon criterion scores is referred to as criterion contamination. The latter also affects the relationship between construct being measured and criterion. For example, college professors who account for admission test scores in the grades they give at university level in fact contaminate the criterion (college success). Criterion contamination may strengthen or weaken—the latter being probably the more likely case—a relationship between test and criterion scores. Thus, reported criterion validity coefficients need to be treated with caution especially in contexts where criterion contamination cannot be ruled out.

Restriction of Range: As is well-known from introductory statistics courses, restriction of range can affect markedly a correlation coefficient. For this reason, it can also affect validity coefficients. This restriction often leads to attenuation of validity coefficients and occurs because of selection on a variable related to the criterion or the test. For example, carrying out validation of a college admission test based only on students performing above (below) a certain cutoff on GPA, or alternatively above (below) some SAT score, is likely to affect the validity coefficients, because the correlation of these two measures is likely to be impacted. Restriction of range may be explicit or incidental, depending on whether the researcher is aware of it possibly occurring. Restriction of range can also happen because of ceiling or floor effects operating on one or more of the measures involved or because of attrition during the time elapsed between test administration and criterion evaluation. Because range restriction biases the validity coefficients, the general principle to follow in validity studies is to plan them so as to avoid such curtailment of variance.

Reliability of Predictor and Criterion: There is an important relationship between error of measurement in a test under consideration and/or criterion measure, on the one hand, and their correlation on the other hand. (As indicated earlier in the chapter, this discussion assumes that there are true and observed individual differences on the two measures involved; e.g., Chapters 2 and 6.) If we assume the errors in both measures as unrelated, as has been already known for several decades the correlation between test (X) and criterion (Y) cannot exceed the product of their reliability indexes. That is, subindexing true scores with the symbols of variables they pertain to,

$$\rho_{X,Y} = Corr(X,Y) = \frac{Cov(X,Y)}{\sqrt{Var(X)Var(Y)}} = \frac{Cov(T_X + E_X, T_Y + E_Y)}{\sqrt{Var(X)Var(Y)}}$$

$$= \frac{Cov(T_X, T_Y)}{\sqrt{Var(X)Var(Y)}} \leq \frac{\sqrt{Var(T_X)Var(T_Y)}}{\sqrt{Var(X)Var(Y)}} = \rho_{X,T_X}\rho_{Y,T_Y}. \tag{8.1}$$

In the last part of Inequality (8.1), as we recall from Chapter 6, the symbols ρ_{X,T_X} and ρ_{Y,T_Y} are those of the reliability indexes for X and for Y, respectively. (In the second line of (8.1), we have used the fact that a correlation coefficient—that of the true scores involved—cannot exceed 1; see Chapter 2.)

Inequality (8.1) reveals an important relationship between criterion validity and reliability indexes. Specifically, it shows that the product of the test and criterion reliability indexes is an upper bound of the criterion validity coefficient (compare the first and last part of the inequality). Thus, whenever at least one of these reliability indexes is low, criterion validity will typically be even lower (because the other index cannot be larger than 1, being a correlation). For this reason, it is essential that data be collected on the test and criterion in a way that ensures the effect of measurement error on them to be minimal; similarly, small true variance on the test or criterion can deflate criterion validity as well.

Thus far in this section we have been concerned with the case of continuous or approximately so scores on a test (instrument) and criterion, when as a criterion validity coefficient one can use their correlation coefficient (assuming it is defined; see Chapters 2 and 6 for pertinent discussion). In case of a dichotomous criterion, one can instead utilize the mean differences between the two groups involved as a measure informing about criterion validity of the used instrument. Similarly, the tetrachoric or polychoric correlation between test and criterion can be used as a criterion validity coefficient when at least one of them is discrete (i.e., with a limited number of scores possible on it, say up to five or so; see Chapter 4).

Although quite useful, the notion of criterion validity has several limitations that need to be explicitly mentioned at this point (Crocker & Algina, 1986). In some cases, for an instrument of interest there may not be an appropriate criterion with regard to which its validity could be worked out. Moreover, different criterion variables that may be considered can correlate to a different extent with a test being examined, leading possibly to a multitude of validity coefficients; in those cases, the question which one to trust most may not have an easy answer. Last but not least, the validity coefficient is affected by error of measurement in the instrument under investigation as well as in the criterion used. This leads to validity attenuation, and its extent is directly related to the degree to which either of the two measures lacks reliability. We will return to this issue later in the chapter, where we will address it in more detail.

8.5 Construct Validity

Many constructs considered in the behavioral and social sciences may not be completely formulated or well defined at a given stage of theoretical development in their substantive area. As a result, the pertinent domain may not be possible to elaborate well enough for content validity to be evaluated with respect to an instrument under consideration (e.g., Bollen, 1989). In such cases, content validity is hard to use as a means of assessing the instrument's validity. Furthermore, as mentioned in the preceding section, appropriate criterion variables may not be available for some measuring devices. Under those circumstances, corresponding correlation coefficients or relationship indices cannot be worked out in order to address validity-related questions. This makes impossible the use of criterion validity as a means of assessing validity of a particular test. In such settings, the notion of construct validity can be utilized instead.

The relevance of construct validity goes, however, far beyond its possible application in settings where other forms of validity cannot be assessed. In particular, it is construct validity that represents the evidence based on which one can interpret the results of a given measuring instrument or test. More specifically, construct validity can be viewed as the extent to which there is evidence consistent with the assumption of a construct of concern being manifested in subjects' observed performance on the instrument (cf. McDonald, 1999). The notion of construct validity becomes even more important upon realizing that behavioral and social instruments are imprecise (fallible) not only because of the ubiquitous effects of random errors of measurement on the scores they render but also because they are not perfectly capturing the constructs they purport to assess (e.g., Messick, 1989, 1995). Construct validity directly addresses this imperfection, and to the degree to which the latter is salient, an instrument does not possess construct validity.

To define construct validity more fully, it would be helpful to return for a moment to Chapter 1 where we defined 'construct' as an entity of actual interest to obtain information about, which, however, can be only indirectly measured. We also emphasized there that in order for a construct to be useful and contribute to knowledge accumulation in a particular substantive field, it must be interpretable in the context of other constructs already available in it. This requires that for a given construct there exist specific relationships (or lack thereof) between measures of it with (a) measures of other constructs in that domain and (b) measures of specific real-world criteria. That is, the availability of an operational definition for a construct under consideration is not sufficient to proclaim it well defined, important, and useful. We need also to demonstrate how the construct is related to other relevant constructs and measures in the subject-matter domain. Construct validity thus includes evidence in favor of assumptions that an instrument in question relates to other observed measures in such a way that is consistent with predictions derived on the basis of already-available theories and accumulated knowledge in a substantive area.

We can thus view construct validity as the extent to which an instrument assesses a construct of concern and is associated with evidence for points (a) and (b) in the preceding paragraph. That is, to claim that an instrument possesses construct validity implies that one has examined all possible hypotheses—in particular, for positive, negative, or no association—with respect to constructs already developed in the substantive field in question. Thereby all empirical relationships found should parallel the theoretically specified associations based on prior research in that area. The degree to which they do is construct validity. With this in mind, it is realized that construct validity is the most encompassing type of validity. Construct validity thus comprises the evidence and rationales supporting the explanatory-concept-related interpretations of scores resulting from a measuring instrument under consideration (Messick, 1995). The degree to which these interpretations account for subject performance on the instrument and their score relationships with other variables is an integral part of construct validity (McDonald, 1999; Messick, 1989).

Hence, demonstration of construct validity requires multiple pieces of evidence and in fact typically needs more than a single study. In some sense, therefore, one is never done with (construct) validity. From this discussion, it is clear that no single test can determine construct validity. There are, however, certain approaches that can be used to assess construct validity (Messick, 1995). They include (a) correlational analysis, specifically for measures of the construct in question with measures of other constructs, as well as among these constructs; (b) differentiation between groups, e.g., performance comparison for males versus females; (c) factor analysis and latent variable modeling, to address queries pertaining to the latent structure of the measures involved as well as underlying relationships; and (d) a multitrait–multimethod procedure that focuses on convergent validity and discriminant validity coefficients, viz., the correlations with 'similar' measures that are expected to be high and the correlations with other measures that would be expected to be lower (we address this issue in more detail in a later section of this chapter).

When assessing construct validity, of particular relevance is also the consideration of possible rival hypotheses with respect to what is being measured by a given instrument. Specifically, these hypotheses are concerned with (a) construct underrepresentation and (b) construct-irrelevant variance (Crocker & Algina, 1986; Messick, 1995). Construct underrepresentation refers to the extent to which an instrument leaves out important aspects of the construct that is to be measured. This implies narrower meaning of the scores resulting from an application of the instrument than initially intended and expected. The reason for this limitation is typically that the instrument does not capture some types of content encompassed by the construct of concern. Alternatively, construct-irrelevant variance is the degree to which test scores are influenced by processes that have little to do with the intended construct and are not really part of the latter. For instance, reading speed, in a test of arithmetic ability in third graders, can introduce construct-irrelevant variance if of interest is to measure this ability. We will continue the discussion of construct validity later in this chapter, when we use a methodology we familiarized ourselves with earlier in this book, for purposes of assessing this type of validity.

8.6 Correction for Attenuation

The concept of criterion validity, quantified in the correlation between test (instrument) and criterion, leads naturally to the question what their correlation would be if one had access to the true scores on both test and criterion. This query is responded to by the classical correction for attenuation formula that is applicable to any two observed measures, denoted, say, X and Y (with nonzero true and individual differences, as assumed in the rest of this chapter; cf. Lord & Novick, 1968). Accordingly, the correlation between their observed scores is a lower bound of the correlation between their true scores. Indeed, we can rewrite the earlier Inequality (8.1) as follows (the symbol ρ denotes next correlation subindexed by measures involved, whose error scores are assumed uncorrelated as in Section 8.4; see Chapter 5):

$$\rho_{X,Y} = Corr(X,Y) = \frac{Cov(X,Y)}{\sqrt{Var(X)Var(Y)}} = \frac{Cov(T_X + E_X, T_Y + E_Y)}{\sqrt{Var(X)Var(Y)}}$$

$$= \frac{Cov(T_X, T_Y)}{\sqrt{Var(X)Var(Y)}} = \frac{Cov(T_X, T_Y)}{\sqrt{Var(T_X)Var(T_Y)}} \cdot \frac{\sqrt{Var(T_X)Var(T_Y)}}{\sqrt{Var(X)Var(Y)}} \qquad (8.2)$$

$$= \rho_{T_X, T_Y} \sqrt{\frac{Var(T_X)}{Var(X)}} \cdot \sqrt{\frac{Var(T_Y)}{Var(Y)}} = \rho_{T_X, T_Y} \sqrt{\rho_X \rho_Y} \leq \rho_{T_X, T_Y}.$$

The Inequality chain (8.2) has two important implications. First, observed correlation is a lower bound of true correlation, as we alluded to before (see beginning and final parts of (8.2)). Thereby, equality between the two correlations holds only when measurement is perfect, i.e., in cases with reliability of 1 on both measures X and Y. Such cases would be, however, extremely rare, if possible, to find in empirical behavioral and social research. Hence, taking in the role of X and Y a test and criterion score, respectively, we can consider their observed correlation $\rho_{X,Y}$ typically as a strict lower bound of their true score correlation ρ_{T_X, T_Y}. (We emphasize that this strict lower bound feature applies to all measures with nonzero observed and true variances, as seen from (8.2), where at least one of the measures is imperfect, i.e., evaluated with error.)

Second, Inequality (8.2) contains in its penultimate part also what is called the correction for attenuation formula. Hence, if one wants to evaluate the true score correlation for two measures, ρ_{T_X, T_Y}, all one needs to do is divide their observed correlation $\rho_{X,Y}$ with the product of the square roots of their reliabilities, $\sqrt{\rho_X \rho_Y}$, i.e., with the product of the reliability indexes of the measures involved. This process is often referred to as correction for attenuation or alternatively as disattenuation. In an empirical setting, the resulting estimate of true score correlation, $\hat{\rho}_{X,Y} / \sqrt{\hat{\rho}_X \hat{\rho}_Y}$, is therefore called disattenuated correlation (estimate) between test and criterion.

Because of the difference between observed and true score correlation, which is explicated in Inequality (8.2), it would be meaningful as well as desirable in a criterion validation study to provide both the attenuated correlation (observed correlation) and the correlation corrected for attenuation, i.e., the true score correlation estimate. In this way, a better picture of the relationship between test and criterion will be obtained, which will allow more informed conclusions to be reached about the measurement qualities of an instrument under consideration.

8.7 The Relationship Between Reliability and Validity

We emphasized at the beginning of this chapter that the concepts of reliability and validity are distinct, with the latter being the bottom line of measurement in the social and behavioral sciences. At the same time, such a perspective may create the impression that the two notions can or should be dealt with separately, especially because conceptions relating to the quality and adequacy of measurement have historically tended to be categorized into one of the two areas (Marcoulides, 2004). A fragmentary approach like this has also fostered, however, a lack of appreciation of the interrelationships and interdependencies among the various aspects of measurement theory. As a result, some researchers seem to even believe that 'reliability and validity are independent of each other', whereas assertions like reliability being 'the poor man's validity' can also be found (e.g., Rozeboom, 1966, p. 375). Marcoulides (2004) emphasized, 'The distinction between reliability and validity should be seen as that between two different regions on the same continuum rather than between fundamentally different categories' (p. 183). Cronbach, Gleser, Nanda, and Rajaratnam (1972) also supported this idea when they indicated, 'The theory of reliability and the theory of validity coalesce' (p. 234; see also McDonald, 1999).

These two main concepts in behavioral and social measurement are indeed related, and there is an important relationship between them that is quite helpful to highlight. This relationship provides the connection between reliability and validity and is obtained when one compares a reliability coefficient (index) with a criterion validity coefficient. To this end, first we observe from the preceding section that the correlation between a test score, X, and its true score, T_X, is at least as high as the correlation between the test and any other measure, Y; in other words, the correlation between observed score X and true score T on a given measure is the highest possible correlation between observed score and any other random variable. (As indicated earlier in this chapter, we assume throughout that all correlations considered in it exist, i.e., are well defined; see, e.g., Chapter 2. Similarly, as before, error scores in X and Y are treated as uncorrelated; see Chapter 5.) Indeed, comparing the first with the second-last part of Inequality (8.2) we see that

$$\rho_{X,Y} = \rho_{T_X,T_Y} \sqrt{\rho_X \rho_Y} \leq \sqrt{\rho_X} = \rho_{X,T_X},$$

which is the reliability index for X (Chapter 6). This inequality holds because none of the correlations and reliability coefficients involved in its middle part are larger than 1. Therefore (in the alternative correlation notation),

$$Corr(X, T_X) \geq Corr(X, Y) \tag{8.3}$$

for a given X and any choice of the variable Y (for which ρ_Y exists; Chapter 6). Taking the criterion in the role of Y, and using the definition of reliability index (Chapter 6), we reexpress Inequality (8.3) as

$$\rho_{X,T_X} \geq Corr(X, Y). \tag{8.4}$$

That is,

$$\text{Criterion validity} \leq \text{Reliability index.} \tag{8.5}$$

Hence, the reliability index for a given measuring instrument is an upper bound for the criterion validity of that instrument. We stress that it is the reliability index that stands in the right-hand side of Inequality (8.5), not the reliability coefficient.

Although informally one might interpret Inequality (8.5) as suggesting that validity is never higher than reliability, which seems to be a very widely circulated statement in the social and behavioral science literature, strictly speaking such a claim would not be correct. Specifically, what Inequality (8.5) says is only that criterion validity is never higher than the reliability index rather than coefficient. In fact, it is possible that validity is higher than reliability (i.e., the reliability coefficient), and there is no logical contradiction in such a possibility. What is not possible, however, is that (criterion) validity is higher than the reliability index. For example, if reliability is .50, validity still could be as high as .70, as Inequality (8.5) states, and thus markedly higher than the reliability coefficient. Note that then Inequality (8.5) is not violated because $.70 < \sqrt{.05}$, with the latter being the reliability index. Hence, it is possible that validity is higher than reliability (i.e., the reliability coefficient), and what is true in this context is only that validity is never higher than the reliability index itself.

Inequality (8.5) also does in part justice to the past and ongoing interest in the concept of reliability in behavioral and social research. This is because the inequality asserts that the higher the reliability, the 'more room' there is for validity to lie—in the hope that it may be high for a particular measuring instrument with high reliability. Although the last is a fairly informal statement, typical well-informed efforts to enhance reliability are not unlikely to increase validity as well (possibly up to a certain point). Hence, methods helping one improve reliability may pay off by an accompanied increase in validity also (see next).

Inequality (8.5) further shows that high reliability (index) is a necessary condition for high validity. This means that high validity cannot occur unless the reliability (index) is high. It is in this sense that one can claim high reliability as necessary for high validity, because the latter implies the former. However, as indicated earlier, having a high reliability index is not sufficient, i.e., not enough, in order for an instrument to possess high validity. That is, high reliability does not suffice or guarantee high validity, because the former does not imply the latter. The intelligence-test-related example at the beginning of this chapter demonstrates empirically that high reliability is not sufficient for high validity, i.e., high reliability does not represent any guarantee for high validity.

8.8 Estimation of Criterion Validity and Revision Effect on It

As mentioned earlier in this chapter, criterion validity is quantified by the correlation between a criterion variable and a given score, e.g., on a single measure or on a multiple-component measuring instrument. In an empirical setting, it is therefore important to be in a position to point and interval estimate the criterion validity for a measure under consideration, which is the subject of the present section. We assume for most of the remainder of this chapter that the variables of interest are (approximately) continuous, and we address the issue of variable distribution at the end of each following subsection.

8.8.1 Estimation With Large Samples

8.8.1.1 The Case of Normal Data

Denote the criterion variable by C and the measure of concern by X, whose criterion validity is of concern, and assume they are bivariate normal. (We will relax this assumption in the next subsection.) We are interested here in point and interval estimation of the correlation coefficient $\rho = Corr(C, X)$, which represents the (population) criterion validity coefficient of the score X resulting from an instrument under consideration. Once we have a confidence interval for this correlation, we can also readily conduct if need be tests of hypotheses with regard to its population value. Indeed, suppose we were interested in testing the hypothesis

$$H_0: \rho = \rho_0,$$

where ρ_0 is a prespecified number, at a given significance level, say .05, against a two-tailed alternative. Because a confidence interval represents a range of plausible population values for a parameter in question (e.g., King & Minium, 2003), all we need to do is check whether ρ_0 falls within the confidence interval constructed at confidence level $(1 - .05)100\% = 95\%$, i.e., in the 95%-confidence interval. If it does, we need not reject H_0; if it does not, however, we can reject H_0.

In addition to allowing testing of simple (point) hypotheses like H_0, with pertinent confidence intervals we obtain below, one may also examine if needed some one-tailed (composite) null hypotheses, such as criterion validity being at least ρ_0, a prespecified number of substantive relevance in a given setting. Such a hypothesis is, for instance, the following one:

$$H_0^*: \rho \geq \rho_0,$$

which is further considered below. We stress, however, that in order to carry out interval estimation of criterion validity, one does not have to be interested in testing any particular hypothesis about this coefficient. In fact, in general a confidence interval for a parameter under consideration is provided as an alternative to testing hypotheses about that parameter by representing a range of plausible population values for this parameter (e.g., Wilkinson & The Task Force on Statistical Inference, 1999). With this feature, as is well-known, a confidence interval permits also examining hypotheses if need be.

We can accomplish these interval estimation goals, including in particular obtaining a standard error of criterion validity, using latent variable modeling (LVM) that can in many regards be seen as the modeling framework of this book. We demonstrate this activity with the following example. Suppose a researcher is concerned with evaluating the criterion validity of a reading ability test for second graders that he or she has newly developed, whose overall score is denoted X. For this purpose, the researcher uses as a criterion a well-established measure in the field of reading assessment, denoted C. In a study of $n = 300$ second graders, the latter measure and the newly developed test exhibit the covariance matrix in Table 8.1. (As mentioned earlier, in this chapter we will not be interested in variable means as they are inconsequential for criterion validity, being a correlation coefficient.)

The researcher is interested in point and interval estimation of criterion validity for his or her test. In addition, the researcher also wishes to examine the hypothesis that this validity is at least .75, say. (We observe that the relevant null hypothesis is $H_0: \rho \geq .75$, i.e., a composite hypothesis, with the alternative being $H_1: \rho < .75$, which is similarly one-tailed.) To accomplish these aims we employ LVM as follows. (See Chapter 4 and its appendix for some activities prior to using the LVM program M*plus* for model fitting and parameter estimation purposes.) We utilize the fact that if for any given set of observed variables

Table 8.1. Covariance matrix for a criterion (C)
and test score (X)

Variable:	C	X
C	1.03	
SBR	.66	1.11

one introduces as many latent variables that are defined correspondingly identical to the former, then the resulting latent correlation matrix will be identical to the observed correlation matrix (for details, see Raykov, 2001c, or Raykov & Marcoulides, 2008, 2010c, in a slightly different context). These aims are readily achieved with *Mplus* using the following command file. (Explanatory comments are given in the file, after exclamation mark in the pertinent line; in the text following it, we provide further discussion of some of them. Before proceeding with using this input file, one should first save the contents of Table 8.1 into a separate text-only file, called TABLE8_1.DAT.)

```
TITLE:       POINT AND INTERVAL ESTIMATION OF CRITERION VALIDITY
             (ALLOWING ALSO TESTING OF SIMPLE AND SOME ONE-SIDED
             HYPOTHESES).

DATA:        FILE = TABLE8_1.DAT; ! See Table 8.1
             TYPE = COVARIANCE;
             NOBSERVATIONS = 300;

VARIABLE:    NAMES = C X;

MODEL:       F1 BY C*1;
             F2 BY X*1;
             C-X@0; ! sets error variances = 0
             F1-F2@1; ! sets latent variances = 1

OUTPUT:      CINTERVAL;
```

In this command file, the only new features relative to prior applications of the software *Mplus* in this book are to be found in the MODEL section. In it, first we introduce the latent variables F1 and F2 as effectively identical, for our purposes, to the criterion C and instrument score X. To accomplish this, we set their error variances at 0 and the latent variances at 1 and estimate the latent standard deviations in the single loadings of each observed variable on its pertinent latent variable (e.g., Raykov, 2001c). With this parameterization, we ensure that the correlation between C and X, i.e., the criterion validity coefficient of the test under consideration, is estimated in the latent correlation $Corr$(F1,F2), which equals here the latent covariance Cov(F1,F2). Thus, the standard error obtained for the latter is in fact the standard error of the former. This input file produces the following output (we comment after appropriate sections):

```
THE MODEL ESTIMATION TERMINATED NORMALLY
TESTS OF MODEL FIT

Chi-Square Test of Model Fit

             Value                              0.000
             Degrees of Freedom                     0
             P-Value                            0.0000

Chi-Square Test of Model Fit for the Baseline Model

             Value                            143.896
             Degrees of Freedom                     1
             P-Value                            0.0000

CFI/TLI

             CFI                                1.000
             TLI                                1.000
```

```
Loglikelihood

          H0 Value                                -798.501
          H1 Value                                -798.501

Information Criteria

          Number of Free Parameters                      3
          Akaike (AIC)                            1603.002
          Bayesian (BIC)                          1614.114
          Sample-Size Adjusted BIC                1604.600
             (n* = (n + 2) / 24)

RMSEA (Root Mean Square Error Of Approximation)

          Estimate                                   0.000
          90 Percent C.I.                            0.000     0.000
          Probability RMSEA <= .05                   0.000

SRMR (Standardized Root Mean Square Residual)

          Value                                      0.000
```

The fitted model is saturated because it has three parameters (two loadings and a latent correlation) while being fitted to three data points—two empirical variances (of X and C) and their covariance (e.g., Raykov & Marcoulides, 2006a). Hence, the model fits the analyzed covariance matrix (Table 8.1) perfectly. (In fact, any model that has as many latent variables as observed variables, with the former being defined as identical to the latter or as in the last M*plus* input file, will be saturated and therefore fitting the pertinent covariance matrix perfectly [Raykov, 2001c].) Strictly speaking, because of it being saturated, we cannot test this model. This is not a limitation of the model, however, for our purposes. Given its perfect fit, we wish to use it as a means of point and interval estimation of criterion validity. (We stress that the model fits not only the analyzed covariance matrix in Table 8.1 perfectly but also the population covariance matrix for the two involved measures, if it were available.) With this in mind, we look next for the latent correlation estimate, as well as its standard error and z-value.

```
MODEL RESULTS

                                                            Two-Tailed
                        Estimate        S.E.     Est./S.E.    P-Value
 F1        BY
     C                     1.013       0.041       24.495      0.000
 F2        BY
     X                     1.052       0.043       24.495      0.000
 F2        WITH
     F1                    0.617       0.036       17.273      0.000

 Variances
     F1                    1.000       0.000      999.000    999.000
     F2                    1.000       0.000      999.000    999.000

 Residual Variances
     C                     0.000       0.000      999.000    999.000
     X                     0.000       0.000      999.000    999.000
```

The criterion validity of the reading ability test under consideration, which is the correlation between the latent variables F1 and F2 (i.e., their covariance here), is estimated at .617, with a standard error .036 and is significant (at a conventional level of .05). With these results, we can use the R function 'ci.pc' presented in Section 4.6 (Subsection 4.6.2) in order to obtain a confidence interval for the criterion (correlation) coefficient of interest, say at confidence level 95% (see next section for an alternative approach; we stress that this R function 'ci.pc' is appropriate for obtaining a confidence interval for any type of correlation estimated from a model). All we need to do for this purpose is enter in the call of that R function .617 for its argument 'c' and .037 for 'se'. (That is, after starting R and pasting that function at the R prompt, '>', we enter 'ci.pc(.617, .037)' and submit it to R.)

This activity yields (.539, .684) as a 95%-confidence interval (CI) for the validity coefficient of concern. That is, we can suggest with high confidence that in the studied population of second graders, from which the available sample was drawn, the criterion validity of the new reading ability measure may be as low as .54 and as high as .68. Because this CI contains by definition the plausible population criterion validity values (at the used confidence level), yet does not have any intersection with the null hypothesis tail that is $\rho \geq .75$, it follows that no population value above .75 is plausible for the validity coefficient in question. Hence, it can be concluded that at the used significance level, the data provide evidence warranting rejection of the null hypothesis that the validity of this reading ability measure is at least .75. Therefore, if the researcher desires that his or her measure be associated with higher validity, as would likely be the case here, the reading ability test needs further work in order to enhance its criterion validity.

8.8.1.2 *The Case of Nonnormal Data*

The described modeling approach is also applicable with nonnormal data, which can be (approximately) continuous or alternatively discrete with perhaps at least five or seven values possible on the measures C and X (see Chapter 4). The only change required then in the above command file is the addition of the command ANALYSIS: ESTIMATOR = MLR. (Access to the raw data is then needed in order to proceed with modeling, rather than only the covariance matrix as in Subsection 8.8.1.1, which would be sufficient under the normality assumption made there.) This option invokes a robust ML estimator that is trustworthy with deviations from normality and possibly not very large samples, yet with no piling of cases at either end of the scales of C and X and no pronounced clustering effect (hierarchical data; Muthén & Muthén, 2010).

We conclude this section on large-sample estimation of criterion validity by stressing the following point. Although there is no answer in general to the question how large a sample would be appropriate for this method to be used, we would recommend it with several hundred subjects. Somewhat smaller samples may be handled with the robust ML method, but currently there is no conclusive research allowing one to definitively state so. With lower sample sizes, application of the method discussed next may well be considered, assuming its own assumptions are fulfilled.

8.8.2 Estimation With Small Samples

With samples that are small, say smaller than 100, use of the so-called Fisher's z-transform can be made in case of normality for the criterion and test (instrument) under consideration (see also Section 4.6). (We observe that with small samples, a test of normality is hard to consider trustworthy; e.g., Raykov and Marcoulides [2008]. We find this circumstance as an additional motivation for striving to obtain as large as possible samples in empirical research on criterion validity.) For a given correlation coefficient r, Fisher's z-transform is defined as follows (e.g., King & Minium, 2003; $r \neq 1$ is assumed throughout the remainder of this section):

$$z = \frac{1}{2} \ln \frac{1+r}{1-r}, \tag{8.6}$$

where ln(.) is the natural logarithm function (i.e., the logarithm with base $e = 2.712$). For illustration purposes here, Figures 8.1 and 8.2 graphically display the logarithmic function $y = \ln(x)$ and Fisher's z-transform (8.6), respectively. We observe that both functions are monotonically increasing in their arguments (viz., in x and r, respectively; in Figures 8.1 and 8.2, y and z are formally denoted by the corresponding formula used with the software R to obtain the graphs of these functions; see the appendix to Chapter 11 for details on constructing them).

(As an aside, the apparently discontinued graph in the lower-left corner of Figure 8.1 and both corners of Figure 8.2 results from the fact that the depicted function decreases unboundedly when the values of x approach 0 or 1 in absolute value, respectively; to create this graph using R, we employed a 'grid' with a width of .005 that becomes inadequate for a smooth graphical representation at such extreme values of the argument; see the appendix to Chapter 11 for details.)

The benefit of using Fisher's z-transform consists of the fact that with sample size n of at least 10 cases, it is approximately normally distributed with a mean ρ and variance $1/(n-3)$, i.e.,

$$z \sim N(\rho, 1/(n-3)), \tag{8.7}$$

where ρ is the population correlation coefficient (criterion validity coefficient). We notice from (8.7) that the variance of this normal distribution does not depend on the population correlation, ρ, a feature sometimes referred to as a variance-stabilizing property of Fisher's z-transform. (On the contrary, the variance of the distribution of the conventional Pearson product–moment correlation coefficient estimator given in Chapter 2 is $(1 - \rho^2)^2/n$ and thus

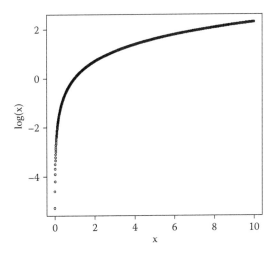

FIGURE 8.1
Graph of the logarithmic function.

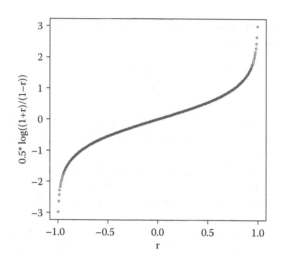

FIGURE 8.2
Graph of Fisher's z transform.

depends on ρ.) We note from Equation (8.6) that if one knew z, then r would be obtained by using the inverse of Fisher's z-transform:

$$r = (e^{2z} - 1)/(e^{2z} + 1). \tag{8.8}$$

Thus, to obtain a confidence interval (CI) for the criterion validity coefficient in the presently considered case, the following SPSS file (or its counterpart with another software, e.g., R) can be used that is based on Equations (8.6) through (8.8). In order to invoke this procedure in an empirical setting, all one needs to supply is (a) the empirical estimate of the criterion validity coefficient (correlation of X and C) and (b) the sample size n at the end of the third and fourth lines of this file, respectively.

```
TITLE 'INTERVAL ESTIMATION OF CRITERION VALIDITY WITH SMALL SAMPLES'.

* ENTER NEXT SAMPLE ESTIMATE OF CRITERION VALIDITY & SAMPLE SIZE N.

COMP R= #.
COMP N= #.

* NEXT COMPUTE FISHER'S TRANSFORM OF CRITERION VALIDITY

COMP Z=.5*LN((1+R)/(1-R)).

* NEXT WORK OUT PERTINENT STANDARD DEVIATION.

COMP Z.SE=1/SQRT(N-3).

* FIND NEXT THE LOWER AND UPPER ENDPOINTS OF THE CI FOR Z.

COMP CI.Z.LO=Z-1.96*Z.SE.
COMP CI.Z.UP=Z+1.96*Z.SE.

* FIND LOWER AND UPPER ENDPOINT OF THE CI FOR CRITERION VALIDITY.

COMP CI.CV.LO=(EXP(2*CI.Z.LO)-1)/(EXP(2*CI.Z.LO)+1).
COMP CI.CV.UP=(EXP(2*CI.Z.UP)-1)/(EXP(2*CI.Z.UP)+1).

EXECUTE.
```

The following example illustrates this procedure. Consider a newly developed measure for mathematics anxiety of fourth graders by an educational researcher, who wishes to validate it. In a study with $n = 25$ children, using also a well-established criterion variable, she obtains an estimated criterion validity coefficient of .77 for her measure, X. To furnish a confidence interval for the population criterion coefficient of this new measure, we use the above SPSS input file. After entering .77 in its third line and 25 in its fourth line, it renders the 95%-CI (.54, .89). We can thus suggest with high confidence that in the studied population the criterion validity of the new instrument could be as low as in the mid .50s and as large as in the high .80s. We note that this interval is relatively wide, indicating other than high precision of estimation, which is due to the sample size being small. We also observe that this CI is not symmetric about the empirical estimate of .77. The reason is that the sampling distribution of the correlation coefficient is in general not symmetric (unless the population correlation is 0; e.g., Agresti & Finlay, 2009).

An important limitation of this approach based on Fisher's z-transform is that it is not strictly applicable with other than bivariate normal data on the criterion and measure validated. Relatedly, this approach is not applicable with data that cannot be considered (approximately) continuous. In the latter two cases, one may consider using the method described in the preceding Subsection 8.8.1, if a large sample is available.

8.8.3 Estimation of Change in Criterion Validity Due to Instrument Revision

Many times in empirical research, one is interested in revising a tentative test (scale, test, multiple-component measuring instrument) so as to improve its psychometric quality. To this end, a scholar may consider conducting a revision of the instrument, which consists of deletion of some components already in the instrument or addition of others not contained in it initially. This revision involves excluding from the overall score the components to be deleted or adding to that score the components to be included into the revised instrument (along with its original components, assuming they all are measured on the same sample of subjects). Revisions consisting of deletion of some and at the same time addition of other components can also be considered—as long as data on them are available from the same sample of subjects—and in fact the following method is equally applicable in those setups as well.

Although we already addressed the issue of instrument revision in Chapter 7, with a view of enhancing composite reliability, perhaps the most important criterion for possible instrument improvement thereby is the gain or loss in validity. This question can be addressed by examining criterion validity and revision effect on it. Hence, a main query in an instrument development endeavor would be whether criterion validity of the revised scale is higher (smaller or the same) than the criterion validity of the prerevised scale. This can be answered by extending the discussion earlier in this Section 8.8.

To describe this extension, we suppose C denotes a criterion variable, SBR denotes the score on the scale (instrument) before the revision was carried out, and SAR denotes the score on the scale after the revision. That is, SBR and SAR are the sum scores on the instrument components before the revision and after it, respectively. There would be no change in validity if the two measure–criterion correlations are the same, which we treat as the null hypothesis to be tested here:

$$H_0: Corr(C, SBR) = Corr(C, SAR).$$

We can consider a one-tailed or two-tailed alternative that we can test in pair with this hypothesis H_0. However, a generally preferable approach—as indicated before—would be to obtain at a given confidence level a confidence interval (CI) of the critical difference, viz., criterion validity after revision less criterion validity before revision:

$$\Delta = Corr(C, SAR) - Corr(C, SBR). \tag{8.9}$$

In the search for a CI of this validity gain or loss Δ, one should first note that the two correlations involved are dependent rather than independent, because they are based on variables observed on the same subjects. A test of H_0 with dependent correlations, which utilizes the important information on their interrelationship, can be carried out employing an alternative approach described in Steiger (1980). However, that earlier approach is applicable only for testing H_0 and not nearly as readily for obtaining a CI for the change in validity in question here. Yet as mentioned earlier, one should generally be interested in obtaining a CI, because of a number of advantageous features of interval estimation relative to hypothesis testing (e.g., Wilkinson & The Task Force on Statistical Inference, 1999).

To furnish the sought CI for the difference in two interrelated correlations, i.e., the loss or gain in criterion validity following revision that is of concern in this section, we can extend the model for obtaining a CI of a single criterion validity coefficient, which we used earlier in this section. To this end, we add in it one more latent variable, denoted F3, and then focus on the difference in the two correlations of concern, which we point and interval estimate as follows. The first latent variable, F1, is formally used here to denote the scale score before revision, the second latent variable (F2) is that score after revision, and the third latent variable (F3) is the criterion measure. We then introduce a new parameter, the difference Δ—denoted DELTA below—in the MODEL section, in a way similar to the one we followed in the preceding chapter. The point and interval estimates of the variance of DELTA, with the latter estimate resulting from an application of the delta method, represent correspondingly the point and interval estimates of the gain or loss in criterion validity due to revision. Hence, the needed *Mplus* input file for these aims is as follows. (Note that we assign the parameter symbols P1 and P2 to the criterion validity coefficients of the scale before and after the revision, respectively, with DELTA being their difference.)

```
TITLE:      ESTIMATING CHANGE IN CRITERION VALIDITY

DATA:       FILE = TABLE8_2.DAT; see covariance matrix in Table 8.2
            TYPE = COVARIANCE;
            NOBSERVATIONS = 480;

VARIABLE:   NAMES = C SBR SAR;

MODEL:      F1 BY SBR*1;
            F2 BY SAR*1;
            F3 BY C*1;
            C-SAR@0;
            F1-F3@1;
            F1 WITH F3*.1 (P1); ! gives start value to Corr(F1,F3)
            F2 WITH F3*.1 (P2); ! gives start value to Corr(F2, F3)
```

```
MODEL CONSTRAINT:
          NEW (DELTA);
          DELTA = P2-P1; ! this is the revision effect on validity

OUTPUT:      CINTERVAL;
```

To illustrate, we use this input file on data from a study concerned with developing a test of writing ability for sixth graders. In that study, $n = 480$ students were initially given five topics to write a short essay on. An educational researcher suspects on substantive grounds that discounting the last two essays would improve the criterion validity of the overall sum score. She decides to use as a criterion the students' grades at the end of the first semester. Table 8.2 provides the empirical covariance matrix for the criterion (denoted *C*), the scale score before revision (i.e., the sum of all five components, denoted *SBR*), and the scale score after the revision consisting of dropping the last two essays (instrument components, i.e., the sum score of the first three essays, denoted *SAR*), assuming normality is plausible for these measures.

Table 8.2. Covariance matrix for three measures involved in examining change in criterion validity due to revision

Variable:	C	SBR	SAR
C	1.03		
SBR	.66	1.11	
SAR	.77	.82	1.23

The last-presented M*plus* command file renders on these data the following output. We insert comments where the output sections are not self-explanatory.

```
THE MODEL ESTIMATION TERMINATED NORMALLY

TESTS OF MODEL FIT

Chi-Square Test of Model Fit

          Value                           0.000
          Degrees of Freedom                  0
          P-Value                         0.0000

Chi-Square Test of Model Fit for the Baseline Model

          Value                         663.156
          Degrees of Freedom                  3
          P-Value                         0.0000

CFI/TLI

          CFI                             1.000
          TLI                             1.000
```

```
Loglikelihood

        H0 Value                           -1792.016
        H1 Value                           -1792.016

Information Criteria

        Number of Free Parameters               6
        Akaike (AIC)                      3596.032
        Bayesian (BIC)                    3621.075
        Sample-Size Adjusted BIC          3602.031
          (n* = (n + 2) / 24)

RMSEA (Root Mean Square Error Of Approximation)

        Estimate                             0.000
        90 Percent C.I.              0.000  0.000
        Probability RMSEA <= .05             0.000

SRMR (Standardized Root Mean Square Residual)

        Value                                0.000
```

Similarly to the earlier-fitted model in this chapter, the present one is saturated. The reason again is the fact that this model is fitted to as many nonredundant variances and covariances as it has parameters (viz., three latent variable variances and three latent covariances; e.g., Raykov & Marcoulides, 2006a). The fact that the model perfectly fits the data is not the reason why we are interested in it here, but instead we wish to use it as a means of point and interval estimation for the revision effect on criterion validity. Given this model's perfect fit, we turn next to the estimate of validity change, its standard error, and its corresponding z-value.

```
MODEL RESULTS
```

		Estimate	S.E.	Est./S.E.	Two-Tailed P-Value
F1	BY				
SBR		1.052	0.034	30.984	0.000
F2	BY				
SAR		1.108	0.036	30.984	0.000
F3	BY				
C		1.014	0.033	30.984	0.000
F1	WITH				
F3		0.617	0.028	21.845	0.000
F2	WITH				
F3		0.684	0.024	28.170	0.000
F1		0.702	0.023	30.293	0.000
Variances					
F1		1.000	0.000	999.000	999.000
F2		1.000	0.000	999.000	999.000
F3		1.000	0.000	999.000	999.000

```
Residual Variances
  C                        0.000        0.000      999.000      999.000
  SBR                      0.000        0.000      999.000      999.000
  SAR                      0.000        0.000      999.000      999.000

New/Additional Parameters
  DELTA                    0.067        0.025        2.630        0.009
```

The last entry is the estimate of change in criterion validity. That is, the deletion of the final two of the five original components of this measure was associated with an estimated increment of .067 in criterion validity, with a standard error of .025, which is significant. We look further below in this output for a confidence interval of this revision effect on validity.

```
CONFIDENCE INTERVALS OF MODEL RESULTS
                  Lower.5%   Lower 2.5%   Estimate   Upper 2.5%   Upper.5%
  F1      BY
    SBR            0.965       0.986       1.052       1.119       1.140
  F2      BY
    SAR            1.016       1.038       1.108       1.178       1.200
  F3      BY
    C              0.930       0.950       1.014       1.078       1.098
  F1      WITH
    F3             0.544       0.562       0.617       0.673       0.690
  F2      WITH
    F3             0.622       0.636       0.684       0.732       0.747
    F1             0.642       0.656       0.702       0.747       0.761

  Variances
    F1             1.000       1.000       1.000       1.000       1.000
    F2             1.000       1.000       1.000       1.000       1.000
    F3             1.000       1.000       1.000       1.000       1.000

  Residual Variances
    C              0.000       0.000       0.000       0.000       0.000
    SBR            0.000       0.000       0.000       0.000       0.000
    SAR            0.000       0.000       0.000       0.000       0.000

  New/Additional Parameters
    DELTA          0.001       0.017       0.067       0.117       0.132
```

To find the lower and upper limits of the 95%-confidence interval (CI) of the change in criterion validity, we locate in the output line pertaining to this parameter—called DELTA here—the entries in the columns 'Lower 2.5%' and 'Upper 2.5%' (which thus 'enclose' a confidence level of 100% − 2.5% − 2.5% = 95%; if we were interested in a 99%-CI, we would look at the entries in the columns labeled in this output section 'Lower .5%' and 'Upper .5%'). Hence, the 95%-confidence interval for validity change, which is furnished by the delta method (internally invoked by M*plus* as a result of the last input command, OUTPUT: CINTERVAL), is (.017, .117). This result suggests that the gain in validity could be, with high degree of confidence, as low as .02 and as high as .12 in the studied population of sixth graders. Because a CI represents a range of plausible values for the corresponding population parameter, given that the obtained 95%-CI in this example is entirely above 0, it is suggested that the revision under consideration by the researcher leads to gain in validity. She next needs to invoke further substantive considerations in order to decide whether to proceed with this revision. If one wishes at this point to find out what the criterion validity would be before and after revision, the estimates and standard errors are located in the MODEL RESULTS part of the presented output. Specifically, the criterion validity coefficient before revision is represented by the parameter Corr(F1,F3) and that after revision by the parameter Corr(F2,F3) (see also their standard errors, and use the earlier-employed R function 'ci.pc' to obtain confidence intervals for them, as demonstrated in Subsection 8.8.1.1).

The modeling approach followed in this Section 8.8.3 was concerned with overall test (scale) scores. This method can also be applied with large samples and not necessarily normal test scores on the variables *SBR*, *SAR*, and *C*. With deviations from normality, application of the robust ML method is recommended (using the command ANALYSIS: ESTIMATOR = MLR;), as long as there is no piling of cases at the minimal or maximal scores possible on any of the scale versions involved (and no pronounced clustering/nesting effect; access to the raw data needs to be ensured in order for this robust method to be applicable). Similarly, this estimation procedure may be applicable with discrete data, so long as each of the three variables involved exhibits at least five to seven distinct values in the sample (see Chapter 4). Last but not least, when interested in examining simultaneously the factorial structure of the instrument under consideration, an alternative method can be used that is described in Raykov (2007a).

8.9 Examining Construct Validity Using Confirmatory Factor Analysis

Confirmatory factor analysis (CFA) can be profitably used to address issues pertaining to the complex process of construct validity assessment. As can be recalled from earlier parts of this chapter, construct validity of a given instrument (test, scale, composite) is supported when the hypotheses are retainable, stating that results from it show (a) strong interrelationships with measures of supposedly closely related constructs and (b) weak interrelationships with measures of presumably unrelated constructs, based on available theory and accumulated knowledge in a given substantive area. The question of whether (a) and (b) are the case can be addressed using CFA. We discuss next its applications for this purpose.

8.9.1 Evaluation of Construct Correlations

To demonstrate this approach, we may use the following example where we are interested in assessing construct validity of a three-component scale of mathematics test anxiety and wish to examine it in relation to measures of algebra, geometry, and trigonometry as indicators of a presumably closely related (negatively) construct of mathematics ability. The covariance matrix for this study, with plausibility of normality for the six measures involved, is shown in Table 8.3. (Since the models fitted in the remainder of this chapter do not impose restrictions that are consequential for observed variable means, there is no loss of generality if fitting these models to the covariance structure of the manifest measures.)

We would like to see if these data provide some evidence for construct validity of the scale of mathematics test-taking anxiety that is based on the first three components, denoted MA1 through MA3. This would be the case if these three measures could be considered indicators of a construct, viz., mathematics test-taking anxiety, which correlates notably with the construct behind the remaining three measures of mathematics test performance that may be called mathematics ability. Such a finding would provide some empirical evidence in favor of what is also referred to as convergent validity of the mathematics test-taking anxiety scale (e.g., Campbell & Fiske, 1959), the degree to which scores

Table 8.3. Covariance matrix of 3 measures of mathematics test-taking anxiety (variables 1 to 3) with tests of algebra, geometry, and trigonometry knowledge (variables 4 –6) for n = 300 high school juniors.

Var.:	MA1	MA2	MA3	ALG	GEOM	TRIGON
MA1	1.11					
MA2	.66	1.21				
MA3	.72	.74	1.33			
ALG	-.66	-.71	-.67	1.28		
GEOM	-.55	-.61	-.71	.73	1.33	
TRIGON	-.65	-.71	-.61	.73	.69	1.37

Note: MA#i = Mathematics anxiety measure #i (i = 1, 2, 3); ALG = algebra test score, GEOM = geometry test score, TRIGON = trigonometry test score.

on a studied instrument are related to measures of other constructs that can be expected on theoretical grounds to be close to the one tapped into by this instrument. To accomplish this aim, we fit a two-factor model with a factor for each of the two constructs involved, which is measured by the first and by the last triple of above observed variables, respectively (see Table 8.3), and point and interval estimate their interrelationship. Finding a strong—viz., significant, sizeable, and negative—latent correlation, in addition to marked and significant (positive) factor loadings, would provide some support for construct validity of the three-component instrument of mathematics test-taking anxiety. We achieve this with the following M*plus* input file:

```
TITLE:        CFA EXAMINING CONSTRUCT VALIDITY
              ASSESSING CONVERGENT VALIDITY

DATA:         FILE = TABLE8_3.DAT; ! SEE TABLE 8.3
              TYPE = COVARIANCE;
              NOBSERVATIONS = 300;

VARIABLE:     NAMES = MATHANX1-MATHANX3 ALG GEOM TRIGON;

MODEL:        F1 BY MATHANX1*1 MATHANX2-MATHANX3;
              F2 BY ALG*1 GEOM-TRIGON;
              F1-F2@1;

OUTPUT:       CINTERVAL;
```

We note that in order to point and interval estimate the latent correlations of interest, we free all loadings of their indicators and fix at 1 their variances, an approach we used on a few occasions earlier in this book. (In this way, as mentioned before, their covariance equals their correlation, and a standard error for the latter easily becomes available.) The following output results:

```
THE MODEL ESTIMATION TERMINATED NORMALLY

TESTS OF MODEL FIT

Chi-Square Test of Model Fit

          Value                           16.397
          Degrees of Freedom                   8
          P-Value                         0.0370
```

```
Chi-Square Test of Model Fit for the Baseline Model
              Value                              784.911
              Degrees of Freedom                      15
              P-Value                           0.0000
CFI/TLI
              CFI                                0.989
              TLI                                0.980
Loglikelihood
              H0 Value                        -2380.879
              H1 Value                        -2372.680
Information Criteria
              Number of Free Parameters              13
              Akaike (AIC)                    4787.757
              Bayesian (BIC)                  4835.907
              Sample-Size Adjusted BIC        4794.678
                (n* = (n + 2)/24)
RMSEA (Root Mean Square Error Of Approximation)
              Estimate                           0.059
              90 Percent C.I.                    0.014    0.100
              Probability RMSEA <= .05           0.310
SRMR (Standardized Root Mean Square Residual)
              Value                              0.022
```

These findings suggest that the fitted model can be considered plausible for the data analyzed (see in particular the left endpoint of the RMSEA confidence interval). Hence, we can trust, for our purposes, the following parameter estimates and related indexes:

```
MODEL RESULTS
                                                          Two-Tailed
                      Estimate      S.E.      Est./S.E.    P-Value

F1        BY
   MATHANX1            0.798       0.055        14.513      0.000
   MATHANX2            0.851       0.057        14.923      0.000
   MATHANX3            0.868       0.060        14.375      0.000

F2        BY
   ALG                 0.879       0.059        14.891      0.000
   GEOM                0.813       0.062        13.090      0.000
   TRIGON              0.843       0.063        13.453      0.000

F2        WITH
   F1                 -0.920       0.029       -31.473      0.000

Variances
   F1                  1.000       0.000       999.000    999.000
   F2                  1.000       0.000       999.000    999.000
```

Residual Variances

MATHANX1	0.469	0.050	-9.411	0.000
MATHANX2	0.483	0.053	-9.104	0.000
MATHANX3	0.573	0.060	9.507	0.000
ALG	0.502	0.057	8.742	0.000
GEOM	0.664	0.066	10.038	0.000
TRIGON	0.655	0.067	9.832	0.000

We first note that the measurement models for both constructs of interest here—mathematics test-taking anxiety and mathematics ability—are well defined. In particular, the estimates of the factor loadings on their pertinent measures are significant, positive, and of sizable magnitude (compare these estimates to the variances of the observed variables; see Table 8.3). Furthermore, the obtained estimate -.92 of the latent correlation provided in the last line of the MODEL RESULT section before the variable variances is that of the (linear) relationship between these two constructs, which is significant and strong. We observe that this correlation is also negative, as one would expect—children high (or alternatively low) on math ability would be expected to have low (high) mathematics testing anxiety. These findings present evidence in favor of construct validity of the mathematics test-taking anxiety scale under study. To interval estimate this critical correlation, one could use as earlier in this chapter the R function 'ci.pc' from Chapter 4 (Section 4.6.2). To this end, all one needs to do when calling this function (once pasting its text at the R prompt), is enter -.92 for 'c' and .029 for 'se' as its arguments (and then submit it to R). This activity yields (-.961, -.839) as a 95%-confidence interval for the correlation between mathematics test-taking anxiety and mathematics ability. That is, with high degree of confidence, the population correlation between mathematics test-taking anxiety and ability—which is a 'true' correlation, as the correlation between the two unobservable constructs of actual interest to study—may lie between -.96 and -.84. This is possibly a fairly strong correlation, which as mentioned above provides a piece of evidence in favor of construct validity, and specifically of convergent validity, of this mathematics test-taking anxiety scale.

As indicated earlier in this chapter, the process of instrument validation consists of multiple steps whereby one aims to obtain at each of them additional evidence in favor of construct validity. In empirical research, such additional evidence could be provided when fitting a CFA model for an instrument in question and measures of a construct(s) that on substantive grounds cannot be expected to correlate highly with the one under consideration, in the present example mathematics test-taking anxiety. Suppose we have available two (or preferably more) measures of U.S. history knowledge. We could fit the same model as above in this section, with the latter two measures taking over the role of the three mathematics ability measures used there. If we find then a weak correlation between the two involved constructs—mathematics test-taking anxiety and history knowledge—we could consider it an additional piece of evidence in favor of construct validity of the scale in question. Such a finding would provide empirical evidence for what is also referred to as discriminant validity. This is the degree to which scores on a studied instrument are differentiated from behavioral manifestations of other constructs, which on theoretical grounds can be expected not to be related to the construct underlying the instrument under investigation (e.g., Campbell & Fiske, 1959). To illustrate, we suppose the following data were available for this purpose (with plausibility of the normality assumption of the five measures involved; see Table 8.4).

Table 8.4. Covariance matrix of 3 measures of mathematics anxiety (variables 1 to 3) with tests of algebra, geometry, and trigonometry knowledge (variables 4 -6) for n = 300 high school juniors.

Variable	MA1	MA2	MA3	HIST1	HIST2
MA1	1.11				
MA2	.66	1.21			
MA3	.62	.64	1.33		
HIST1	.16	.21	.22	1.22	
HIST2	.15	.11	.17	.66	1.31

Note: MA#*i* = Mathematics anxiety measure #*i* (*i*= 1, 2, 3); HIST1 = first grade in history, HIST2 = second grade in history.

To accomplish the above aims, we use the following M*plus* input file:

```
TITLE:      CFA ADDRESSING CONSTRUCT VALIDITY
            EVALUATING DISCRIMINANT VALIDITY

DATA:       FILE = TABLE8_4.DAT; ! SEE TABLE 8.4
            TYPE = COVARIANCE;
            NOBSERVATIONS = 300;

VARIABLE:   NAMES = MATHANX1-MATHANX3 HIST1-HIST2;

MODEL:      F1 BY MATHANX1*1 MATHANX2-MATHANX3;
            F2 BY HIST1*1 HIST2;
            F1-F2@1;

OUTPUT:     CINTERVAL;
```

This command file furnishes the output presented next.

```
THE MODEL ESTIMATION TERMINATED NORMALLY

TESTS OF MODEL FIT

Chi-Square Test of Model Fit

        Value                            2.606
        Degrees of Freedom                   4
        P-Value                         0.6258

Chi-Square Test of Model Fit for the Baseline Model

        Value                          346.731
        Degrees of Freedom                  10
        P-Value                         0.0000

CFI/TLI

        CFI                              1.000
        TLI                              1.010
```

```
Loglikelihood

        H0 Value                         -2111.197
        H1 Value                         -2109.894

Information Criteria

        Number of Free Parameters              11
        Akaike (AIC)                     4244.394
        Bayesian (BIC)                   4285.135
        Sample-Size Adjusted BIC         4250.250
          (n* = (n + 2) / 24)

RMSEA (Root Mean Square Error Of Approximation)

        Estimate                            0.000
        90 Percent C.I.                     0.000    0.072
        Probability RMSEA <= .05            0.856

SRMR (Standardized Root Mean Square Residual)

        Value                               0.014
```

These fit indexes suggest that the model is tenable, and so we move on to interpreting its parameter estimates.

```
MODEL RESULTS
                                                 Two-Tailed
                  Estimate      S.E.    Est./S.E.   P-Value

F1       BY
   MATHANX1         0.793      0.062     12.809      0.000
   MATHANX2         0.825      0.065     12.769      0.000
   MATHANX3         0.779      0.068     11.505      0.000

F2       BY
   HIST1            0.951      0.182      5.235      0.000
   HIST2            0.691      0.140      4.932      0.000

F2       WITH
   F1               0.253      0.077      3.265      0.001

Variances
   F1               1.000      0.000    999.000    999.000
   F2               1.000      0.000    999.000    999.000

 Residual Variances
   MATHANX1         0.477      0.067      7.095      0.000
   MATHANX2         0.525      0.073      7.163      0.000
   MATHANX3         0.719      0.079      9.061      0.000
   HIST1            0.311      0.333      0.933      0.351
   HIST2            0.828      0.188      4.402      0.000
```

As in the preceding analysis with regard to convergent validity, the measurement models for the constructs of concern here—mathematics test-taking anxiety and history knowledge—are well defined. The latent correlation presented in the last line of the MODEL RESULTS section before the variable variances is weak, although significant. We note that it explains only about 6% of variance in either of the two constructs involved, in terms of such in the other construct. To interval estimate it, we can use again the R function 'ci.pc' (Section 4.6.2 in Chapter 4), entering in its call .253 for 'c' and .077 for 'se' as its arguments. This yields (.097, .397) as a 95%-confidence interval for the correlation between mathematics test-taking anxiety and history knowledge. Hence, we could suggest with a high degree of confidence that this correlation could indeed be rather small in the studied population—as low as .10; alternatively, it could be as high as .40, but even that is a weak correlation, as it explains merely 16% of the (linear pattern) relationship between the two latent constructs of interest. Therefore we conclude that in the analyzed data, there is evidence for up to a weak (linear) relationship between mathematics test anxiety and history knowledge. (As an aside, we note that one would likely not expect grades for different subjects taught in school to be completely unrelated, and so the significance of this correlation that was found above should not come as a surprise.)

We note that the results of both empirical analyses presented in this section are supportive of construct validity of the mathematics test-taking anxiety scale under consideration. At the same time, we stress that even though fit of the models used in this section was good, that finding alone does not provide a formal proof of existence of the mathematics test anxiety construct or of the mathematics ability or history knowledge constructs. However, we can interpret the plausibility of the two models assuming these constructs as providing complementary pieces of evidence in support of construct validity of the mathematics test-taking anxiety instrument being studied.

In conclusion of this section, we emphasize that the CFA approach used in it is equally well applicable with deviations from normality, other than violations due to highly discrete observed variables, ceiling–floor effects, or pronounced clustering effects (as in hierarchical data studies). Such a CFA application is accomplished if one adds in either input file used in this Subsection 8.9.1 the command ANALYSIS: ESTIMATOR = MLR, thus invoking a robust ML estimator (which needs access to the raw data, as emphasized before). The latter estimator choice may also yield trustworthy results with observed variables that exhibit as few as, say, five to seven possible values per measure.

8.9.2 The Multitrait–Multimethod Matrix Approach

The preceding Subsection 8.9.1 discussed what may be considered a two-phase procedure for examining construct validity as determined by empirical support for theoretically predictable relationships of constructs of interest with other constructs and their measures. In the first of its stages, we dealt with the evaluation of the correlations between a studied construct and others that are expected on theoretical grounds to be closely related to it, e.g., exhibit marked positive or negative correlations with it (i.e., relatively close to 1 or −1). In the second phase, we evaluated correlations between the construct in question and other constructs that based on the accumulated knowledge in a substantive domain could be expected to be only up to weakly related to it (i.e., correlated with the studied construct in the vicinity of 0 of marginally above in absolute value).

A related, alternative approach that can contribute considerably to the process of construct validation is based on the so-called multitrait–multimethod (MTMM) matrix, which in part focuses specifically on observed measure correlations. (The remainder of this section draws substantially from Raykov [2010a].) This method was advanced about a half century ago in a landmark paper by Campbell and Fiske (1959) that quickly became very influential in the field of behavioral and social measurement, particularly for purposes of studying construct validity. The MTMM approach is applicable when several constructs (multiple traits) are examined simultaneously, and each of them is evaluated by a number of measures or measurement methods (multiple methods). As elaborated by Campbell and Fiske, the following two types of validity coefficients are of special interest then, which we alluded to earlier in this section: (a) convergent validity coefficients and (b) discriminant validity coefficients. The convergent validity coefficients are the correlations between observed measures of the same construct with different measurement methods. These correlations are at times called monotrait–heteromethod (MTHM) coefficients (or alternatively monotrait–multimethod coefficients). Owing to the fact that they reflect the (linear) relationships between indicators of the same construct, a finding of them being consistently high would lend partial support for construct validity with regard to that construct. The evaluation of these coefficients thus represents an important part of the process of construct validation via the MTMM method.

On the other hand, discriminant validity coefficients are correlations of two types. The first consists of the correlations between manifest measures of different constructs furnished by the same method of measurement. These correlations are typically called heterotrait–monomethod coefficients (HTMM coefficients or alternatively multitrait–monomethod coefficients; e.g., Crocker & Algina, 1986). The other type of discriminant validity coefficients represents correlations between observed measures of different constructs obtained using different measurement methods and for this reason are called heterotrait–heteromethod coefficients (HTHM coefficients or multitrait–multimethod coefficients). A finding that the HTMM and HTHM coefficients are consistently lower than the MTHM coefficients would lend also partial support for validation with regard to each of the constructs involved. This is because one would usually expect indicators of a given construct to be more closely related among themselves than proxies (measures) of different constructs. Therefore, examination of the HTMM and HTHM correlations represents another important part of the construct validation process using the MTMM approach. In the remainder of this section, for simplicity of reference, we will often call the HTMM, HTHM, and MTHM collectively 'convergent and discriminant validity coefficients' (abbreviated CDVCs).

We reiterate that the CDVCs are indexes of relationship between observed variables. In this feature, they differ in an important way from the correlations that were of interest in Subsection 8.9.1, which were correlations between latent variables. With this distinction in mind, we note that the approach followed in the present Subsection 8.9.2 complements that of the preceding one, as a means of assessing construct validity in empirical behavioral and social research, as well as alternative latent variable modeling procedures for MTMM-based validation (e.g., Eid, 2000; Marsh, 1989; Marsh & Hocevar, 1983).

Multitrait–multimethod correlation matrices have been used for a number of years by social and behavioral scientists as a means for examining construct validity in various substantive areas. Many of those studies, however, have focused on empirical correlations and their relative magnitude in available samples from studied populations. Thereby, typically only point estimates of the above three types of CDVCs (MTHM, HTMM, and HTHM correlations) have been of interest to scholars using the MTMM approach to construct validation. Moreover, little attention if any has been paid then to the relationships existing among the population values of these coefficients. In particular, only the magnitudes of the sample values of these correlations have been usually compared with one another in an effort to find out whether HTMM and HTHM (i.e., discriminant validity) coefficients are lower than MTHM (i.e., convergent validity) coefficients in a given study. Sampling error affecting their empirical estimates has typically not been taken into account in those efforts. Hence, incorrect conclusions with respect to construct validity of examined measuring instruments may have been reached in the past, especially when such inferences have been based primarily on a finding of HTMM and HTHM correlations being smaller than MTHM coefficients in available samples.

To counteract such a possibility of reaching incorrect conclusions about construct validity, in the remainder of this section, we outline a readily employed method for (a) point estimating and in particular interval estimating the convergent and discriminant validity coefficients (correlations) and (b) studying their population relationships. A special feature of this method is that it is also developed using the latent variable modeling framework, which is the analytic basis of this text, despite the method being focused primarily on observed variable correlations.

To outline this approach, we make use of confirmatory factor analysis (CFA). Specifically, in order to evaluate the discussed three types of validity coefficients, we employ a special CFA model that is described in detail in Raykov and Marcoulides (2010b; see also references therein; the following method is equally applicable with missing data, under the assumption of multinormality and missing at random; e.g., Little & Rubin, 2002). Accordingly, denote by X the $p \times 1$ vector of available measures on all c constructs involved in a MTMM study ($p, c \geq 2$), where $p = mc$ is the product of the number m of measurement methods used for each construct with their number c (cf. Raykov, 2010c). That is, let $\underline{X}_1 = (X_1, ..., X_c)'$ be the measures obtained on all constructs with the first method and correspondingly denote by $\underline{X}_2 = (X_{c+1}, ..., X_{2c})', ..., \underline{X}_m = (X_{(m-1)c+1}, ..., X_p)'$ their measures obtained with the remaining $m - 1$ methods; then $\underline{X} = (\underline{X}_1' | \underline{X}_2' | ... | \underline{X}_m')'$ is their concatenation (representation of all of them sequentially after each other). Then the model of interest in the rest of this section is

$$\underline{X} = A\,\underline{f} + \underline{u}, \tag{8.10}$$

where A is a diagonal matrix of size p with main diagonal elements being model parameters (and otherwise containing zeros), $\underline{f}$ is a set of p dummy latent variables with variance 1 and whose covariances are also model parameters, and $\underline{u}$ is a $p \times 1$ zero-mean vector with zero covariance matrix, i.e., the $p \times p$ matrix consisting of zeros only. With this parameterization, obviously each observed variable (measure), X_i, is identical to its corresponding latent variable, f_i, up to a scaling factor (multiplication constant) that equals that measure's standard deviation ($i = 1, ..., p$; Raykov & Marcoulides, 2010b). Hence, the covariance matrix of the random vector $\underline{X}$ is the same as its correlation matrix, i.e.,

$$Cov(\underline{x}) = Corr(\underline{x}) = Cov(\underline{f}) = Corr(\underline{f}). \tag{8.11}$$

Therefore, point and interval estimation of the correlations among elements of the vector $\underline{X}$ is accomplished by point and interval estimation of the corresponding covariances among the elements of $\underline{f}$ (see also Raykov, 2001c). These correlations are the above convergent and discriminant validity correlations, positioned at appropriate places in $Corr(\underline{f})$.

To illustrate, we consider the following example, where for our purposes we use contrived data. Suppose we were interested in measuring guilt by self-report inventories (cf. Crocker & Algina, 1986, Chap. 10, and references therein; the data in Table 8.5 stem from Raykov, 2010c). We focus on the constructs of hostility guilt and morality conscience and assume they are measured by three methods: true–false, forced–choice, and

Table 8.5. *Correlations among 6 measures of 2 constructs, resulting from 3 measurement methods, with standard deviations (underneath) and means (bottom line; n = 435; Raykov, 2010c).*

Measure	M1T1	M1T2	M2T1	M2T2	M3T1	M3T2
M1T1	1					
M1T2	.45	1				
M2T1	.85	.40	1			
M2T2	.35	.80	.30	1		
M3T1	.65	.15	.70	.25	1	
M3T2	.20	.55	.20	.65	.35	1
Means:	42.25	48.33	52.35	45.23	49.31	51.86
StdDev:	202.35	331.26	298.35	255.67	322.78	301.34

Note. MiTj = Measure with the ith method of the jth trait ($i = 1, 2$, $j = 1, 2, 3$). StdDev = standard deviation.

incomplete sentences tests (subscales). The correlation matrix, standard deviations, and means of these six observed measures from $n = 435$ cases, for which the assumption of multinormality is viewed as plausible (we will relax this assumption later in the section), are presented in Table 8.5.

The CFA model defined in Equation (8.10) (see also assumptions stated immediately after them) is readily fitted to these data using the LVM program M*plus*. This is accomplished with the following input file, which is a direct extension to the case with $p = 6$ observed variables of the command files used for validity estimation earlier in this chapter (Section 8.8; Raykov, 2010c).

```
TITLE:     MULTITRAIT-MULTIMETHOD MATRIX BASED VALIDATION USING LATENT
           VARIABLE MODELING.
           ANALYSIS 1.

DATA:      FILE = TABLE8_5.DAT; ! See Table 8.5
           TYPE = CORRELATION MEANS STDEVIATIONS;
           NOBSERVATIONS = 435;

VARIABLE:  NAMES = M1T1 M1T2 M2T1 M2T2 M3T1 M3T2; ! See note to Table 8.5.

MODEL:     F1 BY M1T1*1; M1T1@0;
           F2 BY M1T2*1; M1T2@0;
           F3 BY M2T1*1; M2T1@0;
           F4 BY M2T2*1; M2T2@0;
           F5 BY M3T1*1; M3T1@0;
           F6 BY M3T2*1; M3T2@0;
           F1-F6@1;
```

This command file in effect performs the first analytic step consisting of laying the ground for interval estimation of the convergent and discriminant validity coefficients discussed above, and for this reason we add the subtitle ANALYSIS 1 as last line of its title command. Subsequently, we indicate in the DATA command the type of data analyzed by using the subcommand TYPE = CORRELATION MEANS STDEVIATIONS. This is because we have in Table 8.5 data in the form of observed variable correlations, means, and standard deviations. In this way, the software is in a position to work out the associated covariance matrix and fit to it the model of concern (Equation (8.10); recall that under multinormality, the means and the covariance matrix are sufficient statistics; e.g., Roussas, 1997). The MODEL command defines each of the six dummy latent variables, denoted F1 through F6, as identical to its corresponding observed measure up to a constant, because the error term associated with that measure is set at 0 in the same command line. In the last line of this section, we fix all latent variances at 1 to achieve model identification (e.g., Chapter 4). As a result, the proportionality constant just mentioned becomes equal to the standard deviation of the pertinent observed measure.

This command file yields the following output. (We insert comments after sections that are not self-explanatory and are relevant for the present example.)

```
THE MODEL ESTIMATION TERMINATED NORMALLY

TESTS OF MODEL FIT

Chi-Square Test of Model Fit

            Value                               0.000
            Degrees of Freedom                      0
            P-Value                             0.0000

Chi-Square Test of Model Fit for the Baseline Model

            Value                            2465.874
            Degrees of Freedom                     15
            P-Value                             0.0000

CFI/TLI

            CFI                                 1.000
            TLI                                 1.000

Loglikelihood

            H0 Value                        -17188.006
            H1 Value                        -17188.006

Information Criteria

            Number of Free Parameters              27
            Akaike (AIC)                     34430.011
            Bayesian (BIC)                   34540.046
            Sample-Size Adjusted BIC         34454.362
            (n* = (n + 2) / 24)

RMSEA (Root Mean Square Error Of Approximation)

            Estimate                            0.000
            90 Percent C.I.                     0.000       0.000
            Probability RMSEA <= .05            0.000

SRMR (Standardized Root Mean Square Residual)

            Value                               0.000
```

The model fit is perfect because here we are dealing again with a saturated model (see Section 8.8; Raykov, 2001c). This feature is not a limitation of the model, for our goals, but rather it is of particular interest to us. This is because we employ the model only to obtain standard errors for the analyzed variable correlations that we will use in the next step of our overall validation procedure.

F1	BY				
M1T1		202.117	6.852	29.496	0.000
F2	BY				
M1T2		330.879	11.218	29.496	0.000
F3	BY				
M2T1		298.007	10.103	29.496	0.000
F4	BY				
M2T2		255.376	8.658	29.496	0.000
F5	BY				
M3T1		322.409	10.931	29.496	0.000
F6	BY				
M3T2		300.993	10.205	29.496	0.000
F2	WITH				
F1		0.450	0.038	11.769	0.000
F3	WITH				
F1		0.850	0.013	63.885	0.000
F2		0.400	0.040	9.932	0.000
F4	WITH				
F1		0.350	0.042	8.319	0.000
F2		0.800	0.017	46.348	0.000
F3		0.300	0.044	6.876	0.000
F5	WITH				
F1		0.650	0.028	23.475	0.000
F2		0.150	0.047	3.201	0.001
F3		0.700	0.024	28.627	0.000
F4		0.250	0.045	5.562	0.000
F6	WITH				
F1		0.200	0.046	4.345	0.000
F2		0.550	0.033	16.446	0.000
F3		0.200	0.046	4.345	0.000
F4		0.650	0.028	23.475	0.000
F5		0.350	0.042	8.319	0.000
Intercepts					
M1T1		42.250	9.691	4.360	0.000
M1T2		48.330	15.864	3.046	0.002
M2T1		52.350	14.288	3.664	0.000
M2T2		45.230	12.244	3.694	0.000
M3T1		49.310	15.458	3.190	0.001
M3T2		51.860	14.432	3.594	0.000

```
Variances
    F1                1.000      0.000      999.000      999.000
    F2                1.000      0.000      999.000      999.000
    F3                1.000      0.000      999.000      999.000
    F4                1.000      0.000      999.000      999.000
    F5                1.000      0.000      999.000      999.000
    F6                1.000      0.000      999.000      999.000

Residual Variances
    M1T1              0.000      0.000      999.000      999.000
    M1T2              0.000      0.000      999.000      999.000
    M2T1              0.000      0.000      999.000      999.000
    M2T2              0.000      0.000      999.000      999.000
    M3T1              0.000      0.000      999.000      999.000
    M3T2              0.000      0.000      999.000      999.000
```

As could be expected, the means, standard deviations, and correlations are estimated precisely at their sample counterparts. The reason is that the fitted model is saturated. However, of more interest to us are the latent correlation standard errors. This is because as shown above these correlations are the ones between the different measures of the studied constructs. From the output part within the MODEL RESULTS section, which presents the correlations among the dummy latent variables F1 through F6, we see for instance the standard error of .038 for the correlation of .450 between the true–false method measures of the hostility guilt and morality–conscience constructs. (This is the correlation between F1 and F2, i.e., between the variables X_1 and X_2 in our above notation used in Equation (8.10).) We stress that this standard error is obtained as a result of fitting the model in (8.10), rather than provided with the analyzed data in Table 8.4 (see also subsection 8.8.1.1).

Although this estimate is in a sense a best numerical guess for the population correlation between these two measures of the pair of constructs under consideration, it does not contain any information as to how far the estimate may be from their 'true' correlation in the studied population that is of actual interest. To obtain such information, in the form of a confidence interval (CI), we can use the interval estimation procedure outlined in Chapter 4 (Section 4.6; see also Section 8.8; Browne, 1982; Raykov, 2010c). For a given convergent or discriminant validity coefficient, this procedure involves first applying Fisher's z-transform, obtaining then its standard error, furnishing next a CI for this transformed correlation, and finally back transforming its limits to render these of the CI for the convergent or discriminant validity coefficient of actual concern. All these activities can be implemented in an extended Mplus command file, as discussed in detail in Chapter 4, or alternatively one can use for this interval estimation the R function 'ci.pc' defined in that chapter and employed on a few occasions earlier in this chapter.

To illustrate, suppose we were interested for the currently considered example in obtaining a 95%-CI for the discriminant validity coefficient for Method 1 (true–false test) applied to measure the hostility guilt and morality conscience constructs (Raykov, 2010c). The pertinent correlation is that between variables X1 and X2 in Table 8.5, i.e., F1 and F2 in the output of the last Mplus command file. As indicated earlier in this section, we found that this correlation was estimated at .45 (which is identical to its sample value, as pointed out before), with a standard error of .038. We now enter these two quantities as arguments correspondingly in the call of the R function 'ci.pc' just mentioned. This renders the 95%-CI for the discriminant validity coefficient of interest—the HTMM correlation between the true–false measures for the hostility guilt and morality conscience constructs—as (.372, .521). This suggests, with high degree of confidence, that the population value of this discriminant validity coefficient is moderate, between the high .30s and low .50s. Such a finding is not unexpected for a discriminant validity coefficient, in this case the correlation between same-method measures of different constructs. We stress that although these are measures resulting with the same method, this is not really contributing a great deal to their correlation; the more influential fact is that they are measures of different constructs, which impacts their correlation.

Alternatively, suppose one were interested in obtaining a CI of the convergent validity coefficient for the true–false and forced choice measures of the construct of hostility guilt, i.e., the variables X_1 and X_3 in Equation (8.10). From the results of the M*plus* output for ANALYSIS 1 presented earlier in this section, we see that this MTHM correlation is estimated at .85 (which is its sample value, as pointed out before) with a standard error of .013. Entering these two quantities correspondingly as arguments of the call of the same R function 'ci.pc', we obtain the 95%-CI for this convergent validity coefficient as (.822, .874). This finding suggests, with high degree of confidence, that the population convergent validity coefficient for these measures of the hostility guilt construct is in the mid-.80s. Such a finding could be expected from different indicators (measures) of the same construct, as we are dealing with here.

Although the CIs obtained with the outlined method for different convergent and discriminant validity coefficients represent plausible ranges for their population values, a comparison of these CIs could not be used as a means of studying their population relationship, i.e., for answering questions as to which of the two pertinent population coefficients is larger/smaller. The reason is that these CIs are obtained using the same data, so they are not independent of one another. In order to examine the population relationship of convergent and discriminant validity coefficients (CDVCs) of interest, one can use a slightly modified approach. To this end, one can consider the difference in these coefficients, and using the popular delta method (e.g., Raykov & Marcoulides, 2004), obtain a confidence interval for it. (This CI will take into account the relationship between the estimates of these CDVCs, unlike a simple comparison of their CIs.) We accomplish this goal by using the same approach as above, but similarly to the earlier developments when interval estimating the change in validity following revision in this chapter, we proceed in two steps. In the first, we define in the MODEL CONSTRAINT section a new parameter the difference of interest. In the second, we request its CI based on the delta method by including in the end the command OUTPUT: CINTERVAL;.

To illustrate, suppose we wanted to see in the above example whether in the studied population a convergent validity coefficient is indeed larger than a discriminant validity coefficient, as one would expect on theoretical grounds (e.g., Raykov, 2010c). To take for instance the last two validity coefficients considered, we are interested in examining if in the population of actual concern, the correlation ρ_1 between the true–false and forced choice measures of the hostility guilt construct is indeed larger than the correlation ρ_2 between the true–false measures of this construct with that of morality conscience. That is, we are interested in a CI of the correlation difference $\Delta\rho = \rho_2 - \rho_1$. To obtain a 95%-CI for this difference, which is based on the delta method, all we need to do is use the last M*plus* input file in which we first assign the parametric symbols RHO1 and RHO2 to these two correlations, then define in the MODEL CONSTRAINT section their difference DELTA as a new parameter, and finally request in the OUTPUT command a confidence interval. All this is achieved with the following M*plus* input file, which for ease of reference we subtitle ANALYSIS 2.

```
TITLE:          MULTITRAIT-MULTIMETHOD MATRIX BASED VALIDATION.
                ANALYSIS 2.

DATA:           FILE = TABLE8_5.DAT; ! see Table 8.5
                TYPE = CORRELATION MEANS STDEVIATIONS;
                NOBSERVATIONS = 435;

VARIABLE:       NAMES = M1T1 M1T2 M2T1 M2T2 M3T1 M3T2;

MODEL:          F1 BY M1T1*1; M1T1@0;
                F2 BY M1T2*1; M1T2@0;
                F3 BY M2T1*1; M2T1@0;
                F4 BY M2T2*1; M2T2@0;
                F5 BY M3T1*1; M3T1@0;
                F6 BY M3T2*1; M3T2@0;
                F1-F6@1;
                F1 WITH F3 (RHO1);
                F1 WITH F2 (RHO2);

MODEL CONSTRAINT:
                NEW(DELTA);
                DELTA = RHO1 - RHO2;

OUTPUT:         CINTERVAL;
```

We note that the model being fitted is still the same model defined in Equation (8.10). Hence, the same fit indices and results are obtained here as those presented at the beginning of this Subsection 8.9.2, with the only difference being that now we obtain the following confidence interval of interest here:

```
New/Additional Parameters
   DELTA              0.303     0.326    0.400    0.474      0.497
```

Therefore, the 95%-CI for the difference in the convergence validity and discriminant validity coefficients of concern is (.326, .474). This result suggests, with a high degree of confidence, that the convergent validity coefficient under consideration is substantially higher in the studied population than the discriminant validity coefficient involved in this comparison. Such a finding would also be consistent with theoretical expectations, given that the convergent validity coefficient ρ_1 is a correlation between two indicators of the same construct, whereas the discriminant validity coefficient ρ_2 is a correlation between same-method measures of different constructs and thus could be expected to be markedly lower in the population.

This discussion was concerned with comparison of population values of only two CDVCs. Yet, as pointed out earlier in this section, when using the MTMM approach to construct validation, one is interested in whether the convergent validity coefficients exhibit an overall tendency of being higher than the discriminant validity coefficients. This query can be addressed by comparing, for instance, the mean of the former coefficients with the mean of the latter. To be more specific, in the context of the example under consideration in this subsection, we can ask the question whether the mean of the 6 convergent validity coefficients (MTHM correlations) is higher in the population than the mean of the 9 discriminant validity coefficients (HTMM and HTHM correlations). With the approach outlined

in ANALYSIS 2 just conducted, we can interval estimate the difference in these two population means by introducing first parameteric symbols for all these 15 correlations, then
introducing this difference as a new parameter, and finally requesting a CI for the latter,
obtained with the delta method. The following M*plus* input file accomplishes this goal (see
appendix in Raykov, 2010c; note that the convergent validity coefficients are positioned
along the second lower diagonal of the correlation matrix in Table 8.5, and all remaining
off-diagonal correlations are discriminant validity coefficients).

```
TITLE:      MULTITRAIT-MULTIMETHOD MATRIX BASED VALIDATION
            ANALYSIS 3.

DATA:       FILE = TABLE8_5.DAT; ! see Table 8.5
            TYPE = CORRELATION MEANS STDEVIATIONS;
            NOBSERVATIONS = 435;

VARIABLE:   NAMES = M1T1 M1T2 M2T1 M2T2 M3T1 M3T2;

MODEL:      F1 BY M1T1*1; M1T1@0;
            F2 BY M1T2*1; M1T2@0;
            F3 BY M2T1*1; M2T1@0;
            F4 BY M2T2*1; M2T2@0;
            F5 BY M3T1*1; M3T1@0;
            F6 BY M3T2*1; M3T2@0;
            F1-F6@1;
            F1 WITH F2(P1);
            F1 WITH F3(P2);
            F1 WITH F4(P3);
            F1 WITH F5(P4);
            F1 WITH F6(P5);
            F2 WITH F3(P6);
            F2 WITH F4(P7);
            F2 WITH F5(P8);
            F2 WITH F6(P9);
            F3 WITH F4(P10);
            F3 WITH F5(P11);
            F3 WITH F6(P12);
            F4 WITH F5(P13);
            F4 WITH F6(P14);
            F5 WITH F6(P15);

MODEL CONSTRAINT:
            NEW(CV_DV);
            CV_DV = (P2+P7+P11+P14+P4+P9)/6
            - (P1+P3+P5+P6+P8+P10+P12+P13+P15)/9;

OUTPUT:     CINTERVAL;
```

In this modeling effort, of main interest is the CI for the population difference between
mean convergent validity coefficient and mean discriminant validity coefficient, which
is symbolically denoted CV_DV when introduced as a new parameter in the MODEL
CONSTRAINT section in the last command file. The latter produces the same output as
any of the preceding analyses in this Subsection 8.9.2, as far as fit and model parameter

estimates are concerned (and for this reason they are not presented next), while in addition providing the following confidence interval section of interest to us:

```
New/Additional Parameters
   CV_DV              0.323      0.343      0.406      0.468      0.488
```

This result shows that the 95%-CI of the population mean difference between convergent and discriminant validity coefficients is (.343, .468). This finding suggests, with high degree of confidence, that in the studied population the convergence validity coefficients exceed on average the discriminant validity coefficients by an amount that could be as low as .343 and as high as .468. This is consistent with theoretical expectations, given that the convergent validity coefficients reflect relationships between different measures of the same trait, whereas the discriminant validity coefficients reflect considerably weaker relationships between different indicators of different constructs.

We conclude this chapter by observing that we discussed in it what may well be considered the bottom line of measurement, validity, and specifically several useful approaches to the assessment of validity in empirical behavioral and social research that were developed using the framework of latent variable modeling. Although we were not able to extensively cover all aspects related to validity, we aimed at examining most if not all essential issues for this introductory text. For further discussions of validity and closely related matters, we refer readers to Allen and Yen (1979), Borsboom (2006), Crocker and Algina (1986), Magnusson (1967), McDonald (1999), Messick (1989, 1995), Pedhazur and Schmelkin (1991), and references therein.

9

Generalizability Theory

In several of the preceding chapters, we made substantial use of classical test theory. These chapters were based on the premise that the set of components in an instrument under consideration was prespecified, i.e., fixed throughout our pertinent discussion. Although one could make decisions as to which components to include in revised versions of instruments being investigated, the sets of possible components for them were considered as given beforehand. Within this framework, sometimes called statistical, sampling is typically carried out only from a population(s) being studied, rather than from a large pool of test components.

In this chapter, we will adopt an alternative approach that we already referred to in the first chapter of the book when discussing domain sampling. Specifically, here we will utilize a framework that is sometimes called psychometric, where sampling is usually carried out from a large pool of components (items) or related populations and from a population(s) of individuals being examined. This framework is characteristic of a psychometric modeling approach that has become known as generalizability theory and has a relatively long history. Although many scholars have contributed to its early development (e.g., Burt, 1936, 1947; Hoyt, 1941; Lindquist, 1953), it was formally introduced by Cronbach and his associates (Cronbach, Gleser, Nanda, & Rajaratnam, 1972; Cronbach, Rajaratnam, & Gleser, 1963; Gleser, Cronbach, & Rajaratnam, 1965). More recent developments in generalizability theory have elaborated in different directions the fundamental work by these researchers (e.g., Gessaroli & Folske, 2002; Hagtvet, 1997, 1998; Marcoulides, 1996; Raykov & Marcoulides, 2006b).

9.1 The Nature of Measurement Error

The major decomposition underlying classical test theory (CTT) is that any observed score (X) for an individual obtained through use of a measurement device is the joint result of a true score (T) and random error $(E;$ see Chapter 5, and in particular Equation (5.1)). A characteristic feature of CTT is that all factors affecting the observed instrument (test, scale) score X fall into these two main components, T and E. Specifically, the fundamental CTT equation states that observed score is the sum of the latter two, i.e., $X = T + E$. In Chapter 5, we emphasized the complexity of the sources of variability contributing to the error score. Despite this acknowledgment, the error score E is handled within the CTT framework as a unitary, global entity. In particular, CTT does not make any statement about what specifically contributes to measurement error. Furthermore, no particular assertion is made with respect to systematic error of measurement, which as indicated earlier in this book is absorbed into the true score T within the CTT approach. That is, in actual fact CTT is concerned with only 'one type' of error, viz., the unity of all factors that contribute to the error score E in its above decomposition equation.

In many empirical settings, however, advanced knowledge of the sources of error of measurement may well be beneficial as well as needed. This is in particular the case when one is interested in generalizing from a given set of test scores to situations beyond those under which the scores were obtained. A natural question that may be posed at this point is why one would be concerned with a generalization from a single test score. As we have already emphasized on quite a few occasions throughout this book, measuring instrument results (test, scale scores) are usually employed for making decisions about persons. Therefore, we would typically be interested in coming up with a generalization from a test score when we wish to make such a decision about an individual(s) based on that score. Then the question of real concern is to what degree our decision is dependable, i.e., to what degree that score is accurate, veridical, and trustworthy as a means of making that decision. To begin to answer this question, one needs to address more thoroughly the concept of error of measurement than its treatment within CTT accomplishes.

Additional motivation for elaborating this concept relates to the observation that a good understanding of the composition of error associated with a measuring device facilitates a more veridical evaluation of the effects of error on scores obtained with that instrument. In this connection, it would be helpful to revisit for a moment the notion of reliability in CTT, which is defined as the ratio of the true score variance (σ_T^2) to the observed score variance (σ_X^2, or equivalently $\sigma_T^2 + \sigma_E^2$), i.e., as the proportion of observed score variability that is attributable to true score variability across individuals (see Chapter 5). To evaluate reliability in an empirical setting, a number of traditional methods have been used in the past. As discussed in Chapter 7, a test–retest reliability estimate could be utilized to provide an indication of how consistently a measurement device rank orders individuals over time. This method requires that the instrument be administered on two different occasions and examines the correlation between observed scores on them to evaluate stability over time. Internal consistency (coefficient alpha) could be a different approach to obtaining a reliability estimate that would be dependable under certain conditions and considers the degree to which test items provide similar and consistent results about individuals. A third procedure for estimating reliability involved administering two forms of the same test at different times and examining the correlation between the forms. A common feature of all these methods is that unfortunately it is not always clear which interpretation of error is most suitable when each of them is used. To make things worse, one must face the uncomfortable, at least, fact that scores obtained from measurement devices used on the same individuals in general yield different values, depending on method, for the resulting reliability estimates.

In contrast with those earlier approaches that do not explicitly handle possibly diverse sources of error, generalizability theory (a) acknowledges the fact that multiple sources of error may simultaneously occur in measurement (e.g., errors attributable to different testing occasions and/or different test items, raters, etc.) and (b) enables estimation of the multifaceted error effects. These goals are achieved by a different handling of the error term in the generalizability theory modeling approach. A special benefit of the theory is that it allows one to accomplish generalization to a wider set of conditions than those under which a particular measurement is conducted. We easily recognize that once administering an instrument (test) and obtaining an individual's score on it, this score is only one of many scores that one could have obtained from that person, which might serve the same purpose of decision making about him or her. In particular, one could have obtained from that individual scores across pertinent test forms, occasions, raters, tasks, etc. All these scores might as well be considered interchangeable for the same decision-making purpose. For this reason, we call these idealized scores admissible for that purpose. Hence, the best datum on which to base the decision would be a score that is representative of all such acceptable or admissible observations. Specifically, in their original formulation of generalizability theory, Cronbach et al. (1972) provided the following argument in this respect:

> The score on which the decision is to be based is only one of many scores that might serve the same purpose. The decision maker is almost never interested in the response given to the particular stimulus objects or questions, to the particular tester, at the particular moment of testing. Some, at least, of these conditions of measurement could be altered without making the score any less acceptable to the decision maker. That is to say, there is a universe of observations, any of which would have yielded a usable basis for the decision. The ideal datum on which to base the decision would be something like the person's mean score over all acceptable observations, which we shall call his "universe score." The investigator uses the observed score or some function of it as if it were the universe score. That is, he generalizes from sample to universe. (Cronbach et al., 1972, p. 15)

Hence, the notion of a universe lies at the heart of generalizability theory. In fact, all measurements are deemed to be sampled from a universe of admissible observations. A universe is defined in terms of those aspects (called facets) of the observations that determine the conditions under which an acceptable score can be obtained. For example, the facets that define one universe could be personality tests administered to new employees during their first week of employment. Because it is possible to conceive of many different universes to which any particular measurement might generalize, it is essential that investigators define explicitly the facets that can change without making the observation unacceptable or unreliable. For example, if test scores might be expected to vary from one occasion to another, then the 'occasions' facet is one defining characteristic of the universe, and multiple testing times must be included in the measurement procedure. The same would hold true for the choice of test items and other aspects of the measurement procedure. Ideally, that measurement procedure should yield information about an individual's universe score over all combinations of facets, but in reality investigators are limited in their selection of particular occasions, items, etc.

The need to sample facets introduces error into the measurement procedure and can limit the precision of estimation of the universe score. For this reason, the classical test theory concept of reliability is replaced in generalizability theory by the broader notion of generalizability (Shavelson, Webb, & Rowley, 1989). More specifically, instead of asking 'how accurately observed scores reflect corresponding true scores', generalizability theory asks 'how accurately observed scores permit us to generalize about persons' behavior in a defined universe' (Shavelson et al., 1989). Although in most instances some attribute of persons will usually be the object of measurement, it is also possible to consider other facets as the object of measurement. In such a case where the object of measurement is not persons, the facet for persons is then treated as an error component. This feature has been termed the 'principle of symmetry' (Cardinet, Tourneur, & Allal, 1976).

A fundamental assumption of generalizability theory is that the object of measurement is in a steady state. For example if the object of measurement is persons, then any measured attribute of theirs like attitude, knowledge, or skill is assumed not to be changing. As a result, any observed differences among scores obtained for a given person on, say, different occasions of measurement are due only to sources of error rather than to any systematic changes in the individual as a consequence of maturation or learning (Shavelson & Webb, 1991). If this assumption is not fulfilled, generalizability theory can provide potentially misleading results and conclusions.

9.2 A One-Facet Crossed Design

In order to discuss specific settings where generalizability theory is applicable, let us assume that a multiple-choice test consisting of a random sample of n_i items from a universe of items is administered to a random sample of n_p persons from a population of interest. (In this chapter, we will attach at times subindexes as part of the symbol for number of units considered.) Such a design is called a one-facet person-crossed-with-items ($p \times i$) design because the items facet is the only potential source of error in the measurement procedure (other than residual effect; see below). A one-facet design can be viewed as an analysis of variance (ANOVA) design with a single random factor, because of the fact that the set of items used is randomly drawn from the universe of items (e.g., Brennan, 2001). Denoting the observed score of person p on item i as X_{pi}, one can decompose that score as follows (in equation form, and following verbal form):

$$X_{pi} = \mu + (\mu_p - \mu) + (\mu_i - \mu) + (X_{pi} - \mu_p - \mu_i + \mu)$$

$$= \text{grand mean} + \text{person effect} + \text{item effect} + \text{residual effect},$$

(9.1)

where $\mu_p = E_i X_{pi}$ is the person's universe score (i.e., the expected value of the random variable X_{pi} across items), $\mu_i = E_p X_{pi}$ is the person population mean for item i, and $\mu = E_p E_i X_{pi}$ is the mean over both the person population and the universe of possible scores (the symbol $E_{()}$ is used here to denote expectation with respect to the universe/population indicated as subindex). Because there is only one observation for each person–item combination in this design, the residual effect corresponds to score effect attributable to the interaction of person p with item i confounded with experimental error (Cronbach et al., 1972). Cronbach et al. (1972) represented this confounding with the notation pi,e (typically used as a subindex). The associated observed variance decomposition with these effects is as follows (e.g., Shavelson & Webb, 1991):

$$\sigma^2(X_{pi}) = \sigma_p^2 + \sigma_i^2 + \sigma_{pi,e}^2,$$

(9.2)

where the symbols on the right-hand side correspond respectively to the variance due to persons, items, and residual (cf. Equation (9.1)).

  In generalizability theory, of main importance are the variance components of the effects in the model adopted, because their magnitude provides information about the potential sources of error influencing a measurement procedure. The reason is that the variance

Table 9.1. Computational formulas for the variance components in a one-facet crossed design

Source of variance	df	Mean square (MS)	E(MS)
Examinee (p)	$n_p - 1$	$SS_p/(n_p - 1)$	$\sigma_{pi,e}^2 + n_i\sigma_p^2$
Rater (i)	$n_i - 1$	$SS_i/(n_i - 1)$	$\sigma_{pi,e}^2 + n_p\sigma_i^2$
Residual (pi, e)	$(n_p-1)(n_i-1)$	$SS_{pi,e}/[(n_r-1)(n_r-1)]$	$\sigma_{pi,e}^2$

Note: p, i, and pi, e = symbols for person, item, and residual, respectively (used in subindexes); n_p, n_i = number of persons and items, respectively, in the study; $\sigma_{(.)}^2$ = population variance pertinent to source (see subindex); E(MS) = expected mean square (mean square, MS, insecond-last column).

components are the basis for evaluating the relative contribution of each potential source of error and the dependability of a measurement. Determining the variance components is typically achieved using mean sum of squares from the corresponding ANOVA setting. Table 9.1 provides the computational formulas for the variance components associated with the score effects in a one-facet design (e.g., Shavelson & Webb, 1991).

In empirical research, estimation of the variance components can be accomplished by substituting mean square estimates from the analysis of variance for their expected values and solving the corresponding equations resulting thereby. In particular, the estimated variance components for the one-facet design in Table 9.1 are determined as follows (see last column of Table 9.1):

$$\hat{\sigma}_p^2 = \frac{MS_p - MS_{pi,e}}{n_i}, \quad \hat{\sigma}_i^2 = \frac{MS_i - MS_{pi,e}}{n_p}, \quad \hat{\sigma}_{pi,e}^2 = MS_{pi,e}, \tag{9.3}$$

where the subindexed symbols MS_p, MS_i, and $MS_{pi,e}$ designate correspondingly the mean squares for persons, items, and residual.

Although this is the conventional variance estimation procedure, other procedures can also be used to estimate variance components. For example, Marcoulides (1987, 1989, 1990, 1996), Raykov and Marcoulides (2006b), and Shavelson and Webb (1981) have described several alternative methods that can be used to provide variance component estimates, including Bayesian, minimum variance, restricted maximum likelihood, and covariance structure modeling approaches (see, e.g., the section on a structural equation modeling approach below). Appropriate decompositions from these methods can provide more accurate estimates of variance components than ANOVA in cases involving small sample sizes, dichotomous data, unbalanced designs, or data with missing observations (Marcoulides, 1987, 1996; Muthén, 1983). The ANOVA approach is currently considerably easier to implement, however, and is the most commonly used estimation method in generalizability theory applications (Shavelson & Webb, 1981).

To obtain standard errors and construct confidence intervals for variance components, one can use two general classes of procedures. The first and more traditional procedure makes normality assumptions about the distribution of the effects, whereas the other class uses resampling methods like bootstrap and jackknife. Within the traditional procedures for standard errors and confidence intervals, a number of alternative approaches have been proposed. Searle (1971) showed that for a one-facet design, the following standard errors can be used ($\hat{\sigma}[.]$ denotes next standard error associated with the estimator within brackets):

$$\hat{\sigma}[\hat{\sigma}_p^2] = \sqrt{\frac{2MS_p^2}{n_i^2(n_p-1)} + \frac{2MS_{pi}^2}{n_p^2(n_p-1)(n_i-1)}},$$

$$\hat{\sigma}[\hat{\sigma}_i^2] = \sqrt{\frac{2MS_i^2}{n_p^2(n_i-1)} + \frac{2MS_{pi}^2}{n_p^2(n_p-1)(n_i-1)}}, \text{ and}$$

$$\hat{\sigma}[\hat{\sigma}_{pi,e}^2] = \sqrt{\frac{2MS_{pi,e}^2}{(n_p-1)(n_i-1)}}.$$

Satterthwaite (1946; see also Graybill, 1976, pp. 642–643) proposed what is usually considered a better approach to construct a confidence interval for a variance component (Brennan, 1983). Accordingly, an approximate 100(1-α)% confidence interval is

$$\frac{\hat{\sigma}_p^2}{\chi_{1-\alpha/2,v}^2} \leq \sigma_p^2 \leq \frac{\hat{\sigma}_p^2}{\chi_{\alpha/2,v}^2},$$

where $v = 2\left[\frac{\hat{\sigma}_p^2}{\hat{\sigma}(\hat{\sigma}_p^2)}\right]^2$ and [.] denotes largest integer not exceeding the quantity within brackets (0 < α < 1). To popularize this approach, Brennan (2001) provided complete tables to determine Satterthwaite confidence intervals for v = 2, 3, 4, …, 20000. Several other traditional approaches have also been proposed (e.g., Burdick & Graybill, 1992; Ting, Burdick, Graybill, Jeyaratnam, & Lu, 1990) but seem to be variations of the above two outlined approaches.

Resampling procedures like the bootstrap and jackknife have also been proposed for obtaining standard errors and confidence intervals for variance components. Both are resampling procedures and primarily nonparametric methods (see also Efron, 1982; Marcoulides, 1989). Some research, however, has suggested that it is not always clear how to draw a bootstrap or jackknife sample from the matrix of observed scores (Brennan, Harris, & Hanson, 1987; Marcoulides, 1989; Wiley, 2000). For example, for the $n_p \times n_i$ matrix of observed scores in a one-facet design, to use the bootstrap it is not clear whether to sample persons (to provide a so-called boot-*p*), to sample items (to provide boot-*i*), or to sample persons, items, and residuals (to provide boot-*p,i,r*)—see also Wiley (2000) for a discussion on a number of other methods to draw bootstrap and jackknife samples. Unfortunately, to date, it is also not clear which resampling procedure is optimal (Brennan, 2001).

9.3 Types of Error Variances

Generalizability theory distinguishes between two types of error variance that correspond to relative decisions and absolute decisions. The former are decisions about individual differences between persons, whereas the latter are decisions about level of performance. Relative error variance, also called δ-type error, relates to decisions that involve the rank ordering of individuals. In such instances, to determine this error variance, all sources of variation that include persons, except σ_p^2, are considered measurement error (e.g., Shavelson & Webb, 1991). For example, in a one-facet design, the relative error variance is $\sigma_\delta^2 = \frac{\sigma_{pi,e}^2}{n_i}$ and includes the variance component due to residual averaged over the number of items used. The square root of this variance, σ_δ, is considered the δ-type (or relative) standard error of measurement. Using σ_δ, a confidence interval at a given confidence level $(1-\alpha)100\%$ for the universe score can be constructed as

$$(X - z_{\alpha/2}\,\sigma_\delta, X + z_{\alpha/2}\,\sigma_\delta), \tag{9.4}$$

where $z_{\alpha/2}$ denotes the $\alpha/2$th quantile of the standard normal distribution (Brennan, 1983; $0 < \alpha < 1$). Thereby, normality of observed scores is assumed, and in order to obtain this interval in an empirical setting, an appropriate estimate of the δ-type standard error of measurement needs to be substituted in Equation (9.4), which is furnished as above via the estimate of residual variance (see last of Equations (9.3)). We note that although generalizability theory per se makes no distributional assumptions about the observed scores or effects in order to accomplish their variance decomposition, such an assumption is required for constructing the above confidence interval within this framework (see also next section).

When concerned with whether an examinee can perform at a prespecified competence level, it is the absolute error variance that is of relevance (e.g., Brennan, 2001). This variance, called Δ-type error, reflects both information about the rank ordering of persons and any differences in average scores. For example, in the one-facet design, the absolute error is $\sigma_\Delta^2 = \frac{\sigma_i^2}{n_i} + \frac{\sigma_{pi,e}^2}{n_i}$ and includes in addition to $\frac{\sigma_{pi,e}^2}{n_i}$ the variance components due to item averaged over number of items used. The square root of this index (σ_Δ) can also be used to construct a confidence interval, at level $(1-\alpha)100\%$, for the universe score as follows:

$$(X - z_{\alpha/2}\,\sigma_\Delta, X + z_{\alpha/2}\,\sigma_\Delta). \tag{9.5}$$

This confidence interval is evaluated empirically by substituting an appropriate estimate of the absolute error variance, like the interval in Equation (9.4) (Brennan, 1983).

9.4 Generalizability Coefficients

Although generalizability theory underscores the importance of variance components, it also provides generalizability coefficients that can be used to index the dependability of a measurement procedure. Their values range from 0 to 1.0, with higher values reflecting more dependable measurement procedures. Generalizability coefficients are available when relative error is of concern (symbolized by $E\rho_\delta^2$) and when absolute error is of relevance (symbolized by ρ_Δ^2 or Φ—the notation is often used interchangeably). For the one-facet design, these coefficients are correspondingly as follows (Cronbach et al., 1963, 1972):

$$E\rho_\delta^2 = \frac{\sigma_p^2}{\sigma_p^2 + \sigma_\delta^2} \quad \text{and} \tag{9.6}$$

$$\rho_\Delta^2 = \Phi = \frac{\sigma_p^2}{\sigma_p^2 + \sigma_\Delta^2}.$$

We note that the value of $E\rho_\delta^2$ in the one-facet design is equal to coefficient α for continuous items and to KR-20 when items are scored dichotomously (Cronbach et al., 1972).

Brennan (1983) indicated that the generalizability coefficient ρ_Δ^2 (or Φ) may be viewed as a general purpose index of dependability for domain-referenced (criterion-referenced or content-referenced) interpretations of examinee scores. The observed examinee score is interpreted as representative of the universe or the domain from which it was sampled, and interest is placed on the dependability of an examinee's score that is unrelated to the performance of others (i.e., unrelated to the universe scores of other examinees). However, if emphasis is placed on the dependability of an individual's performance in relation to a particular cutoff score (e.g., when considering a domain-referenced test that has a fixed cutoff score and classifies examinees who match or exceed this score as having mastered the content represented by the domain), a different generalizability index is of relevance (Brennan & Kane, 1977). The index is denoted by $\Phi(\lambda)$ and represents domain-referenced interpretations involving a fixed cutoff score λ. Thus, for different cutoff scores, the value of $\Phi(\lambda)$ is determined by

$$\Phi(\lambda) = \frac{\sigma_p^2 + (\mu - \lambda)^2}{\sigma_p^2 + (\mu - \lambda)^2 + \sigma_\Delta^2}. \tag{9.7}$$

For computational ease, an unbiased estimator of the term $(\mu - \lambda)^2$ is obtained by using

$$(\overline{X} - \lambda)^2 - \sigma_{\overline{X}}^2, \tag{9.8}$$

where $\sigma_{\overline{X}}^2$ is the mean error variance and represents the error variance involved in utilizing the mean $(\overline{X})$ over the sample of both persons and items as an estimate of the overall mean (μ) in the population of persons and the universe of items (Brennan & Kane, 1977). The smaller the mean error variance, the more stable the population estimate (Marcoulides, 1993). Thus, for a one-facet design, the mean error variance is equal to

$$\sigma_{\overline{X}}^2 = \frac{\sigma_p^2}{n_p} + \frac{\sigma_i^2}{n_i} + \frac{\sigma_{pi,e}^2}{n_p n_i} \tag{9.9}$$

and is estimated by substituting estimates of the three variances in the right-hand side (see preceding section).

Confidence intervals for the generalizability coefficients for both relative and absolute decisions can also be constructed. Brennan (2001) conducted simulations to show that the intervals obtained for relative coefficients perform reasonably well with both normally and nonnormally distributed data (in the used conditions). Intervals obtained for absolute decisions also perform reasonably well with normally distributed data but with nonnormal data are less accurate, although still probably usable for most practical purposes. For relative decisions in the one-faceted design considered above under normality, the resulting interval for $E\rho_\delta^2$ is identical to that derived by Feldt (1965)—see also discussion in Chapter 7 (Brennan, 1983). For the ρ_Δ^2 or Φ generalizability coefficients again under normality, the approach developed by Arteaga, Jeyaratnam, and Graybill (1982) can be used. Alternatively, resampling procedures like the bootstrap and jackknife can also be used generally to construct confidence intervals for relative and absolute generalizability coefficients.

We note that to date, no specific guidelines are available with regard to a preferable method for confidence interval construction of generalizability coefficients. However, it may be suggested that when using large samples, the methods would possibly furnish similar intervals. We hope that future research will examine this issue in detail and, perhaps after some extensive simulation studies, provide guidelines for choosing an optimal approach.

9.5 G Studies and D Studies

As seen from the preceding discussion, a generalizability analysis enables the pinpointing of the sources of measurement error and the determination of how many conditions of each facet are needed in order to achieve optimal generalizability for making different types of future decisions (e.g., relative or absolute; Marcoulides & Goldstein, 1990, 1991, 1992). Indeed, generalizability coefficients for an assortment of studies with alternate numbers of items can be computed in much the same way the Spearman-Brown prophecy formula can be used to determine the appropriate length of a test.

Generalizability theory refers to the initial study of a measurement procedure as the generalizability (G) study (Shavelson & Webb, 1981). However, it is quite possible that, after conducting a generalizability analysis, one may want to design a measurement procedure that differs from the G study. For example, if the results of a G study show that some sources of error are small, then one may elect a measurement procedure that reduces the number of levels of that facet (e.g., number of items) or even ignores that facet (which can be critically important in multifaceted designs; see next section). Alternatively, if the results of a G study show that some sources of error in the design are very large, one may increase the levels of that facet in order to maximize generalizability. Generalizability theory refers to the process in which facets are modified on the basis of information obtained in a G study as a decision (D) study.

Unfortunately, there appears to be considerable confusion in the literature concerning the differences between a G study and a D study. Cronbach et al. (1972) indicated that the distinction between a G study and a D study is just an affirmation that certain studies are carried out while developing a measurement procedure and then the procedure is put into use or action. In general, a D study can be conceptualized as the point at which one looks back at the G study and examines the measurement procedure in order to make recommendations for change. A D study can be thought of as tackling the question 'What should be done differently, relative to a preceding G study, if one were going to rely on the measurement procedure involved for making future decisions or drawing conclusions?' In the case where no changes should be made, the G study acts as the D study (i.e., with the same sample of items as in the initial study).

Although generalizability will generally become better as the number of conditions in a facet is increased, this number can potentially become somewhat unrealistic. More important is the question of a 'trade-off' between conditions of a facet within some cost considerations (Cronbach et al., 1972). Typically, in multifaceted studies there can be several D study designs that yield the same level of generalizability. For example, if one desires to develop a measurement procedure with a relative generalizability coefficient of 0.90, there might be two distinct D study designs from which to choose. Clearly, in such cases one must consider resource constraints in order to choose the appropriate D study design. The question then becomes how to maximize generalizability within a prespecified set of limited resources. Of course, in a one-faceted person by item ($p \times i$) design, the question of satisfying resource constraints while maximizing generalizability is simple. One chooses the greatest number of items without violating the budget. When other facets are added to the design, obtaining a solution is much more complicated. Goldstein and Marcoulides (1991), Marcoulides and Goldstein (1990, 1991), and Marcoulides (1993, 1995) developed various procedures that can be used to determine the optimal number of conditions that maximize generalizability under various constraints (see also discussion in next section).

A One-Facet Nested Design: Another way in which G studies and D studies may differ is in terms of the actual data collection design. In the above discussion, for example, both the G and the D studies might be conducted using the originally conceived crossed $p \times i$ design (i.e., every person is administered the same sample of test items). It is possible, however, that a researcher might use a D study design in which each person is administered a different random sample of items. Such a situation may arise in computer-assisted or computer-generated test construction (Brennan, 1983). Hence, although the facets that define the universe of admissible observations are crossed, an investigator may choose to use a nested measurement design in conducting a D study. This one-facet nested design is traditionally denoted $i{:}p$, where the colon indicates 'nested within'. For such a design, a model for observed scores is

$$X_{pi} = \mu + \mu_p^* + \mu_{i:p,e}{}^*,\tag{9.10}$$

where μ is the overall mean in the population of persons and universe of items, μ_p^* is the effect attributable to person p, and $\mu_{i:p,e}^*$ is the residual effect (Cronbach et al., 1972).

A comparison of this nested design model (9.10) with the crossed design in Equation (9.1) reveals that the items-nested-within-persons effect ($\mu_{i:p,e}^*$) relates to a confounding of the μ_i and $\mu_{pi,e}$ effects in the crossed design. The reason for this confounding is that in the nested design the item effect cannot be estimated independently of the person-by-item interaction, because different persons are administered different items (Shavelson & Webb, 1991). Hence, the variance of the observed scores for all persons and items is the sum of only two variance components, i.e., $\sigma_X^2 = \sigma_p^2 + \sigma_{i:p,e}^2$. In the nested one-facet design, therefore, σ_δ^2 equals σ_Δ^2, and only one generalizability coefficient for relative or absolute decisions can be estimated (Cronbach et al., 1972).

Unfortunately, a major drawback of using a nested design is that it is not possible to obtain a separate estimate of the item effect. Whenever feasible, therefore, generalizability studies should use fully crossed designs so that all the sources of variability in the measurement design can be estimated (Cronbach et al., 1972). However, a researcher may elect to change a crossed generalizability study design to a nested design whenever the results from a crossed G study show that the sources of error for a particular facet are negligible. In the case where there is natural nesting in the universe of admissible observations, a researcher has no choice but to incorporate that nesting into both the G study and the D study.

9.6 Software for Generalizability Analysis

The computational requirements involved in estimating variance components in a generalizability theory analysis can be quite demanding, especially in multifaceted designs. As a consequence, computer programs generally need to be used in order to obtain parameter estimates. Several tailored computer programs have been developed for conducting univariate and multivariate generalizability analyses, including GENOVA, urGENOVA, mGENOVA (Brennan, 1983, 2001), and EduG (Cardinet, Johnson, & Pini, 2010; the program is also available with manuals from http://www.ird.ch/edumetrie/eduGeng.htm). These programs are relatively straightforward to use and provide excellent procedures for handling most of the computational complexities of generalizability theory. Other general purpose programs that can be utilized to estimate variance components in a generalizability analysis include REML (Robinson, 1987), the SAS-PROC VARCOMP and SAS-PROC MIXED procedures (SAS Institute, 2004), the SPSS VARIANCE COMPONENTS procedure (SPSS Inc., 2004), and with some designs also covariance structure modeling programs (e.g., Marcoulides, 1996; Raykov & Marcoulides, 2006b; see Section 9.11 below).

9.7 Example of One-Facet Design Analysis

To illustrate some of the preceding developments in this chapter, let us consider an example one-facet design, in which the mathematics skills of a sample of 285 seventh-grade students based on QUASAR Mathematics assessment tasks are rated by six raters using a holistic scoring rubric ranging from 1 to 8 (see Lane, Liu, Ankenmann, & Stone, 1996). In order to estimate the variance components and generalizability coefficient for this study, we can apply the two-factor ANOVA procedure using the popular software SPSS.

Assuming that the data may be provided in a format similar to that in Table 9.2, in which for illustrative purposes data for just 10 examinees and three raters are presented, a simple restructuring of the data to an appropriate format is needed before using SPSS.

Table 9.2. Illustrative Ratings by 3 teachers for 10 students

Examinee (Person)	Rater 1	Rater 2	Rater 3
1	2.00	3.00	2.00
2	8.00	5.00	7.00
3	4.00	2.00	2.00
4	4.00	3.00	6.00
5	8.00	5.00	5.00
6	8.00	5.00	7.00
7	6.00	4.00	5.00
8	4.00	3.00	3.00
9	3.00	2.00	2.00
10	1.00	2.00	3.00

This restructuring is readily obtained with SPSS by choosing the 'Data' option and then the 'Restructure' function (following the prompts leading to procedure execution). We note that the restructuring activity is quite useful whenever one needs to move from what may informally be called a 'flat' data format (i.e., a data matrix containing data from n subjects [rows] by p variables [columns]) to a so-called vertical data format—usually containing just one measurement per row in the data matrix. The vertical data format (sometimes also called 'univariate' as opposed to 'multivariate', which is a more formal reference to the above 'flat' format) is very often utilized in repeated measure studies, as well as in multi-level/mixed modeling contexts. Restructuring the 'flat' (multivariate) data format presented in Table 9.2 would provide the 'vertical' (univariate) data layout given in Table 9.3.

Table 9.3. Restructured example data set

Examinee (Person)	Rater	Score/Rating
1.00	1	2.00
1.00	2	3.00
1.00	3	2.00
2.00	1	8.00
2.00	2	5.00
2.00	3	7.00
3.00	1	4.00
3.00	2	2.00
3.00	3	2.00
4.00	1	4.00
4.00	2	3.00
4.00	3	6.00
5.00	1	8.00
5.00	2	5.00
5.00	3	5.00
6.00	1	8.00
6.00	2	5.00
6.00	3	7.00
7.00	1	6.00
7.00	2	4.00
7.00	3	5.00
8.00	1	4.00
8.00	2	3.00
8.00	3	3.00
9.00	1	3.00
9.00	2	2.00
9.00	3	2.00
10.00	1	1.00
10.00	2	2.00
10.00	3	3.00

Once the data have been restructured, the following SPSS sequence of commands can be used on the entire data set, which includes 285 students and six raters, to obtain the desired estimates:

```
Analyze → General Linear Model → Univariate (choose the variable 'Score'
as dependent, while the variables 'Examinee (Person)' and 'Rater' as
factors); then click OK
```

We note that the SAS procedures PROC ANOVA and PROC VARCOMP can also be used for the present analytic purposes. The resulting output of the ANOVA source table would be similar to that furnished below by SPSS, with the added advantage that the values of the estimated variance components are provided directly. To accomplish this activity in SAS, the following command statements can be used (for further details see *SAS User's Guide* by SAS Institute, Inc., 2004, or Raykov & Marcoulides, 2008):

```
DATA Chapter9-EX9.7;
INPUT PERSON RATER RATING;
INFILE 'data file';
```

```
PROC ANOVA;
CLASS PERSON RATER RATING;
MODEL RATING = PERSON RATER;
RUN;
PROC VARCOMP;
CLASS PERSON RATER RATING;
MODEL RATING = PERSON RATER;
RUN;
```

The above SPSS command sequence yields the output below (because of space consid-erations, we present only the first 25 observations; the entire output would contain all 285 observations listed).

Univariate Analysis of Variance

Between-Subjects Factors

		N
Person	1	6
	2	6
	3	6
	4	6
	5	6
	6	6
	7	6
	8	6
	9	6
	10	6
	11	6
	12	6
	13	6
	14	6
	15	6
	16	6
	17	6
	18	6
	19	6
	20	6
	21	6
	22	6
	23	6
	24	6
	25	6
Rater	1	285
	2	285
	3	285
	4	285
	5	285
	6	285

We note that for the purposes of this analysis, formally we need to treat the variable 'Examinee (Person)' as a factor with 285 levels, within each of which there are six measurements. (This is the reason why in the last two columns of the output section shown below there are no entries; this fact can be safely ignored here, however, because of this treatment of 'Examinee (Person)'.) The variable 'Rater' is the second factor with six levels that have each 285 observations. This is just a formal arrangement that we use in this example in order to obtain the important mean square statistics and use with them the above formulas of the variance components, error variances, and generalizability coefficient estimates.

Tests of Between-Subjects Effects

Dependent Variable: Rating

Source	Type III Sum of Squares	df	Mean Square	F	Sig.
Person	858.218	284	3.022	.	.
Rater	830.800	5	166.160	.	.
Person * Rater	1412.150	1417	.997	.	.
Total	11598.000	1707			

On the basis of this observed variance decomposition, we can readily obtain the earlier discussed generalizability coefficient estimate for a relative decision using the six raters as (see Equation (9.6))

$$E\hat{\rho}_\delta^2 = \frac{\hat{\sigma}_p^2}{\hat{\sigma}_p^2 + \hat{\sigma}_\delta^2} = \frac{(MS_p - MS_{pr,e})/n_r}{(MS_p - MS_e)/n_r + MS_{pr,e}/n_r}$$

$$= \frac{(3.022 - 0.997)/6}{(3.022 - 0.997)/6 + 0.997/6} = .66,$$

(9.11)

which is not a substantial coefficient of generalizability (especially when we consider that six raters were used in this study). Furthermore, using pertinent results in the above SPSS output and Equations (9.3), the estimated variance component associated with the object of measurement, examinees (persons), is furnished as $\hat{\sigma}_p^2 = 0.3258$, that associated with raters as $\hat{\sigma}_r^2 = 0.579$, and the residual variance estimate is $\hat{\sigma}_{pr,e}^2 = 0.997$. These findings indicate that most of the variability is not due to persons (in fact, only approximately 17% of the total variability is due to persons). In addition, there is considerable disagreement with respect to the actual scores awarded to students by each rater (viz., approximately 30% of the total variability) and the rank ordering of persons (approximately 53% of the total variability). These results can be interpreted as supportive of the earlier suggestion that one may not generalize over raters. As indicated in Section 9.5, if the results of a G study show that some sources of error in the design are large, one may examine various D studies in which an increase in the number of levels of that facet is considered in order to maximize generalizability. For example, if the number of raters were doubled in this example, the generalizability coefficient estimate for a relative decision using 12 raters would increase to 0.80 (all else being the same).

9.8 Two-Facet and Higher-Order Crossed Designs

Generalizability theory can also be used to examine the dependability of measurements in multifaceted designs. For example, a generalizability study might be conducted to determine the dependability of measures of student ratings of their essay performance on different topics. Such a design might involve students (symbolized by p next) being observed by raters or judges (symbolized by j) on their essay writing performance in different subject areas (symbolized by s). A study of this type can be considered as based on a completely crossed $p \times j \times s$ design in which each teacher rates each student on each subject area. (We note, however, that in this study, subject area is considered a random facet selected from a universe of possible subject areas.)

Several sources of variability can contribute to error in this two-faceted study of dependability of the performance measures in which students (persons) are the object of measurement. Using the ANOVA approach, variance components for the three main effects in the design (persons, raters, and subject areas), the three two-way interactions, and the three-way interaction (confounded again with random error) must be estimated. The total variance of the observed score is equal to the sum of these variance components:

$$\sigma^2_{X_{pjs}} = \sigma^2_p + \sigma^2_j + \sigma^2_s + \sigma^2_{pj} + \sigma^2_{ps} + \sigma^2_{js} + \sigma^2_{pjs,e}, \tag{9.12}$$

where the σ's on the right-hand side denote the last-mentioned variance components (see Cronbach et al., 1972). To obtain the estimated variance components for a two-facet design using the ANOVA framework, the following computations would be necessary (Cronbach et al., 1972):

$$\hat{\sigma}^2_{pjs,e} = MS_{pjs,e}$$

$$\hat{\sigma}^2_{ps} = \frac{MS_{ps} - MS_{pjs,e}}{n_j}$$

$$\hat{\sigma}^2_{pj} = \frac{MS_{pj} - MS_{pjs,e}}{n_s}$$

$$\hat{\sigma}^2_{js} = \frac{MS_{js} - MS_{pjs,e}}{n_p} \tag{9.13}$$

$$\hat{\sigma}^2_p = \frac{MS_p - MS_{pjs,e} - n_j\sigma^2_{ps} + n_s\sigma^2_{pj}}{n_j n_s}$$

$$\hat{\sigma}^2_j = \frac{MS_j - MS_{pjs,e} - n_p\sigma^2_{js} + n_s\sigma^2_{pj}}{n_p n_s}$$

$$\hat{\sigma}^2_s = \frac{MS_s - MS_{pjs,e} - n_j\sigma^2_{ps} + n_p\sigma^2_{js}}{n_p n_j}.$$

Following Cronbach et al. (1972), the relative error variance associated with this measurement procedure is given by

$$\sigma_\delta^2 = \frac{\sigma_{pj}^2}{n_j} + \frac{\sigma_{ps}^2}{n_s} + \frac{\sigma_{pjs,e}^2}{n_j n_s}, \tag{9.14}$$

and the generalizability coefficient for a relative decision is

$$E\rho_\delta^2 = \frac{\sigma_p^2}{\sigma_p^2 + \sigma_\delta^2}. \tag{9.15}$$

The absolute error variance associated with this measurement procedure is

$$\sigma_\Delta^2 = \frac{\sigma_j^2}{n_j} + \frac{\sigma_s^2}{n_s} + \frac{\sigma_{pj}^2}{n_j} + \frac{\sigma_{ps}^2}{n_s} + \frac{\sigma_{js}^2}{n_j n_s} + \frac{\sigma_{pjs,e}^2}{n_j n_s}, \tag{9.16}$$

with a generalizability coefficient for an absolute decision equal to

$$\rho_\Delta^2 = \Phi = \frac{\sigma_p^2}{\sigma_p^2 + \sigma_\Delta^2}. \tag{9.17}$$

As previously mentioned, a variety of D studies with different combinations of judges and subject areas can be examined. For example, if it is evident that the subject-areas facet is a major source of measurement error, increasing the number of subject areas in the measurement procedure would be expected to increase the generalizability coefficients. We note again that when selecting between various D studies, one should always consider possible resource or other constraints imposed on the measurement procedures before making final decisions about a D study design (Marcoulides & Goldstein, 1990). For example, Marcoulides and Goldstein (1990) showed that if the total available budget (B) is given and if the cost (C) for each judge to observe a teacher in a subject area is also given, then the optimal number of judges can be readily determined using the following equation (we note that similar formulas can be used to determine the optimal number of conditions for other facets in the design):

$$n_j = \sqrt{\frac{\hat{\sigma}_{pj}^2}{\hat{\sigma}_{ps}^2}\left(\frac{B}{C}\right)}.$$

Therefore, D studies are very important when attempting to improve the dependability of measurement procedures, because they can provide values for both realistic and optimal numbers of measurement conditions.

9.9 Example Two-Facet Analysis

Here we consider an example in which the essay writing skills of a random sample of 101 students are rated in two subject areas by nine teachers using a holistic scoring rubric ranging from 1 to 8. In this case, we are interested in finding out whether the grades can be generalized over both subject areas and teachers. This study exemplifies a typical situation where one would be interested in applying a two-facet design with subject areas (s) and teacher raters (j) as facets (specifically, a *two-facet p × j × s crossed design*).

Using SPSS to obtain the pertinent estimates, we apply the following command sequence to the data:

```
Analyze → General Linear Model → Univariate (Score as dependent
variable; Examinee, Teacher, Topic as fixed factors; OK)
```

This yields the selectively presented output shown in the output below (using 'person' as a reference to 'examinee' or student).

Univariate Analysis of Variance

Tests of Between-Subjects Effects

Dependent Variable: SCORE

Source	Type III Sum of Squares	df	Mean Square	F	Sig.
PERSON	255.80	100	256	.	.
RATER	1.38	8	0.17	.	.
SUBJECT AREA	0.16	1	0.16	.	.
PERSON*RATER	26.90	800	0.03	.	.
PERSON*SUBJECT AREA	8.80	100	0.09	.	.
RATER*SUBJECT AREA	0.18	8	0.02	.	.
PERSON*RATER* SUBJECT AREA	7.40	800	0.01	.	.
Total	466489.000	3524			

Substituting these values in Equations (9.13), the estimated variance components associated with the object of measurement (students) is rendered as $\hat{\sigma}_p^2 = 0.156$, the one associated with raters (teachers) is rendered as $\hat{\sigma}_j^2 = 0.0008$, that associated with subject areas is rendered as $\hat{\sigma}_s^2 = 0.0001$, and the residual variance estimate is rendered as $\hat{\sigma}_{pjs,e}^2 = 0.01$. The remaining components are estimated as $\hat{\sigma}_{ps}^2 = 0.1$, $\hat{\sigma}_{pj}^2 = 0.01$, and $\hat{\sigma}_{js}^2 = 0.0001$. These findings indicate that most of the variability is due to persons (students; approximately 88%) and that there is very little disagreement with respect to the actual scores awarded to students by each rater (approximately 5%) and the rank ordering of persons (approximately 5%), indicating that one may generalize over both subject areas and raters.

On the basis of this observed variance decomposition, we can readily obtain the following generalizability coefficient estimate for a relative decision using the nine raters and two subject areas as (see Equation (9.15)):

$$E\hat{\rho}_\delta^2 = \frac{\hat{\sigma}_p^2}{\hat{\sigma}_p^2 + \hat{\sigma}_\delta^2} = \frac{1.56}{1.56+(0.01/9+0.01/2+0.01/18)} = .99, \tag{9.18}$$

which is a substantial coefficient of generalizability. Given the very high relative generalizability coefficient obtained with these data, we might even consider several D studies in which the number of teachers and/or subject areas is markedly reduced. For example, a D study in which the number of raters is reduced to three (but keeping the number of subject areas at two) still provides a relative generalizability coefficient in excess of 0.90 (all else being the same), indicating that additional reductions to the number of levels in the design can be considered.

9.10 Extensions to Multivariate Measurement Designs

Behavioral measurements may also involve multiple collected scores in order to describe an individual's aptitude or skills (e.g., Raykov & Marcoulides, 2008). For example, the Revised Stanford-Binet Intelligence Scale (Terman & Merrill, 1973) uses subtests to measure four dimensions: short-term memory, verbal reasoning, quantitative reasoning, and abstract/visual reasoning. The most commonly used procedure to examine measurements with multiple scores is to assess the dependability of the scores separately (i.e., using a univariate generalizability analysis; Marcoulides, 1994). In contrast, an analysis of such measurement procedures via a multivariate approach can provide information about facets that contribute to covariance among the multiple scores that cannot be obtained in a univariate analysis. This information can also play a central role in designing optimal decision studies that maximize the dependability of measurement procedures.

The two-facet design examined in the previous section aimed at evaluating in particular the dependability of the measurement procedure using a univariate approach (i.e., one in which judges and subject matter were treated as separate sources of error variance, viz., as facets). However, by treating the subject matter as a separate source of error variance, no information was utilized about covariation (correlation) that might exist between its two examined conditions. Such information may be important for correctly determining the magnitude of sources of error influencing the overall measurement procedure and can potentially influence the estimated variance components in a generalizability analysis (Marcoulides, 1987). One way to overcome this problem is to conduct a multivariate G study. If the covariation between the examined conditions is negligible, one may expect no marked differences between results obtained with this multivariate approach and those of corresponding univariate analyses.

The easiest way to discuss the multivariate case is by analogy to the univariate. As illustrated in the previous section, the observed score for a person in the two-facet crossed p x j x s design was decomposed into error sources corresponding to judges, subject matter, and their interactions with each other and with persons. In extending the notion of multifaceted error variance from the univariate case to the multivariate, one must not treat subject matter as a facet contributing variation to the design but use instead a vector of outcome scores (i.e., a vector with two components, or dependent variables; e.g., Raykov & Marcoulides, 2008). Thus, using the prefix v to symbolize vector (with elements pertaining to the subject matter/topics on which scores are obtained in the used measurement design), the vector of obtained scores can be decomposed as

$$v X_{pj} = v\mu \qquad\qquad \text{(grand mean)}$$
$$+ (v\mu_p - v\mu) \qquad \text{(person effect)}$$
$$+ (v\mu_j - v\mu) \qquad \text{(judge effect)}$$
$$+ (v X_{pj} - v\mu_p - v\mu_j - v\mu) \qquad \text{(residual effect)}$$

The total variance–covariance matrix of the observed scores, denoted $\sigma_v^2 X_{pj}$, which is the counterpart here to the observed score variance in the univariate case, is

$$\sigma_v^2 X_{pj} = \sigma_{vp}^2 + \sigma_{vj}^2 + \sigma_{vpj,e}^2,$$

with the correspondingly denoted variance–covariance matrix of the person, judge, and residual effects in the right-hand side of this equation. For example, the decomposition of the variance–covariance matrix of observed scores with two subject areas or conditions is as follows:

$$
\begin{bmatrix} \sigma_1^2 X_{pj} & \sigma_1 X_{pj2} X_{pj} \\ \sigma_1 X_{pj2} X_{pj} & \sigma_2^2 X_{pj} \end{bmatrix} = \begin{bmatrix} \sigma_{1p}^2 & \sigma_{1p2p} \\ \sigma_{1p2p} & \sigma_{2p}^2 \end{bmatrix} + \begin{bmatrix} \sigma_{1j}^2 & \sigma_{1j2j} \\ \sigma_{1j2j} & \sigma_{2j}^2 \end{bmatrix} + \begin{bmatrix} \sigma_{1pj,e}^2 & \sigma_{1pj,e2pj,e} \\ \sigma_{1pj,e2pj,e} & \sigma_{2pj,e}^2 \end{bmatrix},
$$

where measure variances are positioned along the main diagonals and measure covariances off it, or more compactly represented as

$$
\Sigma_{Xpj} = \Sigma_p + \Sigma_j + \Sigma_{pj,e},
$$

using corresponding matrix notation.

As discussed in the previous section, univariate G theory focuses on the estimation of variance components because their magnitude provides information about the sources of error influencing observed scores in a given measurement design. Because in a multivariate analysis the focus is on variance and covariance components, the observed score matrix is decomposed, as above, into matrices of components of variance and covariance. And, just as the analysis of variance (ANOVA) can be used to obtain estimates of variance components in the univariate case, multivariate analysis of variance (MANOVA) provides estimates of variance and covariance components in the multivariate case. It is important to note that if the two subject areas are uncorrelated (i.e., the covariance $\sigma_1 X_{pj2} X_{pj} = 0$), the diagonal variance estimates for $\sigma_1^2 X_{pj}$ and $\sigma_2^2 X_{pj}$ would be equivalent to the observed score variance in which subject areas are examined separately.

It is also straightforward to extend the notion of a generalizability coefficient to the multivariate case (Joe & Woodward, 1976; Marcoulides, 1995; Woodward & Joe, 1973). For example, a generalizability coefficient for the above multivariate study could be computed as

$$
\rho^2 = \frac{\underline{a}' \Sigma_p \underline{a}}{\underline{a}' \Sigma_p \underline{a} + \dfrac{\underline{a}' \Sigma_{pj,e} \underline{a}}{n_j}},
$$

where $\underline{a}$ is a weighting scheme, i.e., a vector of weights, for the dependent variables used in the multivariate measurement design. For instance, in the presently considered example design, this would correspond to a weight vector for the subject areas in question. We note that the determination of appropriate weights to use for the computation of a multivariate generalizability coefficient is not without controversy in the literature. A detailed discussion of different approaches to the estimation of weights is provided by Srinivasan and Shocker (1973), Shavelson et al. (1989), Weichang (1990), and Marcoulides (1994). These approaches are based on either empirical or theoretical criteria and include (a) weightings based on expert ratings, (b) weightings based on models examined through a confirmatory factor analysis, (c) equal or unit weights, (d) weightings proportional to observed reliability estimates, (e) weightings proportional to an average correlation with another subcriteria, or (f) weightings based on an eigenvalue decomposition criteria. Parameter estimates within a multivariate generalizability model are commonly obtained using either general purpose statistical programs like SAS and SPPS or specialized programs like mGENOVA (Brennan, 2001). In the next section we also discuss how such parameters can be estimated using a latent variable modeling approach and the software M*plus*.

9.11 Alternative Modeling Approaches to Generalizability Theory Analyses

Over the past several decades, alternative analytic approaches to generalizability analysis have received considerable attention. These developments were primarily concerned with variance component estimation outside of the traditional method-of-moment estimation procedures within the ANOVA framework. More specifically, the relationship between covariance structure analysis for estimating variance components and the random effects ANOVA approach has enjoyed marked interest among methodologists. This interest can be traced back to earlier work by a number of authors (Bock, 1966; Bock & Bargmann, 1966; Creasy, 1957; Jöreskog, 1971; Linn & Werts, 1977; Wiley, Schmidt, & Bramble, 1973), although the original idea for analyzing measurement designs in this manner is probably attributed to Burt (1947).

Another stream of research has been concerned more recently with applications of reliability estimation procedures using structural equation modeling (SEqM) for evaluation of generalizability coefficients and related indexes. Work by Gessaroli and Folske (2002), Hagtvet (1997, 1998), Höft (1996), Marcoulides (1996, 2000b), and Raykov and Marcoulides (2006b) has contributed to popularizing the SEqM approach to reliability estimation in the generalizability theory framework. In particular, applying the method in the last-cited source to data from several measurement designs, one can readily obtain an estimate of a relative generalizability coefficient (see further details in the next section).

A third line of research has dealt with comparisons between the generalizability theory and item response theory (IRT) approaches (particularly the Rasch model; e.g., Bachman et al., 1993; Bachman, Lynch, & Mason, 1995; Harris, Hanson, & Gao, 2000; Lynch & McNamara, 1998; MacMillan, 2000; Marcoulides, 1999; Marcoulides & Kyriakides, 2002; Stahl, 1994; Stahl & Lunz, 1993). These works show how both approaches can be used to provide information with respect to measurement designs, especially those that involve judges using defined rating scales. Although estimating a person's ability level is considered by many researchers to be fundamentally different in the two theories (Embretson & Hershberger, 1999), Marcoulides (1997a, 1999, 2000a) argued that its estimation can be conceptualized as merely alternative representations of similar information. Marcoulides (1999) also introduced an extension of the traditional generalizability theory model (called the MD model; see also Marcoulides & Drezner, 1993, 1995, 1997, 2000) that can be used to estimate examinee ability, rater severity, and item difficulties, to name a few. This extension can be considered a special type of IRT model capable of estimating latent traits of interest. Somewhat similar to IRT, where detecting a person's trait level is considered to be analogous to the clinical inference process, the MD model infers trait levels on the basis of the presented behaviors and places each individual on a trait continuum.

9.12 Structural Equation Modeling Applications

As mentioned earlier, reliability estimation using structural equation modeling (SEqM) has received considerable attention in the literature. As discussed in Chapters 6 and 7, work by a number of researchers has contributed to popularizing the SEqM (latent variable modeling) approach to reliability estimation. This approach has been mainly developed within the framework of classical test theory and utilizes primarily the model of congeneric measures (items).

The applicability of this SEqM approach for generalizability theory analyses was originally considered in earlier discussions by Marcoulides (1996 and references therein) and extended more recently by Raykov and Marcoulides (2006b) for the purpose of estimation of some generalizability indexes. For example, in the context of a two-facet design, a confirmatory factor analysis model can be used to estimate all variance components that involve persons (i.e., σ_p^2, σ_{pr}^2, σ_{ps}^2, and $\sigma_{prs,e}^2$).[1]

Indeed, using as a basis the factor analysis model $\underline{X} = A\underline{f} + \underline{u}$ considered in Chapter 3, where $A = [a_{jk}]$ is the matrix of factor loadings while $\underline{X} = (X_1, X_2, ..., X_p)'$, $\underline{f} = (f_1, f_2, ..., f_m)'$, and $\underline{u} = (u_1, u_2, ..., u_p)'$ are the vectors of observed variables, common factors, and unique factors, respectively, the covariance matrix of the observed variables (Σ_{xx}, considered for this argument as given) for the two-facet design is (see Chapter 2)

$$\sum_{xx} = A\,\Phi\,A' + \Theta,$$

where Φ is the covariance matrix of latent variables, and Θ is the covariance matrix of the unique factors. In particular, in the context of the example two-facet design used previously, in which students were rated by nine teachers in two subject areas, the matrices A, Φ, and Θ are specified as follows:

$$A = \begin{bmatrix}
1 & 1 & 0 & 0 & 0 & 0 & 0 & 0 & 0 & 0 & 1 & 0 \\
1 & 0 & 1 & 0 & 0 & 0 & 0 & 0 & 0 & 0 & 1 & 0 \\
1 & 0 & 0 & 1 & 0 & 0 & 0 & 0 & 0 & 0 & 1 & 0 \\
1 & 0 & 0 & 0 & 1 & 0 & 0 & 0 & 0 & 0 & 1 & 0 \\
1 & 0 & 0 & 0 & 0 & 1 & 0 & 0 & 0 & 0 & 1 & 0 \\
1 & 0 & 0 & 0 & 0 & 0 & 1 & 0 & 0 & 0 & 1 & 0 \\
1 & 0 & 0 & 0 & 0 & 0 & 0 & 1 & 0 & 0 & 1 & 0 \\
1 & 0 & 0 & 0 & 0 & 0 & 0 & 0 & 1 & 0 & 1 & 0 \\
1 & 0 & 0 & 0 & 0 & 0 & 0 & 0 & 0 & 1 & 1 & 0 \\
1 & 1 & 0 & 0 & 0 & 0 & 0 & 0 & 0 & 0 & 0 & 1 \\
1 & 0 & 1 & 0 & 0 & 0 & 0 & 0 & 0 & 0 & 0 & 1 \\
1 & 0 & 0 & 1 & 0 & 0 & 0 & 0 & 0 & 0 & 0 & 1 \\
1 & 0 & 0 & 0 & 1 & 0 & 0 & 0 & 0 & 0 & 0 & 1 \\
1 & 0 & 0 & 0 & 0 & 1 & 0 & 0 & 0 & 0 & 0 & 1 \\
1 & 0 & 0 & 0 & 0 & 0 & 1 & 0 & 0 & 0 & 0 & 1 \\
1 & 0 & 0 & 0 & 0 & 0 & 0 & 1 & 0 & 0 & 0 & 1 \\
1 & 0 & 0 & 0 & 0 & 0 & 0 & 0 & 1 & 0 & 0 & 1 \\
1 & 0 & 0 & 0 & 0 & 0 & 0 & 0 & 0 & 1 & 0 & 1
\end{bmatrix}$$

$$\Phi = \begin{bmatrix}
\sigma_p^2 & 0 & 0 & 0 & 0 & 0 & 0 & 0 & 0 & 0 & 0 & 0 \\
0 & \sigma_{pr1}^2 & 0 & 0 & 0 & 0 & 0 & 0 & 0 & 0 & 0 & 0 \\
0 & 0 & \sigma_{pr2}^2 & 0 & 0 & 0 & 0 & 0 & 0 & 0 & 0 & 0 \\
0 & 0 & 0 & \sigma_{pr3}^2 & 0 & 0 & 0 & 0 & 0 & 0 & 0 & 0 \\
0 & 0 & 0 & 0 & \sigma_{pr4}^2 & 0 & 0 & 0 & 0 & 0 & 0 & 0 \\
0 & 0 & 0 & 0 & 0 & \sigma_{pr5}^2 & 0 & 0 & 0 & 0 & 0 & 0 \\
0 & 0 & 0 & 0 & 0 & 0 & \sigma_{pr6}^2 & 0 & 0 & 0 & 0 & 0 \\
0 & 0 & 0 & 0 & 0 & 0 & 0 & \sigma_{pr7}^2 & 0 & 0 & 0 & 0 \\
0 & 0 & 0 & 0 & 0 & 0 & 0 & 0 & \sigma_{pr8}^2 & 0 & 0 & 0 \\
0 & 0 & 0 & 0 & 0 & 0 & 0 & 0 & 0 & \sigma_{pr9}^2 & 0 & 0 \\
0 & 0 & 0 & 0 & 0 & 0 & 0 & 0 & 0 & 0 & \sigma_{ps1}^2 & 0 \\
0 & 0 & 0 & 0 & 0 & 0 & 0 & 0 & 0 & 0 & 0 & \sigma_{ps2}^2
\end{bmatrix}$$

$$\Theta = \begin{bmatrix}
\sigma_{prs,e}^2 & 0 & 0 & 0 & 0 & 0 & 0 & 0 & 0 & 0 & 0 & 0 & 0 & 0 & 0 & 0 & 0 & 0 \\
0 & \sigma_{prs,e}^2 & 0 & 0 & 0 & 0 & 0 & 0 & 0 & 0 & 0 & 0 & 0 & 0 & 0 & 0 & 0 & 0 \\
0 & 0 & \sigma_{prs,e}^2 & 0 & 0 & 0 & 0 & 0 & 0 & 0 & 0 & 0 & 0 & 0 & 0 & 0 & 0 & 0 \\
0 & 0 & 0 & \sigma_{prs,e}^2 & 0 & 0 & 0 & 0 & 0 & 0 & 0 & 0 & 0 & 0 & 0 & 0 & 0 & 0 \\
0 & 0 & 0 & 0 & \sigma_{prs,e}^2 & 0 & 0 & 0 & 0 & 0 & 0 & 0 & 0 & 0 & 0 & 0 & 0 & 0 \\
0 & 0 & 0 & 0 & 0 & \sigma_{prs,e}^2 & 0 & 0 & 0 & 0 & 0 & 0 & 0 & 0 & 0 & 0 & 0 & 0 \\
0 & 0 & 0 & 0 & 0 & 0 & \sigma_{prs,e}^2 & 0 & 0 & 0 & 0 & 0 & 0 & 0 & 0 & 0 & 0 & 0 \\
0 & 0 & 0 & 0 & 0 & 0 & 0 & \sigma_{prs,e}^2 & 0 & 0 & 0 & 0 & 0 & 0 & 0 & 0 & 0 & 0 \\
0 & 0 & 0 & 0 & 0 & 0 & 0 & 0 & \sigma_{prs,e}^2 & 0 & 0 & 0 & 0 & 0 & 0 & 0 & 0 & 0 \\
0 & 0 & 0 & 0 & 0 & 0 & 0 & 0 & 0 & \sigma_{prs,e}^2 & 0 & 0 & 0 & 0 & 0 & 0 & 0 & 0 \\
0 & 0 & 0 & 0 & 0 & 0 & 0 & 0 & 0 & 0 & \sigma_{prs,e}^2 & 0 & 0 & 0 & 0 & 0 & 0 & 0 \\
0 & 0 & 0 & 0 & 0 & 0 & 0 & 0 & 0 & 0 & 0 & \sigma_{prs,e}^2 & 0 & 0 & 0 & 0 & 0 & 0 \\
0 & 0 & 0 & 0 & 0 & 0 & 0 & 0 & 0 & 0 & 0 & 0 & \sigma_{prs,e}^2 & 0 & 0 & 0 & 0 & 0 \\
0 & 0 & 0 & 0 & 0 & 0 & 0 & 0 & 0 & 0 & 0 & 0 & 0 & \sigma_{prs,e}^2 & 0 & 0 & 0 & 0 \\
0 & 0 & 0 & 0 & 0 & 0 & 0 & 0 & 0 & 0 & 0 & 0 & 0 & 0 & \sigma_{prs,e}^2 & 0 & 0 & 0 \\
0 & 0 & 0 & 0 & 0 & 0 & 0 & 0 & 0 & 0 & 0 & 0 & 0 & 0 & 0 & \sigma_{prs,e}^2 & 0 & 0 \\
0 & 0 & 0 & 0 & 0 & 0 & 0 & 0 & 0 & 0 & 0 & 0 & 0 & 0 & 0 & 0 & \sigma_{prs,e}^2 & 0 \\
0 & 0 & 0 & 0 & 0 & 0 & 0 & 0 & 0 & 0 & 0 & 0 & 0 & 0 & 0 & 0 & 0 & \sigma_{prs,e}^2
\end{bmatrix}$$

Thus, by employing the approach proposed by Marcoulides (1996; see also Raykov & Marcoulides, 2006b), the variance component estimates are readily obtained. We note that computationally these estimates can be furnished using appropriate elements of the above matrices, leading to

$\hat{\sigma}_p^2$ = first diagonal element in the Φ matrix,

$$\hat{\sigma}_{pr}^2 = \frac{\sigma_{pr1}^2 + \sigma_{pr2}^2 + \sigma_{pr3}^2 + \sigma_{pr4}^2 + \sigma_{pr5}^2 + \sigma_{pr6}^2 + \sigma_{pr7}^2 + \sigma_{pr8}^2 + \sigma_{pr9}^2}{9}$$

= average of next nine diagonal elements in Φ,

$\hat{\sigma}_{ps}^2 = \dfrac{\hat{\sigma}_{ps1}^2 + \hat{\sigma}_{ps2}^2}{2}$ = average of next two diagonal elements in Φ, and

$\hat{\sigma}_{prs,e}^2$ = average across homogeneous values in Θ.

Applying these estimates using the data from the example two-facet crossed design, one can also readily obtain an estimate of the relative generalizability coefficient. For ease of computation, the LVM program M*plus* can be employed to obtain all these estimates. The only added complexity from the discussion offered in Chapters 3 and 4 is that we must first specify the constrained values in the factor loading matrix A before requesting the analysis. For example, the following M*plus* input lines can be used to obtain the variance component estimates in the example two-facet design in the preceding section:

```
TITLE: ESTIMATION OF VARIANCE COMPONENTS IN TWO FACET G-STUDY EXAMPLE
DATA:   FILE is teach3.txt;
        TYPE = COVARIANCE;
        NOBSERVATIONS = 101;
VARIABLE:    NAMES = X1 X2 X3 X4 X5 X6 X7 X8 X9
        X10 X11 X12 X13 X14 X15 X16 X17 X18;
MODEL: F1 BY X1-X18@1;
        F2 by X1@1 X10@1;
        F3 by X2@1 X11@1;
        F4 by X3@1 X12@1;
        F5 by X4@1 X13@1;
        F6 by x5@1 X14@1;
        F7 by X6@1 X15@1;
        F8 by X7@1 X16@1;
        F9 by X8@1 X17@1;
        F10 by X9@1 X18@1;
        F11 by X1-X9@1;
        F12 by X10-X18@1;
```

Because the estimates that would be obtained from such a SEqM approach are essentially identical to those already presented in Section 9.9 using the appropriate ANOVA procedure, we do not repeat the output generated by the M*plus* program.

9.13 Conclusion

Generalizability theory is a comprehensive method for designing, assessing, and improving the dependability of measurement procedures. Generalizability analysis thus most certainly deserves the serious attention by researchers using measurement procedures. As discussed in this chapter, the results obtained from a generalizability analysis can

245

provide important information for determining the psychometric properties of many types of measurement procedures. Generalizability analysis is also essential for determining what modifications can or should be made to a measurement procedure. Although the examples used in this chapter were purposely kept simple, it would be relatively easy for applied researchers to adapt the discussion to other types of measurement designs that are encountered in empirical applications.

Note

1. Marcoulides (2000b) also elaborated that instead of analyzing the covariance matrix among observed variables, with which only variance components for persons and any interactions with persons can be estimated, analyzing the matrix of correlations among persons leads to estimation of the variance components for the other facets, and hence all potential sources of measurement error in a design can be estimated.

10

Introduction to Item Response Theory

10.1 What Is Item Response Theory?

The discussion in the last few chapters evolved mainly within the framework of classical test theory (CTT). An important limitation of CTT is that it does not place routinely in the center of its concerns how individuals at different levels of the construct studied (ability, trait, attribute) perform on the components, or items, of an instrument aimed at measuring that underlying latent dimension. This information is focused on by an alternative approach to test development, item response theory (IRT), at times also referred to as latent trait theory (cf., e.g., McDonald, 1999). Informally, a main assumption in IRT is that the responses on items of a test under consideration (and consequently overall test performance) can be accounted for by one or more latent abilities or constructs, which are usually much fewer in number than the items. Most current applications of IRT assume that there is a single latent trait behind the responses to items on a given instrument. Although much progress has been made in the past 20 years or so in multidimensional IRT (e.g., Reckase, 2009), the majority of empirical utilizations of IRT still seem to be concerned with single traits. Given this tendency, in addition to the confines of this book, in its remainder we will assume (unless otherwise indicated) that there is a single underlying latent dimension along which individuals differ and that accounts for the relationships among their responses on a given set of components or items comprising a measuring instrument under consideration.

Characteristic features of IRT are that the construct studied is assumed to be (a) continuous and (b) of a latent nature, as in our earlier applications of factor analysis (FA). The basis of most of our preceding discussions of FA (e.g., Chapter 3) was its traditional model

$$\underline{Y} = A\underline{f} + \underline{u}, \tag{10.1}$$

where $\underline{f}$ is a vector of m factors, $\underline{Y}$ is a vector of k observed variables, and $\underline{u}$ is the corresponding vector of unique factors with zero means that are also assumed uncorrelated among themselves and with the elements of $\underline{f}$ ($m < k$). The FA model in Equation (10.1) describes the relationships between the set of manifest measures and the underlying latent variables, typically assumed much fewer in number than those measures. We stress that Equation (10.1) represents a linear model. In fact, it is the same as the general linear model (with zero intercepts; see Section 10.5), except that the independent variables collected in the vector $\underline{f}$ are not observed.

A main difference between these traditional FA utilizations, on the one hand, and IRT, on the other, is that in the latter one is typically dealing with discrete items, e.g., binary test components or such with a limited number of possible scores (3 to 5 say). Furthermore, at the core of IRT lies a mathematical model that describes how subject responses on the instrument components (typically referred to as 'items' in an IRT context) relate to an unobservable trait, such as a studied ability, which model is nonlinear. This is a main point of departure of IRT from FA as we have used it in the preceding chapters of this book, except in Sections 4.5 and 4.6, where the case of discrete items was similarly considered. In particular, the IRT models focus on how individuals with different ability levels respond to each of a given set of items that represent the components of a studied instrument. This feature is a main reason for the high popularity of the IRT models, especially in achievement evaluation contexts. (This is not an exclusive property of IRT models, however, and we will also see later that appropriately developed FA models can account for this type of relationships between items and underlying traits as well; see also Section 4.5 of Chapter 4.)

At the same time, a main similarity feature between FA and IRT is the earlier-mentioned property of conditional independence in the context of FA (Chapter 3). According to the traditional FA model, for a fixed set of factor values, the observed variables are not correlated (i.e., they are independent in case of normality; e.g., Roussas, 1997). A very similar property holds in IRT models, which we will discuss in more detail later. Accordingly, for a fixed value of the latent trait(s), the responses on the given set of items are independent from one another. This property of conditional independence, as mentioned in Chapter 3, is of fundamental relevance for many latent variable models that are used in contemporary applied statistics and the behavioral and social sciences.

10.2 Basic Statistical Relationships for Item Response Theory

In Chapter 2, we reviewed a number of important statistical concepts and relationships. When discussing in particular expectation of random variables, we did not make the assumption that we were dealing with continuous observed variables. That is, our discussion in Chapter 2 regarding expectation of a random variable is just as applicable when these variables are discrete (e.g., binary, or with few scores possible to attain). Hence, as mentioned before, all developments in Chapter 5 on classical test theory, for instance, are equally applicable in case of discrete manifest measures (observed scores) Y, e.g., binary instrument/test components (as long as the mean of Y exists, which is a fairly mild if at all restrictive assumption in most social and behavioral research—see pertinent discussion in that chapter; Lord & Novick, 1968). In the present section, we discuss explicitly a few further details relating to expectation when concerned with discrete random variables, in particular binary random variables, as we will be most of the time in the remainder of this book.

10.2.1 Expectation and Probability of Correct Response

If Y is a binary random variable, we can formally define it as follows:

$$Y = \begin{cases} 1, \text{ with probability } p, \text{ i.e., } P(Y = 1) = p, & \text{and} \\ \\ 0, \text{ with probability } 1 - p, \text{ i.e., } P(Y = 0) = 1 - p, \end{cases}$$

where P(.) denotes probability. This distribution is often referred to as a Bernoulli distribution or alternatively Bernoulli model. For a binary random variable following the Bernoulli distribution, as is well-known from introductory statistics courses (e.g., Agresti & Finlay, 2009),

$$E(Y) = p, \quad \text{and} \quad Var(Y) = p(1 - p) \tag{10.2}$$

hold (with $E(.)$ and $Var(.)$ denoting expectation and variance, respectively). That is, the probability of responding 1 to an item—e.g., correctly solving it—actually equals the expectation of the random variable Y defined as 1 for a correct answer and 0 for an incorrect one.

We note further from Equations (10.2) that once we know this probability p, we know both the expectation (mean) and the variance of the corresponding random variable. That is, its variance is completely determined by its expectation. This is a property that we have not dealt with so far in the book and in particular a feature that does not hold for normally distributed random variables—for them, mean and variance are represented by two distinct parameters (e.g., Chapter 2). Given its special relevance for what follows in this chapter and the next chapter, we reformulate the first of Equations (10.2) as stating that if one were interested in the mean of a binary variable, all one would need to do is take the probability with which it assumes the value of 1. We also note that even if one were concerned with a polytomous item (i.e., one on which there are more than two possible answers), as long as the correct answer(s) was known, one could consider an associated random variable that equals 1 for the correct answer(s) and 0 otherwise. This random variable, being defined as the ultimate score on the item, is obviously binary, and hence the discussion so far in this section—as well as in the rest of the book when a binary variable is considered—holds for it also.

10.2.2 What Is Being Modeled in Conventional Regression Analysis?

In the well-known multiple regression model (univariate regression model), a dependent variable Y and a given set of independent variables (predictors, covariates, explanatory variables), denoted $Z_1, ..., Z_k$, are assumed to be related as follows:

$$Y = a + b_1 Z_1 + b_2 Z_2 + \cdots + b_k Z_k + e \tag{10.3}$$

where a and b_1 through b_k are the intercept and partial regression coefficients, while e denotes the model error term that is assumed with mean of 0 and unrelated with Z_k ($k \geq 1$). Taking expectation from both sides of Equation (10.3), one obtains another form of this familiar regression analysis model

$$E(Y) = a + b_1 Z_1 + b_2 Z_2 + \cdots + b_k Z_k \tag{10.4}$$

for a given set of predictor values, $Z_1, ..., Z_k$. That is, this regression model represents the expectation of a dependent variable as a linear combination of a set of used explanatory variable values (including an intercept term). Equation (10.4) is often presented also as

$$E(Y | Z_1, ..., Z_k) = a + b_1 Z_1 + b_2 Z_2 + \cdots + b_k Z_k, \tag{10.5}$$

where conditional expectation appears in the left-hand side of Equation (10.5), viz., the expectation of the response measure Y at a given set of values for $Z_1, ..., Z_k$. We stress that according to the model in Equation (10.5), it is the conditional expectation of the response variable, *Y*, given the independent variables, that is being modeled in terms of the latter. Thereby, this conditional expectation is assumed to be a linear function of the predictors, where all unknown coefficients (parameters) are involved in a linear fashion. Indeed, no other function of the *a*s or *b*s appears in the right-hand side of Equation (10.5). This feature of the conditional expectation of a response variable is what is typically meant when referring to a model being linear.

These developments highlight an important fact about the traditional FA model that we were concerned with in several of the preceding chapters. Specifically, taking conditional expectation with regard to the factors from both sides of Equation (10.1) for a given observed variable (say, the *s*th, $1 \leq s \leq p$; see also Chapter 3), we obtain

$$E(Y_s | f_1, \ldots, f_m) = a_{s1}f_1 + a_{s2}f_2 + \cdots + a_{sm}f_m, \tag{10.6}$$

that is, as indicated earlier, we are indeed dealing with a linear model here also (despite the lack of observations on the latent variables f_1 through f_m). This fact will be of special relevance in the next developments of this chapter that will be based on a very comprehensive and highly popular modeling framework in contemporary applied statistics that we next turn to.

10.3 The Generalized Linear Model

A modeling framework that encompasses many more models than the conventional ones considered in typical introductory and intermediate statistics texts and courses in the social and behavioral sciences is provided by the generalized linear model (abbreviated GLIM). A special case of it is the general linear model (GLM) that could also be considered a multivariate multiple regression model. In this chapter, we will discuss the framework of GLIM and place emphasis on a few important ideas underlying it that will allow us to shed further light on the conceptual basis of IRT.

10.3.1 Relationship to the General Linear Model

When using the conventional general linear model, e.g., the multiple regression model, a researcher has the flexibility of choice with regard to the explanatory variables and in particular is not concerned with their distribution (e.g., Agresti & Finlay, 2009). That is, the predictors used can be dichotomous, nominal, categorical (ordinal), or continuous (interval or ratio scaled). However, with regard to the dependent variable(s), it is required that it be continuous. Under this assumption, the GLM postulates the linear relationship(s) between the dependent and explanatory variables, and this is the cornerstone of the GLM that is very widely applicable and used throughout the behavioral and social sciences.

The generalized linear model extends the linear relationship idea underlying the GLM to cases where the dependent variable need not be continuous. That is, the GLIM relaxes the above-mentioned continuity assumption of GLM with respect to the response variable.

For example, the dependent (response, outcome) variable can be dichotomous—as is quite often the case in behavioral measurement contexts, especially when response on an item is under consideration—or more generally a discrete measure. The GLIM does keep, however, the linear relationship idea but after an important modification is made.

To introduce this modification, we take a look at Equation (10.3), which describes what can be viewed for our purposes as a single equation from the general linear model:

$$Y = a + b_1 Z_1 + b_2 Z_2 + \cdots + b_k Z_k + e \qquad \text{(10.3, repeated)}$$

As indicated earlier, an alternative representation for this equation is

$$E(Y) = a + b_1 Z_1 + b_2 Z_2 + \cdots + b_k Z_k = \mu, \text{ say,} \qquad \text{(10.4, repeated)}$$

for a given set of predictor values. In the ordinary least squares (OLS) approach to model fitting and parameter estimation, one further assumes, usually for inferential purposes, that the error term in Equation (10.3) is normal and homoscedastic (e.g., King & Minium, 2003). Either of these two assumptions will not be fulfilled, however, if Y were a dichotomous or discrete variable, as discussed at length in categorical data analysis treatments (e.g., Agresti, 2002). Even if one relaxes both of these assumptions and uses the method of weighted least squares for parameter estimation instead of OLS (e.g., Timm, 2002), Equation (10.3) shows that a direct application of the ideas of the GLM can yield predicted probabilities (i.e., individual response value estimates) that lie outside of the [0,1] interval, in which interval, however, these probabilities must reside.

To deal with these problems, the GLIM is based on the idea that not μ itself but a function of it that is called 'link function' (or just 'link') is still linearly related to a given set of explanatory variables involved in a modeling effort. Denoting this function by $g(\mu)$, which is appropriately chosen (as discussed further below), a GLIM stipulates the following relationship (e.g., Skrondal & Rabe-Hesketh, 2004):

$$g(\mu) = a + b_1 Z_1 + b_2 Z_2 + \cdots + b_k Z_k, \qquad \text{(10.7)}$$

that is,

$$g(E(Y)) = a + b_1 Z_1 + b_2 Z_2 + \cdots + b_k Z_k. \qquad \text{(10.8)}$$

We note that Equation (10.8) is—for our aims here—the 'same' equation as (10.4), with the 'only' difference that it is not the mean itself but a function of it, viz., $g(\mu)$, that is linearly related to the given set of predictors, Z_1 through Z_k. That is, the GLIM preserves the linear relationship idea in the right-hand side of its modeling equation (10.7) but provides a number of options with respect to the quantity appearing in its left-hand side. In particular, if $g(.)$ is the identity function, i.e., $g(\mu) = \mu$, then a GLIM is identical to a corresponding GLM, as we will see in further detail later.

The comprehensiveness of the GLIM framework derives from the multitude of options that are available within it with respect to the link function $g(.)$. Before we elaborate with respect to two of them that will be of special relevance to us in the rest of this book, we state more formally what a GLIM is built of, i.e., its 'building' blocks or elements.

10.3.2 The Elements of a Generalized Linear Model

Any GLIM consists of three main elements (e.g., Skrondal & Rabe-Hesketh, 2004; see also Bartholomew & Knott, 1999; Dobson, 2002):

1. a *random component*, also referred to as 'sampling model' or at times 'variable distribution';
2. a *link function*, viz., $g(.)$; and
3. a *systematic component*, i.e., the expression in the right-hand side of Equation (10.7).

Element 1 of a GLIM refers to the distribution of the dependent (response, outcome) variable. For example, as is often the case when considering in an IRT context a single test item, this variable may be dichotomous, i.e., binary. In this case, it is said that the variable follows a Bernoulli distribution, with a probability of taking the value of 1, say, being p and probability of taking the value of 0 being $1 - p$. In the GLIM, the distribution of the dependent variable stems from what is referred to as exponential family. This is a set of very often and widely used distributions, which allows unified mathematical and statistical treatment of many features of GLIMs. For a formal definition of this concept, we refer to specialized literature on GLIMs (e.g., Dobson, 2002) and note that the exponential family includes effectively all variable distributions of relevance in this book, such as the normal, logistic, and Bernoulli distributions.

Element 2 of a GLIM refers to the function $g(.)$ that is applied on the mean of the dependent variable before its linear relationship to a set of predictors is considered. In this sense, $g(.)$ provides the link between the predictors, on the one hand, and an appropriately chosen modification of the mean of the dependent variable, on the other hand. Preempting some of the discussion to follow, in IRT one uses more often the logit function as a link or alternatively the probit function. These functions will be discussed in detail later.

Element 3 of a GLIM describes what is frequently referred to as the 'linear predictor'. The latter is a linear combination of the variables under consideration for use in an explanatory role with respect to the response variable. Just like in traditional regression analysis, the distribution of the explanatory variables is not of interest, i.e., is unrestricted (not modeled or parameterized). In particular, the explanatory or independent variables can be measured on a nominal, ordinal, interval or ratio scale, i.e., can be continuous or discrete (e.g., dichotomous or ordered/categorical). The explanatory variables participating in the linear predictor are, however, assumed, like in regression analysis, to be measured without error. (We will have to say more on this matter in a later section when we relax this assumption.)

Looking now at Equations (10.7) and (10.8), we observe that there is no error term appearing in their right-hand sides. The reason is that the error has already been 'dealt with' or 'taken care of', because stipulated in those equations is a relationship between a function of the mean and a set of predictors. That is, because the left-hand sides of these two equations are presented in terms of the mean, the latter has been in a sense already taken of the dependent variable, leading to evidently dropping the error term from the resulting modeling Equations (10.7) and (10.8).

As a simple example, which we alluded to earlier, the conventional (univariate) regression analysis model with a normal error is a special case of GLIM. Indeed, as mentioned before, $g(.) = identity(.)$ in the GLM, and a normal sampling model is postulated, with the systematic component involving the predictors of interest. (The identity function leaves its argument unchanged: $g(\mu) = \mu$, if that argument is denoted μ.) That is, if in a GLIM one uses the identity link, $g(\mu) = \mu$, and in addition postulates a normal sampling model with the systematic component being a linear combination of a set of predictors of interests, then the result is the familiar GLM (e.g., a regression analysis model).

10.4 The Relevance of the Generalized Linear Model for Behavioral and Social Measurement

Oftentimes in a behavioral measurement setting, a set of binary scored items may be presented to a group of individuals from a studied population. Considering then the result on a given of these items as a dependent variable, we have a situation where the GLIM approach is directly applicable. To explicate this, we need to first familiarize ourselves with several important functions.

10.4.1 The Logit and Logistic Functions

In the measurement setting just described, one can readily see the connection to an appropriate GLIM by noticing first that the dependent variable is binary, viz., follows a Bernoulli sampling model. This variable takes the value of 1 for correct response on a given item (or alternatively a 'yes', 'present', 'endorsed', or 'agree' response) and 0 for an incorrect response (or a 'no', 'absent', 'not endorsed', or 'disagree' response). Second, the systematic component of this model is the regular one, the so-called 'linear predictor'. This is a linear combination of predictor variables, which we will say more about shortly. Third, the link function can be chosen to be the *logit*:

$$\mu \rightarrow \ln[\mu/(1-\mu))] = \ln[p/(1-p)], \tag{10.9}$$

where ln(.) is the natural logarithm (with base $e = 2.712...$), and p is the probability of correct response, i.e., the mean μ of the random variable being the response on the item in question. (Recall from Equations (10.2) that $\mu = p$; the sign '$\rightarrow$' stands in Equation (10.9) to denote transformation: μ is transformed thereby into the expression following that sign. We also note, for this and the next chapter, that we assume $0 < p < 1$, to avoid cases when the logit does not exist, which, however, lead to triviality considerations.) Hence, with Equation (10.9), we have actually defined a one-to-one function that transforms a probability into a real number that can lie anywhere on the real axis (of course, depending on p itself).

The transformation defined by Equation (10.9) is very popular in empirical applications of statistics, especially the biobehavioral and biomedical disciplines, and is called the logit transformation. For future reference, we denote the right-hand side of Equation (10.9) as *logit(p)*, i.e.,

$$logit(p) = \ln[p/(1-p)],$$

where p stands for a probability, e.g., the probability of a correct response on an item in the currently considered measurement setting. We observe that the logit of a given probability can be any real number, that is, the logit is not constrained within any pre-specified interval of real numbers. Specifically, the logit is positive if $p > .5$, negative if $p < .5$, and 0 if $p = .5$. The graph of the logit transformation, as a function of a probability, is presented

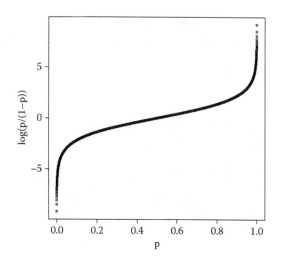

FIGURE 10.1
Graph of the logit function.

in Figure 10.1. (See the appendix to Chapter 11, which discusses how the software R could be used to obtain the figures in the present and next chapter, related curves of relevance in IRT, as well as the graphs of the logarithmic and Fisher's z-transform functions used in Chapter 8.)

A very important property of the logit function is that it represents the inverse of the so-called *logistic function*. The logistic function, denoted $f(z)$, is defined for all real numbers z as follows:

$$f(z) = \frac{e^z}{1+e^z} = \frac{1}{1+e^{-z}}. \tag{10.10}$$

We stress that the denominator in Equation (10.10) is never 0 for a given real number, and hence the logistic function is always defined. In addition, the logistic function value is always between 0 and 1, i.e., can itself be viewed as a probability. In other words, the logistic function $f(.)$ defined in Equation (10.10) takes any real number z and transforms it into one that lies between 0 and 1, i.e., into a probability. We will use the notation *Logistic(.)* for the right-hand side of Equation (10.10), i.e., (10.10) can now be rewritten as

$$f(z) = Logistic(z).$$

An interesting feature of the logistic function, which is of particular relevance for us, is that it is a continuous, smooth (i.e., differentiable) function and monotone increasing. The latter means that there are no two distinct real numbers, for which f takes the same value (i.e., there are no numbers z_1 and z_2, such that $z_1 \neq z_2$ and $f(z_1) = f(z_2)$). Furthermore, if one pictorially depicts the logistic function $f(z)$, as done in Figure 10.2, a gradually increasing graph will be obtained. Thereby, in the central part of it, the function will be increasing most rapidly, unlike in its two tails. Simplistically, the continuity of the function is observed by noting that its graph can be drawn without lifting the pen (or a means of drawing it,

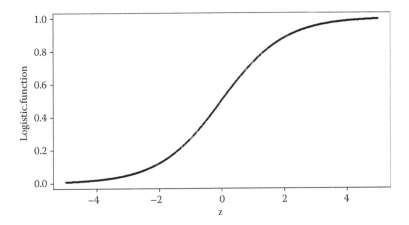

FIGURE 10.2
The logistic function $f(z)$ (see Equation (10.10)).

say, on a piece of paper); its smoothness is observed by realizing that thereby one does not need to make sudden changes of direction because there are no sharp changes (edges) in its graph. Moreover, we notice that because the logistic is a monotone-increasing function of z, it is invertible itself. That is, for each point (number) chosen on the vertical axis, there is a unique number z on the horizontal axis with the property that $f(z)$ equals that point (number). We represent graphically the logistic function in Figure 10.2.

Because the logistic function $f(z)$ is invertible, we can obtain the function that has the reverse effect of $f(z)$, viz., takes a number between 0 and 1, or a probability, and transforms it into a real number. (We stress that not all functions have this property of being invertible; in particular, the function $h(x) = x^2$, as defined for x being any real number, does not have an inverse.) To obtain the inverse function to the logistic in (10.10), all one needs to do is solve Equation (10.10) in terms of the argument z of $f(z)$. This leads after some algebra to

$$z = \ln(p/(1 - p)), \qquad (10.11)$$

where for simplicity we denote $p = f(z)$ (recall, $f(z)$ could be considered a probability).

The right-hand side of Equation (10.11) is, however, precisely the logit function in Equation (10.9) (with μ used as argument in the latter). In fact, as with any pair of inverse functions, the graph of the logit (logistic) can be obtained from the graph of the logistic (logit) by a symmetry transformation or reflection about the equidistant line (the one running through the origin at $45°$ to the horizontal and vertical axes). The point at which the logarithm in Equation (10.11) is taken, viz., $p/(1 - p)$, is often called odds, especially in the biobehavioral and biomedical sciences, as it represents the odds for the event 'correct solution' (say, in a testing context) to occur. For this reason, the logit is also called log-odds. In fact, this is the name under which it is very widely known in those disciplines.

We observe also that the logit (denoted for simplicity by w, say) is an increasing function of the probability p. This is readily seen from the representation $p = w/(1 + w)$, which follows with direct algebra from the equation $w = p/(1 - p)$ used to define the odds w. Furthermore, we notice that p is also increasing in the logit, i.e., the probability $p = p(w) = w/(1 + w)$ is an increasing function of the logit, w. Moreover, from Figure 10.1 it is readily seen that as p approaches 1, the logit increases without limit; conversely, as p approaches 0, the logit decreases without limit; and when $p = .5$, the logit is 0. That is, as the probability p ranges from 0 to 1, the logit (i.e., the log-odds) spans the entire set of real numbers, usually denoted by $\mathbb{R}$.

For simplicity, inverse functions are typically denoted by the power (–1) attached to the functions that they are inverses to. Because the logit is the inverse of the logistic function (and vice versa), we can now rewrite Equation (10.11) as follows, in order to communicate explicitly this fact:

$$z = Logistic^{-1}(p).$$

Therefore, we can also rewrite by substitution Equation (10.10) as

$$f(Logistic^{-1}(p)) = \frac{1}{1 + e^{-z}} = p.$$

Alternatively, it is seen in the same way that

$$logit(f(z)) = z = logit(p) = Logistic^{-1}(p), \qquad (10.12)$$

which is merely a rewrite of Equation (10.11). That is, logit and logistic, considered as functions, annihilate the effect of each other when one is applied on the result of the other. This is a characteristic property more generally of any two functions that are inverse of one another. [Consider for example the function $f(x) = x^2$ defined only for positive x, and its inverse $h(y) = \sqrt{y}$ defined as the positive root. Then f and h are inverse functions of one another; that is, $f(h(y)) = y$, and $h(f(x)) = x$.]

Looking once again at Figure 10.2, we can see some partial (i.e., local) 'similarity' of the logistic function to a straight line in a specific area of the argument of the former. Indeed, this similarity is nearly complete in the middle part of the figure (which is what we mean with the word 'local' used in the preceding sentence). In its upper-right corner, however, it seems like one has 'taken' the right infinite leg of the straight line and (gradually and smoothly) 'bent' it to the right in order to place it within the frame of the figure, i.e., to limit it by 1 from above. Conversely, in the lower-left corner of the figure, it seems like one has 'taken' the left infinite leg of that straight line and (gradually/smoothly) 'bent' it to the left, so as to limit it by 0 from below. This effect of 'bending' is in fact accomplished by the logistic function $f(z)$, which may be viewed as transforming in a one-to-one fashion the real line, $\mathbb{R}$, into the interval [0,1].

10.4.2 The Normal Ogive

If we take a look again at Figure 10.2, we will observe that as z increases from a very small number to a very large number, the logistic function describes an extended or stretched-out S-shaped curve that appears very similar to a cumulative distribution function (abbreviated in this chapter to CDF). Indeed, by definition, the CDF for a random variable increases from 0 to 1 and is monotone (e.g., Agresti & Finlay, 2009). In particular, if one takes the CDF of the standard normal distribution, often referred to as *normal ogive*, it can be shown that with an appropriate scaling of the horizontal axis, it is nearly indistinguishable from a logistic function. Hence (after that rescaling),

$$f(z) = Logistic(z) \approx \Phi(z), \qquad (10.13)$$

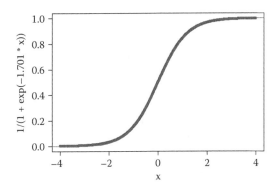

FIGURE 10.3
The normal ogive (thin line) and logistic functions (thick line).

where $\Phi(z)$ denotes the CDF of the standard normal distribution, i.e., the normal ogive. More precisely,

$$f(1.701z) = Logistic(1.701z)$$

differs by no more than .01 from $\Phi(z)$ for any real number z (e.g., Lord, 1980). In fact, for most practical purposes, the two functions are not really distinguishable from one another, as can be seen from Figure 10.3. In it, we generated the normal ogive as a thin line and the logistic function as a thick line and overlaid them on top of each other. (This is the reason for the particular 'name' of the vertical axis; note, x is formally used as argument in lieu of z, for graphing-software-related reasons; see appendix to Chapter 11 for details about how to create this graph.)

From this discussion it follows that for a given probability p we can write also

$$p = \Phi(z) = \text{(Normal ogive function)} (z) \tag{10.14}$$

with an appropriate real number z or alternatively

$$z = \Phi^{-1}(p). \tag{10.15}$$

Equations (10.14) and (10.15) are also approximately valid if we use $p = f(z)$ from our earlier discussion about the logistic function $f = f(z)$ (after rescaling of the units on the horizontal axis by 1.701, as indicated above).

10.4.3 Expressing Event Probability in Two Distinct Ways

The last section shows that we have a choice of two functions to represent a probability of an event, such as a correct response to a given item on a test or measuring instrument more generally. These are (a) the logistic (i.e., inverse logit) function and (b) the normal ogive function. They will be of special help to us in this chapter and the next chapter, when dealing with the probability of the event 'Correct response to a given item'. In particular, we will be concerned with expressing this probability as a function of other, more fundamental and substantively interpretable quantities, as usual called parameters, which are not limited in magnitude. Primarily for mathematical convenience, it turns out that the logistic function is easier to work with for many of these purposes, but the normal ogive function also has a number of important utilizations and in fact is no less applicable, as we will see later.

10.4.4 How Is the Generalized Linear Model Framework Relevant in Behavioral Measurement and Testing Settings?

The discussion so far in this chapter indicated that in a typical behavioral measurement or testing setting with a dichotomous outcome, the GLIM framework is directly applicable. In particular, we already have a handle on two of the building blocks of a GLIM in such a situation. One, we have a sampling model, viz., the Bernoulli model, which as mentioned earlier is the first element of a GLIM. According to this model, the random variable—say, Y—which is the correct or false response obtained on an item under consideration, takes the value of 1 with probability p and the value of 0 with probability $1 - p$. In addition, we have a link function, which is the second element of a GLIM. Indeed, recall that $p = E(Y)$ holds for a dichotomous random variable Y, where p is the probability with which it takes its value of 1. Equations (10.12) and (10.15), and the discussion following them, offer two choices of a link function: the inverse logistic (logit) or alternatively the inverse normal ogive (also called probit) functions, respectively. Each of these two equations presents in z the result of an application of the corresponding link function—logit or probit—upon the probability of the event 'correct solution', i.e., upon the expectation of the random variable Y of concern here, viz., the individual response to an item under consideration.

What we are missing so far is the 'linear predictor', which as indicated before is the third element of a GLIM. To obtain the linear predictor, all we need to do is select explanatory variables of interest in a particular application, e.g., a behavioral measurement setting (such as a testing situation). Once we do so, we simply set their linear combination—with unknown weights, or parameters—to be equal to the result of the application of the link function chosen, i.e., to z in Equation (10.14) or (10.15), respectively. This will finalize the construction of a GLIM.

We note that we are completely 'free' (while of course being guided by a given substantive research question) with regard to our choice of explanatory variables to be included into the 'linear predictor' required by a GLIM. In particular, we may choose a set of observed variables, such as individual background characteristics, like gender, age, education, socioeconomic status, race, religion, geographical region, type of school attended, etc. If we do so, we make the tacit assumption that each one of them is measured without error in order to use the routinely available GLIM framework. In many cases, this may be a plausible assumption, whereas in others it may be violated only to a marginal degree that may not affect the trustworthiness of ensuing results and interpretations.

In yet other cases, however, this may be too strong an assumption, and by making it results may follow that may be misleading. Then it would be prudent to consider one or more latent variables, such as an underlying ability of interest, as explanatory variables participating in the 'linear predictor'. The latter choice is what IRT models effectively do (e.g., Bartholomew & Knott, 1999; cf. McDonald, 1967b, 1983, 1986, 1999). We emphasize, however, that the nature of explanatory variables—whether observed or latent—does not affect the applicability of the GLIM framework discussed in this section, at least conceptually, which is just as relevant and beneficial in either of these two cases.

10.4.5 Other Generalized Linear Models and What Underlies the Process of Model Fitting

Up to this point, we have shown how the GLIM framework is important for behavioral measurement settings with binary outcomes. More generally, there are other link functions and sampling models that are appropriate with other types of data. In particular, the logarithm link function is highly useful when the data are in terms of counts, e.g., the number of times a particular event occurs within a given interval, such as, say, the number of errors made in a learning experiment. In general, the GLIM framework is a highly comprehensive one that covers many different types of data collection designs, with optimal statistical procedures for parameter estimation and testing purposes available within it.

Generalized linear models were formally introduced in the early 1970s by Nelder and Wedderburn. Their work was further brought to fruition and disseminated in particular by McCullagh. The research by these and other statisticians has demonstrated that one can use a single numerical method, the so-called iteratively reweighted least squares (IRLS), to accomplish maximum likelihood estimation. Subsequent statistical research has extended their findings and contributed substantially to the wide circulation of GLIMs in applied statistics, as relevant in many research fields and disciplines within as well as outside the behavioral and social sciences (e.g., Skrondal & Rabe-Hesketh, 2004, and references therein). With this brief historical account, we turn next to the issue of how to apply a GLIM in a particular measurement situation. We will consider initially the case where the explanatory variables are assumed to be measured without error, regardless of their scale (nature). We will relax this assumption in the following chapter.

10.4.6 Fitting a Generalized Linear Model Using Popular Statistical Software

There are various statistical analysis programs that allow one to fit a GLIM in a given empirical setting. The widely available and comprehensive software R (or its somewhat extended, in terms of graphics and user interface, commercial version *Splus*), which we already utilized on a number of occasions earlier in this book, has a lot to recommend then. In the present section, we illustrate how one can use R to fit a model predicting the probability of a correct response on a given item (test component) in terms of a set of observed predictors (assumed measured without error). To indicate a helpful analogy for our purposes in the rest of the text, one can consider IRT as a methodology accomplishing the same aim, among others, when using unobserved predictor(s). Along the same lines, latent variable modeling (LVM; e.g., Chapter 4) can be viewed as a methodology that allows achieving these aims with a mixture of explanatory variables, including covariates that explain individual differences in underlying latent traits; the latter could be viewed as an extension of traditional IRT models to include trait as well as item predictors.

For our illustrative purposes here, we will deal with the following application of GLIM with observed predictors. (The latter implies that they are measured without error or only with a negligible such.) In this example, $n = 248$ seniors were given the following problem:

> Find out the next term, denoted by question mark, in the following sequence of numbers: 3, 5, 9, 17, 33, 65, 129, ?

Thereby, their inductive reasoning ability was measured by a pertinent test, whose score is referred to as IR below. In addition, data on their socioeconomic status (SES; low and high) were collected, as well as whether they took part in cognitive training that aimed at enhancing their fluid intelligence. (Inductive reasoning may be considered a main subability of the cluster of intellectual abilities comprised in fluid intelligence; e.g., Horn [1982].)

To this end, after starting R, we can read in the observed raw data with the following command (using a particular path for the data file, in this example):

```
> d = read.table("C://Data/Chapter.10.1.dat", header=T)
```

In this way, R creates an object that is named d and is identical to our data set to be analyzed, including variable names (in the top line of the data file). (Use next the command ITEM = d$ITEM, and similarly for the remaining variables in the original data file, in order to define available 'conventional' variables within R with the names given above, viz., ITEM, Group, IR, and SES, which variables can be utilized as outlined next. Alternatively, the same goal can be achieved with the command 'attach(d)'.)

Suppose now we are interested in the question of how the probability of correct response on the above item (named ITEM in the analyzed data file) depends on induction reasoning score (named IR there), SES (named SES), and whether or not the subject had participated in the cognitive training sessions (named Group in the data file). Thus, given the dichotomous nature of the variable of main interest, ITEM, in order to answer this question, we fit the GLIM that consists of the following three elements:

1. *Bernoulli sampling model,* referred to as 'binomial' family in R, because the response on ITEM is 0 or 1, with a certain probability for the latter, say, p;

2. *logit link,* because we are interested in using a dichotomous dependent variable here, ITEM, and hence formally wish to predict the probability of it being 1, i.e., p; and

3. *linear predictor* being the linear combination

$$a_0 + a_1 \text{ IR} + a_2 \text{ SES} + a_3 \text{ Group}.$$

Hence, the model to be fitted is

$$ln(p/(1-p)) = a_0 + a_1 \text{ IR} + a_2 \text{ SES} + a_3 \text{ Group} \tag{10.16}$$

or alternatively rewritten (after solving for p in Equation (10.16))

$$p = \frac{e^{a_0+a_1 IR+a_2 SES+a_3 Group}}{1+e^{a_0+a_1 IR+a_2 SES+a_3 Group}} = \frac{1}{1+e^{-(a_0+a_1 IR+a_2 SES+a_3 Group)}}. \tag{10.17}$$

We note that Equation (10.17) can be used, after the model is fitted, to work out predicted probability of correct response on the item for a given set of individual predictor values (i.e., for an individual with available data on the used predictors). Similarly, we stress that the right-hand side of Equation (10.17) is never larger than 1 or smaller than 0, just like any probability.

To fit the GLIM defined in points 1 through 3, which addresses our research question in this illustration section, we need to indicate to R the GLIM elements described in these three points. To this end, we

1. invoke the R command *glm*, requesting binomial sampling model (which by default invokes also the logit link function), and then

2. indicate the predictors just mentioned, which we want to use for our modeling purpose.

Activities 1 and 2 are achieved with the following R command:

```
> model.1=glm(ITEM~IR+SES+Group, data=d, family=binomial)
```

In this way, we assign the object name `model.1` (but one can choose any other name unreserved previously) to the entire output produced by R for this analysis of the data set d that was read in previously. To look at the summary of the results, we next use the command

```
> summary(model.1)
```

that returns the following output:

```
Call:
glm(formula = ITEM ~ IR + SES + Group, family = binomial, data = d)

Deviance Residuals:
    Min      1Q   Median      3Q     Max
-1.5198 -1.2048  0.9265  1.1214  1.4241

Coefficients:
              Estimate   Std. Error   z value   Pr(>|z|)
(Intercept) -0.777370     0.602933    -1.289     0.1973
IR           0.016079     0.007303     2.202     0.0277 *
SES          0.053174     0.274449     0.194     0.8464
Group        0.114755     0.274817     0.418     0.6763
---
Signif. codes:  0 `***' 0.001 `**' 0.01 `*' 0.05 `.' 0.1 ` ' 1

(Dispersion parameter for binomial family taken to be 1)

    Null deviance: 342.77 on 247 degrees of freedom
Residual deviance: 337.04 on 244 degrees of freedom
AIC: 345.04

Number of Fisher Scoring iterations: 4
```

According to these results, in the context of SES and Group, IR is significant. However, in the context of IR and SES (i.e., controlling for IR and SES), Group is not significant; in the context of IR and Group, SES is not significant. We stress the result interpretation that is obtained just like in conventional regression analysis: Significance of any predictor is judged in the context of the others having being controlled or accounted for, i.e., being taken into account (held constant). With this in mind, for persons with the same SES and from the same group (with intervention vs. no-intervention status), any difference in their inductive reasoning score does matter for the probability of correct response on the item in question. We also note the Akaike Information Criterion (AIC) index of 345.04 for this model, which we will refer to next as well. At this moment, a very important part of the output is also the line labeled 'Residual deviance', and so we notice its value and pertinent degrees of freedom. The deviance is similar to the chi-square goodness-of-fit index we used earlier in the book for latent variable models but in general cannot be employed as an index of fit for a single model considered. Instead, we will use it to compare the fit of a pair of models (see below).

Suppose we wish to evaluate next alternatively whether the inductive reasoning score contributes significantly over and above SES and group, that is, has a significant unique contribution to the prediction of the probability of correct response on the item under consideration. To achieve this, we can also use the likelihood ratio theory (i.e., a likelihood ratio test, LRT), which is applicable more generally and not only when we are interested in examining significance of a single predictor, as we do here for illustration purposes only. In the context of GLIM, this LRT has as a statistic the difference in the deviances of the two pertinent nested models. (We stress the analogy to the process of testing parameter restrictions with latent variable models of the kind used earlier in the book.) In our case, these are the initial model, and the one that does not have the predictor IR in it, which is therefore nested in the starting model. (The next fitted model can be considered identical to the first fitted model except that the weight of IR is set equal to 0.) Hence, we need to fit now the same model but without the predictor IR:

```
> model.2=glm(ITEM~SES+Group,data=d,family=binomial)
```

This yields the following output (we use the above command summary to obtain it):

```
Call:
glm(formula = ITEM ~ SES + Group, family = binomial, data = d)

Deviance Residuals:
   Min     1Q  Median    3Q     Max
-1.269 -1.268   1.089  1.089   1.187

Coefficients:
              Estimate Std. Error z value  Pr(>|z|)
(Intercept) -0.0240209  0.4907626  -0.049     0.961
SES          0.0006319  0.2704563   0.002     0.998
Group        0.2349275  0.2670170   0.880     0.379

(Dispersion parameter for binomial family taken to be 1)

    Null deviance: 342.77 on 247 degrees of freedom
Residual deviance: 341.99 on 245 degrees of freedom
AIC: 347.99

Number of Fisher Scoring iterations: 3
```

To conduct the likelihood ratio test indicated above, we subtract the two deviances (note that the more restrictive model will have higher deviance, 'just like' in a confirmatory factor analysis a more restricted model has a higher chi-square value, assuming both models involved are identified). Carrying out this deviance subtraction, we observe that the resulting difference—the test statistic for the null hypothesis that IR does not have a significant unique predictive power for the probability of correct response on ITEM—is significant. Indeed, this difference is $341.99 - 337.04 = 4.95$ and is significant relative to the gain of $245 - 244 = 1$ degree of freedom (recall that the chi-square cutoff is 3.84 for df = 1, at the conventional significance level of .05; e.g., King & Minium, 2003). Hence, we conclude that the inductive reasoning test score does have significant unique contribution to prediction of the probability of correct response on the item under consideration, over and above what is furnished for this purpose by the Group and SES explanatory variables. We observe also that the first fitted model had a smaller AIC value, another indication of it being a better means of data description and explanation when compared with the last fitted model that is nested in it. We note further that the approach we have just used in fact is based on the comparison of a full model (the first fitted model) and a reduced model (the last fitted model), because in the latter model one of the predictors had a 0 weight, viz., IR. This approach of what is also called nested models is similarly applicable, and in the same way as above, when one is interested in comparing models that differ by more than a single predictor.

In conclusion of this section, we would like to mention that we could have carried out the above modeling session using a method that is widely known and popular in social and behavioral research as logistic regression (e.g., Kleinbaum, 2005). The present subsection in fact empirically exemplifies that logistic regression is a special case of a GLIM, as well as the much wider applicability of the GLIM modeling approach.

10.5 The General Factor Analysis Model and Its Relation to Item Response Models

Throughout a number of the preceding chapters we have used or referred to the traditional factor analysis model, which was defined as follows (the next is a repeat of Equation (10.1) for convenience in this section, using the earlier chapters' notation):

$$\underline{X} = A \underline{f} + \underline{u}. \tag{10.18}$$

In Chapter 5, we slightly deviated from this model by considering for a moment intercepts associated with observed variables, which we denoted d_k for the kth manifest measure there ($k = 1, ..., p$; p being the number of those measures). We revisit this idea next and show its usefulness in the IRT context subsequently.

10.5.1 A General Factor Analysis Model

When the observed variable intercepts d_k are included in Equation (10.18), the factor analysis model takes the more general form

$$\underline{X} = \underline{d} + A \underline{f} + \underline{u}, \tag{10.19}$$

where $\underline{d} = (d_1, ..., d_p)'$ denotes the $p \times 1$ vector of intercepts, and all else (including distributional assumptions) is the same as in the FA model defined in Chapter 3 (cf. McDonald, 1962, 1967b, 1999). We refer to (10.19) as the *general factor analysis model* (GFA) in the rest of this book, because it extends the earlier-used traditional FA model in Equation (10.1) (see also Chapter 3) to the more general case of nonzero observed variable intercepts. We note that the traditional FA model in Equation (10.18) is a special case that results from the GFA in (10.19) by setting the vector of intercepts $\underline{d} = \underline{0}$, where $\underline{0}$ denotes the $p \times 1$ vector consisting of zeros only. That is, the FA model we used predominantly up to this point is the GFA model (10.19) when the assumption of zero means on all variables is made. We also observe that the GFA model is in most aspects 'the same' as the general linear model (multivariate multiple regression analysis model), with the important difference, however, that its predictors, $\underline{f}$, are not observed.

In many situations the earlier-made assumption in this book, $\underline{d} = \underline{0}$, does not lead to loss of generality of certain considerations, given the fact that origins of used scales are often irrelevant if not arbitrary—at least for some concerns like disclosing underlying factors, as is typically the case in traditional FA (e.g., Raykov & Marcoulides, 2008). In particular, no loss of generality follows from this assumption in a setting where the scale underlying a given measure has meaningless, arbitrary units of measurement and especially zero point location, and for our aims in Chapters 6, 7, and 8 as mentioned earlier. Assuming then zero intercepts in Equation (10.19) implies that no information is lost when moving from the original data to such resulting after mean centering, i.e., subtraction of the mean from each variable involved. However, loss of information will occur as a result of the assumption $\underline{d} = \underline{0}$ in cases where observed variables do have relevant or meaningful origins of measurement scales, or substantive questions are raised that require consideration of the intercepts, as, for example, in longitudinal or multiple-group studies (e.g., Raykov & Marcoulides, 2008). For this reason, from now on we will adopt the GFA model (10.19) as being generally appropriate. We reiterate that the GFA model has the same defining equations in (10.19) as the general linear model, specifically when the observed variable intercepts are included, with the distinction that its explanatory variables are not observed and thus there are no observations available on them. This fact has implications that will be relevant through the remainder of the book.

An added benefit resulting from adopting the GFA model is seen when realizing that it can be viewed also as effectively underlying several IRT models. This relationship is perhaps easiest to reveal if one uses the context of the generalized linear model, GLIM. Specifically, for a given test (instrument) component or item, say X_k, Equation (10.19) shows that random variable as regressed upon a set of latent variables collected in $\underline{f}$ ($k = 1, ..., p$). This may be most readily realized when X_k is continuous—the case we have dealt with in several previous chapters ($k = 1, ..., p$). Then, from (10.19) follows that for its expectation (given the values of the m factors)

$$E(X_k) = d_k + a_{k1} f_1 + a_{k2} f_2 + \cdots + a_{km} f_m \qquad (k = 1, ..., p) \qquad (10.20)$$

holds. That is, the expected value of the instrument component X_k is a linear function of the factors (including an intercept, as usual in regression analysis). In their complete version, the set of p Equations (10.20) are written as

$$E(X_1) = d_1 + a_{11} f_1 + a_{12} f_2 + \cdots + a_{1m} f_m$$
$$E(X_2) = d_2 + a_{21} f_1 + a_{22} f_2 + \cdots + a_{2m} f_m$$
$$\cdots$$
$$E(X_p) = d_p + a_{p1} f_1 + a_{p2} f_2 + \cdots + a_{pm} f_m$$

or in the compact matrix form as

$$E(\underline{X}) = \underline{d} + A \underline{f}, \qquad (10.21)$$

where the symbols in the left-hand side denote the vector consisting of the expectations of the components of the vector of manifest measures $\underline{X}$. Equation (10.21) simply says that the expectations of the observed variables are linearly related to the underlying factors.

A special case of this discussion, which is of particular relevance in many measurement, testing, and test development contexts, is obtained from Equation (10.21) in case of a single factor, i.e., when $m = 1$. Then (10.21) is rewritten as

$$E(\underline{X}) = \underline{d} + \underline{a}\,f, \tag{10.22}$$

where f is that single factor and $\underline{a}$ is the vector of observed variable loadings on it.

10.5.2 Nonlinear Factor Analysis Models

The conceptual idea underlying the GFA model in Equation (10.19) and in particular its consequence (10.21), which is the idea of relating a dependent variable to a set of explanatory variables, is equally beneficial when X_k is a discrete variable ($k = 1, \ldots, p$). This is possibly most easily seen in case of a binary dependent variable, as oftentimes the response (or ultimate score) on a given item is in a test, a case that is elaborated on next (cf. Etezadi-Amoli & McDonald, 1983; McDonald, 1962, 1967b, 1983, 1999; Wall & Amemiya, 2007).

10.5.2.1 A Nonlinear Factor Analysis Model Based on the Logit Link

With a binary observed variable (item, score), the GLIM approach will postulate via, say, the logit link function the following relationship if using the latent variables (factors) f_1 through f_m as predictors (explanatory variables) with respect to the response X_k:

$$logit(E(X_k)) = d_k + a_{k1}f_1 + a_{k2}f_2 + \cdots + a_{km}f_m \tag{10.23}$$

($k = 1, \ldots, p$). We stress that the right-hand side of Equation (10.23) is a linear function of the unobserved variables f_1 through f_m and is linear in the parameters involved—the ds and as appearing there. At least as important, Equation (10.23) is directly related to the GFA model in case of a binary response variable, after the logit is taken of its expectation. In terms of empirical application, we have not dealt so far with such a model including unobserved variables, yet we underscore that (10.23) is nothing else but an extension of the GFA model in Equation (10.20) using the GLIM framework. This is because (10.23) merely relates linearly a function of the mean of an item score (not just its mean) to a set of predictors—in this case the latent factors. Compactly, the p Equations (10.23) are written as follows:

$$logit(E(X_1)) = d_1 + a_{11}f_1 + a_{12}f_2 + \cdots + a_{1m}f_m$$
$$logit(E(X_2)) = d_2 + a_{21}f_1 + a_{22}f_2 + \cdots + a_{2m}f_m$$
$$\cdots \tag{10.24}$$
$$logit(E(X_p)) = d_p + a_{p1}f_1 + a_{p2}f_2 + \cdots + a_{pm}f_m$$

or, in matrix form,

$$\underline{logit}(E(\underline{X})) = \underline{d} + A\,\underline{f}, \tag{10.25}$$

where $A = [a_{ij}]$ is the matrix comprising the loadings of the factors, $\underline{d} = (d_1, d_2, \ldots, d_p)'$ is the vector of pertinent intercepts, and the symbol $\underline{logit}\,(E(\underline{X}))$ stands for the $p \times 1$ vector consisting of the logits of the expectations of individual observed variables.

Looking at the right-hand side of Equation (10.23), we see that it is identical to the right-hand side of the GFA model, in which, however, the error term is not present. (The reason for the lack of error term in (10.23) is that it is an equation that expresses the logit of the mean of the observed variable involved, as mentioned earlier in this chapter.) On the other hand, the left-hand side of Equation (10.23) is clearly a nonlinear function of that mean, rather than just the latter as would be the case if one were to take expectation from both sides of the GFA model (see Equation (10.19)). For these reasons, Equation (10.23) can be seen as defining a nonlinear factor analysis (NLFA) model, which is based on the logit link (cf. McDonald, 1962, 1967b, 1983, 1999; Wall & Amemiya, 2007).

10.5.2.2 A Nonlinear Factor Analysis Model Based on the Probit Link

Alternatively, the GLIM framework provides also the opportunity to connect the linear predictor, i.e., the right-hand side of (10.20), with a discrete response variable via the probit link function:

$$probit(E(X_k)) = \Phi^{-1}(E(X_k)) = d_k + a_{k1} f_1 + \cdots + a_{km} f_m \qquad (10.26)$$

($k = 1, \ldots, p$). By analogy to the developments in the preceding subsection on the NLFA model based on the logit link, Equations (10.26) are compactly written as

$$\underline{probit}(E(\underline{X})) = \underline{d} + A\,\underline{f}, \qquad (10.27)$$

where $A = [a_{ij}]$ is the matrix of factor loadings, $\underline{d} = (d_1, d_2, \ldots, d_p)'$ is the vector of pertinent intercepts, and the symbol $\underline{probit}\,(E(\underline{X}))$ stands for the $p \times 1$ vector consisting of the probits of the expectations of the observed variables under consideration. Hence, in analogy to the preceding subsection, Equation (10.27) can be seen as defining a nonlinear factor analysis model based on the probit link (cf. Etezadi-Amoli & McDonald, 1983; McDonald, 1967b, 1999; Wall & Amemiya, 2007).

10.5.3 Nonlinear Factor Analysis Models as Generalized Linear Models and the Generalized Latent Linear Mixed Model

When looking at Equations (10.25) and (10.27) of the two NLFA models considered, we see that they share one important feature. This is the fact that they are based on a Bernoulli sampling model, which reflects the random mechanism behind a binary random variable—the response (score) on any given binary item. In addition, these two model-defining equations are based on a link function that is applied on the probability of observing a correct response on the items $X_1, \ldots, X_p$, which is the mean for them. Furthermore, in the right-hand sides of these two equations, (10.25) and (10.27), the same linear predictor is present, viz., a linear function of a set of underlying latent variables denoted $f_1, f_2, \ldots, f_m$. Hence, these two nonlinear factor analysis models, (10.25) and (10.27), can alternatively be also viewed as generalized linear models.

Having made this observation, we next attend to the fact that in the right-hand sides of these two GLIM-based extensions of the general FA model (10.19), there are unobserved variables, the m latent factors. For this reason, we can call the two considered nonlinear FA models in Equations (10.25) and (10.27) generalized latent linear models (GLLMs) (e.g., Bartholomew & Knott, 1999). The extension of GLLM to the mixed modeling context, e.g., the multilevel setting, is referred to as generalized latent linear and mixed model

(GLLAMM; e.g., Skrondal & Rabe-Hesketh, 2004). We will not be concerned with the comprehensive GLLAMM framework in this book, because hierarchical (multilevel) data are outside of the confines of this text, and we refer readers to Skrondal and Rabe-Hesketh (2004) for a thorough treatment of this framework.

In conclusion, we stress that in the present Section 10.5 we discussed an extension of the GFA model (10.19) to the case of noncontinuous observed variables (measures). These were specifically binary response variables or ultimate scores on items in a measuring instrument. This extension was accomplished using the GLIM framework. With this in mind, we also see that in this way one can extend the GFA model to a nonlinear factor analysis (NLFA) model (cf. Etezadi-Amoli & McDonald, 1983; McDonald, 1967b, 1999; Wall & Amemiya, 2007). We used for this goal, in an essential way, the comprehensive GLIM framework and saw thereby that the NLFA model can also be viewed as a GLIM. In the next chapter, we will use these important connections in a more specific context of considering several IRT models traditionally utilized in behavioral and social measurement.

11

Fundamentals and Models of Item Response Theory

The material presented in the last chapter provided only an introductory coverage of item response theory (IRT). In the present chapter, we will specialize our discussion further by considering several important concepts and models of IRT. We will see that the generalized linear modeling (GLIM) approach used in Chapter 10 will find specific applicability here and will allow us to describe easily notions and relationships of relevance in IRT at the level aimed in this book.

11.1 Latent Traits and Item Characteristic Curves

As could be anticipated from Chapter 10, a central concept in IRT is that of item characteristic curve (ICC). In order to define it, we first make a major assumption of (unidimensional) IRT, which stipulates that there exists an underlying latent trait—e.g., a studied ability—with a particular property. Specifically, this construct underlies performance on a given item or instrument component of interest, and it is this latent dimension that a researcher is actually willing to examine but cannot directly measure. (We note in passing that the same kind of assumption is made in factor analysis as well and in particular in single-factor models.) As mentioned in Chapter 10, in general the number of latent traits is not necessarily limited to one in IRT, similarly to factor analysis where there is no restriction in principle on the number of factors. However, in this chapter we will assume that there is only one trait in a behavioral measurement setting that is to be dealt with from an IRT perspective. (For a detailed coverage of multidimensional IRT, we refer to Reckase [2009]; see also McDonald [1999].) In the remainder of this chapter, we will adopt the frequently used term 'item' in IRT contexts, as referring to a behavior measuring instrument component.

11.1.1 What Does an Item Characteristic Curve Represent?

The ICC represents the relationship between (a) the underlying latent trait of ultimate interest, denoted usually θ in IRT contexts and frequently referred to as 'ability', and (b) the probability of responding correctly to, or endorsing, a given item, say the gth, $g = 1, ..., p$ (p being the number of prespecified items or components under consideration, e.g., the items in a behavioral test, scale, or measuring instrument). This item may or may not be dichotomous, but in this conceptual definition we assume that it is clear which response(s) can be considered (scored) correct and which one(s) incorrect. We would like to note that the ICC idea is meaningful also outside of immediate ability testing contexts and more generally in behavioral measurement settings, e.g., in personality, psychology, and social science, as well as in aging, health, and biomedical research, to mention a few fields of scientific inquiry. One would be interested in these disciplines in relating underlying trait(s) to the probability of providing a particular response. This is the reason why we used alternatively the word 'endorsing' above—in these disciplines at times it may be possible to meaningfully speak not of a correct answer but only of a subject indicating presence or absence of a certain characteristic, symptom, or opinion, in which case we may say he or she 'endorses' or not the item. For ease of presentation, however, in the rest of the chapter we will use the reference 'correct' and 'incorrect' or 'false' for a response to an item under consideration.

With this in mind, the ICC for a given item (say, the gth) represents a particular function, $P_g(\theta)$, which is defined generally on the set $\mathbb{R}$ of real numbers and takes values that are probabilities ($g = 1, \ldots, p$). More specifically, the ICC is a real function whose values are bounded from below and above by the numbers 0 and 1, respectively, denoted formally $P_g : \Theta \rightarrow [0,1]$, where Θ is the set of all possible values of the latent trait (usually $\Theta = \mathbb{R}$). In more generic terms, we will also use the notation $P(\theta)$ to symbolize probability of correct response on an item, as a function of the latent trait θ. (We will use the latter notation when it is not of concern which particular item is meant from a set of such.) As we will see later in the chapter, how exactly this function $P_g(.)$ is defined is an important matter that leads to the differentiation between several IRT models we will discuss. These models have the common feature that the associated ICC is (a) a monotonically increasing function of the trait θ, which is also (b) continuous and (c) smooth (i.e., continuously differentiable). In fact, for all IRT models of concern to us, the ICC is an S-shaped curve like the one presented in Figure 11.1.

Figure 11.1 represents a member of the class of typical ICC curves across items and IRT models. From this figure, it is readily seen that as the latent trait θ increases (i.e., individuals possess to a higher degree the corresponding ability), so does the probability of responding correctly to the item considered, $P(\theta)$. In particular, we observe from Figure 11.1 that the ICC increases most rapidly in the 'central' part of the curve. Conversely, the ICC increases much less steeply as one moves away from that part on the latent trait continuum, either to the left or to the right. Different ICCs may be flatter or steeper in their central part than the one in Figure 11.1, and this steepness will be a very important feature to us in the present chapter. However, all ICCs have the property that they gradually trail off to 0 as one moves sufficiently far from the center (i.e., from their steepest part) to the left and gradually approach 1 as one moves further away from that central part to the right. In a later section, we will specialize the discussion to a particular type of items where the ICC does not approach 0 when moving to the left and away from its central part, but a positive number, and this will be another property of interest to us.

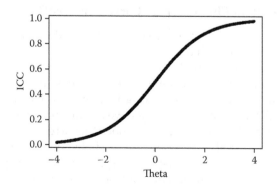

FIGURE 11.1
An item response characteristic curve (ICC).

11.1.2 What Does the Probability of Correct Response Actually Mean?

As discussed in the IRT literature, the notion of probability of correct response has two possible interpretations (Lord, 1980). According to the first, which we will use throughout the remainder of the chapter, if for a given θ and item, say the gth, one were to randomly sample from a subpopulation of individuals possessing that ability level θ, then the probability of the drawn person to correctly respond to the item is $P_g(\theta)$, i.e., equals the value of the ICC of this item at the point θ ($g = 1, ..., p$). (Imagine all persons from this subpopulation have already been administered the item and responded to it, but we do not have access to their responses; once an individual is randomly drawn from that subpopulation, his or her response on the item becomes known—$P_g(\theta)$ is then the probability of this response being correct.)

There is also another meaningful interpretation that is less often used, which we will not adopt in this chapter (Lord, 1980). Accordingly, consider a subpopulation of items that all have the same ICC. Then $P(\theta)$ is the probability of a person with ability θ to correctly respond on a randomly chosen item from that subpopulation. We note that in both interpretations only two 'objects' are fixed but not all three involved. Specifically, in the first interpretation fixed are the item and θ, and then an individual is randomly drawn from a relevant subpopulation of persons. In the second interpretation, fixed are the person and θ while the item is randomly drawn from a relevant (sub)population of items with the same ICC. We easily realize that because we are interested in interpreting $P(\theta)$, the value of θ has to be fixed in either of the two interpretations of this probability. In addition, in the first interpretation the item is fixed while a subject is randomly drawn. Alternatively, in the second interpretation the individual is fixed while the item is randomly drawn. We will keep in mind these interpretations, and especially the first that, as mentioned before, is adopted throughout the remainder of the chapter. In simple terms, $P_g(\theta)$ can be viewed as the probability of correct response to a given item, viz., the gth, by an individual possessing the relevant ability at the level of the value θ ($g = 1, ..., p$).

11.1.3 What Changes Across Item Characteristic Curves in a Given Measuring Situation?

Taking now another look at Figure 11.1, let us formalize further a point we mentioned earlier in this section. Specifically, different IRT models postulate different functions for $P_g(\theta)$ and thus are associated, strictly speaking, with different ICCs, in addition to the latter differing in some aspects across items within a set of such under consideration. Typically, for a chosen IRT model, all items in an instrument in question are assumed to have ICCs that come from the same class, with only one or more parameters differing across items. That is, once an IRT model is chosen—on whatever grounds—all items in a given set (test, scale) are automatically assumed to have ICCs that are described with the same functional form (i.e., represent the same generic function of θ). However, although their ICCs follow that function (functional form), they can have different particular features, i.e., be characterized by different values of the parameters involved in the function. For this reason, IRT models differ from one another in (a) the assumed class of functions describing the ICCs (one function/functional form per IRT model) and (b) the number of parameters on which these functions depend. Also, items differ from one another not in (a) or (b) but in the values that the parameters mentioned in (b) take—each item is characterized by a specific set of numerical values for these parameters, whereas their number and functional form of the ICC are typically the same across all members of a measuring instrument under consideration.

In the IRT models of main interest in this chapter, the ICCs for all items do have a very important property in common. This is the feature that as one approaches the 'central' part of the ICC, with values of θ from either above or below that part (i.e., from the right or left of it), small changes in ability lead to more pronounced changes in the probability of correct response, than further away from that central part. Specifically, in the 'middle' of the central part of the ICC, the gradient (tilt, steepness) of the ICC is highest. Furthermore, as one moves from one end of the central part of the ICC to the other end of it, the ICC is actually positioned at different sides of the pertinent tangent or gradient line. This is because right in the middle of that central part, all models' ICCs have what is called in calculus an inflection point (i.e., their second derivative is 0). We will address this matter in more detail in a following section.

11.1.4 How Could an Item Characteristic Curve Be Thought to Have 'Emerged'?

It is worthwhile noting that the S-shaped ICC in all IRT models of interest in this chapter could be considered resulting from a step-function. Such a function could be viewed as being essentially the same as an ICC (see Figure 11.1) with an extremely steep gradient (tangent) in its central part and is presented in Figure 11.2. (To make our next point clearer, its vertical axis is referred to as 'step-function'; see also the appendix to this chapter with respect to how this curve was obtained and in particular the graphical representation of its central part.)

For purely illustrative purposes here, we imagine next a function like that in Figure 11.2 as being made of nonrigid material (e.g., rubber) and 'pull' it gradually by the upper-right end to the right then 'pull' it by the lower-left end to the left. Doing this in a smooth fashion yields an S-shaped curve that resembles well an ICC in an IRT model.

Conversely, one could consider a step-function as a limit of an ICC (e.g., Figure 11.1) when the gradient or tangent to the central part—at the inflection point—of this curve is allowed to become infinitely large or steep. We will return to this issue later in the chapter, but we mention here that step-functions have not been found to fit well many real data sets and for this reason have rarely been used in applications of IRT.

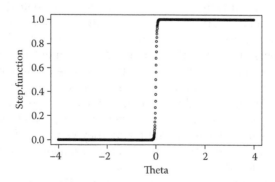

FIGURE 11.2
An ICC with extreme steepness in its central part.

11.2 Unidimensionality and Local Independence

In many applications of statistics in the behavioral and social sciences, it is common to talk about association, relatedness, or unrelatedness, e.g., correlation and/or lack thereof between considered random variables. This is particularly the case when involved variables are continuous (or could be treated as such), especially when they are normally distributed. When these variables are discrete, however, as is typically the case with observed measures in IRT, it is in fact more beneficial to discuss matters in terms of random variable dependence or independence. We mention in passing that correlation and dependence are in general two different notions (e.g., Roussas, 1997); specifically, as is well-known, independence implies lack of correlation, but the reverse is then true only when the two random variables involved are bivariate (and hence univariate) normally distributed.

11.2.1 Independence of Discrete Random Variables

With discrete random variables, the notion of independence can be derived from a more general definition of random variable independence (cf. Agresti & Finlay, 2009). Accordingly, two random variables are independent if their joint distribution (probability when considered together) is representable as the product of the individual, also called marginal, variable distributions (probabilities). In the special case of discrete variables, and in particular binary responses that are of relevance for the rest of this book, the pertinent definition can be specialized further (e.g., Crocker & Algina, 1986). To this end, denote by $P_i(+)$ the probability of a 'positive' response on item i and by $P_i(-)$ that of 'negative' response on it ($i = 1, ..., p, p > 1$). Denote further by $P(+,+)$ the probability of obtaining two positive responses on two items under consideration, the ith and jth say (i.e., positive on the one and positive on the other), and correspondingly define the notation for probability of the other three types of responses ($i, j = 1, ..., p, i \neq j$).

With this notation, we can give the following definition of special relevance in this chapter. Two random variables defined as responses on two binary items, say ith and jth among a set of dichotomous items, are called (statistically) *independent* if and only if the following four equalities hold:

$$P(+,+) = P_i(+) \, P_j(+),$$

$$P(+,-) = P_i(+) \, P_j(-),$$

$$P(-,+) = P_i(-) \, P_j(+), \quad \text{and}$$

$$P(-,-) = P_i(-) \, P_j(-).$$

(11.1)

If at least one of Equations (11.1) is not fulfilled, the two items are called (statistically) *dependent*. That is, two random variables defined as scores on two binary items are independent if one can work out the probability of any response pattern on both (i.e., pair of responses on each item) by simply multiplying the probabilities for pertinent response on each of the two items. If this is not possible, i.e., if some of these products do not equal the probability for the corresponding bivariate response pattern, then the items are not independent.

To illustrate, consider the following example. Suppose the probability of correct response (+) on item i is .40, while on item j it is .70. Then the two items would be independent if for their joint distribution the following holds:

$$P(+,+) = .28,$$

$$P(+,-) = .12,$$

$$P(-,+) = .42, \quad \text{and} \tag{11.2}$$

$$P(-,-) = .18.$$

The four equations in (11.2) define the joint distribution of the two items, because they specify the probability of occurrence of any pair of possible answers on both items. (We note that the sum of the four probabilities listed in the right-hand sides of Equations (11.2) is 1, as it should be, given that they define the joint distribution of the two items in question.) However, if for these two items, $P(+,-) = .42$ and $P(-,+) = .12$, say, were to hold, then the items would not be independent. (We keep in mind that the joint distribution is in general not determined by the marginal distributions, unless of course the items are independent; e.g., Agresti [2002].) One would in general anticipate items to be statistically dependent (in an overall population under study) if they evaluate at least one common latent dimension.

In the context of a given set of binary items, as of relevance in this chapter, statistical dependence is the formalization of the intuitive notion of relationship between items. Two or more items will be dependent when one of them contains information about the response pattern of another item. When a researcher is interested, for example, in constructing a test measuring a single underlying trait (ability), he or she typically would be willing to work with items that are not independent. Their dependence will then be expected to be explainable by the underlying construct that one aims at evaluating.

11.2.2 What Does Unidimensionality Mean in an IRT Context?

How many traits underlie studied individuals' performance on a set of interrelated items that presumably have something in common (from a substantive viewpoint)? The answer to this question depends on the specifics of the item set considered. Whenever we say that a set of items is unidimensional, we mean informally that only one trait can be used to explain the lack of statistical dependence among them (see below for a more formal definition). That is, unidimensionality in this case means that the statistical dependence among the items can be accounted for by a single underlying latent trait. This notion is similar to that of unidimensionality of components in a measuring instrument, which we considered in the context of factor analysis in Chapters 3 and 4. In fact, conceptually this unidimensionality notion is the same across the two contexts considered, viz., the IRT and the general factor analysis frameworks (cf. Takane & de Leeuw, 1987; see also Chapter 10).

More formally, a measuring instrument (test) is referred to as unidimensional if (a) its items (components) are statistically dependent in the entire population of subjects of interest, i.e., in the population for which the instrument has been developed, and (b) a single latent trait can be assumed to exist, such that the items are statistically independent in each subpopulation of individuals that are homogeneous with regard to the trait, i.e., have the same value on it. Because point (b) considers a subpopulation located at a single point on the latent dimension (latent trait scale), this feature of statistical independence is also called *local independence*. We note that requirement (b) is the same as that of conditional independence that we encountered first in Chapter 3 in the context of the traditional FA model (with the assumption of normality of observed variables).

This discussion brings us to the more generally valid notion of dimensionality of a behavior measuring instrument (test, scale). Dimensionality is defined as the number of latent traits needed to achieve local independence (cf. Hambleton, Swaminathan, & Rodgers, 1991). Specifically, if for a given test (set of items), m is the smallest integer number with the property that m latent traits are needed to be taken into account (assumed to exist) in order to achieve local independence, while any fewer than m traits would not accomplish it, then the instrument is referred to as m-dimensional.

11.2.3 Another Look at Local Independence

We stress that unidimensionality is ensured only in the special case of $m = 1$, i.e., a single latent trait, and hence is not the same as the notion of local independence. In fact, the notion of local independence has relevance also for multidimensional tests (e.g., Reckase, 2009) and is qualitatively different from the concept of unidimensionality. Simply put, unidimensionality and conditional independence are two different notions.

We notice also that the concept of latent trait is of instrumental relevance for the above definition of local independence. Thereby, a latent trait may or may not be the same as a construct of actual interest to the scientist. Just like a scale (composite) may have poor validity even though it may be unidimensional, so can a set of items be measuring a trait distinct from the one of substantive concern in a given setting. This can happen even if that set of items is unidimensional—it may just be measuring poorly the construct of actual interest, while still being unidimensional. This fact motivates us for a more formal definition (cf. McDonald, 1999). Accordingly, a set of p items $X_1, X_2, \ldots, X_p$ is called locally independent if for a given (i.e., fixed) set of values on m latent traits ($m > 0$), denoted $f_1, \ldots, f_m$, the joint probability of any response pattern on the p items is the product of the probabilities of pertinent response on any of the items at that set of values for the traits, i.e., if

$$\Pr(X_1 = x_1, X_2 = x_2, \ldots, X_p = x_p \mid f_1, \ldots, f_m) =$$

$$\Pr(X_1 = x_1 \mid f_1, \ldots, f_m) \Pr(X_2 = x_2 \mid f_1, \ldots, f_m) \ldots \Pr(X_p = x_p \mid f_1, \ldots, f_m) \tag{11.3}$$

holds, where $\Pr(.|.)$ denotes probability under the condition stated after the vertical bar (i.e., conditional probability).

We stress that in this definition only conditional probabilities are involved, rather than any unconditional ones (and for this reason the defined concept is often also referred to as *conditional independence*). That is, this definition does *not* say anything particular about the *un*conditional probability $P(X_1 = x_1, X_2 = x_2, \ldots, X_p = x_p)$ of observing the pattern $x_1, x_2, \ldots, x_p$ on the corresponding items $X_1, X_2, \ldots, X_p$. In other words, this definition is not concerned with the probability of a certain response pattern in the entire subject population being studied. Similarly, the definition says nothing about the unconditional probabilities for single items, viz., $P(X_1 = x_1)$, $P(X_2 = x_2)$, ..., and $P(X_p = x_p)$, i.e., the population probabilities for particular responses on each of the set of items under consideration. Moreover, the local independence definition does not say anything about the nature of the latent traits. In fact, there are several possibilities with regard to the trait nature that are very important for different branches of present-day applied statistics (e.g., Bartholomew & Knott, 1999). These are the following.

1. The latent traits may be continuous. In this case, we are in the framework of IRT, and the last definition based on Equation (11.3) pertains to the concept of local independence as relevant in IRT.

2. The traits may be categorical. In this case, we are in the framework of latent class analysis (LCA; assuming categorical items as throughout the rest of this book, unless otherwise indicated; e.g., Muthén, 2002).

3. If in case 2 the items are continuous, we are in the framework of latent profile analysis (LPA; then Equation (11.3) will have to be reexpressed/represented in terms of probability density functions rather than probabilities; Muthén, 2002).

4. When items and traits are continuous, we are in the framework of factor analysis (e.g., Chapter 3; then (11.3) needs to be reexpressed/represented in terms of densities again).

These points 1 through 4 emphasize a basic idea that holds together several branches of applied statistics, some of which were mentioned in the preceding paragraph. This is the notion of local independence, alternatively also referred to as conditional independence (Bartholomew, 2007). According to this basic idea, for IRT, FA, LCA, and LPA the fundamental goal is to find the minimum number of latent traits with which Equation (11.3) holds (or its corresponding modification in case of continuous observed variables, indicated in the preceding paragraph). That is, the notion of conditional (local) independence is at the very heart of any of these applied statistical areas, some of which are of special relevance for measurement and testing in the behavioral and social sciences. (For a further statistical discussion of these fundamental relationships across major modeling frameworks, see Bartholomew [2002, 2007] and Bartholomew and Knott [1999].)

11.3 The Normal Ogive and Logistic Functions Revisited

As we indicated in Chapter 10, and earlier in the present one, a possible choice for an ICC is the logistic curve, or alternatively the normal ogive, i.e., the cumulative distribution function (CDF) of the standard normal distribution. Both curves have the following properties that are worth stressing here and in fact could be directly seen from the graphical display provided in Figure 11.1 that is representative for both classes of ICCs (consider next z formally as the argument of either curve):

- the curve rises continually (when z moves from left to right, along the horizontal axis, i.e., covers all real numbers);
- its lower asymptote is 0 (as z approaches $-\infty$, i.e., $z \to -\infty$ symbolically), and its upper asymptote is 1 (as $z \to \infty$);
- the normal ogive graphs (represents), as a function of z, the area to the left of z and below the standard normal density (probability density function)

$$\phi(u) = \frac{1}{\sqrt{2\pi}} e^{-u^2/2},$$

(11.4)

whereby this area is (cf., e.g., King & Minium, 2003)

$$A_\phi(z) = \int_{-\infty}^{z} \phi(u)\,du = \frac{1}{\sqrt{2\pi}} \int_{-\infty}^{z} e^{-u^2/2}\,du; \tag{11.5}$$

- the logistic function graphs, as a function of z, the area to the left of z and below the standard logistic density

$$\psi(v) = \frac{e^v}{(1+e^v)^2}, \tag{11.6}$$

whereby this area is

$$A_\psi(z) = \int_{-\infty}^{z} \psi(v)\,dv = \int_{-\infty}^{z} \frac{e^v}{(1+e^v)^2}\,dv. \tag{11.7}$$

Because the graphs of the logistic and normal ogive functions are essentially indistinguishable (after a minor—for this point—rescaling of the horizontal axis for the former, as mentioned in Chapter 10), we will use Figure 11.1 as a graphical representation of each of them.

With this revisit of the logistic and normal ogive functions, we are ready to discuss next particular IRT models.

11.4 Two Popular Normal Ogive Models

Suppose the normal ogive is used as ICC for a given item in a unidimensional IRT model (assumed of concern in the rest of this chapter, unless otherwise indicated). Then the height of the normal ogive curve at any prespecified value of θ will represent the proportion of examinees at that ability level who can answer the item correctly (see the first interpretation of probability for correct response discussed in Section 11.1). That is, from Equation (11.5) follows that for a given item g,

$$P_g(\theta) = \int_{-\infty}^{z} \phi(u)\,du = \frac{1}{\sqrt{2\pi}} \int_{-\infty}^{z} e^{-u^2/2}\,du = \Phi(z), \tag{11.8}$$

where $\Phi(z)$ denotes the normal ogive function. (In terms of symbols we note parenthetically that it is $\phi(u)$—rather than $\Phi(z)$—that is the probability density function of the standard normal distribution, also typically referred to as its density, probability density function, or just density function; this function $\phi(u)$ is the bell-shaped curve frequently referred to in introductory statistics textbooks. However, it is the cumulative distribution function of the standard normal distribution, $\Phi(z)$, that equals the area under the density curve $\phi(u)$ and to the left of z and that appears in the very end of Equation (11.8). It is this CDF, $\Phi(z)$, that is of main concern in the current section.)

Equation (11.8) implies, by taking inverse function of its both sides, the following relationship, which will become of particular relevance in the next section:

$$z = \Phi^{-1}(P_g(\theta)) = z(\theta), \tag{11.9}$$

whereby the last part of Equation (11.9) expresses only the recognition that z is a function of θ (as being equal to $\Phi^{-1}(P_g(\theta))$ that is itself a function of θ). That is, all one needs to do in order to get the point z, for which $P_g(\theta)$ is the value of the normal ogive at it, is to take the inverse of the latter function Φ at $P_g(\theta)$ ($g = 1, ...,p$).

11.4.1 The Two-Parameter Normal Ogive Model (2PN-Model)

The discussion in the preceding Section 11.3 leads us now easily to a quite popular model especially in the early years of IRT (particularly the 1950s and 1960s). This model is based on Equation (11.9) and assumes further that for a given item

$$z = a(\theta - b), \tag{11.10}$$

where a and b are parameters with important interpretation, discussed in detail below. That is, this model postulates that the dependence of z on θ, which is stated in Equation (11.9), is a linear function of the trait θ, with intercept $-ab = c$, say, and slope a. Because z depends on these two parameters, a and b, within the context of the normal ogive, this model is called two-parameter normal ogive model, oftentimes abbreviated to '2PN-model'.

We stress that Equation (11.10) explicates the way in which the above-mentioned dependence of z on θ occurs (see Equation (11.9)) in the 2PN-model. That is, Equation (11.10) answers the question of how z actually depends on θ, as a follow-up to Equation (11.9), by assuming or postulating this dependence to be in the linear manner stated in (11.10). We notice also that Equation (11.10) defines an item-specific model, i.e., a model that is assumed for a given item (viz., the gth from a collection of $p > 0$ items, $g = 1, ...,p$). Hence, strictly speaking one could attach the subindex g to both a and b, but to avoid notational clutter we dispense with this added notation here, keeping in mind of course that different items need not have the same a and/or b parameters. We will use that elaborated subindex notation later in the chapter, when it will be important to emphasize item specificity, and we will alternatively dispense with it in discussions of more general nature like here when no confusion can arise.

Returning to the right-hand side of Equation (11.10), the parameter a can be shown to be directly related to the steepness of the ICC at its inflection point (e.g., Lord, 1980). The latter, as indicated in Chapter 10, is located at that ability level (point on the horizontal axis) where the probability of correct response is .5. Looking at Equations (11.9) and (11.10), this happens precisely where $b = \theta$. (This is observed by substituting $b = \theta$ in each of them and recalling that the standard normal distribution of relevance here is symmetric around 0.) Hence, the parameter b is that position on the latent trait scale where the probability of correct response is one half, i.e., $P_g(b) = .5$. (We stress that because of the CDF of the standard normal distribution being monotonically increasing, there is a single point with such a property.) Furthermore, it can be shown that a is directly proportional to the tangent of the angle at which the gradient to the ICC at the inflection point intersects with the horizontal axis (Lord, 1980). That is, the steeper the gradient (i.e., the higher the tangent of the line at which that gradient crosses the horizontal axis), the larger the parameter a. For this reason, a is called discrimination parameter of the item under consideration (also at times referred to as 'item discriminating power').

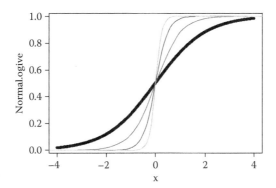

FIGURE 11.3
Illustration of increasing steepness (in central part) of ICC with increasing item discrimination parameter (and same parameter *b*).

Specifically, items having higher *a*s differentiate better between individuals on the trait who are positioned close to the point *b* on the ability dimension. More precisely, those to the right of *b* have considerably higher probability to solve correctly the item than subjects to the left of *b* (how much higher depends on the magnitude of *a*).

To illustrate graphically this feature, Figure 11.3 displays the ICCs of several items that differ from one another only in their discrimination parameter. Specifically, the discrimination parameter of the item with the ICC being flattest in its central part (thickest curve) is smallest and the discrimination parameter for the steepest ICC in that part (thinnest curve) is largest. We emphasize that the gradient to the ICC (in its central part) becomes steeper and steeper with increasing item discrimination parameter (see appendix). We observe also that all curves in Figure 11.3 have the same *b* parameter, as they intersect at the same point, viz., the one at which the corresponding probability of correct response for each item is .5.

Taking another look now at Figure 11.1, or just at Equations (11.9) and (11.10), one readily notices that items having higher *b*s are associated with lower probability of correct solution by subjects with a given (fixed) trait level, because these curves 'come closer' to the horizontal axis at that trait level. This is why the parameter *b* is called *difficulty parameter* of the *g*th item ($g = 1, \ldots, p$), frequently also referred to as 'item difficulty'. This relationship is illustrated in Figure 11.4, which displays the ICCs of several items differing from one another only in their difficulty parameter, i.e., having the same item discrimination parameter *a*. In particular, we note that this parameter for the left-most (thickest) ICC is smallest, whereas the difficulty parameter for the right most (thinnest) curve is largest. We notice also that the entire ICC is moved to the right; as one 'moves' from the thickest to the thinnest curve, the items become also more difficult. (See Section 11.6 for a discussion of the relationship of this parameter to the classical item analysis parameter of item difficulty; see also Chapter 4.)

From this discrimination and difficulty parameter interpretation, it is readily realized that items with flat ICCs are not really differentiating well between individuals with ability levels around (close to) their *b* parameter (see in particular Figure 11.3 for a graphical illustration). These are items with relatively small *a* parameters. Hence, an index of quality of an item (when the aim is to differentiate between subjects with trait levels in the central part of ability range) is the steepness of the ICC, i.e., the magnitude of the *a* parameter. Specifically, the larger *a*, the better the item. For this reason, when given is a set of items with the same *b* parameter but different *a* parameters, and the goal is to choose those that

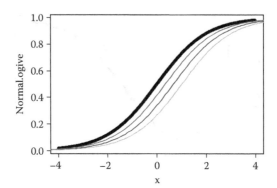

FIGURE 11.4
Illustration of effect of increasing item difficulty parameter (viz., 'translation' of ICC to the right; for fixed parameter *a*).

differentiate best among individuals, one would obviously pick the items with the highest *a* parameters. Similarly, we notice that in addition to items with small *a*, items with negative discrimination parameters (i.e., with *a* < 0) are not desirable for the same purposes (in an item set, test, or instrument where other items have positive discrimination parameters). The reason is that they have a counterproductive contribution to the overall test then (e.g., Hambleton et al., 1991).

11.4.2 The Scale of Measurement Issue

As we repeatedly indicated in this and preceding chapters, the latent trait assumed to be underlying subject performance on a set of items under consideration is not observed and cannot be measured directly. Hence, the scale underlying the trait does not have a natural origin and unit of measurement. In fact, there is no way to come up with such unless they are chosen in an arbitrary fashion. Therefore, it is common to select the origin and unit on the latent trait scale so that the mean of the trait is 0 and its standard deviation is 1 for a population of interest. (We note that this is the traditional assumption in factor analysis as well; see Chapter 3.) Therefore, on any graph of ICC, indication of negative scores on the horizontal axis (representing the latent trait) should not be viewed as unusual—in fact they are just as 'usual' as positive scores.

Another related issue is that the origin and unit of the latent trait scale do affect the values of the *a* and *b* parameters for each item. However, it can be shown that because the probability of correct response $P_g(\theta)$ depends only on the product $a(\theta-b)$ (see Equation (11.9)), this probability itself is not affected by the origin or unit of measurement on the latent scale and is thus unrelated to their choice. That is, the probability of correct response is invariant under changes in origin and location of the underlying latent trait dimension. (This is valid for any IRT model considered in the present chapter.)

We finalize this subsection on measurement scale by stressing that in our discussion we have not made any reference to or used the specific form of the ICC. In particular, we have not assumed it being of any special functional form. Hence, the points made in this Subsection 11.4.2 are valid regardless of whether for a given item (item set) one uses a logistic ICC or a normal ogive ICC. Similarly, although throughout this discussion we assumed that the item considered was fixed, we stress that all points made apply to each given item and its pertinent ICC.

11.4.3 The Two-Parameter Normal Ogive Model as a Generalized Linear Model

Based on our discussion in Chapter 10, from Equations (11.9) and (11.10) it follows that the 2PN-model can be viewed as a generalized linear model. Indeed, we can rewrite Equation (11.10) as follows (denoting the product ab just as b in the next equation, merely to follow traditional notation):

$$z = (-b) + a\theta. \tag{11.11}$$

With Equation (11.11) in mind, from (11.9) it now follows that

$$\Phi^{-1}(P_g) = -b + a\theta. \tag{11.12}$$

Equation (11.12) states that for the gth item, a transformation of its mean (probability of correct response, or P_g) is linearly related to the predictor θ, which is the underlying latent trait ($g = 1, \ldots, p$). Hence, the 2PN-model can be viewed as a GLIM with (a) the Bernoulli model as a sampling distribution, (b) the probit function as a link function, and (c) the latent trait θ as a predictor (explanatory variable). These are exactly the same characteristics, however, that are possessed by the nonlinear factor analysis model based on the probit link (see Chapter 10). Therefore, we can also see that the 2PN-model is a nonlinear factor analysis model (cf. McDonald, 1967b, 1999; Wall & Amemiya, 2007).

The fact that the predictor in this GLIM is *not* observed but instead latent does make quite a bit of difference when fitting this model to data and estimating its parameters from a given set of binary items in an empirical behavioral measurement setting. Well-developed, specific numerical algorithms accomplishing this aim exist within the IRT framework, as well as the FA framework, in addition to estimation of the subject trait levels that are quite often of special interest in their own right (see also Note 1 to this chapter). We will return to this issue later in the chapter.

11.4.4 The One-Parameter Normal Ogive Model (1PN-Model)

A special case of the 2PN-model is the one-parameter normal ogive model (1PN-model). This model is obtained from the 2PN-model when it is in addition assumed that all items have the same discrimination parameter, i.e.,

$$a_g = a_{g'} \tag{11.13}$$

for all $g \neq g'$ ($g, g' = 1, \ldots, p$). Thus, in the 1PN-model all items share the same gradient at the inflection point of their ICC, i.e., are equally steep in the central part of their ICCs and thus parallel to one another. However, in this model the items do differ from one another in the positioning of their ICCs along the latent trait dimension (continuum). Specifically, the items differ in general in their difficulty parameters:

$$b_g \neq b_{g'}, \tag{11.14}$$

for all $g \neq g'$ ($g, g' = 1, \ldots, p$). That is, different items have in general different difficulty parameters, and hence some are positioned 'further to the right' whereas others are 'further to the left' on the continuum of the underlying latent trait.

Because the 1PN-model is obtained as a special case of the 2PN-model, yet the latter is a GLIM itself, it follows that the 1PN-model can be viewed as a GLIM as well. Indeed, the 1-PN model is a GLIM with (a) the Bernoulli model as a sampling distribution, (b) the probit as a link function, (c) the latent trait θ as a predictor, and in addition (d) the same regression weights in the link function (i.e., same as in Equation (11.12)). These are, however, precisely the same characteristics possessed by a special case of the nonlinear FA model we mentioned in the preceding section (as well as in Chapter 10). Hence, like the 2PN-model, it is also true that the 1PN-model is a nonlinear factor analysis model (cf. McDonald, 1967a, 1999; Wall & Amemiya, 2007). At least as important, it is worth stressing that the 1PN-model is a 2PN-model in which the restriction (11.13) is imposed. That is, the 1PN-model is nested in the 2PN-model, because the former results from the latter by imposing a constraint, viz., (11.13). In other words, we can consider the 2PN-model as a 'full' model and the 1PN-model as a 'reduced' model. We will see later in this chapter that the same nestedness property applies to other 1- and 2-parameter models of major relevance within the framework of IRT.

11.4.5 Testing One- and Two-Parameter Normal Ogive Models

Although the 1PN- and 2PN-models certainly represent attractive means for analyzing data from a set of given items, they are built on a restrictive assumption that is empirically testable and falsifiable. This assumption states that there is a single underlying latent trait, denoted θ, which accounts for the relationships between responses on these items. We turn next to the issue of how to test this model and estimate its parameters.

11.4.5.1 Testing the Two-Parameter Normal Ogive Model

As before, let us denote the p items under consideration by $X_1, X_2, ..., X_p$. Then Equations (11.9) and (11.10) entail that the 1PN- and 2PN-models, in terms of equations, are as follows:

$$\Phi^{-1}(P_1(\theta)) = b_1 + a_1\,\theta,$$

$$\Phi^{-1}(P_2(\theta)) = b_2 + a_2\,\theta,$$

$$\cdots$$

$$\Phi^{-1}(P_p(\theta)) = b_p + a_p\,\theta. \tag{11.15}$$

Equations (11.15) represent a special case of the probit model (10.25) with a single latent trait, i.e., of the nonlinear factor analysis model based on the probit link and with a single factor (see Chapter 10; $\Phi^{-1}(.)$ is used here just as a symbol for the probit link function). That is, formally, Equations (11.15) define the 2PN-model with a single latent trait. With the additional assumption

$$a_1 = a_2 = ... = a_p, \tag{11.16}$$

Equations (11.15) yield the 1PN-model (with a single trait). Hence, the ICCs in a 1PN-model are parallel (see Note 1 to this chapter) and are obtained from one another via translation, to the right or to the left along the horizontal axis, by as many units as the difference in their difficulty parameters is.

How does one test the validity of either of these two models? This is possible under an assumption that we first got familiar with in Chapter 4. Accordingly, for the gth of the items there exists a continuous latent, normally distributed variable X_g^* such that when for a given individual this variable's realization is beyond a certain threshold

τ_g a correct response is observed whereas when it is below τ_g an incorrect one ensues (e.g., Skrondal & Rabe-Hesketh, 2004; see also Chapter 4; $g = 1, ..., p$). We note that this assumption may be viewed as plausible in many testing contexts, as mentioned earlier in this book. Following this assumption, and denoting by X_g the response on the gth item ($g = 1, ..., p$),

$$X_g = \begin{cases} 1, \text{ if } X_g^* \geq \tau_g \text{ (i.e., correct response)} \\ \\ 0, \text{ if } X_g^* < \tau_g \text{ (i.e., incorrect response).} \end{cases} \tag{11.17}$$

We note parenthetically that, as mentioned in Chapter 2, for a continuous random variable the probability of it taking a prespecified (i.e., given, fixed) value is 0. Thus, it is irrelevant how one actually defines X_g—whether 1 or 0—when $X_g^* = \tau_g$ ($g = 1, ..., p$). Furthermore, the assumption of existence of X_g^* is akin to the IRT assumption of a single latent trait that accounts for the relationships between the observed responses on the gth item (e.g., Lord, 1980). The former assumption is testable for pairs of items within the framework of latent variable modeling (e.g., Jöreskog & Sörbom, 1996). We will refer to assumption (11.17) as the underlying normal variable assumption (UNV assumption), as before, and a model making this assumption will be referred to in the rest of this chapter as an 'UNV model' (see also Chapter 4).

The UNV assumption is of particular relevance in the present chapter and for our treatment of IRT models. The reason is that according to a main psychometric result by Takane and de Leeuw (1987), the 2PN-model is equivalent to the model (11.15) with the UNV assumption and a single factor underlying the variables X_g^*, $g = 1, ..., p$ (see also Kamata & Bauer, 2008). We refer to the latter model as 1F-UNV model. Its equivalence to the 2PN-model means that both models exhibit the same overall fit to an analyzed data set. We stress that in the 1F-UNV model, parameters are not only the factor loadings of each item on the common latent factor but also the pertinent thresholds (one per item), viz., $\tau_1, \tau_2, ..., \tau_p$ (see (11.17); Chapter 4). The latter can be treated as the corresponding z-scores from the standard normal distribution, which pertain to proportion correct response for the gth item ($g = 1, ..., p$; cf. McDonald, 1999; Muthén, 1984).

Hence, to test the validity of the 2PN-model, it is sufficient to test the 1F-UNV model. Testing the overall fit of the latter is, however, precisely the same as testing the single-factor analysis model with categorical observed variables within the latent variable modeling framework (LVM), which we got familiar with in Chapter 4 and specialized further to this setting in Chapter 7. At the software level, as we saw there, testing of that single-factor model is possible using the LVM program *Mplus*. Furthermore, to test a 1PN-model, as we will see soon, all one needs to do is impose the additional restriction of equal factor loadings in the 1F-UNV model (in case of plausibility of the latter). This can also be easily accomplished within the LVM framework and at the software level with *Mplus*.

Although these two models—the 2PN-model and the 1F-UNV model—are equivalent, i.e., exhibit the same overall fit to the data, their parameters are not the same. Specifically, inversion formulas are available that can be used to obtain the parameters of one model from those of the other (e.g., Kamata & Bauer, 2008; McDonald, 1999). These formulas are also implemented in the software mentioned, and it in fact provides automatically the estimates of item discrimination and difficulty parameters once the single-factor (1F-UNV) model is fitted to the analyzed data. With this in mind, for a given set of binary items the discussion in this section allows one (a) to fit a single-factor model with categorical indicators and from its fit indices to make a conclusion as to whether the 2PN-model provides satisfactory overall fit to the data as an IRT model and (b) to obtain the discrimination and difficulty parameters for each item. These relationships demonstrate yet further similarities between the factor analysis framework underlying this book, on the one hand, and IRT, on the other. We illustrate with the following example.

In a study of preschool children aggression at play, conducted over several weeks, an observer indicated (after multiple observation sessions on separate small groups) whether each of $n = 500$ children exhibited each of $p = 5$ presumed indicators of aggression in a 30-minute observation period of their interactions on a playground. (The resulting data are contained in the file Example_11_1.dat, available at the Web site for this book, with the five items of concern denoted X2 through X6 in that file.) It is of interest to find out whether these five items satisfy the 2PN-model and, if so, to evaluate their discrimination and difficulty parameters. According to the preceding discussion in this section, to respond to these two questions we fit a single-factor analysis model with categorical indicators for the five binary items involved. The pertinent M*plus* input file is as follows (for a detailed discussion regarding the used commands, see Chapter 4) and closely resembles the command file we used for testing unidimensionality of a set of discrete items in Section 7.6 (Chapter 7).

```
TITLE:       FITTING AND TESTING A TWO-PARAMETER NORMAL OGIVE MODEL

DATA:        FILE = EXAMPLE_11_1.DAT;

VARIABLE:    NAMES = X1-X6;
             USEVARIABLES = X2-X6;
             CATEGORICAL = X2-X6;

MODEL:       F1 BY X2* X3-X6;
             F1@1;
```

The only new feature in this input file relative to the corresponding one in Section 7.6 is the selection of variables to be analyzed. This is achieved by using the USEVARIABLES subcommand of the DATA command, which is followed by a list of the names of the items to be actually analyzed (note also their declaration next as 'CATEGORICAL' dependent variables). Also, we prepare the grounds of our subsequent work in this section by freeing in the MODEL section all factor loadings and fixing the latent variance at 1, which is the typical scale setting used in IRT. We will refer to this model as 'full model' in the rest of this Subsection 11.4.5. This model yields the following output:

```
INPUT READING TERMINATED NORMALLY

FITTING A TWO-PARAMETER NORMAL OGIVE MODEL

SUMMARY OF ANALYSIS

Number of groups                                          1
Number of observations                                 500
Number of dependent variables                            5
Number of independent variables                          0
Number of continuous latent variables                    1
```

```
Observed dependent variables

  Binary and ordered categorical (ordinal)
    X2             X3             X4             X5             X6

Continuous latent variables
    F1

Estimator                                                     WLSMV
Maximum number of iterations                                   1000
Convergence criterion                                     0.500D-04
Maximum number of steepest descent iterations                   20
Parameterization                                             DELTA

Input data file(s)
    EXAMPLE_11_1.DAT

Input data format FREE

SUMMARY OF CATEGORICAL DATA PROPORTIONS

    X2
       Category 1    0.412
       Category 2    0.588
    X3
       Category 1    0.432
       Category 2    0.568
    X4
       Category 1    0.436
       Category 2    0.564
    X5
       Category 1    0.410
       Category 2    0.590
    X6
       Category 1    0.400
       Category 2    0.600
```

The last output section presents the sample proportions of correct responses on each item (i.e., the empirical proportions of demonstrating play aggression aspects that each of the items is concerned with). The section immediately before it indicates use of the weighted least squares method for model fitting and parameter estimation purposes (e.g., Muthén, 1984; Muthén & Muthén, 2010). This method is invoked when one wishes to fit a set of probit regressions relating the observed items to the assumed underlying single factor in this model (see Equations (11.15)).

```
THE MODEL ESTIMATION TERMINATED NORMALLY

TESTS OF MODEL FIT

Chi-Square Test of Model Fit

              Value                           7.629*
              Degrees of Freedom                 5**
              P-Value                         0.1779
```

*   The chi-square value for MLM, MLMV, MLR, ULSMV, WLSM and WLSMV cannot
    be used for chi-square difference tests. MLM, MLR and WLSM chi-square
    difference testing is described in the Mplus Technical Appendices at
    www.statmodel.com. See chi-square difference testing in the index of
    the Mplus User's Guide.

** The degrees of freedom for MLMV, ULSMV and WLSMV are estimated
    according to a formula given in the Mplus Technical Appendices at www.
    statmodel.com. See degrees of freedom in the index of the Mplus User's
    Guide.

Chi-Square Test of Model Fit for the Baseline Model

```
            Value                              120.990
            Degrees of Freedom                       9
            P-Value                             0.0000
```

CFI/TLI

```
            CFI                                  0.977
            TLI                                  0.958
```

Number of Free Parameters 10

RMSEA (Root Mean Square Error Of Approximation)

```
            Estimate                             0.032
```

WRMR (Weighted Root Mean Square Residual)

```
            Value                                0.610
```

The model fit indexes suggest that the single-factor model can be considered plausible for the analyzed data (see in particular its RMSEA that is well under the widely adopted threshold of .05). Because this model is equivalent to the 2PN-model, we conclude that the latter model—as an IRT model—is plausible for the analyzed data. We can thus move on to examining the parameter estimates associated with it.

MODEL RESULTS

		Estimate	S.E.	Est./S.E.	Two-Tailed P-Value
F1	BY				
X2		0.512	0.080	6.390	0.000
X3		0.502	0.080	6.265	0.000
X4		0.575	0.081	7.072	0.000
X5		0.535	0.082	6.567	0.000
X6		0.307	0.081	3.773	0.000

```
Thresholds
    X2$1          -0.222    0.057          -3.932         0.000
    X3$1          -0.171    0.056          -3.040         0.002
    X4$1          -0.161    0.056          -2.861         0.004
    X5$1          -0.228    0.057          -4.022         0.000
    X6$1          -0.253    0.057          -4.468         0.000

Variances
    F1             1.000    0.000         999.000       999.000
```

IRT PARAMETERIZATION IN TWO-PARAMETER PROBIT METRIC
WHERE THE PROBIT IS DISCRIMINATION*(THETA - DIFFICULTY)

```
Item Discriminations

  F1      BY
    X2             0.596    0.126           4.717         0.000
    X3             0.581    0.124           4.686         0.000
    X4             0.704    0.149           4.730         0.000
    X5             0.634    0.135           4.684         0.000
    X6             0.323    0.095           3.416         0.001

Item Difficulties
    X2$1          -0.435    0.129          -3.365         0.001
    X3$1          -0.341    0.125          -2.730         0.006
    X4$1          -0.280    0.105          -2.674         0.008
    X5$1          -0.425    0.124          -3.440         0.001
    X6$1          -0.824    0.287          -2.873         0.004

Variances
    F1             1.000    0.000           0.000         1.000
```

These output sections provide the item factor loading estimates and those of the pertinent thresholds, τ_g ($g = 1, ..., 5$). (The particular estimates of the thresholds are not of special interest in the current model fitting and interpretation context, except for obtaining the following discrimination and difficulty parameters that the software produces as well.) The item discrimination and difficulty parameter estimates are also presented subsequently, along with their standard errors and z-values. As can be seen, all factor loadings are significant, which suggests that there are marked relationships between each item (probability of 'correct' response) and the underlying trait they are measuring, children aggressiveness at play. The corresponding item discrimination parameters are also significant, suggesting marked ability by each of the items to discriminate between children possessing this trait to a lower degree versus higher degree. Additional pieces of information with respect to local goodness of fit are provided next.

R-SQUARE

Observed Variable	Estimate	Residual Variance
X2	0.262	0.738
X3	0.252	0.748
X4	0.331	0.669
X5	0.287	0.713
X6	0.095	0.905

Accordingly, most items are associated with considerable percentage explained variance, with that on the last item being notably lower. Given that this item is also associated with a markedly lower discrimination parameter (see earlier output section), it may be suggested that it could be worthwhile considering a version of this five-item instrument of aggressivity, which would consist of the first four items only. Whether a researcher working with this measuring instrument would pursue this avenue, however, depends on validity and substantive considerations, as we indicated in earlier chapters when discussing issues related to instrument construction and development (e.g., Chapters 7 and 8). In addition, consideration may well be given then to the possible population relationship among factor loadings (item discrimination parameters), which is examined next.

11.4.5.2 Testing the One-Parameter Normal Ogive Model

We mentioned earlier in this chapter that the 1PN-model is obtained from the 2PN-model after imposing in the latter the restriction of equal discrimination parameters, i.e.,

$$a_1 = a_2 = \cdots = a_p. \tag{11.18}$$

Equation (11.18) is fulfilled if and only if the loadings on the common factor of the corresponding 1F-UNV model (i.e., a single-factor model with categorical indicators) are identical (e.g., Takane & de Leeuw, 1987). Hence, given validity of the 2PN-model, testing the 1PN-model is tantamount to testing equality of factor loadings in the 1F-UNV model. Returning for a moment to our empirical example, because we found that the 2PN-model was plausible, in order to test if the 1PN-model is plausible as well, we need to restrain the factor loadings for equality and evaluate the decrement in fit incurred thereby. (We refer to the resulting model as 'restricted model', because it implements this constraint of equal factor loadings. By way of contrast, as mentioned before, we refer to the model fitted in the preceding Subsection 11.4.5.1 as a 'full' model.) We can accomplish these aims with the following *Mplus* command file:

```
TITLE:     FITTING A ONE-PARAMETER NORMAL OGIVE MODEL
           THIS IS A CONSTRAINED VERSION OF THE LAST FITTED ('FULL') MODEL
           ('RESTRICTED MODEL').

DATA:      FILE = EXAMPLE_11_1.DAT;

VARIABLE:  NAMES = X1-X6;
           USEVARIABLES = X2-X6;
           CATEGORICAL = X2-X6;

MODEL:     F1 BY X2* X3-X6 (1);  ! THIS IS THE CONSTRAINT OF INTEREST
           F1@1;
```

As seen from this command file, the only difference from the input for the previously fitted model, the unrestrained (unrestricted) or full model, is in the MODEL command (other than the title, of course). This command follows formally the same pattern as discussed in Chapter 5 when we fitted the true score equivalence model (TSEM; a model based on classical test theory [CTT] assuming equality of the factor loadings) by constraining all factor loadings to be the same. This input produces the following output (only the changed parts of the output, relative to that of the unrestricted model, are presented next):

TESTS OF MODEL FIT

Chi-Square Test of Model Fit

                    Value   12.630*
                    Degrees of Freedom   8**
                    P-Value   0.1252

*   The chi-square value for MLM, MLMV, MLR, ULSMV, WLSM and WLSMV cannot
    be used for chi-square difference tests. MLM, MLR and WLSM chi-square
    difference testing is described in the Mplus Technical Appendices at
    www.statmodel.com. See chi-square difference testing in the index of
    the Mplus User's Guide.

** The degrees of freedom for MLMV, ULSMV and WLSMV are estimated
   according to a formula given in the Mplus Technical Appendices at www.
   statmodel.com. See degrees of freedom in the index of the Mplus User's
   Guide.

Chi-Square Test of Model Fit for the Baseline Model

                    Value   120.990
                    Degrees of Freedom   9
                    P-Value   0.0000

CFI/TLI

                    CFI   0.959
                    TLI   0.953

Number of Free Parameters   6

RMSEA (Root Mean Square Error Of Approximation)

                    Estimate   0.034

WRMR (Weighted Root Mean Square Residual)

                    Value   0.930

MODEL RESULTS

		Estimate	S.E.	Est./S.E.	Two-Tailed P-Value
F1	BY				
X2		0.487	0.029	16.529	0.000
X3		0.487	0.029	16.529	0.000
X4		0.487	0.029	16.529	0.000
X5		0.487	0.029	16.529	0.000
X6		0.487	0.029	16.529	0.000

```
Thresholds
     X2$1               -0.222      0.057      -3.932            0.000
     X3$1               -0.171      0.056      -3.040            0.002
     X4$1               -0.161      0.056      -2.861            0.004
     X5$1               -0.228      0.057      -4.022            0.000
     X6$1               -0.253      0.057      -4.468            0.000


Variances
     F1                  1.000      0.000     999.000          999.000
```

IRT PARAMETERIZATION IN TWO-PARAMETER PROBIT METRIC
WHERE THE PROBIT IS DISCRIMINATION*(THETA - DIFFICULTY)

```
Item Discriminations
  F1        BY
     X2                  0.558      0.044      12.604            0.000
     X3                  0.558      0.044      12.604            0.000
     X4                  0.558      0.044      12.604            0.000
     X5                  0.558      0.044      12.604            0.000
     X6                  0.558      0.044      12.604            0.000


Item Difficulties
     X2$1               -0.456      0.121      -3.779            0.000
     X3$1               -0.352      0.118      -2.983            0.003
     X4$1               -0.331      0.118      -2.793            0.005
     X5$1               -0.467      0.121      -3.870            0.000
     X6$1               -0.520      0.121      -4.285            0.000


Variances
     F1                  1.000      0.000       0.000            1.000
```

R-SQUARE

Observed Variable	Estimate	Residual Variance
X2	0.237	0.763
X3	0.237	0.763
X4	0.237	0.763
X5	0.237	0.763
X6	0.237	0.763

We fitted this restricted model, which as evidenced by its goodness-of-fit indices (see above chi-square, associated *p*-value, and RMSEA) is a plausible means of data description, in order to test the assumption of equal factor loading—or item discrimination—parameters. How can this testing be actually achieved in the end? The difference in chi-square values is again applicable, but after an important modification is carried out on it (as indicated in the output of the model immediately after presenting the section with its chi-square value; see starred statements by the software). Because we have fitted the full and restricted models not using the maximum likelihood (ML) method but employing instead that of weighted least squares (as we were interested in fitting normal ogive models), we cannot utilize directly the difference in the chi-square values of the more restrictive and less restrictive (full) models. A corrected chi-square difference statistic is applicable instead, which is based on additional data and fit-related information and also implemented in the software used (Muthén & Muthén, 2010). In order to invoke this statistic for our purpose of testing factor loading (item discrimination) parameter equality, we need to refit the full model and request that information to be saved in a file to use subsequently. To this end, all we need to do is utilize the SAVEDATA command at the end of the command file for the full model, giving a name to the file to be saved with the needed statistics. That is, the needed command file is as follows:

```
TITLE:       FITTING A TWO-PARAMETER NORMAL OGIVE MODEL, PREPARING
             FOR A SUBSEQUENT TEST OF PARAMETER CONSTRAINT
             THIS COMMAND FILE IS IDENTICAL TO THAT OF THE FULL MODEL,
             WITH THE ONLY ADDITION OF THE SAVEDATA COMMAND AT THE END.

DATA:        FILE = EXAMPLE_11_1.DAT;

VARIABLE:    NAMES = X1-X6;
             USEVARIABLES = X2-X6;
             CATEGORICAL = X2-X6;

MODEL:       F1 BY X2* X3-X6;
             F1@1;

SAVEDATA:    DIFFTEST = DERIV.DAT;
```

This command file does not produce any new results that we have not already discussed (see Subsection 11.4.5.1 on testing the 2PN-model, i.e., the full model). Rather, as mentioned in the preceding paragraph, it only prepares the grounds for conducting the corrected difference in chi-square test in order to examine the factor equality constraint of interest in the current subsection. To conduct this restriction test, we use next the same command file for the restricted model but indicate to the software in the added ANALYSIS command where to find the relevant statistics in order to proceed with this test:

```
TITLE:       FITTING A ONE-PARAMETER NORMAL OGIVE MODEL
             TESTING EQUALITY OF FACTOR LOADING (ITEM
             DISCRIMINATION) PARAMETERS.
             THIS COMMAND FILE IS IDENTICAL TO THAT OF THE
             RESTRICTED MODEL, WITH THE ONLY DIFFERENCE BEING THE
             ADDED ANALYSIS COMMAND.

DATA:        FILE = EXAMPLE_11_1.DAT;

VARIABLE:    NAMES = X1-X6;
             USEVARIABLES = X2-X6;
             CATEGORICAL = X2-X6;

ANALYSIS:    DIFFTEST = DERIV.DAT;

MODEL:       F1 BY X2* X3-X6 (1);
             F1@1;
```

This command file produces the same results as the restricted model fitted earlier in this Subsection 11.4.5.2, with the only difference being that the outcome of the test of parameter restriction of interest is now additionally provided. That section is as follows:

```
Chi-Square Test for Difference Testing

          Value                              6.487
          Degrees of Freedom                   4**
          P-Value                            0.1656
```

The result suggests that the tested null hypothesis of equal factor loading (item discrimination) parameters can be considered plausible. This finding allows us to conclude that the five items of aggressiveness exhibit the same relationship to the underlying latent trait, children aggression at play, and are thus associated with the same discrimination parameters. That is, they discriminate equally well among children who are low and those who are high on the studied trait. Given this result, we now revisit the item difficulty parameter estimates in the output associated with the restricted model, which we found above to be also plausible overall for the analyzed data. For completeness of the present discussion, we restate that output section again next and comment on it subsequently:

```
Item Discriminations

 F1        BY
    X2                0.558      0.044      12.604      0.000
    X3                0.558      0.044      12.604      0.000
    X4                0.558      0.044      12.604      0.000
    X5                0.558      0.044      12.604      0.000
    X6                0.558      0.044      12.604      0.000

 Item Difficulties
    X2$1             -0.456      0.121      -3.779      0.000
    X3$1             -0.352      0.118      -2.983      0.003
    X4$1             -0.331      0.118      -2.793      0.005
    X5$1             -0.467      0.121      -3.870      0.000
    X6$1             -0.520      0.121      -4.285      0.000
```

From the lower part of this output section, we see that the last item, X6, appears to be the least difficult (in this sample data set), whereas the middle one, X4, is the most difficult.

In conclusion of this section, we note that we tested not only the overall goodness of fit of the restricted IRT model, the 1PN-model, but also the plausibility of its essential assumption, item discrimination parameters being identical. This equality, as indicated earlier in the chapter, may be seen as an essential feature of the 1PN-model. In this context, we recall an earlier instance in Chapter 5 where we did not reject the overall goodness-of-fit hypothesis for the true score equivalent model fitted there, although its essential assumption of factor loading equality was found not to be fulfilled. That finding highlighted the relevance of testing not only overall fit but also essential assumptions in a given model. We followed this generally valid observation (made first in Chapter 5) also in the current Subsection 11.4.5 and applied it to the examination of the 1PN-model. Because we did not reject the hypothesis of equality of factor loading (item discrimination) parameters, we now have more trust in our conclusion that the 1PN-model of concern here is a plausible means of data description and explanation.

11.5 Logistic Models

We mentioned earlier in this chapter that primarily because of relative simplicity of numerical operations and treatment involved in model testing and parameter estimation, over the past 40 years or so logistic models have become very popular in IRT applications. In this section, we discuss three widely utilized logistic models, beginning with the two-parameter logistic model, and show how we can fit two of them employing the factor analysis framework we used in the preceding Section 11.4. We will progress through the following discussion in complete analogy to the developments in the last one dealing with normal ogive models.

11.5.1 The Two-Parameter Logistic Model (2PL-Model)

The model that most closely resembles the 2PN-model is the two-parameter logistic model, abbreviated 2PL-model. This model is the 'same' as the 2PN-model, with the only difference being that the logistic function rather than the normal ogive underlies it. Hence, in order to introduce the 2PL-model, we commence again with the probability of correct response on a given item (say, the gth, $g = 1, \ldots, p$; see Equation (11.7) that is essentially repeated next):

$$P_g(\theta) = \int_{-\infty}^{z} \psi(v)\,dv = \int_{-\infty}^{z} \frac{e^v}{(1+e^v)^2}\,dv = \text{Logistic}(z), \quad (11.19)$$

where

$$\text{Logistic}(z) = 1/(1 + e^{-z})$$

denotes the standard logistic function (Chapter 10). From Equation (11.19), via taking inverse, we obtain

$$z = \text{Logistic}^{-1}(P_g(\theta)) = logit(P_g(\theta)) = z(\theta), \quad (11.20)$$

that is, z depends on θ, with this fact being expressed in the last part of Equation (11.20). The 2PL-model now assumes, in complete analogy with the 2PN-model, that this dependence of z on θ is described by the following relationship:

$$z = a(\theta - b). \quad (11.21)$$

In other words, the 2PL-model explicates—like the 2PN-model did—the found dependence of z on θ, stated in Equation (11.20), by assuming the validity of (11.21). To make now the results of fitting a logistic (logit) model to data as similar as possible to the results from fitting a normal ogive (probit) model, discussed in the preceding Section 11.5, the following change in underlying latent trait scale is introduced:

$$z = Da(\theta - b),$$

where $D = 1.701$ (see Chapter 10; we use in the right-hand side formally the same notation as in (11.21), as is traditional in the literature). With this scale change, the interpretation of a and b in the 2PL-model is the same as that of the identically denoted parameters in the 2PN-model (see preceding section). That is, a is the item discrimination power, whereas b is the item difficulty parameter.

Equations (11.20) and (11.21) now yield for the gth item ($g = 1, \dots, p$)

$$logit(P_g(\theta)) = Da_g(\theta - b_g). \tag{11.22}$$

In a way similar to that followed with the 2PN-model in the preceding Section 11.5, Equation (11.22) is seen to demonstrate that the 2PL-model is (a) a nonlinear factor analysis model based on the logit link and (b) a GLIM with Bernoulli sampling model, logit link, and linear predictor being the linear function of the underlying latent trait θ as represented by the right-hand side of Equation (11.22) (cf. McDonald, 1967a,b, 1999; Wall & Amemiya, 2007). An important numerical simplicity that is introduced by using logistic models in general is that in taking the logistic (i.e., inverse logit) function of both sides of (11.22), one obtains the following explicit expression for the probability of correct response on the gth item ($g = 1, \dots, p$):

$$P_g(\theta) = \frac{e^{Da_g(\theta - b_g)}}{1 + e^{Da_g(\theta - b_g)}}. \tag{11.23}$$

11.5.2 The One-Parameter and Three-Parameter Logistic Models (1PL- and 3PL-Models)

A special case of the 2PL-model is the 1PL-model, which is nested in the 2PL-model and obtained from the latter by imposing the parameter constraint of equal discrimination parameters across items (the same restriction that yielded the 1PN-model from the 2PN-model in the preceding section):

$$a_1 = a_2 = \dots = a_p = a, \text{ say.} \tag{11.24}$$

The 1PL-model can be viewed as equivalent to the well-known *Rasch model*, named after a famous Danish statistician who developed it using a different rationale in the 1960s.

When this model is correct in a given setting, it follows that all its items have the same discrimination power. Hence, like the case with the 2PN-model, their ICCs are parallel in their central parts and are obtained from one another via a translation—to the right or to the left along the horizontal axis—by as many units as the difference in their difficulty parameters is (see also Note 2 to this chapter). That is, the 1PL-model postulates that for a given item, the logit of the probability of a correct answer is

$$logit(P(\theta)) = \theta - b,$$

where the constant D and the common discrimination parameter a have been absorbed into a single unit of measurement, and the same notation is used as is traditional in the literature—the scale of this quantity is simply its 'old' one, as pertinent to the 2PL-model, rescaled by 1.701 (see Equation (11.25) below; b in the last equation is a symbol for the rescaled in this way 'old' difficulty parameter). Taking now the inverse of the logit, viz., the logistic function, from both sides of the last equation, shows that in the 1PL-model the probability of obtaining a correct response on a given item (say, the gth, $g = 1, ..., p$) is

$$P_g(\theta) = \frac{e^{(\theta - b_g)}}{1 + e^{(\theta - b_g)}}. \tag{11.25}$$

Alternatively, a generalization of the 2PL-model is applicable in contexts where guessing is possible. In those settings, a person not having the knowledge allowing him or her to determine the correct answer may elect to guess it. This is in particular possible with multiple-choice items. In such cases, the generalization of the 2PL-model incorporates an added parameter, the probability of guessing the right answer by individuals with very low values of θ. This parameter, also referred to as the pseudo-guessing parameter, is often denoted c ($0 < c < 1$) and involved in an essential way in the pertinent logistic model that is therefore called a 3PL-model. According to the 3PL-model, the probability of correct response on the gth item is

$$P_g(\theta) = c_g + (1 - c_g) \frac{e^{Da_g(\theta - b_g)}}{1 + e^{Da_g(\theta - b_g)}}, \tag{11.26}$$

$g = 1, ..., p$. An example ICC curve for an item following this model, in case $c = .2$, is given in Figure 11.4. We note that unlike the ICCs for an item following any of the models discussed thus far in this chapter, the lower asymptote of the ICC is the c parameter (e.g., .2 in the example in Figure 11.5) rather than 0.

At this point, it is worth noting that the right-hand side of Equation (11.26) can be obtained with the so-called law of total probability, which is discussed in detail in introductory statistics texts (e.g., Agresti & Finlay, 2009). This law states that if an event A can occur in connection with, say, q ($q > 1$) mutually exclusive events, $B_1, B_2, ..., B_q$, and in no other way, then the probability of A occurring is the sum of the probabilities of A occurring together with any of these events $B_1, B_2, ..., B_q$:

$$Pr(A) = Pr(A\&B_1) + P(A\&B_2) + \cdots + Pr(A\&B_q), \tag{11.27}$$

where Pr(.) denotes probability of the event in parentheses and the symbol '&' is used to denote intersection of events (i.e., their joint occurrence). Equation (11.27) is specialized

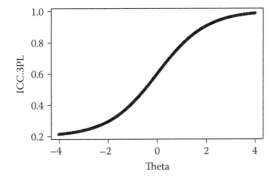

FIGURE 11.5
ICC for an item following a 3PL-model with pseudo-guessing parameter $c = .2$.

with $q = 2$ mutually exclusive events to the following one that will be of relevance next:

$$\Pr(A) = \Pr(A\&B_1) + \Pr(A\&B_2) = \Pr(A\&B_1) + \Pr(A|B_2).\Pr(B_2), \qquad (11.28)$$

where '|' denotes conditional probability (assuming $\Pr(B_2) > 0$), and in the right-hand side we have further expressed $\Pr(A\&B_2)$ as $\Pr(A|B_2).\Pr(B_2)$ according to the definition of conditional probability (Agresti & Finlay, 2009).

Returning to the 3-PL model in Equation (11.26), it is readily realized that a correct response on a given item can occur in two ways. One, it can happen when guessing, and two, it can happen when no guessing is involved. (If one wishes to be more formal, one may invoke here the first interpretation of probability of correct response on a given item, which we dealt with at the beginning of this chapter.) Hence, the probability of correct response can be obtained now from the right-hand side of Equation (11.28). Indeed, one can use here the two mutually exclusive events B_1 = 'guessing' (with an assumed positive probability) and B_2 = 'not guessing'. With them, from Equation (11.28) it follows that

$$\Pr(\text{correct answer}) = \Pr(\text{guessing \& correct answer}) + \Pr(\text{not guessing \& correct answer}).$$
$$(11.29)$$

Although the first probability in the right-hand side of (11.29) is c, the second probability is, from Equation (11.28),

$$\Pr(\text{correct answer \& not guessing}) = \Pr(\text{not guessing}) \Pr(\text{correct answer}|\text{not guessing}).$$

Hence, upon substitution of the involved probabilities, one obtains finally from Equation (11.29) the following equality:

$$P(\theta) = c + (1-c)\frac{e^{Da_g(\theta - b_g)}}{1 + e^{Da_g(\theta - b_g)}}, \qquad (11.30)$$

which is the same as Equation (11.26).

11.5.3 Fitting One- and Two-Parameter Logistic Models

As was the case with the 1PN- and 2PN-models, fitting and testing their counterpart logistic models can be accomplished using the latent variable modeling (LVM) methodology. To this end, one can fit the 1F-UNV model, specifying a single factor and categorical observed variables (items) and requesting application of the maximum likelihood (ML) method. When transforming resulting parameter estimates into discrimination and/or difficulty parameters for corresponding items, the following inversion formulas can be used (e.g., Kamata & Bauer, 2008; Muthén & Muthén, 2010; see also Raykov, Dimitrov, & Asparouhov, 2010):

$$a_{2PL,g} = a_{1F-UNV,ML,g}/1.701, \; b_{2PL,g} = \frac{\tau_{1F-UNV,ML,g}}{a_{1F-UNV,ML,g}}, \qquad (11.31)$$

where the first subindex attached to the a and b parameters denotes the model they pertain to (i.e., the model they are stemming from), whereas the second subindex on the right-hand side of these two equations indicates that the ML method of estimation is used for the 1F-UNV model ($g = 1, ..., p$). We emphasize that we still fit the same single-factor model for the assumed underlying latent variables X_g^* as for the 1PN- and 2PN-models in the preceding Section 11.4 dealing with them, but as a method of parameter estimation we utilize here ML rather than weighted least squares as with those earlier fitted models ($g = 1, ..., p$).[2]

To illustrate this process, we use the same data as in the preceding section dealing with fitting normal ogive models. According to the discussion here, all we need to do in order to fit the 2PL-model is request a different estimator, maximum likelihood (ML). The needed M*plus* input file is therefore as follows (note the only new command used, ANALYSIS: ESTIMATOR = ML;):

```
TITLE:     FITTING A TWO-PARAMETER LOGISTIC MODEL

DATA:      FILE = EXAMPLE_11_1.DAT;

VARIABLE:  NAMES = X1-X6;
           USEVARIABLES = X2-X6;
           CATEGORICAL = X2-X6;

ANALYSIS:  ESTIMATOR = ML;

MODEL:     F1 BY X2* X3-X6;
           F1@1;
```

This input yields the following output:

```
THE MODEL ESTIMATION TERMINATED NORMALLY

TESTS OF MODEL FIT

Loglikelihood

          H0 Value                          -1651.506

Information Criteria

          Number of Free Parameters              10
          Akaike (AIC)                     3323.013
          Bayesian (BIC)                   3365.159
          Sample-Size Adjusted BIC         3333.418
            (n* = (n + 2) / 24)

Chi-Square Test of Model Fit for the Binary and Ordered Categorical
(Ordinal) Outcomes

          Pearson Chi-Square

          Value                              19.968
          Degrees of Freedom                     21
          P-Value                            0.5233

          Likelihood Ratio Chi-Square

          Value                              20.736
          Degrees of Freedom                     21
          P-Value                            0.4751
```

As in a categorical data analysis context, there are two fit indices here—Pearson's and the likelihood-ratio chi-square values (e.g., Agresti, 2002). They both indicate the model as fitting well (i.e., they indicate it as a tenable model). A somewhat different fitting approach is followed in this analysis, relative to the preceding Section 11.4 on normal ogive model fitting. Specifically, the model is fitted here to the observed response frequencies. The latter represent in a sense the $2^5 = 32$ data points that stem from the cells obtained by 'crossing' the two possible values for a subject to attain on each of the five binary items under consideration. Because the sum of probabilities for obtaining all these 32 possible patterns is 1, and the model has $5 + 5 = 10$ parameters (5 factor loadings and 5 thresholds), its degrees of freedom are df $= 32 - 1 - 5 - 5 = 21$.

```
MODEL RESULTS

                                                            Two-Tailed
                   Estimate        S.E.      Est./S.E.      P-Value
F1        BY
    X2              0.978         0.218        4.497         0.000
    X3              0.939         0.214        4.381         0.000
    X4              1.164         0.260        4.473         0.000
    X5              1.044         0.232        4.498         0.000
    X6              0.520         0.155        3.342         0.001

Thresholds
    X2$1           -0.426         0.112       -3.803         0.000
    X3$1           -0.324         0.109       -2.978         0.003
    X4$1           -0.326         0.117       -2.780         0.005
    X5$1           -0.445         0.115       -3.862         0.000
    X6$1           -0.431         0.098       -4.400         0.000
Variances
F1                  1.000         0.000      999.000       999.000


IRT PARAMETERIZATION IN TWO-PARAMETER LOGISTIC METRIC
WHERE THE LOGIT IS 1.7*DISCRIMINATION*(THETA - DIFFICULTY)

Item Discriminations

F1        BY
    X2              0.575         0.128        4.497         0.000
    X3              0.552         0.126        4.381         0.000
    X4              0.684         0.153        4.473         0.000
    X5              0.614         0.136        4.498         0.000
    X6              0.306         0.091        3.342         0.001

Item Difficulties
    X2$1           -0.436         0.131       -3.320         0.001
    X3$1           -0.345         0.128       -2.703         0.007
    X4$1           -0.280         0.107       -2.627         0.009
    X5$1           -0.426         0.125       -3.408         0.001
    X6$1           -0.829         0.289       -2.869         0.004

Variances
F1                  1.000         0.000        0.000         1.000
```

Using Equations (11.31) on the factor loading and threshold estimates in the first part of the MODEL RESULTS output section, we obtain the item discrimination and difficulty parameters as essentially the same as those reported in its last-presented part (titled 'Item Parameterization').

Similarly to the preceding section, one can fit a 1PL-model using the current LVM approach by imposing the constraint of equal item discrimination parameters. Looking at Equations (11.31), this goal is accomplished in the same way as we did in the preceding section in order to obtain the 1PN-model from the 2PN-model, viz., by imposing the constraint of equal factor loadings in the fitted 1F-UNV model (single-factor model with categorical indicators). The needed (single) M*plus* input file is as follows. (Note that the only command in which it differs from the one needed to fit the 1PN-model is the ANALYSIS: ESTIMATOR = ML; line.)

```
TITLE:      FITTING A ONE-PARAMETER LOGISTIC MODEL

DATA:       FILE = EXAMPLE_11_1.DAT;

VARIABLE:   NAMES = X1-X6;
            USEVARIABLES = X2-X6;
            CATEGORICAL = X2-X6;

ANALYSIS:   ESTIMATOR = ML;

MODEL:      F1 BY X2* X3-X6(1);
            F1@1;
```

This input yields the following output:

```
THE MODEL ESTIMATION TERMINATED NORMALLY

TESTS OF MODEL FIT

Loglikelihood

        H0 Value                     -1654.652

Information Criteria

        Number of Free Parameters          6
        Akaike (AIC)                 3321.304
        Bayesian (BIC)               3346.592
        Sample-Size Adjusted BIC     3327.547
          (n* = (n + 2) / 24)

Chi-Square Test of Model Fit for the Binary and Ordered Categorical
(Ordinal) Outcomes

        Pearson Chi-Square

        Value                         27.512
        Degrees of Freedom                25
        P-Value                       0.3308

        Likelihood Ratio Chi-Square

        Value                         27.028
        Degrees of Freedom                25
        P-Value                       0.3545
```

The 1PL-model is thus tenable, as it is associated with such overall fit indices. We note the likelihood ratio chi-square value that we use next to perform a likelihood ratio test (LRF) in order to evaluate the imposed restriction of factor loadings that produced this model as nested in the 2PL-model. As we recall from earlier discussions in the book, to carry out an LRT one needs to subtract the likelihood ratio chi-square of the full model, i.e., the 2PL-model, from that chi-square value of the restricted model, i.e., the 1PL-model. The LRT statistic is thus $27.028 - 20.736 = 6.292$, which is not significant when judged against the chi-square distribution with $25 - 21 = 4$ degrees of freedom (as the pertinent cutoff is 9.47; e.g., King & Minium, 2003). This result is interpreted as suggesting plausibility of the tested hypothesis of equality of the factor loadings of the five involved items. Hence, from the first equation of (11.31) one infers also plausibility of the hypothesis of equality in item discrimination parameters (because the factor loadings need only to be divided by a constant in order to obtain the item discrimination parameters of the 1PL-model currently under consideration). Given in addition the acceptable overall fit indices associated with the 1PL-model, this plausibility of the loading equality hypothesis suggests that the 1PL-model represents a tenable means of data description and explanation. We turn next to the parameter estimates associated with this model for the presently analyzed data.

```
MODEL RESULTS
                                                        Two-Tailed
                       Estimate     S.E.     Est./S.E.   P-Value
    F1        BY
        X2              0.908      0.077      11.735      0.000
        X3              0.908      0.077      11.735      0.000
        X4              0.908      0.077      11.735      0.000
        X5              0.908      0.077      11.735      0.000
        X6              0.908      0.077      11.735      0.000


    Thresholds
        X2$1           -0.417      0.107      -3.903      0.000
        X3$1           -0.321      0.106      -3.021      0.003
        X4$1           -0.302      0.106      -2.844      0.004
        X5$1           -0.427      0.107      -3.991      0.000
        X6$1           -0.476      0.107      -4.429      0.000


    Variances
        F1              1.000      0.000     999.000    999.000


IRT PARAMETERIZATION IN TWO-PARAMETER LOGISTIC METRIC
WHERE THE LOGIT IS 1.7*DISCRIMINATION*(THETA - DIFFICULTY)


    Item Discriminations


    F1        BY
        X2              0.534      0.046      11.735      0.000
        X3              0.534      0.046      11.735      0.000
        X4              0.534      0.046      11.735      0.000
        X5              0.534      0.046      11.735      0.000
        X6              0.534      0.046      11.735      0.000
```

```
Item Difficulties
    X2$1          -0.460    0.121    -3.791         0.000
    X3$1          -0.354    0.119    -2.968         0.003
    X4$1          -0.332    0.119    -2.800         0.005
    X5$1          -0.470    0.121    -3.871         0.000
    X6$1          -0.524    0.123    -4.267         0.000

Variances
    F1             1.000    0.000     0.000         1.000
```

We also notice from the last part of the output that the item X_6 is the least difficult one (in this sample), whereas X_4 is the most difficult among the five items under consideration.

11.6 Relationships Between Item Response Theory and Classical Test Theory

Throughout this chapter, we have benefited substantially from the factor analysis framework underlying most of the book, while pursuing a number of IRT-specific concerns, such as normal ogive and logistic model fitting and parameter estimation. In addition, this FA-based approach allowed us to easily test the overall fit of the IRT models considered to analyzed data. There are yet further connections between the two frameworks of interest in this chapter, FA and IRT, and specifically between CTT and IRT concepts. (We also note that, because as indicated in Chapter 9 the one-facet design for relative decisions within the generalizability theory framework provides the same results as those obtained from an appropriate CTT-based approach, the connections highlighted next between CTT and IRT concepts would also apply in that specific case.)

To highlight these connections, suppose we knew the scores on a studied latent trait θ for each of a group of individuals (whether in a sample or in a population). Upon receiving data on their responses X_g on a given item, say gth, we could calculate the Pearson product–moment correlation between the item and the latent score, denoted $\rho_g = Corr(X_g, \theta)$ $(g = 1,...,p)$. A correlation of this type is frequently referred to as *biserial correlation*, because one of the variables involved—viz., X_g—is binary whereas the other (the trait or ability θ) is continuous.

The correlation ρ_g is the analogue, and in fact an 'improvement', of a statistic also mentioned in Chapter 4. In the early years of test theory, the so-called item-total correlation, $Corr(X_g, X)$, where $X = X_1 + X_2 + \cdots + X_p$ is the score on the test consisting of the items X_1 through X_p, was used quite frequently to study how an item X_g contributes to the total test score, X (cf. Raykov & Mels, 2009). The latter Pearson product–moment correlation is nowadays viewed as providing only limited information about the gth item, but until the 1970s or so it was employed quite often in instrument construction applications. This correlation, $Corr(X_g, X)$, purports to inform about ρ_g, yet can be a seriously biased estimate of the latter because X_g is only a coarse indicator of θ $(g = 1,...,p)$. The biserial correlation between trait and item, ρ_g, is useful in showing that if the latent trait is standard normally distributed, the discrimination parameter a_g of the gth item is an increasing function of ρ_g $(g = 1,...,p)$ (e.g., Lord, 1980). In particular, the following instructive relation holds:

$$a_g = \frac{\rho_g}{\sqrt{1-\rho_g^2}}. \tag{11.32}$$

From Equation (11.32) follows that as the item-trait correlation increases toward 1, the discrimination parameter grows without limit, and the ICC becomes steeper and steeper. Conversely, as this correlation decreases toward 0, so does that parameter, and hence the corresponding ICC becomes flatter. In addition, it can be shown that under the same assumption (Lord, 1980),

$$b_g = \frac{-\Phi^{-1}(p_g)}{\rho_g} = \frac{-probit(p_g)}{\rho_g} \tag{11.33}$$

holds, where p_g is the proportion correct responses—often also referred to as (classical) item difficulty or alternatively item easiness—of the gth item ($g = 1, ..., p$; see also Note 2 to this chapter and Chapters 2 and 4). Equations (11.32) and (11.33) thus demonstrate very insightful relationships between major IRT concepts, such as item discrimination and difficulty parameters, on the one hand, and item-trait correlation as well as proportion correct response, on the other hand, that are closely related to classical item analysis notions (e.g., Chapter 4).

This connection between IRT and CTT extends across other concepts from both frameworks. In particular, the relationship between a true score T corresponding to the sum score X from a set of binary items X_1 through X_p, on the one hand, and the probabilities of correct response on them, on the other, is given as follows (e.g., Crocker & Algina, 1986; Lord, 1980):

$$T = \sum_{g=1}^{p} P_g(\theta) = T(\theta), \tag{11.34}$$

where the last part of the equation emphasizes that the true score T is a function of the ability or trait θ. Equation (11.34) demonstrates that the true score T corresponding to the observed score of number correct responses (often also referred to as 'number correct score') is a nonlinear deterministic function of the latent trait θ. The function given in Equation (11.34) maps any value of the latent trait (ability) into the true score T pertaining to number correct score on the test (set of items, scale, instrument). For this reason, this function is called the *test-characteristic curve* (TCC). We see from Equation (11.34) that the TCC is the sum of the ICCs of the p involved items.

A second look at Equation (11.34) lets us realize that the true score on the test is actually a sum of the true scores on each of the items (this can also be seen alternatively when using the special case of (11.34) for $p = 1$):

$$T = \sum_{g=1}^{p} P_g(\theta) = \sum_{g=1}^{p} T_g(\theta) = T(\theta),$$

where $T_g(\theta) = P_g(\theta)$ denotes the true score on the gth item of an individual with ability level θ. This relationship can be seen from the fact that the true score of the measure X_g, i.e., the gth item, is defined as the mean of the random variable representing the response on this item (e.g., Chapter 5); yet, as mentioned already on a number of occasions (e.g., Chapter 10), this mean is the probability of correct response on the item ($g = 1, ..., p$).

The relationship in (11.34) is true regardless of the ICC underlying an IRT model (as long as X_g is binary, e.g., 0 for incorrect response and 1 for a correct response; $g = 1, ..., p$). In other words, for a given examinee with a trait level θ_i, his or her true score on the composite (sum score) consisting of the g binary items $X_1, X_2, ..., X_p$ is thus

$$T_i = \sum_{g=1}^{p} P_g(\theta_i) \tag{11.35}$$

($i = 1, ..., n$, with n being the number of studied individuals). We stress that all p items considered need not be binary in format but only that their responses be coded (scored) as binary in order for (11.35) to obtain. (That is, they can be, for example, questions with more than two answers, as long as it is known which of them is correct.)

Using the familiar CTT equation $X = T + E$ (Chapter 5), from Equation (11.35) one obtains the relationship between individual observed score on the set of items (test), X_1 through X_p, and underlying latent trait as follows:

$$X_i = \sum_{g=1}^{p} P_g(\theta_i) + E_i \tag{11.36}$$

($i = 1, ..., n$). Because the error term in the right-hand side of (11.36) is a random variable itself, from that equation it follows that the relationship between trait and observed test score is *stochastic* (i.e., nondeterministic, statistical), rather than deterministic like that between true score and ability, as reflected in Equation (11.35).

Given this stochastic relationship, it is meaningful to ask what its strength is. In nonlinear regression, which is closely related to Equations (11.34) through (11.36) (and generally to IRT that can be viewed as nonlinear regression with unobserved predictor or predictors in case of multidimensional IRT), relationship strength is quantified by the so-called nonlinear correlation coefficient (cf. Crocker & Algina, 1986). The latter is defined as

$$\eta_{X.\theta} = \sqrt{1 - \frac{E_\theta[Var(X|\theta)]}{Var(X)}}, \tag{11.37}$$

where $Var(X|\theta)$ is the variance of X for a homogeneous subpopulation of subjects with a given value of the latent trait (all with the same value of it), and $E_\theta(.)$ denotes the expectation (averaging) of that variance with regard to all θ in the overall studied subject population. (We note that $Var(X|\theta)$ depends on θ, so taking its mean with regard to the distribution of θ is a meaningful activity.) Equation (11.37) is a generalization of the formula for multiple correlation in conventional regression analysis to the case of nonlinear regression. We observe in passing that when the ordinary least squares assumptions are fulfilled, for instance, the square of the right-hand side of Equation (11.37) yields as a special case the defining expression for the square-rooted R^2 index in a simple regression model.

Because of the fact that the relationship between latent trait and true score is deterministic, as we saw above, it follows that $Var(X|\theta) = Var(E|\theta)$. This is because for a given θ the variability in X stems only from that in the error term, because once θ is fixed so is the corresponding true score T as well, by virtue of Equation (11.35). Finally, it can also be shown that $E_\theta[Var(E|\theta)] = Var(E)$, the common error variance in CTT (cf., e.g., Crocker & Algina, 1986; Roussas, 1997; see also Chapter 5 for a discussion on the latter variance). Hence, the strength of relationship between X and θ is

$$\eta_{X.\theta} = \sqrt{1 - \frac{Var(E)}{Var(X)}} = \sqrt{1 - \frac{\sigma_E^2}{\sigma_X^2}}. \tag{11.38}$$

The last is, however, the reliability index, as we know from the pertinent discussion in Chapter 6.

This section demonstrated yet another way in which a CTT concept—viz., reliability—can be directly related to IRT-based ones. In particular, within an IRT context, Equations (11.37) and (11.38) show that the reliability coefficient is a function of the average of the relative degree to which observed scores scatter around a deterministic function of fixed levels of the latent trait, whereby this average is taken as those levels are subsequently allowed to cover the entire space of possible values for them, i.e., the set Θ of values for the studied trait or ability (see Chapter 10). All these close connections between CTT and IRT, although not direct and straightforward (in particular, not 'linear'), in addition to our discussion in Chapter 10 on nonlinear factor analysis and related issues, demonstrate the relevance of the fundamental ideas of factor analysis also for a fairly large part of the IRT framework.

Notes

1. The ICCs for two items following the 1PN-model, with distinct difficulty parameters, are technically parallel throughout the entire set of real numbers, because there are no points where they intersect (as can be shown mathematically by solving the equation relating their probability for correct response in terms of underlying parameters). The current paragraph uses the word 'parallel' instead in an informal, graphical sense. (The motivation for this use is the fact that the appearance of approximation of one ICC by the other ICC at lower and higher values of the trait θ, as depicted in the corresponding Figure 11.4—see their lower-left and upper-right corners—may challenge one's possibly usual imagination of parallel curves as staying at the same distance apart regardless of the value of the theta parameter. Yet two ICCs do not need to be the same distance apart across the entire parameter space, i.e., set of possible values for the trait θ, in order for these curves to be parallel in this sense.)

2. The right-hand side of the second equation in (11.31) shows that up to the gth factor loading of the 1F-UNV model, the item difficulty parameter is a function of the proportion correct response (because the threshold is the z-value pertaining to proportion correct responses; e.g., Kamata & Bauer, 2008; Muthén, 1984). (This allows us to view the 'two' item difficulty parameters as related in this 'monotonically increasing' fashion, other things being equal; see also Equation (11.33) for a formalization of this relationship.)

Appendix: A Brief Introduction to Some Graphical Applications of R in Item Response Modeling

This appendix aims to introduce some graphical features of the widely available software R, which are highly useful in the context of behavioral measuring instrument-related modeling using IRT as well as a number of other topics (e.g., graphical representation of various functions). This appendix, which may be viewed as a continuation of Section 2.8 (Chapter 2), only touches upon what R can accomplish in terms of graphics and is simply intended to familiarize readers with several commands that can be readily used for the purpose of representing item characteristic curves (ICCs) in IRT (and functions of many types of empirical relevance in social and behavioral research). We will then also describe how to produce a scree-plot and compute percentage explained variance by a given number of factors (principal components). As it will be recalled from Chapter 4, the scree-plot is particularly useful in exploratory factor analysis (EFA), as is the percentage explained variance by the first n eigenvalues ($n = 1, 2, \ldots, p$, with p being the number of analyzed variables). As one becomes more familiar with R, one will find out further additional subcommands for those below that provide more informative axis labeling, figure titles, plotting symbol/character options, etc. This appendix provides sufficient instruction, however, to display ICCs and scree-plots in an informative way. In the remainder of this appendix, we are using object names that aim at being most informative, but they can be also alternatively chosen. (That is, none of the names appearing in the left-hand side of an equation below, which is entered at the R prompt, is a reserved name for a function of relevance.)

A.1 Producing a 'Grid' for a Figure

We begin with a command producing the 'grid' (or 'net' on the horizontal axis) for a figure representing a function of interest, such as an ICC. This command furnishes a large set of points that are successively positioned very close to one another within a specified interval on the real line. At these points one can calculate, also with R, the values of any function of interest (for which there is a close-form expression; we assume that we are dealing only with such functions of single arguments in this appendix—any function of this type can be represented using an explicit formula in terms of that argument). In the rest of the appendix, we are preceding the presentation of any command by the R prompt, at which one should type the command. (As mentioned earlier in this book, the R prompt, >, appears in red on the computer screen, and what is given below after that prompt sign is what one needs to type in at it and then press 'enter'; see Section 2.8 in Chapter 2.)

The command that produces the 'grid' of a function we would like to obtain later is as follows:

```
> x = seq(-4,4,.005)
```

This command creates an array (i.e., a set of scores) **x** that consists of the sequence of numbers ranging from −4 to +4 at a distance of .005 units successively apart from one another. (We are emboldening arrays in this appendix in order to make them stand out from the remaining text.) At each of these values we compute next those of a function of interest. We use the scale limits of −4 and 4 because practically all standard normal random variable realizations lie within them, with very few exceptions for very large samples that need not be of particular importance here. (We can assume, as usually done in applications of IRT, that a latent trait of relevance in an IRT model considered in this book follows this distribution—at least approximately—within a population of interest.) We stress that the array **x** is unidimensional, i.e., consists of numbers positioned equal distances (viz., .005 units) successively from one another along the real line, the set of all real numbers. (Looked at from an alternative viewpoint, an array is obviously a vector; see Chapter 2.)

A.2 Viewing and Plotting One-Dimensional Arrays (Sets/Sequences of Numbers)

There are two ways to view what one has created with the last command. In the first, one just requests from R the reproduction of all elements of **x**. This is done by merely typing

```
> x
```

As a response, R displays all 1,601 numbers contained in the above array **x**. (There are as many points of the grid we created with the second-last command.) We are listing next only the beginning and final few of them to save space. (As throughout this book, we are presenting R output in a font different from the text font, with the symbol '...' standing for the omitted numbers from the actual output.)

```
[1]  -4.000 -3.995 -3.990 -3.985 -3.980 -3.975 -3.970 -3.965 -3.960 -3.955
[11] -3.950 -3.945 -3.940 -3.935 -3.930 -3.925 -3.920 -3.915 -3.910 -3.905
...
[1601] 4.000
```

Listing such a long set (array) of numbers is not very helpful. (As mentioned earlier, the numbers within brackets indicate only the running index of the next number; e.g., [11] means that immediately next—in the same line—is the 11th consecutive member of **x**, viz., -3.95.) An easier way to look at them is to produce their plot, i.e., the graph of each member of **x** against its own running number (referred to as 'index' below) within the array. This is accomplished with the following command:

```
> plot(x)
```

This causes R to open a new graphics window in which the plot of **x** is provided, which we include in Figure A.1.

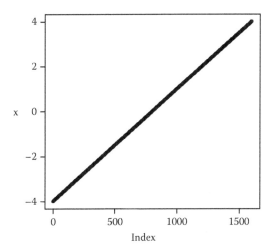

FIGURE A.1
Plot of the array **x**.

A.3 Plotting the Normal Ogive and Logistic Functions

Next, suppose one were interested in graphing the normal ogive, which as discussed in Chapters 10 and 11 underlies the 1PN- and 2PN-models. To this end, let's first calculate the values of the normal ogive. To achieve this, we assign to the array NORMAL.OGIVE the values of the normal ogive across all values contained in the above grid sequence (array **x**), using the following command:

```
> NORMAL.OGIVE = pnorm(x)
```

The command in the right-hand side of the last line produces the values of the cumulative distribution function (CDF) of the standard normal, for each and every element of the set **x** (array **x**), in the same order as those of **x**. Hence, using the last-stated command, we produced the values of the normal ogive for all scores in the array **x** of interest to us. We can look at them by simply entering

```
> NORMAL.OGIVE
```

but this will not be particularly revealing (as we observed above with regard to the array **x**). Alternatively, we could present them graphically on their own, by using the command

```
> plot(NORMAL.OGIVE)
```

Even this will not be very informative, however, because we are interested not in these numbers themselves but only in their connection to their corresponding numbers in the array **x**. This connection is exposed by graphing the array NORMAL.OGIVE against the array **x**. To this end, we use the following command:

```
> plot(x, NORMAL.OGIVE)
```

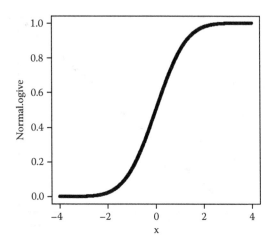

FIGURE A.2
Graph of the normal ogive (cumulative distribution function of the standard normal distribution).

We stress that so far in this Section A.3 we have been referring to the array NORMAL. OGIVE using capital letters. This is an essential feature of R—it is a case-sensitive software, unlike many other specialized programs (e.g., SAS, SPSS, M*plus*). The result of requesting the last plot is presented in Figure A.2. We observe that it displays the ICC for an item in a 2PN-model.

As a next step, suppose we were interested in graphing the logistic function (corresponding to the standard logistic distribution), as discussed in Chapters 10 and 11. This function underlies the 1PL-, 2PL-, and 3PL-models. To this end, let us calculate the values of the logistic function. We achieve this aim by assigning to the array LOGISTIC.FUNCTION the values of the logistic function across all values contained in the above sequence (array) x, using the following command

```
> LOGISTIC.FUNCTION = 1/(1+exp(-x))
```

Let us graph the result, of course against the pertinent values of the array x. This is accomplished with the command

```
> plot(x, LOGISTIC.FUNCTION)
```

The result is presented in Figure A.3.

We see immediately from Figure A.3 that the curve presented in it looks very similar to that of the normal ogive. As discussed in Chapter 10, the two are nearly indistinguishable if a slight change in the scale underlying the logistic function is employed, viz., its argument is multiplied by $D = 1.701$. Let us see how we can visualize this relationship. To this end, we first compute the values of the logistic function in this 'new' scale. This is done with the following command (using the symbol '*' for multiplication, as will be recalled):

```
> LOGISTIC.FUNCTION=1/(1+exp(-1.701*x))
```

Next, we plot the normal ogive and the last logistic function on the same graph. This is accomplished by first plotting any of them and then overlaying its graph with that of the other function. (Note that we are using the same array x as a 'grid' for any of these

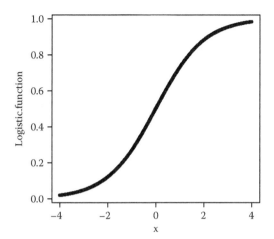

FIGURE A.3
Graph of the cumulative distribution function of the standard logistic function (logistic function).

functions.) Let us use thereby different colors (on the computer screen). Here's how it can be done. First plot, say, the normal ogive in green:

```
> plot(x, NORMAL.OGIVE, col = "green")
```

(Note the added argument, color, of the plot command, followed by the requested color placed within inverted commas.) The resulting graph is identical to that in Figure A.2, with the only difference being that the actual curve is in green on the screen. Let us keep the picture and move on to the next one that is an overlay on it. To superimpose another graph on an existing one, immediately after producing the latter we use the following command:

```
> lines(x, LOGISTIC.FUNCTION, col = "red")
```

This furnishes Figure A.4, where we note how close the two curves are.

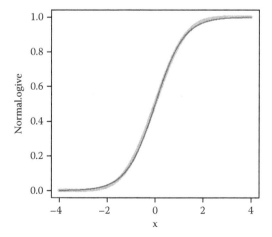

FIGURE A.4
Simultaneous graph of a normal ogive (thick curve) and standard logistic function (with appropriately changed scale; thin curve).

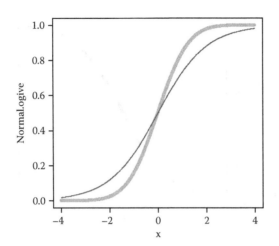

FIGURE A.5
Simultaneous graph of the normal ogive (thick curve) and standard logistic function (without change in under-lying scale for the latter; thin curve).

We can easily do the same but without changing the scale of the logistic function like above. The result is given in Figure A.5.

We notice that the two curves intersect at the point (0, .5). (This can be shown math-ematically by solving the equation relating the two pertinent integrals presented in Chapter 11—one can do it by differentiating both sides of that equation and then solving the resulting equation.)

A.4 Plotting Item Characteristic Curves Pertaining to Normal Ogive Models

So far in the appendix we have not dealt with any particular IRT model and its ICCs, which is the aim here. To accomplish it, first let us get a handle on the situation by graphing the ICC of a particular normal ogive model, say. Suppose we were interested in a 2PN-model for a given item with discrimination parameter $a = 2$ and difficulty parameter $b = 0$. (We are using $b = 0$ next only to fit the central part of the ICC within the resulting figure, given our already-created array x. The essence of the following procedure is applicable with any difficulty parameter b, however. As an aside, recall that $b = 0$ means not that the item has no difficulty at all but that in the chosen scale for it—with an arbitrary origin and unit in general—the difficulty parameter of this item happens to coincide with the previously selected origin point of that scale.)

According to the discussion in Chapter 11, and given that we already have the array x that we now have to treat as containing consecutive scores on the latent trait continuum (i.e., of θ, referred to below as 'theta'), for reference purposes we first assign all values of the array x to the array **theta**. (This is not essential or even needed, but it will make the resulting graph more easily interpretable within an IRT context.)

```
> theta = x
```

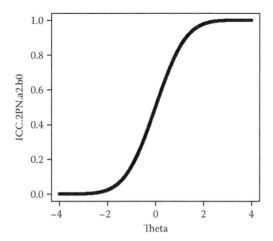

FIGURE A.6
ICC for an item following a 2PN-model with discrimination parameter $a = 2$ and difficulty parameter $b = 0$.

Next we need to produce the values of the ICC for the model chosen for the item under consideration. This is done as follows (note the name of the new array), using the definition of the 2PN-model from Chapter 11 and relevant parts from the preceding discussion in this appendix.

```
> ICC.2PN.a2.b0 = pnorm(2*x)
```

To plot this ICC, we use the command

```
> plot(theta, ICC.2PN.a2.b0)
```

The result is in Figure A.6.
Let us see what the effect is of increasing the discrimination parameter, overlaying the last figure with the ICC of an item with the same class ICC but a discrimination parameter $a = 4$. All we need to do is use the following command:

```
> lines(theta, pnorm(4*x), col="blue")
```

The result is in Figure A.7.
We note that the added thin ICC intersects the thick ICC depicted in Figure A.6, at the point (0, .5), as one would expect given the discussion in the preceding section of the appendix. Also we observe that its slope in the central part is much higher than that of the ICC with $a = 2$ that we dealt with immediately before we created the blue ICC. Continuing this process, with a red ICC having $a = 8$, say, Figure A.8 is furnished.

A.4.1 Graphing (an Approximation of) a Step-Function

In this connection, let us return to a statement made in Chapter 11, which asserted that one can obtain an ICC through 'pulling' to the right and to the left the graph of a step function. Using it, how can we produce the graph of the step function? To this end, let us

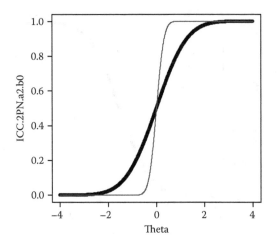

FIGURE A.7
Added ICC (thin curve) for an item following a 2PN-model with discrimination parameter $a = 4$ and difficulty parameter $b = 0$.

first produce an ICC from a probit (or logistic, for the same matter) model with a very large discrimination parameter, say, $a = 40$. This is shown next.

```
> plot(theta, pnorm(40*theta), col="green")
```

Note that the computer could not present the graph really in the central part (because of graphics resolution limits; see Figure A.9).

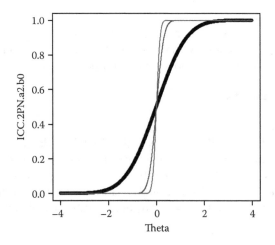

FIGURE A.8
Added ICC (steepest curve) for an item following a 2PN-model with discrimination parameter $a = 8$ and difficulty parameter $b = 0$.

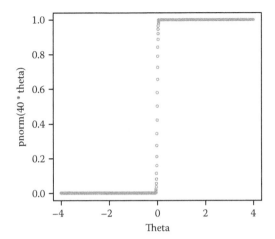

FIGURE A.9
ICC for an item following a 2PN-model with discrimination parameter $a = 40$ and difficulty parameter $b = 0$ (approximating well a step function).

A.5 Graphing ICCs for Logistic Models

Let us now produce the ICCs for items following a 2PL-model with the same parameters as the above ones. First, the following command will produce the ICC for a 2PL-model with parameters $a = 2$ and $b = 0$ (for the same reasons as mentioned in the preceding Section A.4).

```
> ICC.2PL.a2.b0 = 1/(1+exp(2*(-theta)))
> plot(theta, ICC.2PL.a2.b0)
```

The result is in Figure A.10.

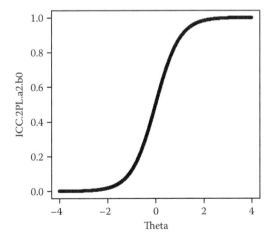

FIGURE A.10
ICC for a logistic model.

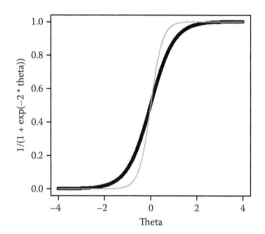

FIGURE A.11
A pair of a logistic model's ICCs.

Let us overlay the curve in Figure A.10 with the ICC for an item following a 2PL-model with $a = 4$ and $b = 0$. (Note next the more economical way of accomplishing this.)

```
> lines(theta, 1/(1+exp(4*(-x))))
```

The result is in Figure A.11, where the thinner line is the added ICC.

Let us next add the ICC for an item following the same model (2PL-model) but with $a = 8$ (and $b = 0$).

```
> lines(theta, 1/(1+exp(-8*theta)))
```

And finally, let us overlay the curves in Figure A.12 with the ICC for $a = 40$ (and $b = 0$), which should pretty well approximate a step function:

```
> lines(theta, 1/(1+exp(-40*theta)))
```

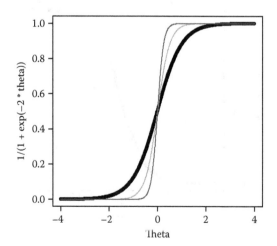

FIGURE A.12
Three ICCs from a logistic model (with the last added being the steepest ICC).

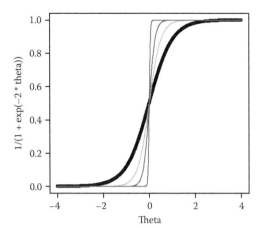

FIGURE A.13
Four ICCs from a logistic model (with the last added being the steepest ICC).

The result is in Figure A.13.

We observe how similar all these four ICCs are, as far as shape is concerned, to their corresponding ones—with the same respective parameters a and b—for the 2PN-model (see preceding Section A.4).

A.6 Producing a Scree-Plot for Exploratory Factor Analysis (Principal Component Analysis), and Calculation of Percentage Explained Variance

To produce a scree-plot, first we need to create the sequence containing the eigenvalues resulting from an exploratory factor analysis or principal component analysis. This is accomplished with the following command ('c' standing for 'concatenate into a vector') for a fictitious example with 10 eigenvalues, say, where 'evalues' is used as the name of an initially defined array (set) containing these eigenvalues:

```
> evalues = c(7, .8, .7, .5, .4, .3, .15, .1, .03, .02)
```

Once we have done so, we need to plot the elements of the vector evalues against their running index as members of this vector. This is achieved as follows ('pch' = 2 asks for using little triangles as plotting symbols to let any underlying pattern emerge more easily):

```
> plot(evalues, pch=2)
```

The result is in Figure A.14.

Note the distinct scree-like profile, with the scree beginning at 2. This suggests considering extracting 1 factor (Chapter 3).

To work out the percentage explained variance by the first eigenvalue (or any number of them), we divide that eigenvalue by the sum of all elements of the vector of eigenvalues. This sum is obtained as follows:

```
> sum(evalues)
```

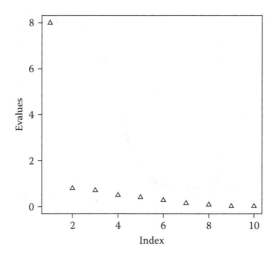

FIGURE A.14
Scree-plot for example with 10 eigenvalues.

For the above set of eigenvalues, this sum is 10. Hence, the percentage explained variance is obtained as follows (recall, 7 was the first eigenvalue):

```
> 7/sum(evalues)
```

This yields 70% explained variance by the first factor. (See Raykov and Marcoulides [2010c] for a latent-variable-modeling-based method allowing one to obtain a confidence interval, at a prespecified confidence level, of this proportion explained variance in a studied population.)

A.7 Conclusion

This appendix showed how the widely available and comprehensive statistical analysis software R can be used as a means for visualizing ICCs that are of fundamental relevance within the framework of IRT, as well as for obtaining scree-plots and calculation of percentage explained variance that is of particular importance when conducting exploratory factor analysis (using, e.g., LVM software as very often employed throughout this book). As indicated above, this appendix was meant only to be a brief introduction to the graphical possibilities of R that are far more comprehensive. In addition, this appendix indicates how to produce readily the graphs of many other functions (available in closed form) that one may be interested in visualizing in empirical behavioral and social research.

Epilogue

This book aimed at providing an introduction to the broad field of psychometric theory. Because of space limitations and the confines of the book, we could not delve in more detail into a number of concepts we discussed, especially in its later part. In addition, we inevitably had to leave out other topics related to those covered. As was made clear from the outset, the major 'working horse' of this text was factor analysis (FA). We started with a discussion of the traditional FA model, which can be viewed as a general linear model with latent predictors (and with vanishing observed variable intercepts, yet we relaxed later this restriction). We showed that FA can be used in a number of instances where various behavioral instrument development concepts and activities are of concern. In particular, one could explore the latent structure of a given test using exploratory FA or alternatively test a hypothesis about that structure using confirmatory FA—of most interest in many of the book chapters being the hypothesis of unidimensionality for the set of measuring instrument components. We then moved on to classical test theory (CTT) and showed how FA could be used to examine a number of interesting models developed based on CTT. Within the framework of CTT, we introduced and discussed important concepts such as reliability and validity and then moved on to generalizability theory. In the last two chapters of this book we introduced item response theory (IRT). Specifically, we discussed a generalization of the FA model used in earlier chapters, leading to a nonlinear FA model (cf. Etezadi-Amoli & McDonald, 1983; McDonald, 1962, 1967b, 1983, 1986, 1999; Wall & Amemiya, 2007). We used for this extension the framework of the generalized linear model (GLIM). We discussed thereby a number of fundamental notions and several models of IRT, using as a general setting the nonlinear FA model within the GLIM approach.

Throughout this book, we assumed that we were not dealing with missing data or with data that are hierarchical in nature. The presence of missing data complicates substantially the discussion of measurement concepts and relationships, and in particular their applications, as does the consideration of hierarchical data. These two topics are the object of more advanced treatments that lie outside of the confines of this text. We hasten to add, however, that under certain assumptions most modeling approaches and procedures used throughout the book can be applied also with missing data (e.g., data missing at random; Little & Rubin, 2002). Extensions of some methods discussed in this book to the case of weighted scale reliability estimation can be found in Raykov (2004), Raykov and Penev (2006, 2009), and Penev and Raykov (2006), while extensions to the case of two-level data are discussed in Raykov and du Toit (2005) and Raykov (2010c; see also Raykov, 2010a, for a possible means to use when it is of concern to select between single-level, two-level, or higher-level modeling approaches; cf. Skrondal & Rabe-Hesketh, 2004).

In retrospect, we hope to have succeeded in showing how useful the factor analysis model is, particularly when appropriately extended and generalized if need be. In our view, it is indeed gratifying to realize that so much in present-day psychometric theory and its utilizations can be traced back to the very powerful ideas of factor analysis, now more than 100 years old (or young), and what could be viewed as its present-day generalization, latent variable modeling. The latter is readily available to behavioral, social, and educational scientists as well as economists and business, marketing, and biomedical scholars for modeling and measuring instrument development purposes (among many others) with the increasingly popular program M*plus*. The latter was used as a software platform for most of the book, and some of its applications were also substantially facilitated by applications of the software R—especially for interval estimation (as well as other purposes). Alternatively, latent variable modeling can also be readily carried out using the software GLLAMM (Skrondal & Rabe-Hesketh, 2004) within the popular statistical analysis package STATA, which similarly easily allows extensions to hierarchical data modeling settings (as does M*plus* in many cases as well; e.g., Muthén & Muthén, 2010).

We conclude with the hope that this introductory book on psychometric theory will be helpful to readers in their subsequent journey into more advanced topics of the impressively comprehensive field of measurement and testing in the behavioral and social sciences.

References

Agresti, A. (2002). *Categorical data analysis.* New York: Wiley.

Agresti, A., & Finlay, B. (2009). *Statistical methods for the social sciences* (4th ed.). Upper Saddle River, NJ: Prentice Hall.

Allen, M. J., & Yen, W. M. (1979). *Introduction to measurement theory.* Monterey, CA: Brooks/Cole.

Arteaga, C., Jeyaratnam, S., & Graybill, F. A. (1982). Confidence intervals for proportions of total variance in the two-way cross component of variance model. *Communication in Statistics: Theory and Methods, 11,* 1643–1658.

Asparouhov, T., & Muthén, B. (2008). Multilevel mixture models. In G. R. Hancock & K. M. Samuelsen (Eds.), *Latent variable mixture models.* Charlotte, NC: Information Age Publishing.

Bachman, L. F., Boodoo, G., Linancre, J. M., Lunz, M. E., Marcoulides, G. A., & Myford, C. (1993, April). *Generalizability theory and many-faceted Rasch modeling.* Paper presented at the joint annual meeting of the American Educational Research Association and the National Council on Measurement in Education, Atlanta, GA.

Bachman, L. F., Lynch, B. K., & Mason, M. (1995). Investigating variability in tasks and rater judgments in a performance test of foreign language speaking. *Language Testing, 12,* 238–257.

Baltes, P. B., Dittmann-Kohli, F., & Kliegl, R. (1986). Reserve capacity of the elderly in aging-sensitive tasks of fluid intelligence: Replication and extension. *Psychology and Aging, 1,* 172–177.

Bartholomew, D. (2002). Old and new approaches to latent variable modeling. In G. A. Marcoulides & I. Moustaki (Eds.), *Latent variable and latent structure models* (pp. 1–14). Mahwah, NJ: Lawrence Erlbaum.

Bartholomew, D. J. (2007). Three faces of factor analysis. In R. Cudeck & R. C. MacCallum (Eds.), *Factor analysis at 100* (pp. 9–21). Mahwah, NJ: Lawrence Erlbaum.

Bartholomew, D. J., & Knott, M. (1999). *Latent variable models and factor analysis.* London: Arnold.

Beck, A. T., Rush, A. J., Shaw, B. F., & Emery, G. (1979). *Cognitive therapy of depression.* New York: Guilford.

Bentler, P. M. (2004). *EQS structural equation program manual.* Encino, CA: Multivariate Software.

Bentler, P. M. (2009). Alpha, dimension-free, and model-based internal consistency reliability. *Psychometrika, 74,* 137–144.

Bock, R. D. (1966). Components of variance analysis as a structural and discriminant analysis of psychological tests. *British Journal of Statistical Psychology, 13,* 507–534.

Bock, R. D., & Bargmann, R. E. (1966). Analysis of covariance structures. *Psychometrika, 31,* 507–534.

Bollen, K. A. (1989). *Structural equations with latent variables.* New York: Wiley.

Bollen, K. A., & Curran, P. J. (2006). *Latent curve models.* New York: Wiley.

Bollen, K. A., & Stine, R. A. (1993). Bootstrapping goodness-of-fit measures in structural equation models. In K. A. Bollen & J. S. Long (Eds.), *Testing structural equation models* (pp. 111–135). Thousand Oaks, CA: Sage.

Borsboom, D. (2006). The attack of the psychometricians. *Psychometrika, 71,* 425–440.

Brennan, R. L. (1983). *Elements of generalizability theory.* Iowa City, IA: American College Testing.

Brennan, R. L. (2001). *Generalizability theory.* New York: Springer.

Brennan, R. L., Harris, D. J., & Hanson, B. A. (1987). *The bootstrap and other procedures for examining the variability of estimated variance components in testing contexts* (ACT Research Report 87-7). Iowa City, IA: American College Testing.

Brennan, R. L., & Kane, M. T. (1977). An index of dependability for mastery of tests. *Journal of Educational Measurement, 14,* 277–289.

Browne, M. W. (1982). Covariance structures. In D. M. Hawkins (Ed.), *Topics in applied multivariate analysis* (pp. 72–141). Cambridge, UK: Cambridge University Press.

Browne, M. W. (2001). An overview of analytic rotation in exploratory factor analysis. *Multivariate Behavioral Research, 36,* 111–150.

Browne, M. W., & Cudeck, R. (1993). Alternative ways of assessing model fit. In K. A. Bollen & J. S. Long (Eds.), *Testing structural equation models* (pp. 136–162). Newbury Park, CA: Sage.

Browne, M. W., & Mels, G. (2005). Path analysis (RAMONA). In *SYSTAT 11: Statistics III* [Computer software and manual] (pp. III-1–III-61). Richmond, CA: SYSTAT Software.

Burdick, R. K., & Graybill, F. A. (1992). *Confidence intervals on variance components*. New York: Marcel Dekker.

Burt, C. (1936). The analysis of examination marks. In P. Hartog & E. C. Rhodes (Eds.), *The marks of examiners*. London: Macmillan.

Burt, C. (1947). Factor analysis and analysis of variance. *British Journal of Psychology, 1*, 3–26.

Campbell, D. T., & Fiske, D. W. (1959). Convergent and discriminant validity by the multitrait–multimethod matrix. *Psychological Bulletin, 56*, 81–105.

Cardinet, J., Johnson, S., & Pini, G. (2010). *Applying generalizability theory using EduG*. New York: Routledge.

Cardinet, J., Tourneur, Y., & Allal, L. (1976). The symmetry of generalizability theory: Application to educational measurement. *Journal of Educational Measurement, 13*, 119–135.

Cohen, J., Cohen, P., West, S. G., & Aiken, L. S. (2002). *Applied multiple regression/correlation analysis for the behavioral sciences* (3rd ed.). Mahwah, NJ: Lawrence Erlbaum.

Cornfield, J., & Tukey, J. W. (1956). Average values of mean squares in factorials. *Annals of Mathematical Statistics, 27*, 907–949.

Creasy, M. A. (1957). Some criticisms of factor analysis with suggestions for alternative methods. *Journal of Mental Science, 105*, 755–761.

Crocker, L., & Algina, J. (1986). *Introduction to classical and modern test theory*. Fort Worth, TX: Harcourt College.

Cronbach, L. J. (1951). Coefficient alpha and the internal structure of tests. *Psychometrika, 16*, 297–334.

Cronbach, L. J., Gleser, G. C., Nanda, H., & Rajaratnam, N. (1972). *The dependability of behavioral measurements: Theory of generalizability scores and profiles*. New York: Wiley.

Cronbach, L. J., Rajaratnam, N., & Gleser, G. C. (1963). Theory of generalizability: A liberization of reliability theory. *British Journal of Statistical Psychology, 16*, 137–163.

Cudeck, R. (1989). Analyzing correlation matrices using covariance structure models. *Psychological Bulletin, 105*, 317–327.

Cudeck, R., & MacCallum, R. C. (Eds.). (2007). *Factor analysis at 100* (pp. 315–336). Mahwah, NJ: Lawrence Erlbaum.

Dickinson, T. L. (1987). Designs for evaluating the validity and accuracy of performance ratings. *Organizational Behavior and Human Decision Processes, 40*, 1–21.

Dimitrov, D. M. (2003). Marginal true-score measures and reliability for binary items as a function of their IRT parameters. *Applied Psychological Measurement, 27*, 440–458.

DiStefano, C. (2002). The impact of categorization with confirmatory factor analysis. *Structural Equation Modeling, 9*, 327–346.

Dobson, A. (2002). *An introduction to generalized linear models*. London: Chapman & Hall.

Efron, B. (1982). *The jackknife, the bootstrap, and other resampling plans*. Philadelphia: SIAM.

Efron, B., & Tibshiriani, R. J. (1993). *An introduction to the bootstrap*. London: Chapman Hall/CRC.

Eid, M. (2000). A multitrait–multimethod model with minimal assumptions. *Psychometrika, 65*, 241–261.

Embretson, S. E., & Hershberger, S. L. (1999). *The new rules of measurement: What every psychologist and educator should know*. Mahwah, NJ: Lawrence Erlbaum.

Embretson, S. E., & Reise, S. P. (2000). *Item response theory for psychologists*. Mahwah, NJ: Lawrence Erlbaum.

Endler, L. C. (1998). *Cognitive development in a secondary science setting*. Unpublished thesis, James Cook University, Townsville, Queensland, Australia.

Etezadi-Amoli, J., & McDonald, R. P. (1983). A second generation nonlinear factor analysis. *Psychometrika, 48*, 315–342.

Feldt, L. S. (1965). The approximate sampling distribution of Kuder-Richardson reliability coefficient twenty. *Psychometrika, 30*, 357–370.

Feldt, L. (1969). A test of the hypothesis that Cronbach's alpha or Kuder-Richardson coefficient is the same for two tests. *Psychometrika, 34*, 363–373.

Gessaroli, M. E., & Folske, J. C. (2002). Generalizing the reliability of tests comprised of testlets. *International Journal on Testing, 2*, 277–295.

Gleser, G. C., Cronbach, L. J., & Rajaratnam, N. (1965). Generalizability of scores influenced by multiple sources of variance. *Psychometrika, 30*(4), 395–418.

Goldstein, Z., & Marcoulides, G. A. (1991). Maximizing the coefficient of generalizability in decision studies. *Educational and Psychological Measurement, 51*(1), 55–65.

Graybill, F. A. (1976). *Theory and application of the linear model.* Belmont, CA: Duxbury.

Graziano, A. M., & Raulin, M. L. (2009). *Research methods: A process of inquiry* (7th ed.). Boston: Allyn and Bacon.

Green, S. B., Lissitz, R. W., & Mulaik, S. A. (1977). Limitations of coefficient alpha as an index of test unidimensionality. *Educational and Psychological Measurement, 37*, 827–838.

Green, S. B., & Yang, Y. (2009a). Commentary on coefficient alpha: A cautionary tale. *Psychometrika, 74*, 121–136.

Green, S. B., & Yang, Y. (2009b). Reliability of summed item scores using structural equation modeling: An alternative to coefficient alpha. *Psychometrika, 74*, 155–167.

Guilford, J. P., & Fruchter, B. (1978). *Fundamental statistics in psychology and education.* New York: McGraw-Hill.

Guttman, L. (1945). A basis for analyzing test–retest reliability. *Psychometrika, 10*, 255–282.

Hagtvet, K. A. (1997, March). *The error structure of constructs: A joint application of generalizability analysis and covariance structure modeling.* Paper presented at the annual meeting of the National Council on Measurement in Education, Chicago, IL.

Hagtvet, K. A. (1998). Assessment of latent constructs: A joint application of generalizability theory and covariance structure modeling with an emphasis on inference and structure. *Scandinavian Journal of Educational Research, 42*, 41–63.

Haladyna, T. M. (2004). *Developing and validating multiple-choice test items.* Mahwah, NJ: Lawrence Erlbaum.

Hambleton, R. K., Swaminathan, H., & Rodgers, J. (1991). *Fundamentals of item response theory.* Thousand Oaks, CA: Sage.

Hancock, G. R., & Mueller, R. O. (2001). Rethinking construct reliability within latent variable systems. In R. Cudeck, S. H. C. du Toit, & D. Sörbom (Eds.), *Structural equation modeling: Present and future—A Festschrift in honor of Karl G. Jöreskog.* Lincolnwood, IL: Scientific Software International.

Harris, D. J., Hanson, B. A., & Gao, X. (2000, April). *A comparison of generalizability theory and IRT methodology in estimating domain scores.* Paper presented at the annual meeting of the American Educational Research Association, New Orleans, LA.

Hayashi, K., & Marcoulides, G. A. (2006). Identification issues in factor analysis. *Structural Equation Modeling, 13*, 631–645.

Höft, S. (1996). *Generalisierbarkeits-theorie über Strukturgleichungsmodelle: Eine Darstellung und Anwendung auf die Konstruktvalidität von Assessment Centern* [Generalizability theory using structural equation modeling: A presentation and application for construct validation of assessment centers]. Stuttgart, Germany: University of Hohenheim.

Horn, J. L. (1982). The aging of human abilities. In B. B. Wolman (Ed.), *Handbook of developmental psychology* (pp. 847–870). New York: McGraw-Hill.

Hoyt, C. J. (1941). Test reliability estimated by analysis of variance. *Psychometrika, 6*, 153–160.

Jennrich, R. (2007). Rotation methods, algorithms, and standard errors. In R. Cudeck & R. C. MacCallum (Eds.), *Factor analysis at 100* (pp. 315–336). Mahwah, NJ: Lawrence Erlbaum.

Joe, G. W., & Woodward, J. A. (1976). Some developments in multivariate generalizability. *Psychometrika, 41*, 205–217.

Johnson, D. R., & Creech, J. C. (1983). Ordinal measures in multiple indicators models: A simulation study of categorization error. *American Sociological Review, 48*, 398–407.

Johnson, R. A., & Wichern, D. W. (2002). *Applied multivariate statistical analysis.* Upper Saddle River, NJ: Prentice Hall.

Jöreskog, K. G. (1969). A general approach to confirmatory maximum likelihood factor analysis. *Psychometrika, 34,* 183–202.

Jöreskog, K. G. (1971). Statistical analysis of sets of congeneric tests. *Psychometrika, 36,* 109–133.

Jöreskog, K. G. (1978). Structural analysis of covariance and correlation matrices. *Psychometrika, 43,* 443–477.

Jöreskog, K. G. (1994). On the estimation of polychoric correlations and their asymptotic covariance matrix. *Psychometrika, 59,* 381–389.

Jöreskog, K. G., & Sörbom, D. (1996). *LISREL8 user's guide.* Chicago: Scientific Software International.

Kamata, A., & Bauer, D. J. (2008). A note on the relationship between factor analytic and item response theory models. *Structural Equation Modeling, 15,* 136–153.

Kerlinger, F. N. (2001). *Multiple regression in behavioral research.* Fort Worth, TX: Harcourt College.

Kerlinger, F. N., & Lee, H. B. (1999). *Foundations of behavioral research* (4th ed.). Orlando, FL: Harcourt College.

King, B. M., & Minium, E. W. (2003). *Statistical reasoning in the behavioral sciences.* New York: Wiley.

Kleinbaum, D. (2005). *Logistic regression.* New York: Springer.

Krishnamoorthy, K. (2006). *Handbook of statistical distributions with applications.* London: Chapman & Hall.

Lane, S., Liu, M., Ankenmann, R. D., & Stone, C. A. (1996). Generalizability and validity of a mathematics performance assessment. *Journal of Educational Measurement, 33,* 71–92.

Leite, W., Huang, I.-C., & Marcoulides, G. A. (2008). Item selection for the development of short forms of scales using an ant colony optimization algorithm. *Multivariate Behavioral Research, 43,* 411–431.

Li, H. (1997). A unifying expression for the maximal reliability of a linear composite. *Psychometrika, 62*(2), 245–249.

Li, H., Rosenthal, R., & Rubin, D. (1996). Reliability of measurement in psychology: From Spearman-Brown to maximal reliability. *Psychological Methods, 1,* 98–107.

Lindquist, E. F. (1953). *Design and analysis of experiments in psychology and education.* Oxford, UK: Houghton Mifflin.

Linn, R. L., & Werts, C. E. (1977). Covariance structure and their analysis. In R. E. Traub (Ed.), *New directions for testing and measurement: Methodological developments* (No. 4, pp. 53–73). San Francisco: Jossey-Bass.

Liou, M., & Chang, C. H. (1992). Constructing the exact significance level for a person fit statistic. *Psychometrika, 57,* 169–181.

Little, R., & Rubin, D. B. (2002). *Statistical analysis with missing data.* New York: Wiley.

Lynch, B. K., & McNamara, T. F. (1998). Using g-theory and many-facet Rasch measurement in the development of performance assessments of the ESL speaking skills of immigrants. *Language Testing, 15,* 158–189.

Lord, F. M. (1980). *Applications of item response theory to practical testing problems.* Hillsdale, NJ: Lawrence Erlbaum.

Lord, F. M., & Novick, M. R. (1968). *Statistical theories of mental test scores.* Reading, MA: Addison-Wesley.

MacCallum, R. C. (1986). Specification searches in covariance structure modeling. *Psychological Bulletin, 100,* 107–120.

MacMillan, P. D. (2000). Classical, generalizability and multifaceted Rasch detection of interrater variability in large, sparse data sets. *Journal of Experimental Education, 68*(2), 167–190.

Magnusson, D. (1967). *Test theory.* Reading, MA: Addison-Wesley.

Marcoulides, G. A. (1987). *An alternative method for variance component estimation: Applications to generalizability theory.* Unpublished doctoral dissertation, University of California, Los Angeles.

Marcoulides, G. A. (1989). The application of generalizability theory to observational studies. *Quality and Quantity, 23*(2), 115–127.

Marcoulides, G. A. (1990). An alternative method for estimating variance components in generalizability theory. *Psychological Reports, 66*(2), 102–109.

Marcoulides, G. A. (1993). Maximizing power in generalizability studies under budget constraints. *Journal of Educational Statistics, 18*(2), 197–206.

Marcoulides, G. A. (1994). Selecting weighting schemes in multivariate generalizability studies. *Educational and Psychological Measurement, 54*(1), 3–7.

Marcoulides, G. A. (1995). Designing measurement studies under budget constraints: Controlling error of measurement and power. *Educational and Psychological Measurement, 55*(3), 423–428.

Marcoulides, G. A. (1996). Estimating variance components in generalizability theory: The covariance structure analysis approach. *Structural Equation Modeling, 3*(3), 290–299.

Marcoulides, G. A. (1997a, March). *Generalizability theory: Models and applications.* Paper presented at the annual meeting of the American Educational Research Association, Chicago, IL.

Marcoulides, G. A. (1997b). Optimizing measurement designs with budget constraints: The variable cost case. *Educational and Psychological Measurement, 57*, 808–812.

Marcoulides, G. A. (1999). Generalizability theory: Picking up where Rasch IRT leaves off? In S. E. Embretson & S. L. Hershberger (Eds.), *The new rules of measurement: What every psychologist and educator should know* (pp. 129–152). Mahwah, NJ: Lawrence Erlbaum.

Marcoulides, G. A. (2000a). Generalizability theory. In H. E. A. Tinsley & S. Brown (Eds.), *Handbook of applied multivariate statistics and mathematical modeling.* San Diego, CA: Academic Press.

Marcoulides, G. A. (2000b, March). *Generalizability theory: Advancements and implementations.* Paper presented at the 22nd Language Testing Research Colloquium, Vancouver, Canada.

Marcoulides, G. A. (2004). Conceptual debates in evaluating measurement procedures. *Measurement, 2*, 182–184.

Marcoulides, G. A. (2007a). A review of recent developments on structural equation models: Theory and applications. *Applied Psychological Measurement, 31*, 240–244.

Marcoulides, G. A. (2007b, August). *Modeling the etiological structure of the world.* Paper presented at the Symposium on Causality and Structural Equation Modeling: Where Statistics and Philosophy Intersect, Annual Meeting of the American Psychological Association, San Francisco, CA.

Marcoulides, G. A., & Drezner, Z. (1993). A procedure for transforming points in multi-dimensional space to a two-dimensional representation. *Educational and Psychological Measurement, 53*(4), 933–940.

Marcoulides, G. A., & Drezner, Z. (1995, April). *A new method for analyzing performance assessments.* Paper presented at the Eighth International Objective Measurement Workshop, Berkley, CA.

Marcoulides, G. A., & Drezner, Z. (1997). A method for analyzing performance assessments. In M. Wilson, K. Draney, & G. Engelhard, Jr. (Eds.), *Objective measurement: Theory into practice.* Stamford, CT: Ablex.

Marcoulides, G. A., & Drezner, Z. (2000). A procedure for detecting pattern clustering in measurement designs. In M. Wilson, K. Draney, & G. Engelhard, Jr. (Eds.), *Objective measurement: Theory into practice.* Stamford, CT: Ablex.

Marcoulides, G. A., & Goldstein, Z. (1990). The optimization of generalizability studies with resource constraints. *Educational and Psychological Measurement, 50*(4), 782–789.

Marcoulides, G. A., & Goldstein, Z. (1991). Selecting the number of observations in multivariate measurement designs under budget constraints. *Educational and Psychological Measurement, 51*(4), 573–584.

Marcoulides, G. A., & Goldstein, Z. (1992). The optimization of multivariate generalizability studies under budget constraints. *Educational and Psychological Measurement, 52*(3), 301–308.

Marcoulides, G. A., & Hershberger, S. L. (1997). *Multivariate statistical methods: A first course.* Mahwah, NJ: Lawrence Erlbaum.

Marcoulides, G. A., & Kyriakides, L. (2002, April). *Applying the Rasch and extended generalizability theory models: Discrepancies between approaches.* Paper presented at the 11th International Objective Measurement Workshop, New Orleans, LA.

Marsh, H. W. (1989). Confirmatory factor analyses of multitrait–multimethod data: Many problems and a few solutions. *Applied Psychological Measurement, 13*, 335–361.

Marsh, H. W., & Hocevar, D. (1983). Confirmatory factor analysis of multitrait–multimethod matrices. *Journal of Educational Measurement, 20*, 231–248.

Masters, G. N., & Keeves, J. P. (1999). *Advances in measurement in educational research assessment.* The Netherlands: Pergamon.

Maxwell, A. E. (1968). The effect of correlated errors on estimates of reliability coefficients. *Education and Psychological Measurement, 28,* 803–811.

McCall, R. B. (2005). *Fundamental statistics for behavioral sciences.* New York: Cengage Learning.

McCrae, R. R., & Costa, P. T., Jr. (1996). Toward a new generation of personality theories: Theoretical contexts for the five-factor model. In J. S. Wiggins (Ed.), *The five-factor model of personality: Theoretical perspectives* (pp. 51–87). New York: Guilford.

McDonald, R. P. (1962). A general approach to nonlinear factor analysis. *Psychometrika, 27,* 397–415.

McDonald, R. P. (1967a). A comparison of four methods for estimation of factor scores. *Psychometrika, 32,* 381–401.

McDonald, R. P. (1967b). Nonlinear factor analysis. *Psychometric Monograph, No. 15,* 1–90.

McDonald, R. P. (1970). The theoretical foundations of principal factor analysis, canonical factor analysis, and alpha factor analysis. *British Journal of Mathematical and Statistical Psychology, 23,* 1–21.

McDonald, R. P. (1978). Generalizability in factorable domains: Domain validity and reliability. *Educational and Psychological Measurement, 38,* 75–79.

McDonald, R. P. (1981). The dimensionality of tests and items. *British Journal of Mathematical and Statistical Psychology, 34,* 100–117.

McDonald, R. P. (1983). Exploratory and confirmatory nonlinear factor analysis. In H. Wainer & S. Messick (Eds.), *Principals of modern psychological measurement: Festschrift for Frederick M. Lord* (pp. 197–213). Hillsdale, NJ: Lawrence Erlbaum.

McDonald, R. P. (1985). *Factor analysis and related methods.* Hillsdale, NJ: Lawrence Erlbaum.

McDonald, R. P. (1986). Describing the elephant: Structure and function in multivariate data. *Psychometrika, 51,* 513–534.

McDonald, R. P. (1999). *Test theory: A unified treatment.* Mahwah, NJ: Lawrence Erlbaum.

Messick, S. (1989). Validity. In R. L. Linn (Ed.), *Educational measurement* (3rd ed., pp. 13–103). New York: Macmillan.

Messick, S. (1995). Validation of inferences from persons' responses and performances as scientific inquiry into score meaning. *American Psychologist, 50,* 741–749.

Miller, M. B. (1995). Coefficient alpha: A basic introduction from the perspectives of classical test theory and structural equation modeling. *Structural Equation Modeling, 2,* 255–273.

Mooney, C. Z., & Duval, R. D. (1993). *Bootstrapping: A nonparametric approach to statistical inference.* Newbury Park, CA: Sage.

Murphy, K. R., & Davidshofer, C. O. (2004). *Principles of psychological testing: Principles and applications.* Upper Saddle River, NJ: Prentice Hall.

Muthén, B. O. (1984). A general structural equation model with dichotomous, ordered categorical, and continuous latent variables indicators. *Psychometrika, 49,* 115–132.

Muthén, B. O. (2002). Beyond SEM: General latent variable modeling. *Behaviormetrika, 29,* 87–117.

Muthén, B., Kao, C.-F., & Burstein, L. (1991). Instructional sensitivity in mathematics achievement test items: Applications of a new IRT-based detection technique. *Journal of Educational Measurement, 28,* 1–22.

Muthén, L. K. (1983). *The estimation of variance components for dichotomous dependent variables: Applications to test theory.* Unpublished doctoral dissertation, University of California, Los Angeles.

Muthén, L. K., & Muthén, B. O. (2010). *Mplus user's guide.* Los Angeles: Author.

Novick, M. R., & Lewis, C. (1967). Coefficient alpha and the reliability of composite measurement. *Psychometrika, 32,* 1–13.

Pearl, J. (2001). *Causality.* New York: Cambridge University Press.

Pedhazur, E. J., & Schmelkin, L. P. (1991). *Measurement, design, and analysis: An integrated approach.* Hillsdale, NJ: Lawrence Erlbaum.

Penev, S., & Raykov, T. (2006). On the relationship between maximal reliability and maximal validity for linear composites. *Multivariate Behavioral Research, 41,* 105–126.

Rasch, G. (1980). *Probabilistic models for some intelligence and attainment tests.* Chicago: University of Chicago Press. (Original work published 1960)

Raykov, T. (1997). Scale reliability, Cronbach's coefficient alpha, and violations of essential tau-equivalence for fixed congeneric components. *Multivariate Behavioral Research, 32*, 329–354.

Raykov, T. (1998a). A method for obtaining standard errors and confidence intervals of composite reliability for congeneric items. *Applied Psychological Measurement, 22*, 369–374.

Raykov, T. (1998b). Cronbach's alpha and reliability of composite with interrelated nonhomogenous items. *Applied Psychological Measurement, 22*, 375–385.

Raykov, T. (2001a). Bias of coefficient alpha for congeneric measures with correlated errors. *Applied Psychological Measurement, 25*, 69–76.

Raykov, T. (2001b). Estimation of congeneric scale reliability via covariance structure models with nonlinear constraints. *British Journal of Mathematical and Statistical Psychology, 54*, 315–323.

Raykov, T. (2001c). Testing multivariable covariance structure and means hypotheses via structural equation modeling. *Structural Equation Modeling, 8*, 224–257.

Raykov, T. (2004). Estimation of maximal reliability: A note on a covariance structure modeling approach. *British Journal of Mathematical and Statistical Psychology, 57*, 21–27.

Raykov, T. (2005). A method for testing group differences in scale validity in multiple populations. *British Journal of Mathematical and Statistical Psychology, 58*, 173–184.

Raykov, T. (2007a). Evaluation of revision effect on criterion validity of multiple-component measuring instruments. *Multivariate Behavioral Research, 42*, 415–434.

Raykov, T. (2007b). Reliability if deleted, not "alpha if deleted": Evaluation of scale reliability following component deletion. *British Journal of Mathematical and Statistical Psychology, 60*, 201–216.

Raykov, T. (2007c). Reliability of multiple-component measuring instruments: Improved evaluation in repeated measure studies. *British Journal of Mathematical and Statistical Psychology, 60*, 119–136.

Raykov, T. (2008). "Alpha if item deleted": A note on loss of criterion validity in scale development if maximising coefficient alpha. *British Journal of Mathematical and Statistical Psychology, 61*, 275–285.

Raykov, T. (2009a). Evaluation of scale reliability with congeneric measures using latent variable modeling. *Measurement and Evaluation in Counseling and Development, 42*, 222–232.

Raykov, T. (2009b). Interval estimation of revision effect on scale reliability via covariance structure modeling. *Structural Equation Modeling, 16*, 539–555.

Raykov, T. (2010a). Evaluation of convergent and discriminant validity with multitrait–multimethod correlations. *British Journal of Mathematical and Statistical Psychology* (in press).

Raykov, T. (2010b). Proportion of third-level variance in multilevel studies: A note on an interval estimation procedure. *British Journal of Mathematical and Statistical Psychology* (in press).

Raykov, T. (2010c). Scale validity evaluation with congeneric measures in hierarchical designs. *British Journal of Mathematical and Statistical Psychology* (in press).

Raykov, T., Dimitrov, D. M., & Asparouhov, T. (2010). Evaluation of scale reliability with binary measures. *Structural Equation Modeling* (in press).

Raykov, T., & du Toit, S. H. C. (2005). Evaluation of reliability for multiple-component measuring instruments in hierarchical designs. *Structural Equation Modeling, 12*, 536–550.

Raykov, T., & Hancock, G. R. (2005). Examining change in maximal reliability for multiple-component measuring instruments. *British Journal of Mathematical and Statistical Psychology, 58*, 65–82.

Raykov, T., & Marcoulides, G. A. (2004). Using the delta method for approximate interval estimation of parametric functions in covariance structure models. *Structural Equation Modeling, 11*, 659–675.

Raykov, T., & Marcoulides, G. A. (2006a). *A first course in structural equation modeling*. Mahwah, NJ: Lawrence Erlbaum.

Raykov, T., & Marcoulides, G. A. (2006b). Estimation of generalizability coefficients via a structural equation modeling approach to scale reliability evaluation. *International Journal of Testing, 6*, 81–95.

Raykov, T., & Marcoulides, G. A. (2008). *An introduction to applied multivariate analysis*. New York: Taylor & Francis.

Raykov, T., & Marcoulides, G. A. (2010a). Classical item analysis using latent variable modeling: A note on a direct evaluation procedure. *Structural Equation Modeling* (in press).

Raykov, T., & Marcoulides, G. A. (2010b). Group comparisons of observed variable mean and inter-relationship indices in the presence of missing data. *Structural Equation Modeling, 17,* 150–164.

Raykov, T., & Marcoulides, G. A. (2010c). Population proportion of explained variance in principal component analysis: A note on its evaluation via a large-sample approach. *Structural Equation Modeling* (in press).

Raykov, T., & Marcoulides, G. A. (2010d). Evaluation of validity and reliability for hierarchical scales using latent variable modeling. *Structural Equation Modeling* (in press).

Raykov, T., & Mels, G. (2009). Interval estimation of inter-item and item-total correlations for ordinal items of multiple-component measuring instruments. *Structural Equation Modeling, 15,* 449–461.

Raykov, T., & Penev, S. (2006). A direct method for obtaining approximate standard error and confidence interval of maximal reliability for composites with congeneric measures. *Multivariate Behavioral Research, 41,* 15–28.

Raykov, T., & Penev, S. (2009). Estimation of maximal reliability for multiple component instruments in multilevel designs. *British Journal of Mathematical and Statistical Psychology, 62,* 129–142.

Raykov, T., & Shrout, P. E. (2002). Reliability of scales with general structure: Point and interval estimation using a structural equation modeling approach. *Structural Equation Modeling, 9,* 195–212.

Raykov, T., & Zinbarg, R. (2010). Proportion of general factor variance in a hierarchical multiple- component measuring instrument: A note on a confidence interval estimation procedure. *British Journal of Mathematical and Statistical Psychology* (in press).

Reckase, M. D. (2009). *Multidimensional item response theory.* New York: Springer.

Revelle, W., & Zinbarg, R. (2009). Coefficients alpha, beta, and the glb: Comments on Sijtsma. *Psychometrika, 74,* 145–154.

Robinson, D. L. (1987). Estimation and use of variance components. *The Statistician, 36,* 3–14.

Roussas, G. G. (1997). *A course in mathematical statistics.* New York: Academic Press.

Rozeboom, W. W. (1966). *Foundations of the theory of prediction.* Homewoor, IL: Dorsey Press.

Rulon, P. J. (1939). A simplified procedure for determining the reliability of a test by split-halves. *Harvard Educational Review, 9,* 99–103.

SAS Institute, Inc. (1994). *SAS user's guide, Version 6.* Cary, NC: Author.

SAS Institute, Inc. (2004). *SAS user's guide, Version 9.* Cary, NC: Author.

Satorra, A., & Bentler, P. M. (2001). A scale difference chi-square test statistic for moment structure analysis. *Psychometrika, 66,* 507–514.

Satterthwaite, F. E. (1946). An approximate distribution of estimates of variance components. Biometrics Bulletin, 2, 110–114.

Searle, S. R. (1971). *Linear models.* New York: Wiley & Sons.

Shavelson, R. J. (1996). *Statistical reasoning for the behavioral sciences.* Upper Saddle River, NJ: Prentice Hall.

Shavelson, R. J., & Webb, N. M. (1981). Generalizability theory: 1973–1980. *British Journal of Mathematical and Statistical Psychology, 34,* 133–166.

Shavelson, R. J., & Webb, N. M. (1991). *Generalizability theory: A primer.* Newbury Park, CA: Sage.

Shavelson, R. J., Webb, N. M., & Rowley, G. L. (1989). Generalizability theory. *American Psychologist,* 44(6), 922–932.

Short, L., Webb, N. M., & Shavelson, R. J. (1986, April). *Issues in multivariate generalizability: Weighting schemes and dimensionality.* Paper presented at the annual meeting of the American Educational Research Association, San Francisco, CA.

Sijtsma, K. (2009a). On the use, the misuse, and the very limited usefulness of Cronbach's alpha. *Psychometrika, 74,* 107–120.

Sijtsma, K. (2009b). Reliability beyond theory and into practice. *Psychometrika, 74,* 169–174.

Skrondal, A., & Rabe-Hesketh, S. (2004). *Generalized latent variable modeling: Multilevel, longitudinal and structural equation models.* Boca Raton, FL: Chapman & Hall/CRC.

Spearman, C. (1904). "General intelligence" objectively determined and measured. *American Journal of Psychology, 5,* 201–293.

SPSS Inc. (2004). *SPSS base 13.0 for Windows: Users guide*. Chicago: Author.

Srinivasan, V., & Shocker, A. D. (1973). Estimating weights for multiple attributes in a composite criterions using pairwise judgements. *Psychometrika, 38*(4), 473–493.

Stahl, J. A. (1994). What does generalizability theory offer that many-facet Rasch measurement cannot duplicate? *Rasch Measurement Transactions, 8*(1), 342–343.

Stahl, J. A., & Lunz, M. E. (1993, March). *A comparison of generalizability theory and multi-faceted Rasch measurement*. Paper presented at the annual meeting of the American Educational Research Association, Atlanta, GA.

Standards for Educational and Psychological Testing. (1999). Washington, DC: AERA, APA, and NCME.

Steiger, J. H. (1980). Test for comparing elements of a correlation matrix. *Psychological Bulletin, 87,* 245–251.

Steiger, J. H. (2003). Structural equation modeling (SEPATH): User's guide. In *STATISTICA 6.1*. Tulsa, OK: StatSoft.

Steyer, R., & Eid, M. (2001). *Messen und Testen* [Measurement and testing] (2nd ed.). Berlin: Springer.

Suen, H. K. (1990). *Principles of test theories*. Hillsdale, NJ: Lawrence Erlbaum.

Takane, Y., & de Leeuw, J. (1987). On the relationship between item response theory and factor analysis of discretized variables. *Psychometrika, 52,* 393–408.

Terman, L. M., & Merrill, M. A. (1973). *Stanford-Biner Intelligence Scale*. Chicago: Riverside.

Thissen, D. (1991). *MULTILOG user's guide: Multiple, categorical item analysis and test scoring using item response theory*. Lincolnwood, IL: Scientific Software International.

Thissen, D., & Wainer, H. (2001). *Test scoring*. Mahwah, NJ: Lawrence Erlbaum.

Thurstone, L. L. (1947). *Multiple factor analysis*. Chicago: University of Chicago Press.

Timm, N. H. (2002). *Applied multivariate analysis*. New York: Springer.

Ting, N., Burdick, R. K., Graybill, F. A., Jeyaratnam, S., & Lu, T.-F.C. (1990). Confidence intervals on linear combinations of variance components that are unrestricted in sign. *Journal of Statistical Computation and Simulation, 35,* 135–143.

Uliaszek, A., Hauner, K., Zinbarg, R., Mineka, S., Craske, M., Griffith, J., & Rose, R. (in press). An examination of content overlap and disorder-specific predictions in the associations of neuroticism with anxiety and depression. *Journal of Research in Personality*.

Venables, W. N., Smith, D. M., & The R Development Core Team. (2004). *An introduction to R*. Bristol, UK: Network Theory Limited.

Wall, M. M., & Amemiya, Y. (2007). A review of nonlinear factor analysis and nonlinear structural equation modeling. In R. Cudeck & R. C. MacCallum (Eds.), *Factor analysis at 100: Historical developments and future directions* (pp. 337–362). Mahwah, NJ: Lawrence Erlbaum.

Webb, N. M., Shavelson, R. J., & Maddahian, E. (1983). Multivariate generalizability theory. In L. J. Fyans, Jr. (Ed.), *Generalizability theory: Inferences and practical applications*. San Francisco: Jossey-Bass.

Wechsler, D. (1958). *The measurement of adult intelligence*. Baltimore: Williams and Wilkins.

Weichang, L. (1990). *Multivariate generalizability of hierarchical measurements*. Unpublished doctoral dissertation, University of California, Los Angeles.

Wiley, D. E., Schmidt, W. H., & Bramble, W. J. (1973). Studies of a class of covariance structure models. *Journal of the American Statistical Association, 68,* 317–323.

Wiley, E. W. (2000). *Bootstrap strategies for variance component estimation: Theoretical and empirical results*. Unpublished doctoral dissertation, Stanford University.

Wilkinson, L., & The Task Force on Statistical Inference. (1999). Statistical methods in psychology journals: Guidelines and explanations. *American Psychologist, 54,* 594–604.

Woodward, J. A., & Joe, G. W. (1973). Maximizing the coefficient of generalizability in multi-facet decision studies. *Psychometrika, 38*(2), 173–181.

Wright, B. D. (1998). Estimating measures for extreme scores. *Rasch Measurement Transactions, 12*(2), 632–633.

Zimmerman, D. W. (1972). Test reliability and the Kuder-Richardson formulas: Derivation from probability theory. *Educational and Psychological Measurement, 32,* 939–954.

Zimmerman, D. W. (1975). Probability spaces, Hilbert spaces, and the axioms of test theory. *Psychometrika, 40,* 395–412.

Zinbarg, R. E., Mineka, S., Craske, M. G., Griffith, J. W., Sutton, J., & Rose, R. D. (2009). *Cognitive vulnerabilities as non-specific but important facets of neuroticism in cross-sectional associations with adolescent emotional disorders*. Manuscript submitted for publication.

Zinbarg, R. E., Revelle, W., Yovel, I., & Li, W. (2005). Cronbach's α, Revelle's β, McDonald's ωH, their relations with each other, and two alternative conceptualizations of reliability. *Psychometrika, 70*, 123–134.

Zinbarg, R. E., Yovel, I., Revelle, W., & McDonald, R. P. (2006). Estimating generalizability to a latent variable common to all of a scale's indicators: A comparison for estimates of ωH. *Applied Psychological Measurement, 30*, 121–144.

Name Index

Subject Index

A

Absolute error, 229–231
Absolute error variance (*see* Absolute error)
Alpha (*see* coefficient α)
Alternate forms, 147–148
Attenuation (*see* Correction for attenuation)

B

Binomial (*see* Bernoulli)
Bernoulli sampling model, 260–261
Biserial correlation, 301–302
Bootstrap estimates, 228
Budget constraints, 238

C

Categorical items, 175–179
CDF (*see* Cumulative distribution function)
CFA (*see* Confirmatory factor analysis)
Classical item analysis, 98–99
Classical test theory, 115–144
Classical test theory equation, 117–118
Coefficient α, 142–143, 154–155
Coefficient of generalizability (*see* G-theory)
Communality, 49–51
Conditional independence, 42–43, 275–276
Confirmatory factor analysis, 61–113
Congeneric tests, 126–128
Constructs, 4–8
Construct validity, 190
Content validity, 186
Convergent validity (*see* Construct validity)
Correction for attenuation, 191
Correlation, 18–21
Covariance, 18–21
Criterion validity, 187
Cumulative distribution function, 256–257

D

D-Study (*see* Decision study)
Decision study, 229–232
Descriptive statistics, 15–20
Design, crossed (*see* G-theory)
Design, nested (*see* G-theory)
Difficulty, item (*see* Item difficulty)

D (continued)

Discriminant validity (*see* MTMM)
Discrimination, item (*see* Item discrimination)
Divergent validity (*see* Construct validity)

E

EduG software, 232
Epilogue, 305–306
Error of measurement (*see* CTT and G-theory)
Error score, 118–119
Estimation of item difficulty, 99–105
Estimating true scores, 158
Expectation, 248–250
Exploratory factor analysis (*see* Factor analysis)

F

Factorial validity (*see* Construct validity)
Facet (*see* G-theory)
Factor analysis, 37–113
Factor loading, 43–44
Factor rotation, 44–48
Fit of a model (*see* FA and IRT)
Fixed facet (*see* G-theory)

G

G-theory (*see* Generalizability theory)
Generalizability coefficients, 229–231
Generalizability study, 231–232
Generalizability theory, 223–246
General factor analysis model, 263–265
General linear model, 250–252
Generalized latent linear and mixed model, 266–267
Generalized latent linear model, 266–267
Generalized linear model, 250–252
GENOVA program, 232
GFA (*see* General factor analysis model)
GLIM (*see* General linear model)
GLLAMM (*see* Generalized latent linear and mixed model)
GLLM (*see* Generalized latent linear model)
GLM (*see* Generalized linear model)
Group homogeneity, 156–157
Guessing, 295–296
Guttman's method, 151–152